# Transnational *Kaijū*

## Exploitation, Globalisation and Cult Monster Movies

Steven Rawle

EDINBURGH
University Press

Edinburgh University Press is one of the leading university presses in the UK.
We publish academic books and journals in our selected subject areas across the
humanities and social sciences, combining cutting-edge scholarship with high editorial
and production values to produce academic works of lasting importance. For more
information visit our website: edinburghuniversitypress.com

© Steven Rawle, 2022

Edinburgh University Press Ltd
The Tun – Holyrood Road
12 (2f) Jackson's Entry
Edinburgh EH8 8PJ

First published in hardback by Edinburgh University Press 2022

Typeset in Times New Roman by
Manila Typesetting Company, and
printed and bound by CPI Group (UK) Ltd,
Croydon, CR0 4YY

A CIP record for this book is available from the British Library

ISBN 978 1 4744 7580 8 (hardback)
ISBN 978 1 4744 7581 5 (paperback)
ISBN 978 1 4744 7582 2 (webready PDF)
ISBN 978 1 4744 7583 9 (epub)

The right of Steven Rawle to be identified as author of this work has been asserted in
accordance with the Copyright, Designs and Patents Act 1988 and the Copyright and
Related Rights Regulations 2003 (SI No. 2498).

# Contents

| | |
|---|---|
| *List of Figures* | v |
| *Acknowledgements* | viii |

**Introduction: 'Every Country Has a Monster'** — 1
    What is the *Kaijū Eiga*? — 2
    Cult Movies — 11
    Transnational Cinema — 14
    Transnational *Kaijū* — 19

**1. National Films, Transnational Monsters** — 21
    *Kaijū* and the Japanese National Imaginary — 23
    Carl Denham's Giant Monster — 33
    The Lost World and the Beast — 37
    *Kaijū* Emerge — 43

**2. The First Monster Boom** — 48
    *Kaijū* at Tōhō — 52
    *Kaijū* at Daiei — 62
    *Kaijū* at Shōchiku, Nikkatsu and Toei — 70
        Shōchiku — 70
        Nikkatsu — 73
        Toei — 75

**3. Exchanging Monsters: Korean *Kaijū*** — 78
    The *Kaijū* Meme — 80
    *Kaijū* Head West — 83
        *Kaijū* on the Korean Peninsula — 84
        Kim Jong-Il's *Kaijū* — 94
        *Kaijū* in New Korean Cinema — 102

**4. Distributing *Kaijū*: Localisation and Exploitation** — 114
    National Cinema: Quality and Trash — 116
    Popular Cinema to Exploitation Film — 122
    Long Live the King — 125
    *Cozzilla* — 131
    The Return of Steve Martin — 136

| | |
|---|---|
| **5. 'Paul Bunyan Never Fought Rodan'** | **148** |
| Appropriation, Borrowing, Exchange | 151 |
| European *Kaijū* | 155 |
| Hollywood *Kaijū* | 162 |
| *Kaijū* Mockbusters | 183 |
| Kongsploitation | 187 |
| **6. Legendary Monsters** | **196** |
| Legendary Entertainment | 197 |
| Marked/Unmarked Transnational Cinema | 201 |
| *Pacific Rim* | 203 |
| *The Great Wall* | 209 |
| *Pacific Rim: Uprising* | 212 |
| Into the MonsterVerse | 215 |
| **Conclusion: The Limiting Imagination of Transnational Monsters** | **232** |
| National *Kaijū* | 233 |
| Nostalgia and Fandom | 240 |
| *References* | 244 |
| *Index* | 266 |

# Figures

| | | |
|---|---|---|
| I.1 | Godzilla becomes a signifier of Japan in *The Simpsons* | 2 |
| I.2 | Godzilla and Miniya emotionally huddle at the end of *Son of Godzilla* | 6 |
| I.3 | The US military is attacked by a time-travelled Godzillasaurus in *Godzilla vs. King Ghidorah* | 8 |
| 1.1 | The *Eiko-maru*'s sailors are affected by Godzilla's nuclear arrival in *Gojira* | 24 |
| 1.2 | Godzilla smashes the National Diet building | 27 |
| 1.3 | A widow huddles with her children during the *kaijū* attack on Tokyo | 28 |
| 1.4 | The aftermath of Godzilla's attack evokes the devastation of nuclear bombing | 29 |
| 1.5 | Kong destroys a New York train and establishes a *kaijū* motif | 36 |
| 1.6 | A marauding dinosaur visits a national landmark in London as a sign of urban fragility in *The Lost World* | 39 |
| 2.1 | Blackface was often used to represent 'primitive' cultures, here in *King Kong vs. Godzilla* | 55 |
| 2.2 | Varan attacks in the widescreen cinema version of *Daikaijū Baran* | 56 |
| 2.3 | Bowen and Togami share moments of cultural exchange, with traditional food and dress, throughout *Frankenstein Conquers the World* | 62 |
| 2.4 | Gamera attacks a lighthouse in *Gamera*, referencing *The Beast from 20,000 Fathoms* | 65 |
| 2.5 | The animated stone *kaijū*'s angry face resembles the *Oni* from *bunraku* in *Daimajin* | 68 |
| 2.6 | *The X from Outer Space* fetishises both white and Japanese femininity in its 1960s vision of the future | 72 |
| 3.1 | *Yongary, Monster from the Deep* imagines a futuristic and self-reliant Republic of Korea | 88 |
| 3.2 | Yongary destroys the seat of colonial government in Seoul | 89 |

| | | |
|---|---|---|
| 3.3 | The monster dances with Yoo to 'Arirang', the traditional national song | 90 |
| 3.4 | Fiery Pulgasari attacks the overlords who repress the masses | 97 |
| 3.5 | The cute Ninja-Turtle-styled Galgameth spies another meal of delicious metal | 101 |
| 3.6 | The CGI creature is shipped away to its own monster island at the end of *Yonggary* | 106 |
| 4.1 | Martin watches on from an obvious studio background whilst witnessing Godzilla's demise at sea | 127 |
| 4.2 | Steve Martin is inserted into Odo Island ritual as Tomo Iwanaga translates in *Godzilla, King of the Monsters!* | 128 |
| 4.3 | Cozzi cut real footage of the devastation from the nuclear bombings to preface *Cozzilla* | 134 |
| 4.4 | Before unleashing the Oxygen Destroyer, Serizawa watches a shark and octopus fight in *Cozzilla*, a scene lifted from *The Beast from 20,000 Fathoms* | 136 |
| 4.5 | Major McDonough enjoys a refreshing piece of product placement at a high point of tension in *Godzilla 1985* | 145 |
| 5.1 | Gorgo revisits a London landmark familiar from the inception of the *kaijū* film | 157 |
| 5.2 | A still-Blitz-scarred London is attacked by the Giant Behemoth | 159 |
| 5.3 | Emmerich's monster makes a statement in the teaser trailer by crushing the puny T. rex from *Jurassic Park* | 166 |
| 5.4 | *Kraa! The Sea Monster* takes aim at *Godzilla* (1988) as it rampages through a miniature city street | 185 |
| 5.5 | The monster makes a pejorative statement about the US military in *A\*P\*E* | 191 |
| 6.1 | A brief intro to *Pacific Rim* includes a short insert of a Japanese-style TV show | 204 |
| 6.2 | The very non-traditionally styled Tao Tie queen from *The Great Wall* | 211 |
| 6.3 | Tencent's Penguin mascot makes an appearance during a *kaijū*–Jaeger battle in *Pacific Rim: Uprising* | 213 |
| 6.4 | Side-by-side credits from *Godzilla* (2014) and *Kong: Skull Island* help connect its shared universe | 223 |
| 6.5 | *Kong: Skull Island's* post-credits sequence teases *Godzilla: King of the Monsters'* return of King Ghidorah | 225 |
| C.1 | The monster comes ashore as a giant slithering mutated fish before taking on the more familiar shape of Godzilla in *Shin Gojira* | 237 |

C.2 *MST3K* established Gamera as a recurring gag after Sandy Frank's catalogue enabled the show to riff on multiple *Gamera* films    242

# Acknowledgements

Unlike many *kaijū*, this book has been long in gestation. Its development has been enabled by many friends, family and colleagues, of whom there are far too many to mention individually. However, some do merit specific kudos. My undergraduate and postgraduate students at York St John University have been generous in listening to and discussing ideas about *kaijū eiga*, transnational flow and borrowing, contributing to the growth of ideas and highlighting aspects that I hadn't previously considered. Colleagues in the departments of Media Production and Media and Film Studies have supported, discussed, read material or simply helped me manage time along the way. These include Martin Hall, Keith McDonald, Wayne Johnson, Dan Crawforth, Anne Dawson, Kevin Gash, Jonathan Brown, Tracy Willits, Sue Greenwood, Robert Wilsmore, Matthew Reason, Rachel Wicaksono, Mary Murata and Chisato Danjo.

The many scholars of transnational, horror and exploitation cinemas have been instrumental and inspirational in helping to shape my thinking and understand the contexts behind the films that are discussed throughout the book. There are special nods to Neil Jackson and Ed Glaser, however, for sharing useful, difficult-to-find material. Fans of *kaijū* cinema have also been especially generous, in their sharing of collected materials, discussions of media and their scholarly research about the *kaijū eiga*, their production and the personnel behind them. I couldn't have completed this book without their work to draw upon. I'd also like to thank J. D. Lees for sharing his thoughts about *kaijū*'s adoption in the English language.

Finally, as always, I'd like to thank my brilliant wife, Lorna. She has put up with a lot as I've been working on the book. There have been some terrible films to watch, and some rather brilliant ones. While I haven't been able to make her appreciate *Godzilla vs. Megalon*, she is certainly now something of a G-fan, as well as an excellent proofreader. Her parents, Rick and Joyce, shared a lovely recollection of their first date being a trip to see a double bill that included *Gappa: The Triphibian Monster* on its first UK release (naturally, they couldn't remember the other picture on the bill). In some regards, therefore, Lorna owes her very existence to *kaijū* films, and therefore this book is dedicated to her, for all her love, support, encouragement and patience.

## Note on the Text

Throughout the text, Asian names are listed with surname first. This is generally the case for filmmakers and performers, although where authors or performers are credited or published with given name first, the names have been given following western convention. Film titles have been included in their original language using their most common Romanisations. Generally, films' best-known English titles are included, unless otherwise noted.

# Introduction
## 'Every Country Has a Monster'

When *Mystery Science Theater 3000* (*MST3K*) was rebooted in 2017 following a successful crowdfunding campaign, *Reptilicus* (Poul Bang/ Sidney W. Pink, 1961), a cult Danish-American co-production, was the subject of the first episode's riffing. The choice was perhaps not surprising given the original *MST3K*'s passion for 'bad' monster movies. The first run of the show had featured numerous Japanese monster movies. This opening takes its title from a song by Jonah in the reboot episode: 'every country has a monster it's afraid of'. Usually, as Jonah's rap shows, these creatures have roots in folklore or mythology, and while this is true of some big monsters, this isn't necessarily the case for most *kaijū*. As many scholars have shown, *kaijū* were born of the atomic nightmares of the twentieth century. The Godzilla (1954–present) series is really the *kaijū eiga*'s urtext. The genre has grown over a century, and national and international resonances have shifted throughout that time. Transnationalism has therefore become the most useful concept through which to explore how national and global themes have been shaped by cross-border exchanges, appropriations or political and environmental concerns. Even as globalisation undermines the stability of borders, national specificity remains an important concern, and this shifting, mutating form has roots and branches in many countries, and as Deborah Shaw (2013b) has argued, the national film remains a vital concern in transnational cinema studies. Even though every country has a monster, *kaijū* have very specific associations with Japan.

This is really a book about global connectivity. It isn't intended as an authoritative overview of every global *kaijū* movie, but as a look at genre through an interpretative lens. The *kaijū eiga* is thus a case study for a point of view that might be applied to other transnational genres. What is perhaps most immediately revealing about the *kaijū eiga* is that, unlike many international film forms, its name borrows a Romanised Japanese rather than Anglophone term. Fans and critics use the Japanese word to

**Figure I.1** Godzilla becomes a signifier of Japan in *The Simpsons* (20th Century Studios/Disney/Gracie Films)

refer to the genre, and *kaijū* has become a loanword in English-language films such as *Pacific Rim* (Guillermo del Toro, 2013) and *Monster Island* (Mark Atkins, 2019). While much of the core text of the *kaijū eiga* documents cross-border politics, particularly the historic relations between Japan and the US, its association with Japan (Japan and Godzilla in particular, like the 'Godzilla-related turbulence' experienced by The Simpsons in the 1999 episode 'Thirty Minutes over Tokyo' [S10E23], Figure I.1) posits a cinematic centre away from Hollywood. *Kaijū* can help us to understand the sometimes complex relationships between national cinemas and transnational culture. Monster movies are global phenomena, just as monsters are highly contingent upon national and historical context for their meanings and specificities. As we'll see during this study, giant monsters have spread throughout the world. Their roots tend to be transnational despite their close associations with national cinema.

## What is the *Kaijū Eiga*?

One of the things we need to do early in this study is establish the parameters for analysis. The goal of this book is to examine the *kaijū eiga* as a transnational genre. We will return later to how to define or describe transnational cinema, but, for now, it's necessary to establish how the study will define the *kaijū eiga*. This requires two areas of classification: firstly, what is the *kaijū eiga*, and secondly, how do we classify this an object? Is the *kaijū eiga* a genre, distinct from others, such as the Western or the Japanese swordplay *chambara*, does it represent a subgenre, a subset of the science-fiction or horror film, or is it a hybrid genre that mixes elements of different genres with tropes of giant monsters? Finally, we need to consider when a *kaijū* film is indeed a *kaijū* film and how we recognise this.

In its simplest sense, the term *kaijū eiga* (怪獣映画) translates as 'monster movie'. The name is generally used to refer to a particular kind of giant monster spectacle. It is also often, but not universally, applied to monster films made or co-produced by Japanese filmmakers. In *Nightmare Japan: Contemporary Horror Cinema*, Jay McRoy distinguishes further by preferring the term *daikaijū eiga*. *Daikaijū* (大怪獣) is distinguished simply by the *dai-* prefix referring to the scale of the monster – they are literally big. McRoy defines the form through its 'over-the-top representations of Japanese urban centres under assault by giant dinosaurs and insects (among other fantastical and gargantuan creatures)' (2008, 7). However, despite this term being more literally in keeping with the scale and size of the monsters in these films, and being in the title of films such as *Daikaijū Baran* (*Varan the Unbelievable*, Honda Ishirō, 1958) and *Daikaijū Gamera* (*Gamera: The Giant Monster*, Noriaki Yuasa, 1965), *kaijū* has been the preferred term to reference films featuring giant monsters.

The term *kaijū* translates literally as strange or mysterious (怪) beast (獣). This aspect of the strange or mysterious is significant in the ways that the *kaijū eiga* has been codified. Michael Crandol (2019) has discussed how the *kaiki eiga* (怪奇映画), the strange film, problematises the generic definition of the *kaijū eiga*, especially for Japanese critics of the 1950s and 1960s. The *kaiki eiga* came to define a thread of the Japanese horror film, notably the ghost story adaptations of the mid-twentieth century, including Nakagawa Nobuo's *The Ghost Story of Yotsuya* (*Tōkaidō Yotsuya kaidan*, 1959), but which, according to Crandol, later came to describe Hammer Studios' films, such as *The Curse of Frankenstein* (Terence Fisher, 1957). At the time of its release, Crandol demonstrates, the influential critics at *Kinema Junpō*, Japan's premier film journal, had flirted with including *kaijū* in the canon of *kaiki eiga*. This was largely down to their pseudo-religious motifs of vengeance and destruction – analogous with ghost stories, albeit updated for the atomic age.

Nevertheless, as Crandol shows, the themes and spectacles of the monster movie became passé, supplanted by the dread and gory aesthetics of British horror films. By the end of the decade, *Kinema Junpō* had excised the Godzilla films, and their spin-offs, from their definition of the *kaiki* film. This raises several points here about how we codify the *kaijū* film. Firstly, it is difficult to place the *kaijū* film within the horror genre. While the term *kaiki* doesn't fully account for a clear connection with generic traditions usually associated with the horror film, the *kaijū eiga* sits more comfortably as a sub-classification of the science-fiction film, even if it shares traces of the horror film. Secondly, as Crandol concludes, 'the crucial role a minor British film studio and its bloody acts of violence played in defining a genre of Japanese popular film . . . remind[s] us that any discussion of national cinema must account for the transnational nature of the medium' (22). The *kaijū eiga* builds upon a similar relationship of national and transnational threads. Thirdly, the proximity of *kaiki* to *kaijū* more clearly allows us to see the *kaijū* film emerging from Japanese traditions of storytelling, even if its roots are generally modern.

Briefly, a point about genre. In some sense, it's comfortable to refer to the *kaijū eiga* as a genre. As Crandol makes clear, Japanese critics initially saw the films through a lens of *kaiki*, as strange films, where that classification fits closely with globally established horror film conventions. But, as the *kaijū* film develops, it becomes less horrific, especially as the 'monster boom' of the 1960s aligns more with Japanese prosperity and monsters become saviours as well as destroyers. Tropes from science-fiction become more prevalent – more films are set partly in space, and they feature aliens and civilisations with fantastical technology. Also, in many cases, the monsters of *kaijū* films fit uncomfortably with the vampires, werewolves and zombies of horror films.

*Kaijū* share aspects of the gothic with horror texts, although they are often less transgressive than their horror counterparts. As Fred Botting argues, gothic 'texts operate ambivalently: the dynamic inter-relation of limit and transgression, prohibition and desire suggests that norms, limits, boundaries and foundations are neither natural nor absolutely fixed or stable despite the fears they engender' (2014, 9). *Kaijū* do transgress norms and limits, mostly of size, but are rarely morally ambivalent. The stories are often clear-cut in their morality (due to the younger age of their target audiences), although generally engender some form of technological or political fear. However, the ambivalence or abjection of gothic body horror is largely absent in the *kaijū* film. There is, for instance, often no challenge to the frameworks of rationality, morality or ideology: 'frameworks which, in modernity, had shaped the world: freedoms, anxieties, monstrosities associated with otherness, power, bodies, sexuality' (172). As we'll explore in the next chapter, there is something gothic in the *kaijū* film's approach to Otherness, and the monster is always irrational to some degree; nevertheless there are gothic themes that are generally not explored in *kaijū* cinema, especially sexuality. Roger Luckhurst's exploration of monster theory in relation to Gareth Edwards' film *Monsters* (2010) calls attention to some of the problematic dimensions of *kaijū* analyses as they relate to the gothic significance of monstrousness on a social and political level:

> Monstrous scale compels the work of allegorical interpretation, but if this theory ends up merely evoking the monster's 'ambivalence as a symbol' – that Godzilla, for instance, 'means everything and nothing' (Tsutsui [2004] 111) – then the labour of interpretation does not deepen an understanding but disperses into a kind of weak hermeneutic pluralism where anything goes. (Luckhurst 2020, 276)

Such an interpretation, rooted in monster theory's gothic reading of monstrosity as a vehicle for queerness, sexual and gender identity (Cohen 1996, Halberstam 1995, Sedgwick 1993), problematises the signifier of the monster and its role as political and social metaphor. If the metaphor is amorphous (as *kaijū* rarely are), then it would become banal, empty even. However, the *kaijū* monster is perhaps best described in Cohen's terms, referring to Biblical giants, that consider them 'fantastic overabundance, vast signifiers of an untamed landscape that, fecund enough to sprout monstrous excess, poses a threat to the domesticating . . . order' (Cohen 1999, 33–4). *Kaijū* emerge where order has already been threatened, by nuclear terror, ecological disaster or imperialism. Edwards' film even repeatedly plays TV news footage that echoes Cohen's language, where monsters have sprouted (the film uses the Spanish, *brotes*) in an infected zone in the Mexican borderlands, a location Othered and disrupted long before giant alien monsters arrived.

There is certainly something gothic in the text of the *kaijū* film that is shared with the horror film, namely that, as Botting mentions, gothic 'formulas readily produce laughter as abundantly as emotions of terror or horror' (2014, 174). Terror and horror are generally signified through the onscreen surrogates for the audience – the families, couples, adventurers, scientists and journalists who populate *kaijū* films – while the laughter at the formula is often a result of the many changes made to Japanese texts over the years, especially dubbing, that made them an object of mockery. There are therefore gothic elements to the *kaijū* film that position it at the intersection of the horror and science-fiction films. This is something that Vivian Sobchack acknowledges in her classic study *Screening*

*Space: The American Science Fiction Film* (2001) about monsters in science-fiction: 'the Monster film bears a great resemblance to the horror film; we are concerned with an isolated individual who – science or no – is in conflict with his animal nature, who defies law, and who suffers and dies for his personal sins' (52).

The Promethean dimension to the sci-fi monster film – also noted by Jason Barr in his study of the *kaijū* film (2016) – is shared with *kaijū* films. The monster is often a result of some form of human hubris or transgression – of nuclear power or environmental crisis. However, in an important distinction from Sobchack's point above, this doesn't happen to 'isolated individuals'; it happens broadly to societies, whole cities, cultures or even globally, where conflict is generated by the monster's excessive size. The monsters Sobchack discusses are 'object[s] to look at, not one[s] to feel for' (52). This ebbs and flows through the *kaijū* film. The demise of the monster in *Gojira* (Honda Ishirō, 1954)[1] is treated didactically: we aren't invited to feel for the monster (unlike at the end of *Son of Godzilla* [*Kaijū Shima no Kessen: Gojira no Musuko*, lit. *Monster Island's Decisive Battle: Godzilla's Son*, Fukuda Jun, 1967], where Godzilla and Miniya freeze into hibernation as their Pacific island is transformed into an icy wasteland, Figure I.2), but to contemplate the dangers of nuclear experimentation and the proliferation of monsters. The meanings of such monsters position the *kaijū* film somewhere between the horror and sci-fi genres. Their approach to monsters is partly gothic, always engaged with modernity, but more in keeping with the messaging of the science-fiction film and its articulation of Otherness in critiquing humanity's transformative impact on nature. The monsters are often, in

**Figure I.2** Godzilla and Miniya emotionally huddle at the end of *Son of Godzilla* (Tōhō)

Sobchack's terms, victims not of themselves, but of an accident. The *kaijū* film therefore draws on aspects of these two genres, and is more a subgenre that sits at the intersection of these two thematically, although it has, to echo Rick Altman's terms (1984), a semantics of its own – its own monsters – that have deep connections with history.

The term *kaijū* has reasonably ancient roots. It originates in the Chinese *Classic of Mountains and Seas* (*Shan Hai Jing*, approximately third century BC to second century AD). *The Classic* is a tour of the kingdoms by a series of mythical deities. The book describes the landscape and the creatures that roam there, *guàishòu* (怪兽), strange beasts, mainly birds, such as the malignforce-buzzard of Mount Stagcry: 'it looks like a buzzard but it has horns. It makes noise like a baby crying. It eats humans' (Birrell 1999, 7). The many divine birds, horses, foxes and fish often exhibit multiple heads, tails or body parts, their numerology symbolising a variety of earthly or cosmic aspects. There is little resemblance between modern *kaijū* and the beasts of *The Classic*, other than their strangeness, curiousness or paranormality. Nevertheless, the term *kaijū* develops from such roots, and can be found in late nineteenth- and early twentieth-century documents in Japan. The Japanese National Diet's Digital Library contains several documents that evidence use of the word *kaijū*, in tales of monsters (Nakagawa 1874, Suzuki 1908) and Greek myths (Baldwin and Daisui 1909).

As we'll see in later chapters, there is no direct, comparable antecedent in Japanese folklore for giant monsters like Godzilla, Mothra, King Ghidorah or Gamera. However, *kaijū* such as these do share attributes with folkloric creatures. William Tsutsui talks about how Godzilla 'resonated with legends . . . Giant serpent deities [that] inhabited remote mountain valleys, and dragons [that] moved across water, land and sky' (Tsutsui 2004, 15). Godzilla evokes dragon mythology, its connection with the sea, and in *Gojira*, the creature is imbued with mythological (albeit fictional) origins for the inhabitants of Odo Island. In 1991's *Godzilla vs. King Ghidorah* (*Gojira buiesu Kingu Gidora,* Ōmori Kazuki), the *kaijū*'s origins were revised, becoming a nuclear-mutated Godzillasaurus, a specific type of dinosaur (Figure I.3). While this further weakens the folkloric dimension of *kaijū*, it re-emphasises the centrality of motifs of nuclear anxiety in *kaijū* movies. Barr echoes this contention when he points out that the *kaijū* film is, in Susan Sontag's terms, destined always to 'reflect world-wide anxieties' but rarely provides much solace from those fears (2016, 9). Nonetheless, the shades of folklore in understanding *kaijū* do help to define the genre as one that is heavily dependent upon national contexts. In *Japan's Green Monsters* (2018),

Figure I.3 The US military is attacked by a time-travelled Godzillasaurus in *Godzilla vs. King Ghidorah* (Tōhō)

Sean Rhoads and Brooke McCorkle discuss how the performer-in-a-suit technique behind the monsters in the *kaijū eiga* (generally referred to as suitmation) reflect performative traditions of classical Japanese theatre, such as Nō, Kabuki and Bunraku, which depicted many stories of monsters and the supernatural, often through a series of stock characters and voiceless monsters that can be seen reflected in the *kaijū* movie. Rhoads and McCorkle also discuss how *kaijū* may refer to other Japanese monsters, such as *yōkai*. *Yōkai* are described by Michael Dylan Foster as 'creatures of the borderlands, living on the edge of town, or in the mountains between villages, or in the eddies of a river running between two rice fields' (Foster 2015, 5). These are fantastic monsters, mysterious, strange, shape-shifting creatures, often with the mark of the divine: *kami*, in Shinto, Japan's dominant religion, are spirits inhabiting all manner of natural things, such as water, mountains or stones. Some, such as *kappa*, as Rhoads and McCorkle discuss, can resemble turtles, like the giant space *kaijū* Gamera, the star of twelve *kaijū eiga*; Foster describes *kappa* as 'mischievous and sometimes deadly, notorious for pulling horses and cattle into the water; they have also been known to drown young children and extract their internal organs through their anuses' (2015, 157). Gamera, famously the friend to all children, is unlikely to do this. The resemblance, therefore, is likely to be superficial, although it highlights the importance of certain forms for the physical appearance of some monsters, such as *orochi*, an eight-headed dragon whose multiple heads and tails echo King Ghidorah, or *ryū*, a Japanese dragon serpent that resembles Manda, the serpent of underwater kingdom Mu, first seen in *Atragon* (*Kaitei Gunkan*, lit. *The Undersea Warship*, Honda Ishirō, 1963).

Foster gives us a clear indication of the relationship between *kaijū* and *yōkai*:

> Kaijū shares a kanji (*kai*) with yōkai and might be translated as 'strange beast.' The difference between kaijū and yōkai is murky, but kaijū usually encompass gigantic creatures such as Godzilla, Mothra and Gamera that appear in kaijū eiga, or 'monster movies.' Kaijū do not often, if ever, appear in local folktales and legends. Generally speaking, then, kaijū are physically giant creatures whose origins are traceable not to folk roots but to commercial sources – usually a movie. So even though Godzilla (or Gojira as it is known in Japan) is one of Japan's most globally infamous monsters, in Japan Godzilla is not a yōkai. (2015, 22–3)

This is a very important distinction for our purposes here: the *kaijū* is marked by two significant aspects: their size and their modern origins (Foster is here perhaps a little dismissive of the 'commercial' roots of the *kaijū eiga*). In subsequent chapters, we'll see how the *kaijū eiga* is marked by its relationship with contemporary politics and anxieties, as Barr also contends, but this distinction allows the genre to be open to investigation as a transnational genre that is defined more straightforwardly through the presence of a giant monster, its very size determining its 'strangeness'. For Barr, this allows the canon of monsters to encompass not only Japanese *kaijū* but examples as broad as the giant, genetically modified *Indominus rex* of *Jurassic World* (Colin Teverrow, 2004) and the Stay-Puft Marshmallow Man in *Ghostbusters* (Ivan Reitman, 1984). The former is perhaps a more appropriate inclusion in this canon, since the monster's existence relies on genetic modification, given that threats from science are a common theme in *kaijū* movies, and its production by Legendary Pictures also connects it to the MonsterVerse films starring Godzilla, King Kong, Mothra and King Ghidorah. However, the loose inclusion of the Marshmallow Man, a form taken by the God Gozer to attack New York and the heroes, provides a mild form of social criticism that Barr dismisses as 'hollow', but which ultimately would leave the film outside the transnational *kaijū eiga*.

For an alternative approach to classifying *kaijū*, an article by J. D. Lees, editor of fanzine *G-Fan*, takes a biological approach to classifying the genus *kaijū*. Noting that *daikaijū* and *kaijū* have become synonymous,

Lees explores how the distinctions in what qualifies as a *kaijū* lead to a few points:

1. [The *kaijū*'s] size must be beyond the upper limit of natural and enable the entity to destroy buildings.
2. It must present a menacing aspect.
3. It must show some degree of purposeful intelligence beyond that of any comparable animal. (Lees 2006, 71)

Lees' classification of *kaijū* as animal does problematise further Barr's points about the Stay-Puft Marshmallow Man – as a giant corporate icon, it wouldn't fit with Lees' distinction. It would obviously include characters from the 'classic' *kaijū* pantheon: Godzilla, Gamera, Gappa, Girara. But it wouldn't necessarily cover monsters from sci-fi films such as *Them!* (Gordon Douglas, 1954), *The Blob* (Irvin S. Yeaworth, Russell S. Doughten, 1958) or *X: The Unknown* (Leslie Norman, Joseph Losey, 1956). While we might see them as fitting into Barr's generic criterion about anxiety, focusing on similar nuclear or political anxieties, they fall outside our object of study here, simply because the monster either isn't big enough, or, like the giant ants of *Them!*, isn't characterised in ways that fit with many *kaijū*. Lees' reference to intelligence is perhaps a moot point, but if we widen this to encompass some form of performance or characterisation, then many films begin to fit with this, such as *Cloverfield* (Matt Reeves, 2008). Rife with post-9/11 metaphors, the monster, known as Clover, fits comfortably with Lees' classification, and has commonly been discussed as a *kaijū* by fans. Its scale, destructive force and purposefulness make it easy to understand the film as fitting within a canon of *kaijū* cinema.

Perhaps a further key point to take from Lees' article is about nationality. For our purposes here, this is another significant distinction in defining part of the book's approach. Lees notes that there is an argument that *kaijū* can only be defined as such if they come from Japan. He counters that 'country of origin is irrelevant to the basic nature of the entity' (72). This is a particularly salient viewpoint for a transnational exploration of the form. If *kaijū* cinema can originate from any country (because 'every country has a monster'), then we can establish an international canon of *kaijū eiga*. But, as we'll come to see, international and transnational are not synonymous. Transnationalism transcends nation but doesn't make it irrelevant. Texts relating to nationhood and regional distinctions still hold sway, even though cross-cultural interactions might weaken or complicate such traits. 'Nationality', Lees continues, 'could be a subset of kaijū, as in Japanese kaijū, British kaijū, or American kaijū. Whether it is considered an important criterion is another debate' (72). This debate is something that this book will engage with very strongly. Nationality is a key determining characteristic for film industries, cultural content and fandoms. Processes such as cultural flow have meant that cultural products, such as films, have spread globally, adopted or appropriated by audiences and producers, and reworked. If such processes weren't relevant to global film cultures, we wouldn't see forms such as the *kaijū eiga* or the Western spread beyond their originating cultures. The Western has become a globalised genre. Its highly specific relationship with American history and Manifest Destiny hasn't stopped its production spreading to Latin America, Europe or Asia in ways that adapt its source material for local contexts, national histories and according to national cinemas' standards and processes. We'll return to this as we begin to look more closely at transnational cinema.

## Cult Movies

In the first volume of *The Big Book of Japanese Giant Monster Movies* (2017), John LeMay introduces the *kaijū* movie through the lens of the cult movies of the 1960s, which he describes as 'a wild and offbeat time for cinema exports'. For LeMay, the *kaijū eiga* sits alongside several genres that he situates in their respective national contexts:

> Rome introduced the world to Sword and Sandal epics and Spaghetti Westerns via Cinecitta Films, Mexico made colorful lucha-heroes, China [*sic*] showcased the Shaw Brothers and Kung Fu, England gave the gothic Hammer horrors of Peter Cushing and Christopher Lee, and the Japanese had their 'rubber suited giant monsters.' (13)

LeMay's contextualisation of the *kaijū* movie as one that emerged from specific national origins is highly significant here. As every country has a monster that it is afraid of, we can also identify that countries have cult genres with which they become associated. However, as Tim Bergfelder has pointed out, these genres were often 'contained' by both critics and scholars within specific national cultural contexts, and forms like the spaghetti Western or exploitation films were frequently situated within specifically Italian contexts. But, as Bergfelder argues, this often overlooks how those films were regularly designed precisely for their 'cross-cultural appeal' (2005, 141). Such productions underline some of the complexities of the relationships between national cinemas and cult films.

Sangjoon Lee has explored how some of these traditions collided in the Hammer–Shaw Brothers co-production *The Legend of the Seven Golden*

*Vampires* (Roy Ward Baker, 1974). As Lee discusses, the production context in the UK during the 1960s was heavily reliant upon funding from Hollywood, with over 90 per cent of UK film funding coming from the US during the latter part of the decade. *The Legend of the Seven Golden Vampires* was an attempt to capitalise upon the most popular Hammer property, *Dracula*, although, to circumvent the 'crisis' in the British film industry, the studio was forced to look further afield for funding. The Shaw Brothers, based in Hong Kong, provided an opportunity both to plug gaps in the film's budget and provide an avenue through which to sell the film to American distributors due to the popularity of kung fu films in the US. Films like these[2] 'transnational productions, [are] hybrid genres, . . . explicit instances of "genre-mixing"' (2016, 67). Their creolisation problematises the relationship between genres and their national origins, especially when cult films were designed to appeal to a maximum range of cross-cultural spectators. This was frequently achieved through re-editing, retitling and the reworking of elements as the films crossed borders. *The Legend of the Seven Golden Vampires* was released in a 110-minute version for Asia and an 89-minute one for Europe, which shortened the fight sequences. When the film was belatedly released in the US in 1979, it was called *The Seven Brothers Meet Dracula* and just 83 minutes long. As we'll see later, this was repeatedly the fate of *kaijū* movies as they travelled across borders. Perhaps as a footnote to this example, however, it's worth mentioning that in *A History of Horrors: The Rise and Fall of the House of Hammer*, Denis Meikle refers to *The Legend of the Seven Golden Vampires* as 'an unmitigated mishmash on the level of Toho's Godzilla series' (Meikle and Koetting 2009, 212), the *kaijū* film seemingly unfairly standing in as a metonym for the Asian cult film.

The cult film has long been assumed to be an example of hybridity, of being blended, or simply a 'mishmash'. Umberto Eco referred to *Casablanca* (Michael Curtiz, 1942) as a 'hodgepodge', 'ramshackle, rickety, unhinged', 'a palimpsest for future students of twentieth-century religiosity' (1986, 197–8). For Eco, the cult movie

> must provide a completely furnished world so that its fans can quote characters and episodes as if they were aspects of the fan's private sectarian world, a world about which one can make up quizzes and play trivia games so that the adepts of the sect recognize through each other a shared expertise. (198)

Ultimately, 'in order to transform a work into a cult object one must be able to break, dislocate and unhinge it so that one can remember only parts of it, irrespective of their original relationship with the whole' (198). The cult film for Eco is almost always one that is a kind of hybrid rooted in the 'cultural'. When we talk about the cross-cultural dimensions of the cult movie, the national origins of the text are called into question. For Ernest Mathijs and Jamie Sexton, the transgressive quality of cult movies, especially Asian cult movies, is at the core of their appeal for transnational viewers. These authors contend that the cult around Godzilla exists because of this transgression of boundaries. It builds 'on aspects of transnationalism and exoticism'; it is 'transnational because [it is] transgressive, *and* transgressive because [it is] transnational' (2011, 120). For Mathijs and Sexton, part of the transnational appeal of *Gojira*, its many sequels, and the Asian cult film more broadly, is difference. It emphasises an Otherness and opposition from the norms of what Jeffrey Sconce terms 'the parent taste culture' (1995, 376). The monster plays a role as both 'destructor and respected icon' (in Chon Noriega's [1987] terms) and therefore disturbs 'the binary us-versus-them opposition that Western cinema seeks to conform' (Mathijs and Sexton 2011, 120).

Definitions of cult cinema are key to understanding the markers of hybridity and cultural blending that mark the *kaijū* film's origins and legacy. As LeMay has demonstrated for us, cult genres are often marked by their national origins, from their names to their key symbols. In many cases, audiences engage with cult cinema *because* of its difference from Hollywood norms. The *kaijū eiga* even appears in Sconce's list of paracinematic forms (Sconce 1995, 372). Subgenres such as the *kaijū* film, with strong associations with exploitation cinema, allow audiences to articulate subcultural capital, an oppositional stance to the standards of 'high-brow' culture. Many *kaijū* fans have grown up with the films playing on television and later home video, which has now given way to a 'social space' of YouTubers and podcasters that continue to celebrate monster-battle spectacles. As Steve Ryfle explained during Godzilla's fiftieth anniversary, the monster had both cult cachet and serious 'world cinema' credentials:

> Godzilla, that city-smashing, vaguely mammalian-looking mutant reptile with the white-hot radiation breath and that trademark high-pitched roar, is a worldwide pop icon and Japan's most internationally famous movie star. In this corner of the world, he's considered little more than a cartoon character, a low-tech holdover from the time of atomic bug movies and drive-in theaters, and a nostalgia trip for aging boomers and post-boomers who spent the Saturdays of their youth watching creature-feature programs. For any Cold War-era kid fascinated with giants, monsters, outer space, warfare, technological wonders, the future, and the bizarre,

> the Godzilla movies of the sixties and seventies were the ultimate *outré* playground for the imagination. (Ryfle 2005, 46)

Ryfle captures much of the cult charm of *kaijū* films here: their nostalgic attractiveness to childhood eras with simple morality; the films' 'low-tech' approach to special effects; their hybridisation of elements of other genres; and their 'bizarreness'. This all combines to produce an image of paracinematic and cult allure that generally stands apart from the dominant stylistic and technological standards associated with Hollywood. When we add in things like dubbing and the editing of the films alongside these elements, we have a form that is highly applicable to cult appropriation. And, as Ryfle goes on to explain, when Hollywood inevitably produced its own Godzilla film in 1998, directed by *Independence Day*'s (1996) Roland Emmerich, the results were spurned by fans. The design of the monster lacked the charm and distinctiveness of the 'real' Godzilla, and its characterisation was largely absent. The monster is now referred to by fans as GINO (Godzilla in name only), and, in their series continuity, Tōhō re-copyrighted the monster as Zilla. The 1998 film had high Hollywood production values but little of what fans wanted in a Godzilla film. Yet, while the *kaijū* film builds on its cult appeal, it also has roots that are canonised within the most significant works of national cinema in Japan. Looking 'beyond the rubber suits and the flaming Tokyos' (Ryfle 2005, 63), we can see a work – Honda's *Gojira* – that, in its original form, is a classic of world cinema, released by prestigious outlets such as the British Film Institute and the Criterion Collection. We'll look more closely at this in the next chapter, but it's worth pointing out here that the *kaijū* film is typical of cult movies in that, to use Iain Robert Smith's terms, it 'relies precisely on [the] productive tension between celebration and mockery of difference' (2013, 237) that can, on one hand, celebrate the transgressive appeal of transnational cinema, and, simultaneously, be mocked for its perceived badness via difference from the perceived norms of Hollywood cinema.

## Transnational Cinema

Transnational cinema has emerged as a critical focus in film studies during the last decade or so. As the area has firmly established its conceptual and methodological approach to analysing film history and texts, numerous studies have appeared that have explored cinema as a transnational medium that has persistently crossed boundaries and cultures. It is both a product and critique of globalisation. Yet, while globalisation can often be interpreted as a threatening Americanisation, transnational emphases have enabled us to look at how flows of culture, ideas, individuals, capital and technologies can often be multidirectional and interact with local, regional and global power structures that call the stability of borders and national identity into question. Borders have never held giant monsters back (figuratively as well as literally onscreen). Dudley Andrew's comment that '[b]orders are thresholds as much as walls' (2011, 1008) has never been more salient. For those monsters, borders pose as little of a hindrance as the walls of skyscrapers.

Although the term 'transnational' has been in circulation for many decades, it came into academic discourse toward the end of the twentieth century as late capitalism intensified. Transnationalism offers a vision of multiple and plural mobilities, as texts are consumed by diverse audiences in different countries, as film crews travel around the world to work in those countries, production companies draw finance from assorted areas, and ideas are reworked, adopted, consumed in multiple ways in dissimilar cultures. Nations aren't hermetically sealed bubbles, and neither are their cultures. Andrew Higson, one of the principle architects of concepts of national cinema (2002), has argued that national cinema is a limiting concept:

> The movement of films across borders may introduce exotic elements to the 'indigenous' culture. One response to this is the anxious concern about the effects of cultural imperialism, a concern that the local culture will be infected, even destroyed by the foreign invader. A contrary response is that the introduction of exotic elements may well have a liberating or democratising effect on the local culture, expanding the cultural repertoire. A third possibility is that the foreign commodity will not be treated as exotic by the local audience, but will be interpreted according to an 'indigenous' frame of reference; that is, it will be metaphorically translated into a local idiom. (2006, 19)

The metaphor of the foreign invader is highly applicable for the purposes of this study. *Kaijū* represent an 'exotic element'; as we'll see, as films have spread globally, and the subgenre has become established as a transnational one, national cultures remain – *kaijū* expand the repertoire of images and references available to a local culture. And, once those images become interpreted through an indigenous frame of reference, the form of the *kaijū* film is created. If *Gojira* has an originating moment, it is precisely through this indigenising frame of reference, as imported films are filtered through a specifically national consciousness and made relevant to Japanese audiences and producers. The influence of American films like *King Kong* (Ernest B. Schoedsack and

Merian C. Cooper, 1933) and *The Beast from 20,000 Fathoms* (Eugène Lourié, 1953) has long been held as an important precedent in the formation of the *kaijū* film. Lourié's film was the first to become a *kaijū* film in Japan, when it was released as *Genshi kaijū arawaru* (*Atomic Monster Appears*) in December 1954, just after the release of *Gojira* in November. The producers of *Gojira* were, as Ryfle notes, likely to have been aware of the Hollywood film. An early working title for the Tōhō film was *The Giant Monster from 20,000 Miles beneath the Sea* (Ryfle 2005, 49). Kayama Shigeru's story was even published under this title prior to the film's release. But, as Tsutsui argues, the local interpretation of the generic trope becomes more significant in the form realised by Japanese producers: 'the message of the original Godzilla is so much more nuanced, the special effects so different, and the emotions stirred so much more profound that any charges of cinematic plagiarism seem all but irrelevant' (2004, 20).

Transnational cinema has been defined by Daniela Berghahn and Claudia Sternberg (2010) as 'a generic category that comprises different aspects of film production, distribution and consumption which *transcend* national film cultures' (22; emphasis added). This is an important point: transnational cinema does not replace thinking about national cinemas but supplements it. National cinemas remain an important and relevant emphasis in film cultures. As Deborah Shaw outlines in her article 'Deconstructing and Reconstructing "Transnational Cinema"' (2013b), transnational cinema takes fifteen different forms and emphases, from the politics of globalisation to elements of cross-border production (52). She adds 'national films' to this list.[3] This controversial category emphasises the continuing relevance of national cinema for a transnational frame of interpretation and study, namely that the national retains its prominence in terms of cultural policy, identity, economics and ideology. Not all 'national films' receive international distribution, and many have little relevance for global audiences, for reasons of language or theme. They remain within their own borders and tell stories relevant only to local (and perhaps diasporic) viewers. While many of the *kaijū* films we'll consider throughout the book do circulate outside their national borders, it's important to note that not all 'break out'. The Hindi film *Gogola* (Balwant Dave, 1966) has since been lost, the only surviving evidence a promotional poster for its Mumbai release that bills it as 'an action packed story of a Sea-monster with Thrills, Suspense and What Not? [*sic*]' and its soundtrack on YouTube.

Shaw's categories intersect with the production of *kaijū* movies, both historically and more recently. Transnational stars and directors have become higher profile as films have become more defined products of global capital, from the appearances of Nick Adams and Russ Tamblyn in the 1960s to more recent appearances, including Zhang Ziyi in 2019's *Godzilla: King of the Monsters* (Michael Dougherty). Directors such as Guillermo del Toro, Gareth Edwards, Shin Sang-ok and Honda Ishirō have produced films across and beyond borders. Co-productions have been a core ingredient of *kaijū* cinema as American, Chinese, Japanese and British companies have collaborated to produce *kaijū* movies throughout the second half of the twentieth century and into the next. Modes of production, distribution and exhibition are therefore resolutely transnational, as work is produced (and reinterpreted) in global circulation, while audiences adopt and understand the films through local and global lenses. As I've mentioned above, the very form of the *kaijū* movie is a product of cultural exchange and transnational influences that have been integrated into an ongoing process of development, appropriation, hybridisation and production that speaks to the globalisation of the form of the *kaijū* film and demonstrates its place in the film industries of multiple countries. *Kaijū* cinema also engages with the condition of living in a transnationally interconnected world, covering Shaw's categories of the cinema of globalisation; stories of migration, journeying and other forms of border crossing; and the transnational modes of narration that express the condition of living as a transnational subject. Whether this is about the threats of a nuclear-powered world, or in the face of ecological disaster, *kaijū* films have demonstrated the shared threats that make borders obsolete, just as the monsters care little for those borders, right from the first *kaijū* films onwards. From *King Kong* to *The Beast from 20,000 Fathoms* and *Mothra* (*Mosura*, Honda, 1961), the *kaijū* film is globally obsessed with border crossing.

As this book contends throughout, the *kaijū eiga* is a transnational genre. In their introduction to *Global Genres, Local Films: The Transnational Dimension of Spanish Cinema* (2016), Elena Oliete-Aldea, Beatriz Oria and Juan Tarancón view transnational genres through national and regional connections:

> films, regardless of their generic resemblances, engage in a context that is always changing as a consequence of concrete political, social and cultural forces, and genre conventions – although developed in a supranational sphere – always derive their meanings from these forces as much as from the histories and traditions they carry with them. (3)

As we've begun to see, the structures and aesthetics of genre develop in, over and above national boundaries, although, as Oliete-Aldea et al.

describe here, they are given specific forms through their contact with identifiable national contexts: 'genres evolve in a supranational exchange of recognizable narrative and aesthetic choices while engaging in and responding to specific social challenges' (3). *Gojira* was made possible by specific national conditions: the loosening of censorship at the end of the Allied Powers occupation following the Second World War and the national trauma of the Hiroshima and Nagasaki nuclear bombings in August 1945. Yet the genre had begun to establish itself globally prior to this, and the choices made by the production team (of which more in the next chapter) respond to those specific social challenges. As Tsutsui mentions, this elevates the films beyond a simple rip-off of the technologically superior American films made prior to this; it gives the genre its own defined form for the first time. With this experience of occupation, national trauma and the consumption of American movies, the development of the *kaijū* film speaks to cross-border national relationships. As Oliete-Aldea et al. point out, films play a significant role in articulating the different experiences of transnationalism 'both [as] agents and expressions of globalization' (5). Genres are inflected by transnational flows, and do not always represent the nation in the same way:

> generic conventions rest on international interactions that undercut any attempt to put forward a unique and distinctive account of national identity. How we represent the nation to ourselves (or how we imagine our community) is inextricably linked to transnational relations . . . The nation and the transnational – or the local and the global – do not designate different, mutually exclusive conditions. (4)

Nation is always present in some sense, weakly or strongly, in its interactions with supra-, trans- or international conventions or structures, or in conformance with particular blueprints. The blueprint of the *kaijū* movie is always at once both about, and a product of, transnational interconnectedness and speaks to local interpretations of the format in how it examines specifically national contexts.

The *kaijū* movie is therefore a product and representation of Arjun Appadurai's notion of 'global cultural flow'. These flows cover the movement of people, media, technology, capital and ideas that Appadurai argued was representative of a 'new global cultural economy . . . understood as a complex, overlapping, disjunctive order, which cannot any longer be understood in terms of existing center–periphery models' (1990, 296). This globalised economy takes on a 'fluid, irregular' formation (297). Centre–margins models of previous cultural formations that rely upon distinctions between self and Other or 'us and them' (in cinema terms, between Hollywood and the rest) are muddied. Lines of flow become uneven and multidirectional between different regions, industries and nations (for instance, Hollywood and Japan, Japan and China, South and North Korea, Britain and Italy, Germany and Japan), where historical power relations are different, while acknowledging different relationships regionally and globally. The story of the *kaijū eiga* is one that takes its form due to the different lines of flow across and between nations over the last century, producing a type of film that emphasises how a transnational genre thrives on changing political and economic relationships.

## Transnational *Kaijū*

As I mentioned at the outset, this isn't an exhaustive overview of the *kaijū eiga*, or an exploration of giant monster movies and whether they are or aren't *kaijū* films. It's an exploration of how *kaijū* cinema has helped make us aware of our connectedness and how culture moves across borders. Chapter 1 looks at *kaijū* movies' origins, and how *Gojira* established the template for the form moving forward. However, in so doing, I'll examine how the makers of *Gojira* exhibited creativity in their adaptation of films that largely originated in America. Without diminishing the Japaneseness of *kaijū*, the chapter looks back at some of the films that influenced Honda and his associates and the ways in which national films can emerge from transnational origins.

The second chapter starts to investigate the ripple effect of *Gojira*'s impact on national popular cinemas. This is largely through an exploration of how the tropes developed throughout Tōhō's monster films came to be imitated by their competitors and the ways in which a genre started to crystallise. For the purposes of our argument here, the chapter examines how Japanese studios, and the government, came to support a wave of films in the first monster boom that were intentionally transnational in nature. Not all examples of national cinema are intended only to be exhibited locally, and *kaijū eiga* quickly became an attractive market for export and co-production with American producers. Chapter 3 follows these ripples and looks at the regional spread of *kaijū* films by focusing on a case study of Korean monster movies. Korean–Japanese relations have been defined by the latter's occupation of the Korean peninsula. As such, the production of South Korean variants became a means through which South Korean filmmakers could appropriate material for a popular family film form, even though Japanese culture was banned there. The chapter looks at how *kaijū* movies by South Korean filmmakers, albeit produced sporadically, emphasise aspects of transnational mobility for cultural products and personnel who travelled to work on them. Furthermore, the chapter examines how the *kaijū* film continued to be a means of exploring cross-border politics and connections as transnational relationships developed across the twentieth century.

Subsequent chapters continue to head west. Chapter 4 examines the localisation of *kaijū* films and how the work of distributors shaped contemporary understandings of the *kaijū eiga*. It explores how films with giant monsters were adapted to fit other cinemas' standards and became exploitation films in the process, circulating in different forms and often with numerous titles to fit with distributors' catalogues. Chapter 5 then considers western productions that appropriated *kaijū* tropes and memes. It explores the many films produced across low-budget and Hollywood sectors and how they sometimes problematise or adapt the *kaijū* formula to different ends. This includes considering how *kaijū* have become staples of low-budget mockbuster production and the prominence of giant ape films. Finally, in our last chapter, we consider how Legendary Entertainment have shaped contemporary *kaijū* films. Legendary's films have resurrected the shared universe of Tōhō's creations and shifted their texts to fit the demands of themes around climate change. Furthermore, Legendary's Chinese ownership has come to reflect the shifting poles of cultural power and how *kaijū* cinema is now wrapped up with China's policies around soft power, a strategy once inherent in Japanese culture. Nevertheless, despite how connected and mobile cinema has become as it has transnationalised, concepts of nation (and nationalism) still hold sway, and we'll come to discuss this as we wrap up in the Conclusion.

## Notes

1. I will henceforth refer to Honda's film by its Japanese title. While I will generally refer to Japanese films with the titles by which they're known internationally, I'll use *Gojira* to disambiguate between *Gojira* (1954), *Return of Godzilla* (the US title of *Gojira*, 1984), *Godzilla* (1998) and *Godzilla* (2014).
2. Lee cites many, across 'low-end' genres including horror, spaghetti Westerns, blaxploitation, *jidaigeki* (Japanese historical *chambara*, involving swordplay), sci-fi and sexploitation.
3. A different version of the list had previously been published in the first issue of the *Transnational Cinema* (now *Screens*) journal (Shaw and De La Garza 2010).

CHAPTER 1

# National Films, Transnational Monsters

A 2017 post on the Maser Patrol blog poses the question, '怪獣 or 外獣? (Kaiju or Gaiju?)' (Maser Patrol 2017). Its author, Kevin Derendorf, whose reviews are collected in the book *Kaijū for Hipsters* (2018), notes that *kaijū* has 'permeated the English lexicon' as a loanword but that the term *kaibutsu* (怪物, 'strange creature') was often used for translations from English of monster films that originated outside Japan. Yet it is *kaijū* that has spread globally as the most widely used term to describe giant monsters. Derendorf suggests an alternative: 'utilizing the kanji that already exists for foreignness (外), and shortening those "gaikoku kaiju" down to just "gai-jū", like the slang term "gaijin" for foreign people'. Derendorf's comments here highlight a common thread in *kaijū* cinema's reception: its association with Japan. The *kaijū*/*gaijū* distinction essentialises the Japaneseness of the *kaijū eiga* and distinguishes its specifically Japanese historical and social concerns, from the end of the Second World War onwards. Yet it obscures the transnational origins of the giant monster movie. If *gaijū* is useful as a classifying term for the genealogy of monsters, it is in calling attention to the *kaijū eiga*'s continuing relationship with conceptions of national cinema. This is emphasised by the introduction to *The Japanese Cinema Book*, released alongside the British Film Institute's series of films from Japan in 2020 (to coincide with the 2020 Tokyo Olympics, prior to their postponement). Hideaki Fujiki and Alastair Phillips introduce their collection by summarising the main draws of the cinema of Japan: 'from the work of renowned directors such as Ozu Yasujirō, Kurosawa Akira, Miyazaki Hayao and Kore-eda Hirokazu to Samurai and horror films, the Godzilla series and anime' (Fujiki and Phillips 2020, 1).

This strong connection with Japanese national cinema calls into question the relationships between nation and genres or forms of cinema that relate to transnational form. National/international binaries are complicated by, but may also overshadow, the centrality of hybridity in both national and transnational cinemas. Derendorf's *kaijū/gaijū* distinction echoes the opposition of 'the west' and 'the rest' described by Koichi Iwabuchi, in response to Stuart Hall's argument concerning postcolonial hybridity in 'When Was the Post-Colonial? Thinking at the Limit' (1996). Hybridity, Iwabuchi argues:

> fruitfully displaces our conception of clearly demarcated national/cultural boundaries, which have been based upon a binary opposition between 'us' and 'them,' 'the West' and 'the Rest,' and the colonizer and the colonized, with a postcolonial perspective which 'oblige(s) us to re-read the binaries as forms of transculturation, of cultural translation, destined to trouble the here/there cultural binaries forever' (Hall 1996, 247). (Iwabuchi 2002, 51)

The separation of *kaijū* and *gaijū* demarcates national boundaries and downplays hybridity. This is not to deny the importance of nation in understanding the *kaijū* film, since this has generally been the default way of looking at *kaijū eiga* for scholars and critics. As Iwabuchi notes, Japan has traditionally seen itself as part of Asia, but culturally superior, and heavily defined through its cultural and political relationship with the US, and *kaijū* films are no different in this regard. For Iwabuchi, global cultural flows are understood as uneven and hierarchised structures that carry culture across borders, where they can then be reinterpreted, negotiated, remade and indigenised. Japanese products are subject to cultural flows more readily because of their odourless nature (Iwabuchi refers to *mukokuseki*, 無国籍, which translates as borderless or stateless) that makes them particularly open to transcultural appropriation:

> Transnationally circulated images and commodities . . . tend to become culturally odorless in the sense that origins are subsumed by the local transculturation process. By appropriating, hybridizing, indigenizing, and consuming images and commodities of 'foreign' origin in multiple unforeseen ways, even American culture is conceived as 'ours' in many places. (46)

Thus, giant monsters such as King Kong might be *gaijū*, but their global circulation means that their foreignness can be 'subsumed by the local transculturation process' so that what is initially foreign can become localised. This can reveal what Cynthia Erb describes in *Tracking King Kong* as 'questions of international uses of Hollywood films' (Erb 2009, 19). We'll return to these questions later as we consider how *kaijū* cinema transcends national cinema as a hybrid form that is at once both global and national in its origins and ongoing legacy.

The first section of this chapter examines the roots of the *kaijū* film and its relationship with the Japanese national imaginary. The origins of the genre have been well served by scholarship, and this chapter engages broadly with that scholarship to define the ways in which the *kaijū* film has classically been designated as one that is strongly linked with the national cinema of Japan. The opening parts of the first section argue that the focus in scholarship on *kaijū* films has often remained one that is embedded in classical approaches to national cinema (this includes the sustained focus on the first Godzilla film, but little on the subsequent films in the series). The second section of the chapter turns toward the roots and development of the genre by focusing on the ways in which *kaijū* films developed outside Japanese cinema. Much has been made in scholarship and fandom about the roots of the genre in special effects supervisor Tsuburaya Eiji's appreciation of *King Kong* (see Ryfle 1998), but, as Mick Broderick's collection *Hibakusha Cinema: Hiroshima, Nagasaki and the Nuclear Image in Japanese Film* (1996) has made clear, the 1954 *Gojira* has long been held as an example of the national struggles to recognise the nuclear devastation wreaked on the country. Historicising the origins of the genre cinematically will highlight key parts of this book's approach overall, that is, to examine the ways in which transnational genres can draw significantly upon national figures whilst simultaneously emphasising global cultural flows and their impact on conceptions of national cinema.

## *Kaijū* and the Japanese National Imaginary

The Tōhō logo fades up from black as what sounds like thunder pounds. Suddenly, an ear-splitting roar sounds and reverberates multiple times as the thunderous pounding continues. A title rolls up the screen: ゴジラ (*Gojira*). The credits roll over Ifukube Akira's 'Godzilla March' (the main title theme that became associated with the monster in subsequent films). We fade up to the sea, a trawler's wake stretching into the background of the shot as the water bubbles. Cut to the boat's crew relaxing. Some huddle together playing music on guitar and harmonica. Others play games, relax, smoke. The calm is suddenly broken by a blinding light from screen left. The sailors turn towards the source of the light. They run to the side of the boat to investigate, led by the guitarist. The sea then seems to boil up. It explodes, knocking the sailors back. Chaos ensues: the guitar is dropped as a Go board is knocked over. A fierce wind blows across the deck of the ship as the sailors scrabble for safety. Cut to a long shot of the boat on fire, sinking to the stern. Wireless operators try tirelessly to send a distress call but are washed away by torrents flooding into the radio room. As the ship sinks, the message is received.

It finally finds its way to salvage operative Ogata (Takarada Akira, who would become a series regular and fan favourite). A rescue ship is sent, only to suffer the same fate.

The opening of Honda's *Gojira* is extremely efficient in establishing the parameters of the national text of the *kaijū eiga*. The first fishing trawler, the *Eiko-maru no. 5* ('Glory') suffers a fate very similar to a real fishing boat that had inspired the film's producer Tanaka Tomoyuki in the development of the film (Figure 1.1). This origin story is well-trodden ground in scholarship about the Godzilla films, since it provides for the first time the connection between monsters and national trauma that comes to define the first waves of the *kaijū eiga*. It's worth covering this ground again to emphasise the significance of the relationship between *kaijū* films and national cinema. Putting aside for a moment the two nuclear bombs dropped on Hiroshima and Nagasaki on 6 and 9 August 1945 respectively, as well as the firebombing of Tokyo by US air forces in March 1945, a single incident motivates the plot of *Gojira*. As the Cold War escalated following the Second World War, the United States and Russia tested several nuclear devices amid an intensifying arms race. One, tested by the United States on 1 March 1954 at Bikini

**Figure 1.1** The *Eiko-maru*'s sailors are affected by Godzilla's nuclear arrival in *Gojira* (Tōhō)

Atoll as part of Operation Castle – the first test, Castle Bravo – has become significant as a motivating device in the history of *kaijū* films. Alongside its referencing in *Gojira*, it becomes a notable plot device in the Legendary MonsterVerse series, mentioned in *Godzilla* (Gareth Edwards, 2014) and *Kong: Skull Island* (Jordan Vogt-Roberts, 2017), where it's reframed not as a test, but an attempt to destroy a monster by the organisation Monarch (see Chapter 6).

The Castle Bravo test was significantly larger than the devices dropped on Japan in 1945, roughly a thousand times more destructive. But it was an error in calculating the yield that led to disastrous consequences. When the Atoll's reef was vaporised, it fell as ash on an island over a hundred miles away. Within that radius was a Japanese trawler, the *Daigo Fukuryū Maru* ('Lucky Dragon No. 5'). It too was covered in radioactive ash. The crew began to experience burns and hair-loss. One of their personnel died of liver disease weeks later. The experiences of the *Daigo Fukuryū Maru* are a key inspiration for the narrative form of *Gojira*, but they also work strongly to connect the film with national trauma. Rhoads and McCorkle (2018, 29) argue that Tanaka even showed newspaper clippings about the incident to Tōhō executives to persuade them to green-light the film. Likewise, the incident is mentioned in most scholarship about *Gojira*. William Tsutsui mentions that in the wake of the food scare that followed the incident, as many Japanese refused to eat fish landed by tainted boats, the film was an example of 'canny opportunism' or 'bald cynicism', but that it also 'engaged with the most profound, contentious, and chilling issues of the day' (2004, 19). In 'Godzilla and the Japanese Nightmare' (Noriega 1987), Chon Noriega contends that the film emerged from 'no national filmic tradition per se' (1987, 64) but that (drawing on Robin Wood's seminal argument [1985] concerning the American horror film) it developed out of 'the return of the repressed'. The incident involving the *Daigo Fukuryū Maru* had reignited a national debate regarding both the nuclear past and present of the country, as anti-nuclear protests and movements rose in Japan. The US was forced to accept responsibility for the death of the ship's crew member (paying compensation of under $4,000). As Noriega argues, the self/Other distinction more common in western interpretations of monsters is insufficient to explain the nuclear nightmare's embodiment within the monster:

> the monster's American and cold war historical origins, now rooted in Japanese mythology, allow it to serve as an intermediary in the Japanese designating themselves vis-à-vis the United States and, later, the Soviet Union. The plot must then uncover why the *distant* past (embodied in the dinosaur) again confronts the present. (68)

Godzilla is both self and Other, both outsider and insider to Japanese culture, not simply the projection of Otherness onto the United States and its culpability for the attacks and tests that resulted in civilian deaths and suffering:

> The films transfer onto Godzilla the role of the United States in order to symbolically re-enact a problematic United States–Japan relationship that includes atomic war, occupation, and thermonuclear tests. The films, however, in their search for a solution do more than blame and destroy the transferred object, and thereby 'resolve' the 'problem.' 'Other-oriented self-designation' mitigates the sharp division between self and Other implicit in the transference process, so that Godzilla comes to symbolize Japan (self) as well as the United States (Other). (68)

Yomota Inuhiko has also highlighted the significance of the fishing boat incident, as well as identifying the monster with the return of the repressed. Yomota, however, sees the homecoming from the South Seas as metaphorically reflecting the souls of Japan's war dead returning to rest in peace. They are, Yomota contends, 'a mental image of the casualties of the war . . . in an abject relation to those Japanese who had survived the atrocities and who now enjoyed the prosperity and democracy of post-war life' (2007, 108). This highlights the establishment of a prominent national thread in the *kaijū* film. *Gojira* quickly establishes the *kaijū* film's proximity to Japanese national cinema. In *What is Japanese Cinema? A History*, Yomota devotes little time to the *kaijū eiga*, with a greater focus on key auteurs, independent production and a broad overview of studios' rise and fall over a hundred years. However, he calls the genre 'globally unprecedented', yet rooted in the Japanese consciousness:

> an antinuclear film with an ecological perspective . . . The idea of a threat to Tokyo, born in the south seas, is unthinkable without considering the air raids by the American forces that scorched the Japanese archipelago just nine years before the film was shot, as well as offering repose for the Japanese soldiers sent to the south seas. (Yomota 2019, 117)

What is perhaps most surprising about the film is how starkly the film refers to the nuclear tragedy. There are reasons why this remains surprising today, and we'll explore those in Chapter 4 when we look at the exploitation of the film in the United States as *Godzilla, King of the Monsters!* (Honda and Terry O. Morse, 1956). The film engages starkly with the nuclear devastation wreaked on Japan and its people. During the monster's attack on Tokyo, it emerges from the Bay, destroying iconic sites along the way. A train is destroyed at Shinagawa Station. The iconic Wako Department Store in Ginza, one of the buildings that survived the city's bombing in 1945, has its clock torn down. Tōhō's own Nichigeki Theatre is smashed before the National Diet building in Akasaka is reduced partly to rubble (Figure 1.2). Kachidoki Bridge is the last Tokyo landmark to fall to the monster before it returns to the sea. Throughout, the city burns intensely, as though firebombed. The *mise en scène* of the aftermath is redolent of photographs of the real attacks on Tokyo, Hiroshima and Nagasaki. Photographs of the cities after those attacks provide an eerie comparison with the scenes after the monster's attack as the camera tracks across scenes of destruction to the sound of Ifukube's requiem (the 'Prayer for Peace').

Two other moments provide blunt reminders of Japanese national trauma. After news of the monster's attacks at sea emerges in Tokyo, a group of young professionals on a train discuss a story in the newspaper: 'It's terrible', one of them says. The woman in the centre of shot complains of 'atomic tuna and radioactive fallout' (again recalling the *Daigo Fukuryū Maru* incident). 'I barely escaped the atomic bomb at Nagasaki – and now this!', she exclaims. The older man on her right mocks her, saying the monster will get her first, while the younger one frets about needing to evacuate again. At the height of the attack, right before Godzilla destroys the Wako building's clock tower, we see a

**Figure 1.2** Godzilla smashes the National Diet building (Tōhō)

woman huddle with three young children. They are alone and isolated in shot, a high-angle looking down on them (Figure 1.3). The scene cuts back to the monster, framed behind a birdcage, as it screeches, and destroys more of the area. We cut back to the woman as she draws her children more tightly to her. She tells them that they'll be with daddy soon, just a little longer. Their father is presumably one of those soldiers whose unrest is symbolised by the monster's return. Such moments highlight the explicitness of the metaphor in the film.

*Gojira* is not accidentally symbolic – as Tsutsui alluded to, some critics found the explicitness of the metaphors to be not just blunt, but cynical (Figure 1.4). As Steve Ryfle and Ed Godziszewski contend in their biography of Honda, the overt metaphors were very close to the director's personal experience. Throughout the text, these authors emphasise how Honda's world view was strongly shaped by his experiences in the military. Honda had been drafted into the Japanese military in 1934 and saw his filmmaking career interrupted several times as he was reconscripted before and during the war. After a failed coup by his commanding officer, Kurihara Yasushide, on 26 February 1936, Honda was forever tainted by association, even though he hadn't been involved (Ryfle and Godziszewski 2017, 16). He saw service in Imperial Manchukuo

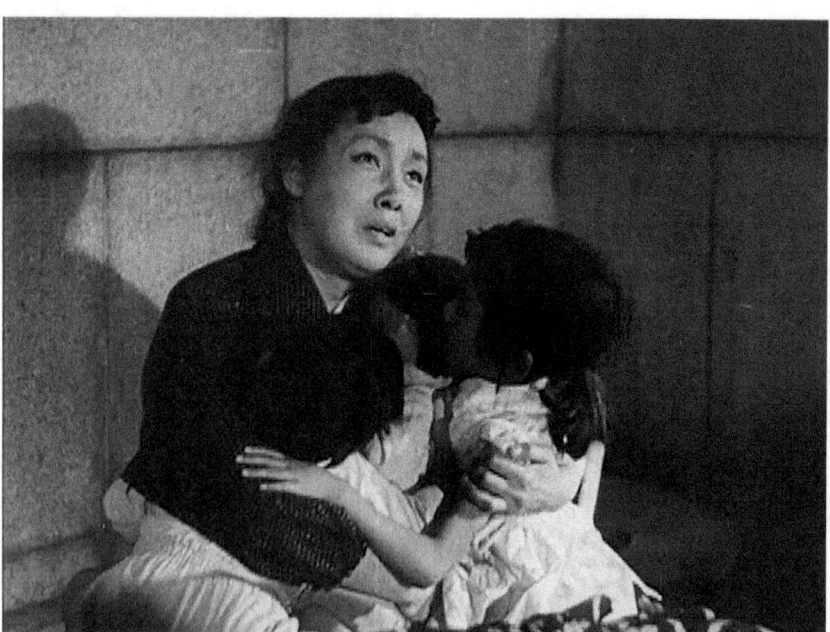

**Figure 1.3** A widow huddles with her children during the *kaijū* attack on Tokyo (Tōhō)

NATIONAL FILMS, TRANSNATIONAL MONSTERS    29

**Figure 1.4** The aftermath of Godzilla's attack evokes the devastation of nuclear bombing (Tōhō)

(at one time overseeing a comfort station, something he wrote candidly about in a 1966 essay, detailed by Ryfle and Godziszewski [28–9]), and during the war, including a spell as a prisoner of the Chinese National Revolutionary Army. His wartime experiences left an indelible mark. Ryfle and Godziszewski note that Honda communicated this to his wife Kimi: 'Having seen the terror of the atomic bomb in real life, it is most important to weave this element into [*Gojira*] as well, so that everyone will understand' (103). Yet, according to the film's assistant director, Honda didn't communicate this to the film's crew. As far as they were concerned, it was a work of pure entertainment.

The anti-nuclear and ecological messages of *Gojira* have been well served by scholarship. They are repeatedly discussed, as mentioned above, and form the basis upon which the *kaijū* film is understood. Hence, I don't want to spend too much time *reading* the film, except to bring out these threads of scholarship that define the film as a classic of national cinema. *Gojira* stands apart from many films in the *kaijū eiga*. Since its global re-emergence at the turn of the twenty-first century, stepping out of the shadow of its Americanised version, its harsh black-and-white photography and serious anti-nuclear message have overcome the cheesy reputation of *Godzilla, King of the Monsters! Gojira*'s international relationship with Japanese national cinema has never been stronger.

Bliss Cua Lim has argued that what she terms a '*national cinema effect*' is problematic when considering Asian cinemas. Discussing Hong Kong in particular (a cinema without a nation), she argues that the 'national cinema paradigm [is] rooted in the *auteurist* model of the postwar European new waves' and 'typically works on a contrastive principle of difference from Hollywood' (Lim 2009, 188). In many regards, this tendency has precluded *Gojira* and its sequels from serious consideration as examples of national cinema. The major auteurs of Japanese cinema – Kurosawa, Ozu and Mizoguchi Kenji – have long been considered representatives of a tradition of national cinema. Yomota attributes this both to the rise of auteurist criticism in Europe during the 1950s, and to the fact that such films 'readily fulfilled Orientalist desires' (2019, 113). Thus, films such as *Gojira* generally fall outside this tendency. This is partly due to how long the film circulated in its international form, dubbed and recut with new scenes, but also down to the lack of both self-Orientalising historical tropes, such as samurai and kimonos (the two features that Yomota attributes to the trend). *Gojira* is a modern film, born of the trauma of the mid-twentieth century, although its genesis is also attributed to the influence of global, particularly Hollywood, cinema that, as we'll see, the film comfortably both drew upon and slotted alongside thematically. As the Godzilla series progressed, its difference from Hollywood standards of production also placed it at odds with global trends. The *kaijū* film is, as other scholars have shown (notably Rhoads and McCorkle, and Igarashi), a relatively conservative form, one which generally promotes Japanese interests and celebrates its growing international confidence during the 1960s. *Kaijū*'s association with younger audiences has also tended to exclude it from more serious interest.

As Andrew Higson points out, a national cinema 'is first of all to specify a coherence and unity; it is to proclaim a unique identity and a stable set of meanings' (2002, 133). *Gojira* is an example of national cinema, but also of *hibakusha* cinema. *Hibakusha* is the term granted to those affected by the nuclear bombings, although it didn't gain legal recognition until three years after the release of *Gojira*, in 1957. The *Daigo Fukuryū Maru* incident had intensified use of the term to refer to victims of nuclear attacks (Naono 2019). Godzilla represents both *hibakusha*, transformed by radiation, its skin ravaged and scarred from exposure, and its cause.

This emphasises Noriega's 'doubled' sense of Otherness in the figure of the monster, as both victim and destroyer. *Gojira* sits alongside films such as Shindo Kaneto's *Children of Hiroshima* (*Genbaku no Ko*, 1952), *Black Rain* (*Kuroi Ame*, Imamura Shohei, 1989) and Kurosawa's *Rhapsody in August* (*Hachigatsu no kyōshikyoku*, 1991). While these still represent more typical auteurist works, *Gojira* is more comfortably assessed, as Broderick notes, alongside anime such as *Barefoot Gen* (*Hadashi no Gen*, Yamada Tengo, 1976), based on Nakazawa Kenji's autobiographical manga, and *Akira* (Otomo Katsuhiro, 1988), with which it shares what Susan Napier calls 'the Japanese imagination of disaster'. First published in 1993, Napier's article also highlights the paucity of serious critique of Japanese mass culture (something since remedied to a large extent, although the *kaijū eiga*, *Gojira* aside, has received limited attention). But she argues that such forms are highly appropriate lenses through which to examine Japan's rapid modernisation and attendant complexities: for her it is the core themes of the science-fiction genre, 'of technological, social, and cultural advancement', that attest to 'the cultural instrumentalities that characterize modern capitalism' (1993, 329). Drawing on Andrew Tudor's notion of 'secure horror' (1989), she suggests that *Gojira* is at once 'cathartic and compensatory': 'collectivity is threatened, but only from the outside, and is ultimately reestablished . . . through the combined efforts of scientists and the government' (1993, 332). As we've seen so far in the chapter, though, the threat is often not from outside, but internalised through prior trauma, specifically in relation to the film's examination of post-war guilt. Nevertheless, what *Gojira* and *Akira* share is destruction. One of the most cathartic pleasures of the *kaijū eiga*, its primary spectacle, is monster destruction. From the Great Kanto Earthquake of 1923 to the Tōhoku Earthquake, tsunami and Fukushima Nuclear Plant meltdown in March 2011, the impact of natural disasters has been a recurring feature of modern Japan that is reflected in the ambivalent spectacle of destruction in the *kaijū* film, from *Gojira* onwards.

This focus on disaster is the subject of perhaps the first critical piece to treat the *kaijū eiga* as serious cinema (although without its Japanese name), Susan Sontag's 1966 article 'The Imagination of Disaster'. Sontag argues that the science-fiction film's primary theme is disaster, mainly the moral disasters that befall humanity's attempted conquests of science and nature, the ones that give rise to the biggest and most deadly of beasts. She notes that the genre 'is concerned with the aesthetics of destruction, with the peculiar beauties to be found in wreaking havoc, making a mess' (Sontag 2009, 213). In their approach to their core subject, *kaijū eiga* are 'strongly moralistic' in their approach to abusive and 'mad' uses of science, something they share with classic horror films (which reminds us of the difficulty of classifying the *kaijū* film, somewhere between the gothic horror and science-fiction films). But it is in the Japanese versions of the imagination of disaster that the issue of mass trauma became most strongly defined: they 'bear witness' to nuclear trauma and 'attempt to exorcise it' (218). The imagination of disaster is strongly ambivalent, as we've explored during this chapter, again something shared with both the horror and science-fiction genres, at once revelling in the spectacle of destruction and devastation, and morally bound to critique the causes of such disaster. One final note to make about Sontag's positioning of the genre, however, and one that relates directly to the *kaijū eiga* as a work of national cinema, is her focus on Honda's cinema (she refers to him as Inoshiro, a common mis-transliteration of his name in the credits of dubbed versions of his films) that allows him to emerge, for once, as an auteur. For a long time, Honda's work was dismissed as too generic for him to be seriously considered as an auteur, and he was therefore someone outside the pantheon of noted Japanese directors. His friendship with Kurosawa, whose career soared whilst Honda's was blighted by his repeated call-ups to the military, had often recuperated Honda's reputation, as he served as assistant to Kurosawa on his later films from *Kagemusha* (1980) onwards. Sontag, perhaps surprisingly, doesn't refer to *Gojira* at all, but she does mention a range of other Honda films, including *Rodan* (*Sora no Daikaijū Radon*, lit. *Giant Monster of the Sky, Radon*, 1956), *The Mysterians* (*Chikyū Bōeigun*, lit. *Earth Defense Force*, 1957) and *Battle in Outer Space* (*Uchū daisensō*, lit. *Great Space War*, 1959). The first of these was Honda's first *kaijū eiga* after *Gojira*, while the latter two are both space invasion movies. So, while there have been more recent attempts to classify Honda as an auteur (particularly Ryfle and Godziszewski's biography), Sontag's focus on Honda's movies fits with 1960s critical attempts to define auteurs through their recurring themes and concerns, a critical tendency often emphasised by constructions of national cinema. Although Honda's work sits apart from the art cinema traditions of national cinema, his contribution to the *kaijū eiga* is an important component in its relationship with discourses of auteurist national cinema. The template of the *kaijū eiga* was determined very quickly by its themes and relationship with national trauma, but its roots also evidence a *'national cinema effect'*. Despite this, the format also has significantly transnational influences that speak to processes of cultural exchange and flows of cultural material across national borders.

## Carl Denham's Giant Monster

Sontag discussed *King Kong* as an 'old monster film' that shared a 'spirit' with Honda's *kaijū* and science-fiction films, namely that of 'primitive gratifications' in the spectacle of city-wide destruction (Sontag 2009, 214). However, this classification of the film as a horror film is something that Erb critiques in her work on *Kong*. Erb places the film in its contemporary location and in relation to the previous works of Ernest B. Schoedsack and Merian C. Cooper in the ethnographic adventure films of the 1920s and 1930s that built problematic binaries between nature (represented by primitivism) and civilisation, equating the camera with the gun (Erb 2009). The opposition of nature and modernity is something that Rhoads and McCorkle argue is central to understanding the *kaijū eiga*, particularly its emphasis on ecological themes. Yet the reclassification of *King Kong* as horror in the 1950s following its twentieth anniversary re-release and reappraisal places it close to the origins of the *kaijū eiga*. Indeed, in many regards, *King Kong* might be considered the first *kaijū eiga*, albeit without its core allegories. As Erb stresses in her own assessment of *Gojira*, the case of *King Kong* can tell us a lot about how a classic of national cinema came to be born of transnational roots and influences. Iain Robert Smith's (2017) concept of the Hollywood meme is relevant here in considering how *King Kong* became adopted by filmmakers outside Hollywood to establish a variant form of the monster genre that is in some sense derivative – albeit as an homage – but that gives rise to a defined subgenre that enters global circulation and is itself subject to further appropriation and revision. While *Gojira* remains the *kaijū eiga*'s urtext, *King Kong*'s formative role cannot be underestimated.

Chapter 1 of David Kalat's book *A Critical History and Filmography of Toho's Godzilla Series* is about *King Kong*, so fused are the two monsters' histories. Kalat refers to legendary special effects director Willis O'Brien's work on the monster in the film as 'pioneering', 'lifelike' and 'unique' (Kalat 1997, 12). *King Kong* therefore becomes a significant originating point for the *kaijū eiga*, despite its American origins. *King Kong*, as Erb demonstrates, has strong affinities with adventure filmmaking and an ethnographic tradition that connects strongly with depictions of colonialist primitivism. Erb argues that:

> King Kong's modernist hybridity stemmed primarily from evolutionist discourses that defined him as both human and animal. Godzilla, who enters at the dawning of the postmodern era, embodies a hybridity born from an intensifying sense of globalization, and from a fear that national destiny is inextricable from international concerns. (Erb 2009, 143)

While Kong's problematic racial and primitivist dimensions emerge from the colonialist trends of jungle adventure films, Godzilla's – and more generally the *kaijū*'s – genesis in a global sphere of national and international concerns strongly emphasises the concerns of our argument here: that transnational genres develop through processes of hybridity. While King Kong's designation as a *kaijū* would be further cemented through the monster's appearance in two Tōhō productions, *King Kong vs. Godzilla* (*Kingu Kongu tai Gojira*, Honda, 1962) and *King Kong Escapes* (*Kingu Kongu no Gyakushū*, lit. *King Kong's Counterattack* Honda, 1967), and the Legendary MonsterVerse, in *Kong: Skull Island* and *Godzilla vs. Kong* (Adam Wingard, 2021), the ape figure has become a staple of giant-monster-on-the-loose movies. This includes Kongsploitation films such as *Konga* (John Lemont, 1961), *A\*P\*E* (*Kingkongui Daeyeokseub*, lit. *King Kong's Counterattack*, Paul Leder, 1976), *Queen Kong* (Frank Agrama, 1976), *The Mighty Peking Man* (AKA *Goliathon*, *Xīngxīng wáng*, lit. *Orangutan King*, Meng Hua Ho, 1977) and *Yeti: Giant of the 20th Century* (Gianfranco Parolini, 1977), as well as the two direct remakes of *King Kong* (John Guillermin, 1976, and Peter Jackson, 2005) and *Rampage* (Brad Peyton, 2018). As we'll see in later chapters, the *kaijū* movie formula became both a staple and a template for exploitation films, a trend that was at once both mocked and celebrated by audiences. *King Kong* became an intrinsic part of that, a generic template for the movies' narratives of urban destruction, hubris and their monstrous stars.

In many regards, *King Kong* cements the formula for the *kaijū* film and its thematic focus on exploitation. A brief plot summary highlights the core elements. Carl Denham (Robert Armstrong) is a successful producer of exotic adventure films. For his latest film, he charters a ship in New York, but, before he can leave, he needs to finalise casting of his leading lady. He meets Ann Darrow (Fay Wray), a down-on-her-luck actress who has to steal food to survive. The expedition sets sail for a mysterious island in the South Pacific that Denham heard about in a Singaporean myth. On the way, Ann forms a bond with the ship's first mate, Jack Driscoll (Bruce Cabot), and rehearses with Denham, imagining something giant and terrifying, a scream in horror. They arrive at the island, and go ashore to begin shooting, finding themselves in a primitive native village dominated by a giant wall that seems built to keep out some gargantuan threat. They witness and interrupt what looks to be a ritual ceremony in which a young woman is to be sacrificed. When the villagers see Ann, they offer a trade for the 'golden woman'. Denham's party refuses and leaves, but Ann is abducted from their ship that night. She is tied to the wall in a replay of the ceremony, and Kong emerges from the wall to take her. This opening act sets up some of the dimensions that we'll see repeated in later *kaijū* movies: the mythic dimensions of the monster and its scale, the hubris and arrogance of the human characters, the sometimes-problematic aspects of binaries between civilisation and nature. These difficulties have long been a focus of criticism of *King Kong*. David N. Rosen, in 1975, pointed to how the film allegorised Depression-era America, and how it highlights the deep racial and social tensions of the times. Not only was this a time when the Ku Klux Klan had expanded its membership, but the economic impacts of the 1929 Wall Street crash had disproportionately disadvantaged African-Americans. Rosen also highlights a reading that has been common, about threads of race (Kong is transported to America in chains) and sexuality:

> Aside from the sexual aspect implicit in the question of race, there's the more direct, and somewhat delirious, sexual imagery in the film. The ape often functions as a most appropriate anthropoid symbol of 'lower,' 'animal' instincts. In this case we have a giant ape (literally a huge, hairy monster) and his unrestrained, headlong pursuit of a 'blonde,' that archetypical Hollywood sex-object, ending on top of the world's foremost phallic symbol. The sexual theme touches on the standard racist myth of the black male's exaggerated sexual potency, and the complementary notion of his insatiable desire for white women. (Rosen 1975)

Rosen highlights a further concern regarding the depiction of revolutionary struggle in the figure of the monster. He points to the prominence of anti-Communist initiatives in the US and the relationships between the Communist Party and black causes, such as that of the Scottsboro Boys, nine African-American teenagers who, in 1931, were accused of raping two white women on a train following a dispute with a group of white men (the case became a landmark racist miscarriage of justice, and the last of the accused men were fully pardoned in 2013). Such associations were escalated in the public consciousness and Kong came to symbolise a fear not just of Blackness but of 'alien elements', in which fears of Communism and racial difference were conflated. Such readings highlight Barr's contention that the *kaijū* film emphasises aspects of anxiety and projects them onto the monster, although Rosen points out that the conservative mechanisms in a film such as *King Kong* are such that the destruction of the beast neutralises its threat. However, these are conventional ways in which *kaijū* films straddle gothic horror and science-fiction in their imagination of Otherness in the form of the monster. As Erb notes, however, this wasn't a contemporary frame through which to view *King Kong*, seen much more in the 1930s as a variant of the jungle adventure film, but reassessed in the 1950s following its re-release labelled as a horror film.

*King Kong*'s second and third acts focus much more on action. After being abducted by Kong, Ann is taken to his mountain lair. Denham and his crew pursue them through the great wall and into the jungle. They encounter several dinosaurs. Denham's crew fight off a Stegosaurus, only to be decimated by a man-eating Brontosaurus. Kong, protecting Ann, kills a Tyrannosaurus rex in hand-to-claw combat, as well as an Elasmosaurus. Ann and Jack escape from Kong's lair after a Pteranodon attempts to swoop away with Ann and the giant ape fights it off. Kong pursues them through the jungle, smashing down the huge gate, but is subdued with gas bombs. In one of cinema's most iconic sequences, Kong is transported to New York City and publicly exhibited as 'The Eighth Wonder of the World'. When flash photography enrages the beast, it breaks loose and rampages through the city. He locates Ann and carries her up the Empire State Building after smashing a commuter train (Figure 1.5). The ape is attacked by biplanes and eventually overcome, falling to the ground as Jack rescues Ann. Denham's line 'it wasn't the

**Figure 1.5** Kong destroys a New York train and establishes a *kaijū* motif (Warner Bros.)

airplanes, it was Beauty killed the Beast' restates the binary between culture and primitivism. The Empire State Building – completed in 1931 – highlights the modernity of New York, as do the technological marvels, trains and planes, that stand in Kong's way. These, and the sequences of monster action in the jungle, emphasise one of the primary appeals of the *kaijū* movie: the spectacle of 'impossible' action and urban destruction that is at the core of most *kaijū* movies, either in the monster-on-monster action of Kong's battle with the T. rex (a form of action repeated in many classic *kaijū* movies, from Kong fighting Godzilla to the updated versions of this tussle in Jackson's remake) and the fragility of the urban landscape that is smashed repeatedly in many a *kaijū* rampage. The presence of the military is another core element of the *kaijū* movie. The deployment of modern technology (often ever more sophisticated, such as the updated technology of the *Heisei* Godzilla movies[1]) becomes a central feature, but rarely with as much success as the biplanes against Kong, where military might is able to overcome the creature, despite Denham's famous comment. So foundational is Kong as a *kaijū* that the ape can be found listed in the *kaijū* wiki, Wikizilla. It lists not just the giant ape itself, but all the monsters that appear in the film: not only all the generically named creatures, the Stegosaurus, Brontosaurus, Elasmosaurus and Pteranodon, but also those with names derived from the script or the 1932 novelisation: The Man-Eater (the name of the T. rex with which Kong fights) and the Two-Legged Lizard and Scavenger Ravens. This also emphasises how comfortable fans have been with incorporating non-Japanese *kaijū* into the genre's canon of monsters.

## The Lost World and the Beast

Before returning to *Gojira*'s inception and the formalisation of the *kaijū eiga* as a form of national cinema, there are two other American films that need to be discussed in setting the *kaijū* formula: Harry O. Hoyt's *The Lost World* (1925) and Eugène Lourié's *The Beast from 20,000 Fathoms*. Hoyt's *Lost World*, the first of several film and television adaptations of Arthur Conan Doyle's 1912 novel,[2] is most notable as a progenitor of the *kaijū* film for its relationship with *King Kong*. Willis O'Brien's special effects are an obvious point of connection, but, as Cynthia Erb discusses, *The Lost World* is further bound to *Kong* as a key intertext, an inspiration and a legal problem in the latter's development. She notes that RKO's lawyers looked at the film's script, then titled *The Beast*, as a network of references to other genre films and stories. They included *Ingagi* (William Campbell, 1930), an ethnographic adventure film in which an expedition sets forth from London to the Belgian Congo to discover a tribe of gorilla-worshipping women, and *Murders in the Rue Morgue* (Robert Florey, 1932), an adaptation of Edgar Allan Poe's detective story in which an ape is eventually found to the killer. However, *The Lost World* proved to be the biggest stumbling block for the producers. Erb argues the studio 'tried to persuade Cooper that the sequence of events in [Edgar] Wallace's script was too similar to the plotting of Doyle's story, so that the project posed a potential case of copyright infringement' (Erb 2009, 37). In Hoyt's version of the story, evidence is presented to the fringe scientist Professor Challenger that dinosaurs still roam the Earth on a plateau in South America. An expedition heads to the lost world and encounters a host of dinosaurs, including several that overlap with *King Kong*'s menagerie of beasts: a Pteranodon, a Brontosaurus and a T. rex, as well as an Allosaurus that battles a Trachodon and an Agathaumas. The film also shares with *King Kong* both the transgression of a border from civilisation to wilderness and the transportation of the beast to the city. In the film of *The Lost World*, the expedition returns a Brontosaurus to London, where it inevitably escapes to wreak mayhem. The dinosaur smashes its way through the streets before reaching Tower Bridge (Figure 1.6). As it crosses, the bridge collapses and the behemoth is swept away by the Thames. Right from this early point, giant monsters were trampling famous landmarks, just as Kong scales the Empire State Building and Godzilla crushes the National Diet building. The construction of the monster's assault on the British capital has some significant similarities with Godzilla's attack on Tokyo in *Gojira*. There are reflections in the cutting between human characters and the special effects sequences. At one point, a woman huddling with her baby is in the dinosaur's path, although she is saved, unlike the mother and children in Tokyo. The influence of some of the special effects sequences would later be evident in *Gojira*, including the detailed city miniatures, and the use of puppetry in close-ups. O'Brien was a strong influence on Tsuburaya, whose initial plans for *Gojira* included working with stop-motion in homage, although this proved too costly (Ryfle 1998, 23).

However, it was another of O'Brien's admirers who was more directly involved in the transnational origins of the *kaijū eiga*. Ray Harryhausen's brand of stop-motion animation had been significantly influenced by O'Brien's work on *King Kong*. Harryhausen's first film as a special effects supervisor had an important effect on the development of *Gojira*. Based on the short story 'The Fog Horn' by Ray Bradbury, *The Beast from 20,000 Fathoms* (which was the story's original title) further develops the giant monster rampage film for the atomic age. We've seen how

Figure 1.6 A marauding dinosaur visits a national landmark in London as a sign of urban fragility in *The Lost World* (1925) (public domain)

earlier movies established some of the core themes of the *kaijū eiga* and envisaged the destruction caused in modern cities when giant primitive beasts become victims of humanity's hubris, but *The Beast* connects this with nuclear anxieties in ways that directly foreshadow the *kaijū eiga*'s inception. Bradbury's story tells a tale of a beast that emerges from the depths to wreck a lighthouse that it mistakes for the call of a long-lost mate. This translates to a short sequence in the film in which the monster, a Rhedosaurus, trashes a lighthouse on the Maine coast while travelling from the Arctic to the north-eastern coast of the US, its ancestral home. The film's producers were particularly inspired by the growing popularity of science-fiction and monster films in the early 1950s, including *The Thing from Another World* (Christian Nyby, 1951) and the 1952 re-release of *King Kong* (Webber 2004, McKenna 2016, 39). They paired the giant monster with anxieties about nuclear testing to create the template for what would eventually become *Gojira*. It's reported that Tanaka Tomoyuki, *Gojira*'s producer, had read a synopsis of the film prior to its Japanese release (which was just after Tōhō's film opened) (McKenna 2016, 37)[3] and developed his film based on that formula, with a working title of *The Giant Monster from 20,000 Miles Beneath the Sea* (Ryfle 1998, 21).

*The Beast*'s genesis as an independently produced film that was later picked up by Warner Bros. belies its significance in the construction of an image of the transnational roots of the *kaijū eiga*, again emphasising the significance of Erb's observation about how Hollywood films become important for international producers. The relationship between US and Japanese culture is problematised by the occupation of Japan following the imperial nation's surrender at the end of the Pacific war. Prohibitions were placed on content relating to the war, the impact of the nuclear bombings and Imperial history, introducing a colonial aspect to the use of the American film. However, it's difficult to see the adoption of the giant monster formula simply as a form of colonial mimicry. As we've seen already in this chapter, the reworking of the American film introduced specific national meanings into the text that made it thoroughly Japanese, despite its hybridity. *The Beast* is less moralistic in its approach both to science and to nuclear anxiety. It begins with a plane taking off on a time-sensitive journey to a specific location. We eventually understand that this is an Arctic nuclear test. This echoes the setting of Nyby's *The Thing from Another World* rather than any specific inspiration from a real nuclear test, the majority of which were carried out in deserts or on Pacific atolls. Presciently, the film's hero, nuclear physicist Thomas Nesbitt (Paul Christian), ponders what the effects of these tests will ultimately be. He doesn't need to wait long, as he becomes the only survivor of an attack by a giant beast, awakened from a long slumber by the blast. Nobody will believe Nesbitt, but he pursues his investigation, enlisting the help of sceptical palaeontologist Professor Thurgood Elson (Cecil Kellaway), who dismisses Nesbitt's claims. Elson's assistant, Lee Hunter (Paula Raymond), is intrigued by Nesbitt's story and assists him by showing him pictures of prehistoric creatures. He recognises one of them: the Rhedosaurus, a fictional dinosaur, approximately 20 metres long, amphibian with a fearsome scaled head. Scuttled boats and destroyed buildings along the Canadian and American coasts suggest the creature is heading towards New York, to an underwater canyon where Rhedosaurus fossils have been found. Nesbitt is determined to prove his story and seeks out survivors of the attacks. The captain of one boat refuses to speak to him, sick of the press hounding him, but another crew member is convinced to leave his hospital bed to corroborate what Nesbitt saw. Looking through a series of dinosaur drawings, he picks the Rhedosaurus as the one that attacked his boat. Now convinced of the existence of Nesbitt's creature, the scientists track it to Hudson Bay, where Elson insists on going into the depths to see the beast for himself. After watching an octopus and shark struggle against one another, he is killed as the Rhedosaurus eats his diving bell. It then heads to the city, where it rampages its way to Wall Street. The military finally injure it and it flees to the sea. Its blood proves to be deadly, though, as those who are exposed to it become sick with radiation poisoning. Nesbitt determines therefore that they can't blow it up – they must use a radioactive isotope, shot directly into its open wound, to vaporise it. Coney Island is the perfect place to do this, they surmise. The monster becomes cornered in the park's rollercoaster and Nesbitt and a sharpshooter (a young Lee van Cleef) climb up to get a better shot. As they do, the monster smashes the rollercoaster, causing cars to careen off and set the wooden frame on fire. Nesbitt and the marksman must climb down into the flames once the isotope is successfully delivered. The film ends abruptly with the monster's death, which is a painful one, but without a moral message about nuclear experimentation.

The ending emphasises the contradictory nature of the film. While it gives us some sense of contemporary nuclear anxiety, this mostly proves exploitative, as the answer to the monster's rampage is to use science, radioactive science at that. With the monster defeated, the film's protagonist is presumably free to continue testing nuclear devices. However, the film becomes the first to connect the figure of *King Kong* – the giant marauding beast – with nuclear anxiety and is therefore foundational for what would become the *kaijū eiga*. It is an evolutionary link, and, as noted in the previous chapter, was the first to be released in Japan with the word *kaijū* in its title. Furthermore, the effects by Harryhausen provide a further link between O'Brien and Tsuburaya. While Tsuburaya would depart from the stop-motion style, the construction of sequences of destruction – although the monster is far more on display in *The Beast* than it is in *Gojira* – continues a style pioneered in *The Lost World*, editing between human victims and the monster's impact on buildings and selected individuals. The humans on the ground provide a focal point for identification and empathy while the spectacle of the monster's attack provides the primary pleasure.

One final question requires some attention: are dinosaur films *kaijū* films? The strangeness of the *kaijū* is a disputed area. While the initial influences imbue strange beasts with multiple heads and mystical powers, the creatures of the *kaijū eiga* are more grounded: their strangeness is a result of nuclear radiation (the Rhedosaurus and Godzilla), genetic modification (Biollante, from 1989's *Godzilla vs. Biollante* [*Gojira tai Biorante*, Ōmori Kazuki]) or other-worldly origins (Gamera, Clover, King Ghidorah), or they are mechanical (Kiryu, the *Heisei*-era MechaGodzilla). Therefore, shouldn't we consider dinosaurs as variants of *kaijū*? Their stories would certainly match the strange origins of *kaiki*. There are shared themes and images. Harryhausen's later film *The Valley of Gwangi* (1969) certainly shares elements of the *kaijū* template. The film is a *Lost World* variation (the film's marketing even used the title of Conan Doyle's story in its tag line), in which some performers from a travelling Wild West show discover a lost valley while pursuing a tiny horse (an Eohippus) stolen from a Mexican village. Gwangi, an Allosaurus, is taken from the valley and exhibited, in King Kong fashion, with inevitably bad results. The dinosaur dies a horrific death in a burning church. It has some affinities with *kaijū* films of the 1960s boom: the fights between Gwangi and a Styracosaurus echo the wrestling matches of Tōhō and Daiei's films, while humanity's repeated failure to tame wilderness harks back to *The Lost World* and *King Kong*. The film also blends genres, straddling the Western and horror films. There is as well a more literal link back to Kong, as the project had initially been developed by O'Brien at RKO in the 1940s and was resurrected by Harryhausen following his mentor's death in 1962. Thus, there are clear affinities between dinosaur films and *kaijū eiga*, although this may partly be down to the presence of large monsters. Dinosaur movies generally lack the characterisation and anthropomorphising impetus of the *kaijū* film. Hence, it's difficult to see the dinosaurs of *Jurassic Park* (Steven Spielberg, 1993) as *kaijū*. They are either too small or too animalistic. This explains the contentious rejection of the first Hollywood *Godzilla* in 1998, where the film too closely resembles a dinosaur film (it very closely mirrors the plot of *The Beast from 20,000 Fathoms*, as the monster makes its way – inexplicably from the South Pacific – to New York City). We therefore observe very close relationships between dinosaur and *kaijū* films, where there are certainly affinities and a shared developmental history. It should also be noted the *Heisei* Godzilla films retconned[4] the *kaijū* as a mutated dinosaur, a Godzillasaurus, and therefore we need to consider such contiguities and relationships as part of the history of the *kaijū eiga*. The Rhedosaurus in some respect is less a *kaijū* than a reawoken dinosaur – it is perhaps less a *kaijū* than the slightly more anthropomorphised Gwanji (the film certainly invites less empathy for the unnamed creature) – but fans have, through the shared history of *The Beast* and *Gojira,* invited the Rhedosaurus into the pantheon of *kaijū*. It even makes a single frame's appearance in *Cloverfield*.

## *Kaijū* Emerge

When we compare *The Beast from 20,000 Fathoms*' conflicted message on nuclear testing with the more cautious tone of *Gojira*'s approach to science, the differences are stark. Returning to *Gojira*, we see reflections of several themes and narrative patterns in its influences. However, it's important to highlight a key concern of transnational film studies as we do so. As Iain Robert Smith has argued, the appropriation and adaptation of Hollywood material need not be seen, as they have been, as a form of 'blanket Americanization': 'borrowings should be understood less through the prism of cultural domination and resistance than through the lens of agency and creativity' (2017, 229). If we accept Smith's argument that the meme-like quality of texts constitutes 'a unit of culture which spreads and replicates' (52) then the adaptation of tropes from American cinema makes up a key part of the fabric of the *kaijū* film, but filtered through a national imaginary of trauma. Yet it is also the 'borderless' (*mukokuseki*) nature of the figure of the *kaijū* that allows it to be adapted to different national contexts. In some sense, this is similar to what Daniel Herbert describes as '*The Ring* intertext', 'a circuit of economic, semiotic, and cultural exchange . . . [that] maps a transnational and macroregional space' (2010, 154) that may also 'reinforce certain cultural boundaries and relations of power' (166). Cultural exchange is a crucial process in the way texts are shaped and reworked in different national contexts, hence the development of *Gojira* as a film that demonstrates Erb's point about how international producers use Hollywood films. As described by Tom O'Regan, cultural exchange is 'a critical component of wider processes of cultural identity formation and cultural development' in the way that it enables 'the lending and redisposition of cultural materials from one filmmaking and cultural tradition to another' (1999, 262). As we've seen, *Gojira* is highly specific in its reference to cultural and political conditions around the time of its production, as well as global in its response to trends in American cinema that are thoroughly repurposed and grounded in the culture reproducing them. There is therefore an element of exploitation to both the timeliness of the film's reference to national tragedy and its capitalisation on popular movies distributed in Japan.

Picking up the film's plot after a look at the precursors of the film, we see a few similarities to and differences from its influences. Following the loss of the ships at sea near Odo Island, the villagers report a shortage of fish. The shortage is put down to a local legend – Godzilla. A delegation is sent to the island, and they briefly witness the monster during a storm.

The development of the plot here mirrors the introduction of King Kong, through a local myth of a primitive island culture, compared with the more modern and sophisticated urban protagonists. Another familiar character is introduced: the noble palaeontologist, here Professor Yamane (played by Tōhō contract star Shimura Takashi, well known internationally from his work with Kurosawa). Yamane plays a role like that of the scientists in *The Beast from 20,000 Fathoms*, with a desire to study and understand the monster rather than destroy it. Yamane discovers giant footprints and a mutated trilobite on Odo Island, and hypothesises that the creature is a giant dinosaur transformed in size by nuclear testing. He presents his findings to the National Diet but struggles to convince the country's leaders of the discovery (the establishment are always slow to be convinced). Meanwhile, Godzilla continues to destroy ships at sea. When frigates are dispatched to kill the monster with depth charges, Yamane protests against the action. He demands the monster be studied. The mission fails to kill the monster, which strengthens the professor's position. Yamane's daughter Emiko (Kōchi Momoko) is betrothed (in an arranged marriage) to a colleague of her father's: Serizawa Daisuke (Hirata Akihiko), an eyepatched chemist who bears the scars of his service in the war. When a journalist asserts that a German contact has suggested that Serizawa has developed a weapon potent enough to destroy the monster, a darker association with his wartime experiences is implied. Yet Serizawa has developed a weapon with the capacity to destroy the monster: the 'Oxygen Destroyer', created in secret, results in a reaction that liquefies flesh when deployed. Serizawa demonstrates its effect for Emiko in a fish tank, and she turns away in horror. Serizawa has strong reservations about unleashing such a powerful weapon on the world and refuses to use it. Emiko, however, has fallen in love with Ogata Hideo (Takarada), the salvage ship captain, who heard one of the first reports of the monster's attacks. With the love triangle in the background (the film's protagonists are onscreen surprisingly little for the first third of the film), Godzilla emerges from Tokyo Bay and proceeds to rampage through Shinagawa. The Japan Self-Defense Forces (JSDF, perhaps the most ineffective military ever presented in a film series) erect a giant electric fence, which the monster destroys with its atomic breath. Ogata pleads with Yamane to kill the monster, but the professor is obstinate in his desire to study the creature. The JSDF continues to be unable to kill the monster, its breath burning the city. It returns to the sea, leaving Tokyo in ruins and survivors blighted with radiation sickness. The attacks on Tokyo mirror those of both *King Kong* (the destruction of a train) and *The Beast* (the destruction of buildings and the sickness suffered by survivors), although the *mise en scène* of the attack at night is much darker (literally and figuratively) than either film, the destruction much more devasting. There is a far stronger echo of trauma in *Gojira*. While the two films that inspired it reflect specific anxieties or cultural binaries, this example of cultural exchange is much more than a straight copy, significantly interpolating the formula of the monster-on-the-loose narrative into a different national setting. In the end, this reflection is bleaker in the film's core themes. Unlike *The Beast*'s embrace of science as the answer to the problem caused by science (making a distinction between 'good science' and 'bad science'), *Gojira* is less ambivalent. After Emiko tells Ogata of the Oxygen Destroyer, he implores Serizawa to use it, but the scientist refuses. He eventually relents, but burns his notes and decides to take the knowledge of how to create the weapon to his grave. They sail to Tokyo Bay, where Godzilla sleeps. Ogata and Serizawa dive with the weapon, but Serizawa cuts his own air pipe. The eruption of the Oxygen Destroyer kills the creature and the scientist. There is no ambivalent message about scientific progress, and no sudden ending. In a coda, Yamane delivers a moral message (one seemingly aligned with Honda's humanist and pacifist stance): 'If nuclear testing continues, then someday, somewhere in the world, another Godzilla may appear.' This imagination of disaster, the monster as victim (as many of the monsters in *kaijū* films tend to be), *hibakusha*, gives a solemn tone to the film entirely in keeping with its national origins. This emphasises how thoroughly the film translates the text of films like *King Kong* and *The Beast from 20,000 Fathoms*. In this form (we'll return to the Americanised version later), it bears the marks of that influence, but is adapted to suit the needs of Japanese producers.

To finish this section, I want to briefly recount some of the production history of the film, which emphasises the consciousness of that translation. The story of *Gojira*'s production has been well told, (Ryfle 1998, Brothers 2015, Rhoads and McCorkle 2018, Kalat 1997), so I won't go into too much detail. But some points are worth noting. In katakana, Gojira is ゴジラ (this is the form used in most advertising, although it can also be written using phonetic kanji), romanised as go-ji-ra (using an alternative system of romanisation, it is rendered as Go-dzi-lla). The word is the combination of two Japanese words: the transliteration of gorilla (katakana: ゴリラ, Rom. *gorira*) and the word for whale (katakana: クジラ, Rom. *kujira*). The origins of the name are disputed. Ryfle recounts a story about how the monster was named for a burly Tōhō employer who has never been identified, a tall story according to Honda's widow (Ryfle 1998, 23). Brothers points to a few sources for the name, from Tanaka himself, to Tōhō's publicity department, a studio-sponsored competition, or producer Sato Ichiro, who was revealed as the inventor of the name in a 1955 report in *Film News* (Brothers 2015, 34). Takayuki Tatsumi calls these tales of the origins of the term 'apocryphal' (Tatsumi 2014, 70), a publicity stunt, and notes that the English version of the name is more accurate, especially the 'God-' part, as the monster is 'a kind of kami (Shinto divinity or spirit)' (71). The term itself echoes the project's development. In March 1954, Tanaka had needed a project to quickly plug a schedule gap following the collapse of a co-produced film due to be shot in Indonesia. On the return flight, he had the idea of a film in the vein of *The Beast from 20,000 Fathoms*. The year 1952 had seen the end of US occupation and censorship in Japan, and therefore topics such as the nuclear bombings had become acceptable for discussion. He commissioned noted science-fiction writer Kayama Shigeru to write a synopsis for *Project-G* (*G-Sakuhin*), the 'G' standing for 'giant' (a shortening of the overtly derivative *The Giant Monster from 20,000 Miles Beneath the Sea*). Kayama's autobiography revealed that Tanaka's vision for the monster was 'a cross between a whale and gorilla [*sic*]' (Ryfle 1998, 22). The monster went through several iterations, variously combining elements of gorillas, whales, an octopus and then dinosaurs. While we might dispute the simplicity of the stories of ゴジラ being a more straightforward reflection of the film's precursors, the film's production history and the development of the monster demonstrate how producers work with ideas, how these are shaped, are revised and reflect originality in the sense of the form of finished ideas, rather than in their genesis. The influence of *King Kong* and *The Beast from 20,000 Fathoms* is reflected not just in the finished form of the film, but in how the story developed. At one stage, the story even included a moment in which Godzilla attacks a lighthouse, a scene more or less lifted from Bradbury's story as well as the film that was adapted from it. This emphasises the agency of producers to appropriate and rework ideas that become more than examples of Americanisation, highlighting more intricate processes of globalisation that reveal differences (the national trauma behind the film's motivating plot point and its *mise en scène*) and resistances (that a film so thoroughly influenced by American cinema could present a viewpoint so anti-American). *Gojira* cemented the Japanese form of the monster movie. As Crandol (2019) has argued, this was comfortably acknowledged by Japanese critics as a variant of *kaiki*, before developing its own generic moniker. This first became a national monster boom as the success of Tōhō's blockbuster inspired its rivals to get in on the act. It is to this we turn in the next chapter, and the ways in which the *kaijū* film continued to develop for export markets and a transnationally influenced and produced genre.

## Notes

1. *Kaijū* films have generally been periodised through reference to Japanese imperial eras. The era of the *Shōwa* Emperor (Hirohito) ran between 1926 and 1989. *Shōwa*-era films include the original monster boom, from *Gojira* in 1954 roughly to *Gamera: Super Monster* in 1980. The period of the *Heisei* Emperor (Akihito) ran between 1989 and his abdication in April 2019, but films of the *Heisei* era are generally considered to begin with 1984's *Gojira*. The third period of *kaijū* is generally known as the Millennium era, signalling a break from the *Heisei* Godzilla series following Roland Emmerich's Hollywood version (1998), while later iterations have become known as the *Reiwa* series. The *Reiwa* era follows the *Heisei* from 2019, but, as with the previous period, the overlap begins earlier, with Tōhō's *Shin Gojira* (Anno Hideaki and Higuchi Shinji) released in 2016. Fans have generally used these time periods to group and classify all *kaijū* films, not just those from Japan.
2. This doesn't include the *Jurassic Park* sequel, *The Lost World* (Steven Spielberg, 1997), even though it does share aspects of the plot with the novel and direct adaptations when a T. rex is transported to San Diego. Inevitably, it gets loose and goes on an urban rampage.
3. This is disputed by Takayuki Tatsumi, however (Tatsumi 2014).
4. The term 'retconned' is short for 'retroactive continuity', in which producers of a series will introduce new elements that change the audience's understanding of a character's backstory or the lore of the universe.

CHAPTER 2

# The First Monster Boom

At the time, *Gojira* was the most expensive Japanese film ever produced and it returned a solid profit for Tōhō. It was the eighth most popular film of the year (with around 9.6 million admissions), behind the studio's prestige *jidaigeki* (period dramas) *Seven Samurai* (*Shichinin no Samurai*, Kurosawa Akira) and *Miyamoto Musashi* (Inagaki Hiroshi) (Ryfle 1998).[1] Tōhō released a sequel just five months later, *Godzilla Raids Again* (*Gojira No Gyakushu*, lit. *Godzilla's Counterattack*). As we heard in the previous chapter, numerous commentators connected the original *Gojira* with Japanese trauma and the 'imagination of disaster'. Igarashi Yoshikuni has argued that the original film had meant that '[m]emories of the war and images of the United States as an enemy country were made visible and reappropriated into postwar society' (Igarashi 2000, 105–6), but that tropes 'of in-betweenness . . . [simultaneously] allowed postwar Japan to leap over this historical disjuncture to identify with American material culture' (105). Both *Gojira* and the popular professional wrestler Rikidōzan fitted with what Igarashi called 'a nationalist project', as both 'embodied the hybrid identity of Japanese who would be capable of defeating both American and traditional Japanese competitors' (127), and thereby bridging the pre-modern and contemporary in Japan. Aaron Gerow has also argued that there is an equivalence in the bodies of *kaijū* and the wrestler: that the monster body came to reflect a 'sutured national body' that ultimately reflected intertextual references to contemporary discourses of nationality and the knowing fictionality of such a body that ultimately resists realist interpretation (2006, 78–9). They both highlighted their hybridity and the ascendance of Japanese forms through their appropriation of American forms of culture. For Igarashi, however, the economic growth of the 1960s and the death of Rikidōzan in 1963 (in a fight with yakuza) would come to erase such memories, and to incorporate monsters into a more 'banal' portrayal of Japanese nationalism and child-friendly movies that sat alongside the economic miracles of modernisation post-occupation:

> As Japan regained its political independence and international status through economic growth, *Nihonjinron* [日本人論, lit. theories of the Japanese] gained ascendance as ideological support for postwar Japanese national pride. It discursively constructed Japan as a liminal, hybrid entity and found historical continuity within this liminality. (Igarashi 2000, 130)

As Yoshio Sugimoto (1999) has argued, the 'nation, ethnicity and culture' dimensions of *Nihonjinron* present a unified, amicable and consensual social structure, centred on the perceived uniqueness of Japanese identity. However, as Sugimoto recognises, globalisation puts significant pressure upon principles of *Nihonjinron* to acknowledge both the diversity of Japan's population, from Okinawans, to Ainu, to returned children of Japanese-Korean parentage, and to naturalised international residents in the country. The acknowledgement of diverse ethnic groups in Japan challenges the monolithic dimensions of Japanese identity. Alongside this, globalisation developed a focus on Japanese culture and 'transferability' that grew as an export culture for forms such as the *kaijū eiga* through the 1950s, 1960s and 1970s, alongside the economic miracle and landmark events such as the 1964 Tokyo Olympics. Nevertheless, the 'more *Nihonjinron* stresses the transferability of Japaneseness, of course, the more it would lose its claim for uniqueness, the very foundation upon which the *Nihonjinron* argument has been constructed' (Sugimoto 1999, 89). The *kaijū eiga* came to embody many of these elements of both the superiority of *Nihonjinron* and the aspects of globalisation that produced outward-looking culture. As Sugimoto also notes, Koichi Iwabuchi has described the ways in which Japanese culture has an 'odorless' quality in relation to the national characteristic, but this produces a contradictory effect:

> If it is indeed the case that the Japaneseness of Japanese animation derives, consciously or unconsciously, from its erasure of physical signs of Japaneseness, is not the Japan that Western audiences are at long last coming to appreciate, and even yearn for, an animated, race-less, and culture-less, virtual version of 'Japan'? (Iwabuchi 2002, 33)

As we've seen already, the *kaijū eiga* is a hybrid form, subject to aspects of localisation, but Iwabuchi argues that the flows in which Japanese culture sits are hierarchical, positing Japan as superior to other East Asian countries, while simultaneously transculturating American culture.

The 'liminal, hybrid entity' that Igarashi described is articulated by the very 'banalization' (Igarashi 2000, 121) of the *kaijū eiga* as it grew in popularity in the first monster boom of the 1960s. Godzilla was not alone in the ways in which the films' text was subsumed by growing Japanese nationalism and ideological independence. As the 1960s progressed, Godzilla was joined by several competitors from rival studios whose films built on or adopted the formula of the hybrid *Kong–Gojira–Beast from 20,000 Fathoms* template. Throughout this chapter, we'll explore the ways in which the *kaijū* genre became a cross-studio phenomenon in Japan. The monster boom of the 1960s shifted the roots of the genre away from the atomic nightmare towards a more child-friendly experience by the 1970s. This overview of the history of the genre explores the ways in which Tōhō's competitors capitalised upon the success of *Gojira* to produce their own versions of the *kaijū* film, from Daiei's *Gamera* (1965–2006) and *Daimajin* series (three films released in 1966, with a television follow-up in 2010), to Shōchiku's 's *The X from Outer Space* (*Uchū Daikaijū Girara*, lit. *Giant Space Monster Guilala*, Nihonmatsu Kazui, 1967) and Nikkatsu's *Gappa, The Triphibian Monster* (*Daikyojū Gappa*, lit. *Giant Beast Gappa*, Noguchi Haruyasu, 1967) across the 1960s. Yet, while this popular form developed alongside Japan's film industry, and waned alongside its decline, the *kaijū eiga* came to emphasise globalising trends in Japanese cinema. Government initiatives to promote and support Japanese film contributed to the growth of transnational aspects in the Japanese *kaijū eiga*.

Joseph L. Anderson and Donald Richie devoted very little space to the *kaijū* eiga in their seminal 1959 book *The Japanese Film: Art and Industry*. There is a short passage on *Gojira* at the beginning of the wave of science-fiction films, including Tōhō's *The Mysterians* and rival studio Daiei's *Warning from Space* (*Uchūjin Tokyo ni arawaru*, lit. *Spacemen Appear in Tokyo*, Shima Koji, 1956), that they contend seem part-designed for the international market ('some snippets of Japanese culture and lots of English spoken') (1959, 262–3). Anderson and Richie's comments reflect Igarashi's concern with how the development of areas of Japanese culture following the end of US occupation opened a space for a liminal, hybrid identity. *Warning from Space* is a case in point. A more conventional science-fiction film rather than a *kaijū* film (there are no big monsters, the aliens more like big starfish), it focuses on the arrival of aliens from the planet Paira. The aliens' warning is that a rogue planet is on course to destroy Earth, whose governments must work together to send all their nuclear weapons to divert the course of the planet and save the world. When that proves unsuccessful, the atmosphere begins to become super-heated, disturbing weather and threatening our protagonists, who take shelter in the basement of an observatory. The film's apocalyptic imagery shares the imagination of disaster, as well as its anti-nuclear stance, not only with *Gojira*, released just over a year before, but also with American films such as *The Day the Earth Stood Still* (Robert Wise, 1951), itself a film about a warning from space. William Tsutsui places *Warning from Space* squarely within the cycle of films that repeatedly imagined the destruction of Tokyo, reflecting the nation's history of recurrent trauma, from the nuclear bombings to natural disasters like the Great Kanto Earthquake of 1923 (2010, 112). Whereas Tsutsui calls the film 'charming', Anderson and Richie dismiss it as produced for the 'foreign market', but add that '[f]oreigners never had a chance to enjoy the film . . . , since Daiei was never able to sell it to anyone' (Anderson and Richie 1959, 263). The film did eventually sell, several years after Anderson and Richie's book was published, to American International Television, along with other sci-fi and monster movies, before later entering the public domain. Much worse in Anderson and Richie's view, though, was the 'pretentious' *The Mysterians*, in which the eponymous aliens launch an attack on Earth, to repopulate their species after being ravaged by nuclear war. It extends the anti-nuclear sentiment that was well established by previous films but marries this with the nascent *kaijū* film by introducing the giant robot Mogera,[2] defeated by the Self-Defense Forces early in the film. For these critics, the film develops the *tokusatsu*[3] formula of destruction, rampaging monsters and the leadership of Japan in bringing peace. Anderson and Richie name the 'Japanese monster picture' in the same breath as other commercial genres that were exploitable for a 'fast profit': ghost stories (another important aspect of Japanese cinema's international exposure in the early twenty-first century); Tōhō's monster movies and musicals; and Nikkatsu's sexy, rebellious adolescent *taiyozoku* (sun tribe) films.

The disreputability of the *kaijū eiga* for serious critics was established fairly quickly. While other critics felt that *Gojira* had been exploitative (Ryfle 1998), production of films accelerated, especially at Tōhō and Daiei, from the mid-1950s until the late 1960s. Following this, and alongside a more general decline in Japanese cinema, production of *kaijū* films slowed while new series on television began to occupy its audience's time. Rhoads and McCorkle synthesise areas of scholarship around this period, concluding that the monster boom was influenced by a number of factors: the exploitation of popular, often well-made entertainment films, the optimism of the accelerated economic growth in the period (including the imagination of Japan as central to global politics) and 'a wide array of Japanese children consumers' (Rhoads and McCorkle 2018, 77). Children became central during this period of *kaijū* film's growth, both as protagonists and as consumers.

In the next section, we'll look at how the *kaijū* boom developed across the Japanese studios and into popular culture more generally. Again, the purpose isn't to be exhaustive or definitive, but to provide an overview of how a popular genre can develop within a national industry and through co-operation with transnational co-production. This is not to essentialise a concept of the national through the development of a genre within borders, but to acknowledge, as Oliete-Aldea et al. put it, that:

> generic conventions rest on international interactions that undercut any attempt to put forward a unique and distinctive account of national identity. How we represent the nation to ourselves (or how we imagine our community) is inextricably linked to transnational relations . . . The nation and the transnational – or the local and the global – do not designate different, mutually exclusive conditions. (Oliete-Aldea, Oria and Tarancón 2016, 4)

As genres are produced with reference to shared or repeated blueprints (Altman 1999), films can be 'both agents and expressions of globalization' (Oliete-Aldea, Oria and Tarancón 2016, 5). Producers combine elements from different genre templates, and audiences and critics become aware of the meanings of those formats. They subsequently rely on local and global conditions for both their production and circulation (and therefore their continued production). As we'll come to see later, many of these films became subject to further development and modification as they spread globally, from editing to dubbing to retitling.

## *Kaijū* at Tōhō

Tōhō are undoubtedly the Japanese studio most associated with the *kaijū eiga*, not solely as the producers of *Gojira*, but in their sustained production of *kaijū* films up to the present, including as distributors of the Legendary monster films in Japan. Following the release of the first Godzilla film, Tōhō found, as Stuart Galbraith writes, that monster movies became their 'most lucrative export for the next fifteen years'. Alongside the *jidaigeki* of Kurosawa and Inagaki, Honda's output in the genre became a regular source of income from the international box office and co-production with American companies (Galbraith 2008, xii). This partly helps to explain some of the critical distain for the films, seemingly cynically produced for export markets and therefore 'not Japanese enough'.

As I've mentioned already, the sequel to *Gojira* hit cinemas a mere five months after the first film. Due to a scheduling conflict, Honda was unavailable, so directing duties went to Oda Motoyoshi, who had recently completed the science-fiction film *The Invisible Avenger* (*Tomei ningen*, lit. *Invisible Man*, 1954) for Tōhō alongside special effects director Tsuburaya. Ryfle (1998, 61–3) documents the production of the film, the rushed circumstances of its genesis and different personnel that meant it fell short of the quality of *Gojira*, but states that it introduces some of the key features of the films moving forward. With no real explanation, a second Godzilla appears near the fictional Pacific Island of Iwato. Two pilots searching for fish at sea witness the second monster fighting a new creature, an Ankylosaurus known as Angirasu (Anglicised as Anguirus). The monsters later find their way to Osaka, where they lay waste the city, including destroying its iconic castle. The last act of the film moves to Hokkaido, where characters are forced to flee after the devastation of Osaka. This reflects a greater inclusion of different parts of Japan, something many *kaijū* films endeavoured to focus upon. While Tokyo experienced the brunt of the devastation (as a quasi-Hiroshima), the damage was spread equally among different parts of the country, from Okinawa to Hokkaido. The tone of the film is not necessarily lighter than the first one, but the anti-nuclear messages are minimised, and there is more focus on the monster-on-monster battles that would become a staple of the series in the 1960s. Only Shimura Takashi returns from the first film, as Dr Yamane, who hypothesises the same origins for these monsters as for the first one. Due to an error in production, the special effects scenes were shot at a slower frame rate, making the monsters faster and less lumbering than before (Ryfle 1998, 63). Despite this, the film was a commercial success, but not at the level of the first. While Tōhō would produce more *kaijū* films in the subsequent few years, Godzilla was left trapped in ice until 1962.

Honda followed *Gojira* with two romantic films, *Lovetide* (*Koi-gesho*, lit. *Love Makeup*, 1955) and *Oen-san* (also known as *Mother and Son* or *Cry-Baby*, 1955), but his next monster film was inspired by global enthusiasm for all things abominable following the mysterious footprints photographed on Mount Everest by Eric Shipton. *Half Human* (*Jū Jin Yuki Otoko*, lit. *Beastman Snowman*, 1955) was released not long after the American film *The Snow Creature* (W. Lee Wilder, 1954), a film more overtly in the mould of *King Kong*, in which a Yeti is discovered in the Himalayas and brought back to Los Angeles by the expedition. *Half Human* was reportedly already in development at Tōhō while *Gojira* was in production, featuring several of the latter's key personnel: Honda,

Tsuburaya and Kayama. Like *The Snow Creature*, it follows an expedition to the mountains where, we're told in an opening framing scene, one of the party has died following a mysterious incident. To find some holidaying college students in the Japanese Alps, a second expedition sets out. They quickly discover that the incident is down to a mysterious creature worshipped by a primitive mountain tribe. But it turns out the party have been followed by the shady businessman Oba, who intends to put the Yeti on show as a circus animal (more shades of *King Kong*). Oba captures the Yeti's offspring, but it is accidentally killed. The Yeti subsequently goes on the rampage to kill all the humans responsible. With the help of Chika, a female member of the mountain tribe, the expedition party discover the monster's cave, where they find remains believed to be the rest of the species, seemingly killed ingesting poisonous mushrooms. When the beast is cornered, it grabs a female member of the party, but Chika tames it. The monster finally falls to its death in a deep pit, dragging Chika down. In its Japanese form, *Half Human* is a fairly forgettable film (slow plotting, too many characters, not one but two flashbacks), yet it's notable for its continuation of the *King Kong* motifs prevalent in the development of *kaijū* movies (it is perhaps not identifiably a *kaijū* film: the Yeti is certainly a strange beast, but not on the scale we would come to expect in later *daikaijū* stories). The anthropomorphised primate monster at its core is attracted to a human female, destroyed by its own humanity and exploitation by selfish businessmen (although, unlike Kong and *The Snow Creature*, it never arrives in the city). The film was released in the US in a much-truncated version, missing around half an hour of running time, and overdubbed with a John Carradine voiceover, but it has been seen little in Japan since the 1950s. This was largely down to its problematic depiction of the mountain tribe in the film, referred to as *baraku*, connoting Japan's *Burakumin*, a group of Japanese people generally considered to be at the bottom of the social strata, and often subject to discrimination. This speaks to the monolithic ethnic image of *Nihonjinron*. The film presents the *baraku* as primitive savages, 'half human' like the film's titular monster, yet portrayed without the film's sympathy for its *Jū Jin* character. As Ryfle and Godziszewski (2017, 116–17) document, references to *Burakumin* have largely been self-censored by Japanese media companies. Nevertheless, their presence echoes a thread of *kaijū* films that have regularly depicted 'natives' in problematic ways, such as the Pacific Islanders depicted in blackface in *Mothra* and *King Kong vs. Godzilla* (Figure 2.1). *Half Human* remains a minor inclusion in the *kaijū* boom, but one that reflects the continued relevance of *King Kong*'s

**Figure 2.1** Blackface was often used to represent 'primitive' cultures, here in *King Kong vs. Godzilla* (Tōhō)

influence, as well as the influence of global trends and fascinations that are reflected in films on a local level.

Between 1955 and the culmination of the *Shōwa Godzilla* series in 1975 with *Terror of MechaGodzilla* (*Mekagojira no Gyakushū*, lit. *MechaGodzilla's Counterattack,* Honda*)*, Tōhō produced or co-produced a string of *kaijū*, monster and sci-fi films that developed the *kaijū* genre and universe. Some of these intersected with their monster universe,[4] such as *Rodan*, *Mothra* and *Atragon*, while others did not, including *Gorath* (*Yōsei Gorasu*, lit. *Demon Star Gorath*, Honda, 1962) and *Dogora* (*Uchū Daikaijū Dogora*, lit. *Giant Space Monster Dogora*, Honda, 1964). I don't want to create an overview here of all of Tōhō's *kaijū* movies – as I've already mentioned, this isn't an exhaustive history – but I do want to focus on a couple of entries in their series that sit in the nexus of national and transnational in the *kaijū eiga*. These are two key non-Godzilla films, *Varan the Unbelievable* and *Frankenstein Conquers the World* (*Furankenshutain tai Chitei Kaijū Baragon*, lit. *Frankenstein vs. Underground Monster Baragon*, Honda, 1965). Both emphasise the swift development of the *kaijū* film from a national to more transnational and outward-looking form, combining aspects of co-production and the hybridisation of local and global content that once more echo the origins of the basic template of the *kaijū eiga*.

*Varan the Unbelievable* stands as one of the first intersections of Japanese *kaijū* cinema with US exploitation cinema. The film was initially conceived as a partnership between Tōhō and AB-PT, following the successful American theatrical release of *Rodan* and television broadcast of the American version of *Gojira* (LeMay 2018). As Kevin Heffernan notes, AB-PT was founded following ABC's purchase of Paramount's theatre chain after the 1948 decree, when studios were forced to sell off their exhibition wings. The company was a means of creating product to fill empty dates in their theatres, and a deal was made with Republic to distribute AB-PT films across their chain (2004, 70–1). The company were also reportedly well capitalised, with a $30-million production fund (Boddy 1985). However, despite AB-PT's existence solely to produce work for the exploitation market (although only two films were ever produced and released), *Varan* was intended as a TV movie, a burgeoning market at the time, and to be split into four parts (LeMay 2018). Steve Ryfle documents how AB-PT, around the same time, funded the development of a film based on *Godzilla Raids Again*, to be expanded with new special effects footage (Godzilla and Anguirus suits were even shipped to Hollywood for filming), and entitled *The Volcano Monsters* (eventually released as *Gigantis, The Fire Monster*) (Ryfle 1998, 67–9). *Varan* began production for the small screen, in black and white and 35-mm Academy ratio, before being switched to widescreen TohoScope for a prestigious big screen release (Figure 2.2). Further scenes of spectacle were added to the schedule to produce a longer film. Ifukube also reportedly produced two scores, one for each medium, although when the film was deconstructed to its original TV format, the soundtrack wasn't included (LeMay 2018). The film was seemingly lower-budget than other *kaijū* films, with a truncated shooting schedule (twenty-eight days as opposed to forty or forty-five [Ryfle and Godziszewski 2017, 149–50]), featured stock footage from previous Godzilla films, and was said to be a great disappointment for Honda. The script also nodded towards future developments in

**Figure 2.2** Varan attacks in the widescreen cinema version of *Daikaijū Baran* (Tōhō)

the series, with Sekizawa Shinichi (who would go on to write many of Tōhō's monster movies) writing scenes featuring children pretending to be Varan, but that were never shot (Ryfle and Godziszewski 2017, 150). *Varan* is another minor entry in the *kaijū* canon, but one that helps to emphasise some of the production trends that would develop across the next decade, from co-production with American studios and engagement with exploitation tropes to declining budget and repetition of stock footage, as well as the further targeting of children as the core audience. There would also be a significantly revised American version, released by Crown International Pictures in 1962, and syndicated for television by Desilu through their acquisition of the Westhampton Film Corporation's Feature Package (Heffernan 2004, 169).

Stuart Galbraith refers to *Varan* as a 'routine *kaijū eiga*' (2008, 149), despite it being only the fourth identifiable *daikaijū* film produced by Tōhō, so clearly had the formula developed. Its story concerns two entomology students who discover a rare species of butterfly near Japan's Kitakami river. The species is normally resident in Siberia, so an expedition is dispatched to investigate (echoing previous visits to Odo Island or the Japanese Alps). Two members of the research team are crushed by a peculiar force, and nearby villagers insist they were killed by their mountain god, Baradagi-sanjin. The villagers are, as in *Half Human*, presented as *baraku*, primitive savages whose appearance is visibly suggestive of inbreeding. This representation led to the film's suppression, although it experienced a slow re-emergence in the 1980s when it was released uncut on VHS in Japan (LeMay 2018, Ryfle and Godziszewski 2017). Another expedition is dispatched – this one funded by a film company producing a show called *20th Century Mysteries Solved* (the exploitative capitalist tropes of previous films). In the group are a respected scientist (a recurring character in most of the films discussed so far) and two staff reporters (characters who would become staples of *kaijū* films in the next decade). Once the expedition meets a village priest who warns them not to anger the beast, Varan emerges from the river to rampage through the village, killing the priest.[5] The JSDF are dispatched to take on the monster, but to little avail as the creature resists their attacks, first on land, then at sea, before it reaches Tokyo. It's only once the monster is seen consuming flares that a plan is hatched to defeat it with bombs filled with special gunpowder to detonate it from the inside. The film marks another step in the shift away from the nuclear allegories of *Gojira* towards themes that pit modernity against nature, as science and media reflect the growing prosperity of modern Japan. Ultimately, though, *Varan* lacks the satire of *King Kong vs. Godzilla* or the direct engagement with ecological themes of what Rhoads and McCorkle describe as 'nature vs. capitalism' in *Mothra vs. Godzilla* (*Mosura tai Gojira*, Honda, 1964) (Rhoads and McCorkle 2018, 63). *Varan the Unbelievable* may not have been produced as a co-production in the end, or shot as a TV mini-series as initially intended, but it marks a departure as the first *kaijū* movie to develop as a transnational production (discounting the heavily edited and dubbed localised versions that do nonetheless represent a form of transnational production). There were many that followed in the subsequent decade and a half. While the film is conceived for a transnational market, like many *kaijū* exports, it strongly depicts a Japan conflicted between pre-modern mysticism, with more problematic depictions of primitive villagers, and a modernising urbanism that is threatened by the ancient forces that rise from the depths. Godzilla rose from nuclear trauma, as *hibakusha*, but Varan is awoken by more mystical forces, and there is none of *Gojira*'s moralising about the threats posed by science or humanity's hubris. Science (eventually) poses an answer, as it did for the Rhedosaurus' defeat in *The Beast from 20,000 Fathoms*.

*Frankenstein Conquers the World* was released just prior to the peak of the monster boom in the mid-1960s. The crest came around 1966–7, when most Japanese studios were releasing *kaijū* movies and Tsuburaya Productions' *Ultra Q* (*Urutora Kyū*, 1966) and *Ultraman* (*Urutoraman*, 1967) were first broadcast on Japanese television. *Frankenstein Conquers the World* opens on the battlefields of Germany in 1945 as the Allied Forces invade. We focus in on a gothic lab where a scientist struggles with Nazi stormtroopers to stop them removing a metal trunk. It's loaded onto a U-boat, where it begins a journey around Western Europe towards the Indian Ocean, where the box is transferred to a Japanese submarine. The camera tracks in on the box as we hear a beating heart. The box is finally transported to an army hospital in Hiroshima, where we discover the box contains the still-beating heart of Frankenstein's creature, the key to giving immortality to soldiers (a mission led by Shimura Takashi in a very brief cameo). But the plans are interrupted on 6 August when Little Boy is dropped. We cut to fifteen years later, and the still-scarred Hiroshima, where Dr Bowen (Nick Adams) works at a hospital treating the victims of radiation poisoning and studying the effects of the atomic bomb on human cells. Later, on her way home, one of Bowen's colleagues, Dr Togami (Mizuno Kimi), is surprised by a young vagrant boy who has killed a family dog. A class of schoolchildren discover a rabbit torn apart in their classroom, setting in motion the first act's central mystery about the identity of this strange boy. The child is eventually captured and taken into the care of Bowen and his colleagues. Before the central enigma is solved, a horned *kaijū* arises from underground. The boy continues to grow at an alarming rate, enamoured of television, rock and roll and Togami's jewellery, but enraged by bright lights. His origins are subsequently traced back to the army hospital in Hiroshima, and the German scientist from the opening scene helps the other scientists confirm that the boy has in fact grown from the irradiated heart of Frankenstein's monster. When a film crew comes to document him, their lights anger him, and he breaks loose, with the crew crushed to death beneath the bars of his cell. Growing ever larger, the boy makes his way across Honshū, from Hiroshima to Okayama, through Hijemi, Osaka, Lake Biwa, to forests near Shirakawa, where the JSDF first encounter him. The search for the boy is then cross-cut with the emergence of the *kaijū* Baragon, an underground tunnelling Mesozoic survivor that wreaks havoc on a mountain retreat on Mount Shirane, for which the boy is blamed. The story draws the two together for an inevitable *kaijū* showdown. They battle in a blazing forest in the shadow of Mount Fuji. The boy defeats Baragon before the earth beneath them collapses and consumes them.

We've heard several times how the *kaijū eiga*'s development relies on aspects of transculturation and the ways in which material is adopted, reworked and localised as it moves across borders, but *Frankenstein Conquers the World* is an excellent example of how the genre developed due to what Mary Louise Pratt termed 'contact zones'. Pratt described these as 'social spaces where cultures meet, clash, and grapple with each other, often in contexts of highly asymmetrical relations of power, such as colonialism, slavery, or their aftermaths as they are lived out in many parts of the world' (Pratt 1991, 34). *Frankenstein Conquers the World* exists in this nexus between national concerns and transnational exchange. The journey of Frankenstein's monster's heart from one Axis country to another and the direct representation of the Hiroshima bombing reflect a national history to which the *kaijū* film repeatedly refers, although such direct representation of the bombing and its aftermath is unusual. The transculturation of Frankenstein's monster as *hibakusha* reflects a continuing focus on the impact of the end of the Second World War in the *kaijū* film, although, as Azumi Sakamoto (2020) has argued, it takes on a different dimension in a rapidly modernising and recuperating Japan following Tokyo's first Olympics. Not only does Bowen's role in the film recuperate science as a positive force in the aftermath of the bombings, but also his romance with Togami is a 'strong and healthy relationship, based on mutual respect, [and becomes] a reflection of the

U.S.–Japan co-production environment itself, [lighting] the way toward peace and prosperity' (Sakamoto 2020, 240). There is a scene early in the film where the doctors say goodbye to a young woman suffering from radiation poisoning caused by the Hiroshima atomic bomb. Sakamoto references Horiaki Yoshii's criticism that the moment '"bleached" away' the horror of the bombing in favour of 'good science' to bring the 'eternal peace and happiness' that Bowen desires (Sakamoto 2020, 234–5). However, the scene also sets a precedent in terms of the scientists' (and Honda's) sympathy for the monster. The traditional abjection of the monster in Shelley's story is mapped onto *hibakusha*. The film never significantly humanises the creature; his portrayal is more akin to the pre-lingual Karloff in James Whale's version (1931), both in look, with prosthetic forehead, and in movement, although the design of this most human *kaijū* is more primitive caveman than the dominating modern figure of Karloff. As a figure of both fascination and abjection, the monster is equated with the dying *hibakusha* of the opening scenes, motivating some scientists to heal the suffering of a victim of the tragedy but others to see the monster as less than human, an object of experimentation that leads another member of the team, Dr Kawaji, to risk his life to gather cells from the monster to continue his work, just as Bowen and his team work on the survivors of the bombing in their hospital.

This transculturation adopts global material and adapts it into a national space. As Pratt attests, '[t]ransculturation . . . is a phenomenon of the contact zone' (1991, 36). *Frankenstein Conquers the World* was one of the first *kaijū* co-productions between Japanese and American companies, and the US–Japanese relationship is embedded within the film's origins and has continued throughout the genre. It's difficult to describe the film as any kind of adaptation of *Frankenstein*, other than through the trope of a scientifically created human, but it helps us to see how Japanese producers, working with American companies, transculturated material to fit national cinemas and the global demands of the film industry. As an example of *hibakusha* cinema, and a positive image of Japanese–US collaboration, it blends aspects of the specificity of national cinema with the transnationalising hybridity of cross-border production. The *kaijū eiga* was, after all, one of Tōhō's key exports.

The concept of a *Frankenstein* adaptation had originated with Willis O'Brien. Ryfle documents how O'Brien developed a treatment in 1960 called *King Kong vs. Frankenstein*. The idea eventually passed through RKO to an opportunistic producer named John Beck, who had produced the James Stewart classic *Harvey* (Henry Koster, 1950). When Beck failed to sell the film to a Hollywood studio (under the title

*King Kong vs. Prometheus*), he looked overseas for investment, and this led to Tōhō. The contact enabled the studio to acquire the rights to King Kong and produce *King Kong vs. Godzilla* (Ryfle 1998, 80–1). A 1963 treatment was developed to create a sequel to Honda's *The Human Vapor* (*Gasu ningen dai 1 gō*, lit. *Gas Human Being No. 1*, 1960), pitting its title character against the monster. However, when Tōhō entered a co-production deal with US animation company United Productions of America (UPA), the Frankenstein idea was resurrected (Ryfle and Godziszewski attribute the decision to UPA's writers), and *Frankenstein vs. Godzilla* was announced (Ryfle and Godziszewski 2017, 222–4).

Henry G. Saperstein, UPA's head, was reportedly more demanding than Japanese producers, insisting on an ending where the giant child fights an octopus. The ending is now available under the original international title of *Frankenstein vs. the Giant Devilfish*. Tsuburaya biographer August Ragone has revealed the confusion behind the scenes for many fans when images of the fight were available but the scene was missing from the film (Ragone 2009). Saperstein had reportedly been impressed with the octopus fight in *King Kong vs. Godzilla*, and wanted more, but was less captivated with the finished version and demanded it be cut. Honda meanwhile had simply never intended it to be in his cut (Ryfle and Godziszewski 2017, 226). While this looks ahead to the many revisions made by exploitation distributors as *kaijū* films crossed borders, it also demonstrates how co-production decisions effected the films. Perhaps the most significantly visible one in *Frankenstein Conquers the World* was casting Adams, whose Hollywood stardom had never really been stratospheric and was waning. The presence of the white American star at the heart of the film and in an honest portrayal of a relationship between a *gaijin* and Japanese woman was uncommon for the time. They joke about cultural differences and share food and clothing from each other's cultures (Figure 2.3). These are key ways in which cultural contact zones are visible in the film. Given Pratt's comments about the asymmetries of such zones, these are also a significant way in which anti-American sentiment is redirected. Since the film's motivating point is the Hiroshima bombing, Adams' role deflects the Otherness of the US, certainly erasing the culpability of the nation that is so prevalent in *Gojira*. Like the scientific narratives in the film, the Good American 'bleaches' the Bad American of two decades previously. *Frankenstein Conquers the World* opened in Japanese cinemas two days after the twentieth anniversary of the Hiroshima bombing. Adams would appear in one more *kaijū* film before his suicide in 1968. Other American actors would appear in Japanese films, including Russ Tamblyn in the Tōhō–UPA co-produced

**Figure 2.3** Bowen and Togami share moments of cultural exchange, with traditional food and dress, throughout *Frankenstein Conquers the World* (Tōhō/MGM)

sequel, *The War of the Gargantuas* (*Furankenshutain no Kaijū: Sanda tai Gaira*, lit. *Frankenstein's Monsters: Sanda vs. Gaira*, Honda, 1966). This one *begins* with an octopus attack and tells the story of two monsters derived from the original monster's cells, one kind, another monstrous.

Tōhō produced around thirty *daikaijū* films in the twenty-one years after the release of *Gojira*, and more that might tenuously be considered *kaijū* films, such as *Half Human*. As the genre boomed in the 1960s, Tōhō capitalised on the popularity of the films in export markets to produce a more transnational form of the genre, through co-productions and licensing to companies such as American International Pictures (AIP), but also created a few films that transculturated popular global trends or source material to blend national and international concerns. As the genre has spread globally or been distributed in different forms, this has developed further. Tōhō proved that *kaijū* films could be profitable. Their annual Champion Festival in the late 1960s and 1970s screened shorter versions of *kaijū* films for a largely young audience at home. However, the films were especially attractive abroad, and this encouraged rival studios to develop their own *kaijū*.

## *Kaijū* at Daiei

Apart from Tōhō, Daiei are generally the studio most closely associated with the Japanese *kaijū eiga* in the 1960s. This is largely down to the creation of a monster who rivalled Godzilla: the giant space turtle Gamera. Daiei were relative newcomers to the Japanese studio system, 'originally created to contribute to national policy', but most at ease with popular entertainment (Kitaura 2020, 115). After producing the first internationally successful Japanese film, Kurosawa's *Rashomon* (1950), Daiei experienced a string of successful series under the production-centred management of Nagata Masaichi, who oversaw major productions such as Misumi Kenji's *Shaka* (1961), the first Japanese 70-mm film, their melodramas known as 'mother films' and the *Zatōichi* films with Katsu Shintaro (twenty-five between 1962 and 1973) (Kitaura 2020). Nagata was reportedly the one who had the idea of producing a rival series to Tōhō's behemoth. Like Tanaka's conception of Godzilla, it happened on a plane journey, Hagata reportedly seeing a cloud shaped like a giant flying turtle (Rhoads and McCorkle 2018, 88).[6] Daiei, like Japanese cinema in general, were experiencing a decline in the mid-1960s; their lack of theatre ownership meant they felt the deterioration more severely than other companies. They eventually filed for bankruptcy in 1971 (Yomota 2019, 134), following which they were purchased by Tokuma Shoten Publishing, and later Kadokawa. Nevertheless, they left a defined mark on the *kaijū* film with the Gamera series, as well as the *Daimajin* trilogy (all three of which were released within eight months in 1966).

Released in 1965, *Gamera* is something of a throwback, given it was distributed alongside Tōhō's colourful widescreen *kaijū* epics. Shot on a relatively low budget, it was filmed in black and white to reduce costs, so its aesthetic echoes that of *Gojira* and its first sequel. It was Nagata who drove the production, influenced by the tremendous success of *King Kong vs. Godzilla* (still the most successful *kaijū* film in terms of admissions in Japan). A production involving giant rats had fallen through, and competitive pitches from Daiei's producers led to a proposal involving a giant turtle (Macias 2020). The naming of the monster (ガメラ) followed the now common convention of using katakana suffixed with ラ (-*ra*), like *Gojira* (ゴジラ), Mothra/*Mosura* (モスラ) or King Ghidorah/*Kingu Gidora* (キングギドラ). The phonetic and typographical similarities to Tōhō's main *kaijū* were no accident – in fact they were deliberately derivative (Milner 2020). The Japanese word for turtle is *kame* (亀 in kanji, カメ in katakana), and this became ガメラ, partly to avoid confusion with *kamera* (camera) (Rhoads and McCorkle 2018), and to emphasise the similarity with Godzilla's name, seemingly on Nagata's orders, although Yuasa Noriaki attributed it to another producer, Takahashi Nisan (Milner 2020). When Gamera was sold to a US distributor, the name was transliterated but amended to Gammera, again to avoid confusion with the word camera (Macias 2020). As Yuasa commented, *Gamera* was designated 'a class B movie' at Daiei, while sequels were elevated to class A, a decision that relegated Yuasa from the first sequel, *Gamera vs. Barugon*, which was directed by Tanaka Shigeo (Milner 2020, 38–9). The Gamera films were strongly targeted at young consumers, as all *kaijū* films became during the first monster boom. Co-production deals with AIP meant that American children (often cast from nearby army bases) regularly featured, and, as the series progressed, films engaged more with the relationship between Gamera, 'friend to all children', and his young friends. Yuasa commented that this meant the films were more violent, as they could present the *kaijū* as more animalistic than Tōhō's monsters, shot in ways that disguised that they were human performers on all fours, and featured blood, which Tsuburaya's effects largely avoided (there is blood in only four of Tōhō's *Shōwa*-era films). This had a secondary impact on the films, as Yuasa described:

> *Gamera the Giant Monster* was intended to show a giant monster on the rampage, and little else. Daiei's executives requested that some human drama be included in *Gamera vs. Barugon*, but discovered that children went to get some food or just ran through the corridors of the theatre during the movie. (Milner 2020, 44)

The background to the film's development emphasises key elements of the discussion here, namely that producers will develop original ideas based on established formats and templates, and that the development of the *kaijū eiga* continued to proceed alongside growing Japanese prosperity and the growth of young consumer markets. However, if we limit our understanding to factors that were within Japan's borders, this essentialises nation. The *kaijū* film relied upon a buoyant export market and growing co-production with American companies, particularly UPA and AIP, later Rankin-Bass. So, again, we see how a thoroughly national cinema creation is reliant on transnational networks to produce hybrid formats, because of economic and cultural globalisation. Cultural flows impact strongly on the *kaijū eiga*, reflecting the growing importance of Japanese soft power and the hierarchised political and economic relationship between Japan and the US. We've seen this already in this chapter, but the connections are further visible as the genre spreads across other Japanese studios.

*Gamera* capitalises on several already well-established *kaijū* tropes. For one, it begins in the Arctic, à la *The Beast from 20,000 Fathoms*. When American fighters shoot down an unidentified plane (the dubbed English dialogue in the Harris Associates version makes it clear the planes are Russian), an atomic bomb detonates. The ice cracks and a giant beast is awoken. By coincidence, a Japanese scientific expedition is also in the area, including Dr Hidaka (Funakoshi Eiji), assistant Kyoko (Kiritachi Harumi) and photographer Aoyagi (Yamashita Junichiro), covering the stock characters that had come to populate the *kaijū eiga*, representing the scientific and investigate threads of the narrative. As Rhoads and McCorkle also discuss, the *kaijū* film had become populated with recurring female stereotypes. While some were assistants to scientists or partners (in *Frankenstein Conquers the World*, Togami fulfils both roles), the emerging focus on alien invasion narratives produced more sexualised female characters equated with subversion. The presence of the expedition at a nearby Eskimo village allows a key element of exposition, as the village chief shows them a stone carving of the giant turtle, named Gamera. Once again, there is a connection between (fictional) mythology and the origins of the creature. *Kaijū*, like many monsters, emerge from outside 'civilisation' (the depiction of the Eskimo village here is certainly less problematic than the depictions of supposedly primitive cultures in other films), from liminal or Othered spaces or cultures to threaten modern centres of urbanity.

Gamera scuttles the expedition's ship and heads for Tokyo. Having been mistaken for a UFO (Gamera flies by retracting its legs inside its shell and spinning, propelled by internal rockets), the monster arrives in Japan. We're first introduced to Toshio, a young boy and his family. His sister and uncle are worried that Toshio is too attached to his pet turtle, and they force him to release it. Immediately after he bids farewell to his pet, the giant turtle arrives. Gamera attacks the family's lighthouse (Figure 2.4 – more echoes of *The Beast from 20,000 Fathoms*), but Toshio has run to the top of the building. He falls from the lighthouse, but is caught by Gamera, whom the boy believes is the pet he has just released. The monster heads inland to a thermonuclear power plant.

**Figure 2.4** Gamera attacks a lighthouse in *Gamera*, referencing *The Beast from 20,000 Fathoms* (Kadokawa Daiei)

After failing to stop Gamera at the power lines (power lines never stop *kaijū*), Hidaka and the military watch as the space turtle devastates the plant and consumes the fire from the resulting destruction (in shots of Gamera's fire-breath reversed). Our protagonists consult the respected scientist Dr Murase (regular Ichikawa Kon collaborator Hamamura Jun mimicking Shimura's roles in the first two Godzilla movies), who speculates that freezing bombs might have an impact on Gamera. The JSDF plant bombs beneath the incapacitated creature and manage to force it onto its back, where they believe the turtle will slowly die. But Gamera draws in its limbs, begins to spin and flies away. The action now heads to Tokyo, where, conveniently, Toshio has also travelled to visit his uncle. They meet with Hidaka, and Toshio insists that Gamera is not evil, just lonely. Eventually, Gamera emerges from Tokyo Bay, where ships have been mysteriously attacked. The monster lands at Haneda Airport and wreaks havoc on Tokyo, while Toshio runs away during the evacuation. Suspecting that the monster is attracted by fossil fuels, the JSDF use burning petrol to attract it to Oshima Island, where they will enact Plan Z to defeat Gamera. Weather thwarts them along the way, but, fortunately, a volcano erupts to drive the monster to the island. Plan Z is finally carried out when Gamera is forced into the capsule of a rocket and blasted into space. Toshio waves goodbye and hopes one day he can visit the monster in space.

While *Gamera* rehashes some of the recurring tropes of the *kaijū* film – the scientist protagonists, scenes of urban destruction, the centrality of identifiable Japanese locations, and the restoration of equilibrium through the application of good science – it also restores the significance of nuclear destruction to the foundations of the monster's genesis, with the bomb at the outset reawakening the beast lost to time. *Gamera* also institutes a focus on the child protagonist. Children had featured in *kaijū* films before *Gamera*, such as Chûjô Shinji in *Mothra*, the younger brother of an anthropologist in the film. Shinji plays a supporting role in that film, providing some comic relief and challenging the main villains after they kidnap the *Shobijin*. Toshio plays a much more central role in *Gamera*. Following Tokyo's evacuation, Toshio is amid the action. Gamera attacks an oil refinery, and Toshio tries to get the monster's attention. He gets on board a train as Gamera pulls the wagons towards him. Yuasa shoots from Toshio's eyeline, not only up at the monster but also when the danger is averted and the boy is surrounded by soldiers. They laugh at him. Yuasa continues to shoot from the boy's point of view, and this becomes a motif to align viewers with Toshio in several scenes. This focus became more pronounced as the *Gamera* series continued, across seven more films in the *Shōwa* period, a *Heisei* trilogy and one more film in the Millennium, *Gamera the Brave* (*Chiisaki Yūsha-tachi Gamera*, lit. *Little Hero: Gamera*, Tasaki Ryūta, 2006). The success of *Gamera* motivated Daiei to elevate the follow-up to an A film, in colour and with a higher budget, but the fortunes of the series declined alongside Japanese cinema, with more recycled stock footage and a final film in the *Shōwa* series, *Gamera: Super Monster* (*Uchū Kaijū Gamera*, lit. *Space Monster Gamera*, Yuasa, 1980) that was almost entirely composed of scenes from the rest of the series.

Daiei's other successful *kaijū eiga* series is a less derivative iteration of the genre. *Daimajin* (大魔神, most closely translated as *Giant Demon*, or *Giant Demon God,* 1966) was directed by Yasuda Kimiyoshi, a contract director at Daiei who also directed six films in the *Zatōichi* series[7] and two entries in the studio's *Yōkai* trilogy.[8] *Daimajin* is an innovate blend of *jidaigeki*, *chambara* and *kaijū* film, set during an unidentified period, probably the Tokugawa period (1603–1867). A village in Tanba worships the Demon God (*majin*) Arakatsuma, the *majin* they believe trapped within the mountain by a giant statue. When tremors convince the villagers that the *majin* is trying to escape, they conduct a ritual ceremony to pacify it. The local *daimyo*'s chamberlain, Samanosuke Ōdate, uses the distraction to stage a coup and take over the village. The lord Hanabasu is killed but his children, Tadafumi and Kozasa, escape with the local priestess, Shinobu, and Kogenta, one of the *daimyo*'s retainers, who spirit them away to the mountain where the *majin* resides. Years pass, and Samanosuke becomes a cruel tyrant, forcing the villagers into slave labour to fortify the castle. Kogenta travels back to the village in an attempt to rally the still-loyal opposition to Samanosuke but is captured and tortured. A young boy, Take, escapes the village to pray to the *majin*, sending word of Kogenta's capture. Tadafumi heads to the village to rescue Kogenta, inadvertently heading into a trap. Meanwhile, Take ventures further into the mountain forest. The forest sequence is disorienting, the boy having visions of being molested by skeletons, while ghosts and animals look on in quick cuts and superimposed effects. He reaches the temple and prays to what he believes is a ghostly priestess (but is really Kozasa). This blends an element of *kaiki* into the film's generic melange. Tadafumi is captured by Samanosuke's samurai, and he and Kogenta await execution. The priestess returns to the village to warn the tyrant of the *majin*'s anger, saying that he should leave the village and take his evil elsewhere. Samanosuke denies the existence of the god and laughs off the villagers' beliefs. He threatens to destroy the statue, to break its spell, and kills the priestess. The sequence of her death is ethereal, with focused low-key studio lighting that theatrically turns the setting to black. She floats like a ghost, cursing the tyrant with her last breaths. Samanosuke's men head for the mountain to destroy the statue. As Take and Kozasa look on, a dropped charm helps the samurai locate and capture them. The samurai find the statue and set about trying to destroy it. It appears impervious to their hammer blows, but when they drive a stake into its forehead, the statue begins to bleed. A furious storm then rages, trapping the samurai on the mountain, where landslips and chasms in the ground swallow them before closing. Samanosuke is undeterred, but Kozasa prays to the *majin* for help to free her brother and Kogenta. She vows to sacrifice herself in return for the god's help. Take stops her from hurling herself into the nearby waterfall. The statue comes to life, its stone face replaced by a demon face, a furrowed brow reminiscent of a *bunraku Oni* mask (Figure 2.5), albeit in a more masculinised form. The villagers revolt, and before Samanosuke's men can quell the revolution, the *majin* arrives to smash the fortress. The *majin* heads straight for the tyrant lord and carries him to the centre of the building, where it removes the stake from its head and pins Samanosuke to a smashed wooden joist. Take prays to the *majin* to stop, but the monster raises its foot to step on him. Kozasa throws herself on top of him and the statue pauses. She pleads with it to return to the mountain. It raises its hand to its face, which returns to the statue façade, and the spirit flies

**Figure 2.5** The animated stone *kaijū*'s angry face resembles the *Oni* from *bunraku* in *Daimajin* (Kadokawa Daiei)

back to the mountain, leaving a bright blue sky behind, while the statue crumbles to a pile of dust and shackles.

The two following films, *Return of Daimajin* (*Daimajin Ikaru*, lit. *Wrath of Daimajin*, Misumi Kenji,[9] 1966) and *Daimajin Strikes Again* (*Daimajin Gyakushū*, lit. *Daimajin's Counterattack*, Mori Kazuo, 1966), follow roughly the same pattern, with the *majin* protecting those who believe in the god and punishing those who would bring injustice upon them. The *kaijū* in this instance perhaps doesn't conform with the conception outlined so far in the formation of the genre. Given the historical setting of the *jidaigeki*, this monster is perhaps more a blending of traditional elements than more modern variants of *kaijū*, partly due, as Jason Barr attests (2016, 11), to the lack of science-fiction elements in the film. As a variant of the *chambara*, the *Daimajin* films bring together one of Daiei's foundational genres with the suitmation special effects that help to define the *kaijū* film as a key Japanese export. The films' monster also seems more specifically rooted in Japanese spirituality than other creatures (that its name is rendered in kanji rather than katakana is a sign of this). *Daimajin*'s Japanese name includes the character *kami* (神, sometimes rendered as *shin* or *jin*), which is generally translated as 'god', but the Shinto understanding of the term is looser than the English translation suggests. *Kami* can be divine spirits or objects of worship.[10] The conception of the *majin* combines *kami* with the demon (*ma*) in the form of both the stone *Dōsojin*, the marker that guards the spirit, and the divine *kami* within. As mentioned before, once the *majin* comes to life, it resembles *Oni*, the Shinto demons that must be appeased, which traditionally can bring destruction as well as protection (in essence, this is the description of the plot of all three films). Consequently perhaps, the *Daimajin* films have travelled less than other examples of the giant monster film but are considered by fans to be *kaijū* films, despite their less modern influences. That the trilogy also includes music by Ifukube Akira, the composer most linked with the *kaijū eiga*, is another palpable link, as is the presence of young protagonists. The first *Daimajin* was also released by Daei in a double bill with *Gamera vs. Barugon* (to maximise admissions, according to Yuasa [Milner 2020]). Statues from the film now adorn the Kadokawa Daiei Studios in Chōfu, west of Tokyo City. Kadokawa would also later resurrect *Daimajin* in their own TV series, *Daimajin Kanon* (2010), a combination of idol, *henshin*, *yōkai* and teen drama shows. As is often the case, the TV series was produced by a committee, bringing together a series of companies to co-ordinate different elements of production, including toy company Bandai, TV Tokyo, clothing producer Cospa and cellular operator NTT DoCoMo, alongside Kadakowa's TV and publishing divisions (Aiken, Ellis and Ashby n.d.).

## *Kaijū* at Shōchiku, Nikkatsu and Toei

### Shōchiku

At the peak of the monster boom in the mid-1960s, all the major Japanese studios contributed to the phenomenon. While Tōhō and Daiei were the major architects of the boom, other studios got involved to capitalise on the success of the *kaijū* film both in Japan and abroad. Shōchiku are one of Japan's oldest studios, home to major Japanese directors such as Ozu Yasujirō, Mizoguchi Kenji and Naruse Mikio. The studio developed an early specialism in *shinpa* melodrama but moved away to cultivate a more modern, aspirational, female (*modan gāru*) audience (Standish 2005, 53–4). Shōchiku's single *kaijū* film of the 1960s is perhaps also one of the strangest, while drawing on many of the now established tropes of *kaijū eiga*: the monster rampages, thirst for UFOs and space exploration, international casts and English dialogue, sexualised female roles and colourful widescreen designs.

Known internationally as *The X from Outer Space, Giant Space Monster Guilala* (*Uchū Daikaijū Girara*) was released in 1967 and directed by Nihonmatsu Kazui. Nihonmatsu had earlier served as an assistant director to significant directors at the studio, including Kurosawa Akira, Kobayashi Masaki and Kinoshita Keisuke. As director, he made just four films, but two stand out for our purposes here: *The X from Outer Space* and *Genocide* (*Konchu daisenso*, lit. *Great Insect War*, 1968), both part of a very brief cycle of horror and *tokusatsu* films produced by Shōchiku. *The X from Outer Space* was one of several *kaijū* films co-financed in the 1960s by the Japan Film Export Promotion Association (Nihon Eiga Yushutsu Shinkō Kyōkai, FEPA). The initiative backed sixty-one films in five years, with 7,333 million yen supplied in loans. With the film industry generally in recession, the loans were issued based on the proportion of overseas sales, and therefore *kaijū* films were perfect for promotion, as a genre in which Japan had a 'competitive advantage' (Uchiyama 2020, 122). *Kaijū eiga* were seen as films ripe for exploitation in foreign markets, and Shōchiku, along with Daiei and Nikkatsu, benefited from the additional funding to develop films that were 'export-appropriate'. The first films supported by the scheme were the third entries in the *Gamera* and *Daimajin* series.[11] The scheme failed to arrest the decline in Japanese cinema, producing films castigated by politicians as 'foolish', and leading to little or no financial returns through export markets (Tanikawa 2020). However, as Tanikawa argues, the scheme provided a basis for future public film industry support that made *kaijū* films Japan's first publicly funded film exports.

*The X from Outer Space* was developed specifically to this end. Tōhō's *Godzilla* films were already internationally successful and had sold to American distributors or gained co-production investment, and Shōchiku's entry built on some of the other-worldly elements that had adorned Tōhō's films. Space themes and alien invaders had been prevalent in *Ghidorah, the Three-Headed Monster* (*Sandai Daikaijū: Chikyū Saidai no Kessen*, lit. *Three Giant Monsters: Earth's Greatest Battle*, Honda, 1964) and *Invasion of Astro-Monster* (*Kaijū Daisensō*, lit. *The Giant Monster War*, Honda, 1965), while Gamera would fight off an alien invasion the following year in *Gamera vs. Viras* (*Gamera tai Uchū Kaijū Bairasu*, lit. *Gamera vs. Outer Space Monster Viras*, Yuasa, 1968). *The X from Outer Space* combines a space exploration narrative, not unlike that of *It! The Terror from Beyond Space* (Edward L. Cahn, 1958), with invasion by a space monster, like King Ghidorah (without the Hydra design). It follows the astronauts of *AAB Gamma* (the 'Astro-Boat') as they investigate previous expeditions to Mars that had gone missing. The crew consists of three Japanese astronauts – Captain Sano (Wazaki Toshiya), Miyamoto (Yanagisawa Shinichi) and Dr Kato (Okada Eiji[12]) – and scientist Lisa Schneider (Peggy Neal[13]). Dr Kato quickly succumbs to space sickness after an encounter with a UFO and is replaced by another foreign character, the reluctant Dr Stein (Mike Daneen), after a stopover at a very fashionably decorated moon base (Figure 2.6). Although the nationality of the western characters is never revealed explicitly, all have German names (Schneider, Stein and Berman), and Lisa gives a gift of German jewellery to Michiko (Harada Itoko), a member of the moon base crew who is in love with Sano. The crew resume their journey to Mars, shadowed by the UFO again, and discover a mysterious substance sprayed on their engine. They return to Earth with the spore-like substance and eventually find it has hatched, with a three-toed talon imprint left on the ground. Investigating the monster's first attack, they find a matching footprint, but this time giant. They[14] name the monster Girara (ギララ, doubling down on the monster-naming convention, with 'gi' simply standing for giant), although it is visibly romanised in the film as Guilala. The monster rampages across Honshū, south from Lake Inawashiro in Fukushima (echoing the *kaijū eiga*'s sharing out of the destruction across Japan) and towards Tokyo. Meanwhile, the astronauts are sent back out to space to

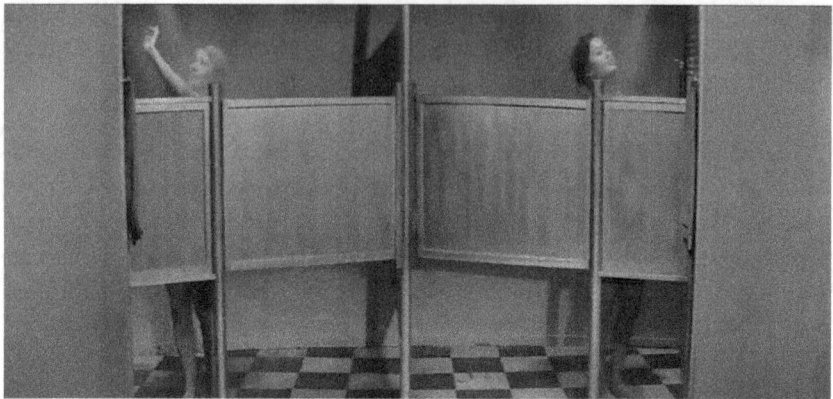

**Figure 2.6** *The X from Outer Space* fetishises both white and Japanese femininity in its 1960s vision of the future (Shōchiku)

collect a substance they believe can kill the monster, Guilalanium. The monster is finally defeated, shrunk back to a spore and returned to space. The ending of the film resolves the main romantic triangle, with Lisa giving up on her attraction to Sano to let him and Michiko be together. Michiko has already sworn to give up science to become a wife and mother. This is emblematic of the film's gender politics. While it does have not just one but two women in science positions who both play active roles in the film, Lisa is presented as a western fetish, blonde with blue eyes, while the film features an out-of-place scene in which the two women converse in the shower. This isn't the only tonal misstep: the film's moon-set sequences are highly contemporary in style, with garish colours and a well-stocked bar. There is also a surprising soundtrack of pop and bossa nova, the latter particularly popular at the time, and there are moments of broad comedy, especially when Miyamoto seals a hull rupture in space with his backside. The film is something of a mishmash of outward-looking tropes and international casting (a feature of FEPA-funded films), with a high degree of *tokusatsu* action: Girara's atomic breath is almost identical to Godzilla's, with very similar shots of tanks being melted by it. Special effects for the film were directed by Kawakami Keiji, whose Japan Tokusatsu Movie Co. Ltd had recently been founded following his departure from Tsuburaya's company.[15] Kawakami's company also provided special effects for other late-1960s *kaijū* movies, the remainder of Shōchiku's horror cycle, including *Genocide*, and Nikkatsu's *Gappa: The Triphibian Monster* (*Daikyojū Gappa*, lit. *Giant Beast Gappa*, Noguchi Haruyasu) later in 1967.

## Nikkatsu

Nikkatsu, originally Nihon Katsudo Shashin (Japan Cinematograph Company), are Japan's oldest film studio. They had initially prospered, before merging with Shinko and Daito studios to form Daiei during the war. Following the war, Nikkatsu flourished with a mix of *taiyozoku* (sun tribe[16]) and 'borderless' action films (Schilling 2007, 12–20). By the late 1960s, they, like most Japanese film studios, were struggling, and no Nikkatsu film made the domestic box office top ten for 1965 and 1966. Like other studios, they turned to FEPA to fund a *kaijū* film. *Gappa* was the only *kaijū* film that the studio produced. In the film title, *Daikyojū* (大巨獣) employs 巨, the kanji meaning 'giant', rather than 怪, the expected kanji for a *kaijū* movie. In the opening scenes, an expedition scouts exotic animals and people for a new theme park, when one of the crew witnesses a monster in the water, and screams 'kaibutsu'.

*Gappa* takes its most significant cue from a foreign *kaijū* film, *Gorgo*, Eugene Lourié's 1961 British *kaijū* movie. This has a plot based on the 'monster on the rampage' template established in both *The Lost World* and *King Kong*, but with an additional element: parental protection. *Gappa* follows yet another expedition, this time to Obelisk Island. The reporters, photographers and scientists on the ship are looking for exhibits for a new park planned by the owner of *Playmate* magazine to celebrate its fifth anniversary. The islanders (once more, 'primitive' islanders portrayed by Japanese actors in blackface) have seemingly previously been colonised or occupied by Japanese travellers. The island also has an erupting volcano, but the visitors are attracted to a giant stone statue. After it collapses due to a tremor caused by the volcano, the crew head inside the cave, accompanied by local boy Saki. Inside, they discover the bones of what they believe to be the long-rotted remains of Gappa, the god of whom the islanders are so afraid. They discover an egg, which hatches to reveal a bird-like lizard, like the *yōkai kappa*. Ignoring Saki's protests, they take the hatchling and return to Japan. Unbeknownst to them, two adult creatures emerge from the underground lake and terrorise the island. The islanders are rescued by a passing submarine and taken to Japan. The expedition, back in Tokyo, have caged the monster, which grows at an alarming rate (not unlike Frankenstein's monster). Photographs of the monster are published in *Playmate*, to great renown, but the two parents have arrived in Japan, emerging from Sagami Bay and laying siege to Atami City before defeating the JSDF with their heat-ray breath and hiding in Lake Kawaguchiro. The two creatures are finally forced from under the lake and head for Tokyo. The *Playmate* team, fearing the city's destruction, take the junior Gappa to Haneda airport, where the two adults arrive. They teach their child to fly and leave.

*Gappa* is a further example of the transnational hybridity of the *kaijū eiga*. Given its development as a form that draws influence from export markets and keeps an eye on international developments through this period, it blends the established template – destruction of Japanese landscape, both urban and rural – with a narrative pattern based on its international forerunners. We also have not one, but two, child protagonists. The connection with mystical island folklore echoes *Mothra* and *King Kong*, while the furious rampage of the monster's parent is so close to that of *Gorgo* that is it really an unauthorised remake (yet it's worth noting that the central 'showman steals monster' trope of *Gorgo* is undoubtedly reliant on *King Kong*'s plot). The monster's design relies on nationally specific imagery, with the beaked, water-dwelling *yōkai* reflected in the design of the Gappas' heads. That *Gappa* was also financed specifically for export makes it no surprise that the film should blend a combination of specifically Japanese traits with transnational influences. As Ramon Lobato and Mark Ryan have argued, in relation to low-budget Australian horror films, a form of 'market-driven textual customization [is] in play at the bottom end of the spectrum' where producers make films exhibiting the preferences of international distributors to gain access to markets beyond the local (2011, 196). As these authors conclude: 'The flourishing of distinctively local content is one unlikely by-product of an increasingly globalized . . . distribution landscape [and] allows national specificity to operate as a marker of difference' (197). The repetition of distinctive features of the *kaijū eiga* from both inside and outside Japan enables this 'textual customization' to develop for export markets. National support schemes can help boost the film industry through the development of work that targets international distribution, even if global circulation comes with strings attached, such as dubbing and editing, two features that helped minimise national specificity. These are exploitative tactics that helped the *kaijū* film develop into a genre that was at once national and transnational. Work that essentialises Japanese cinema as exclusively a national cinema, derived from tradition and historical aspects, problematises how producers and industries develop and engage with international products. Or perhaps more simply, as I. Q. Hunter has argued, '[g]iven cinema's tendency to repetition, imitation, remakes and "sequelitis", it is often difficult to disentangle exploitation, except by its substandard budget, from the usual methods of cashing in on box-office hits' (Hunter 2013, 24). We'll see later that *kaijū* films have often been marked by a 'tendency to repetition, imitation, remakes and "sequelitis"', but this period of the monster boom is difficult to distinguish from exploitation, as an industry struggled to survive in the face of challenges from other media and as the prosperity of mid-to-late twentieth-century Japan offered a range of alternative leisure activities and demands for consumer spending. Yet the *kaijū* boom fully embraced these.

## Toei

Japan's other major studio, Toei, produced just a couple of films featuring *kaijū*, including *The Magic Serpent* (*Kairyū Daikessen*, lit. *Great Mystic Dragon Battle*, Yamauchi Tetsuya, 1966), an adaptation of the nineteenth-century folktale 'Jiraiya Gōketsu Monogatari' ('The Tale of the Gallant Jiraiya'). Its protagonist, Orochimaru, is a master of dragon magic and able to transform into a giant serpent, and battles a series of monsters. Like the *Daimajin* series, it combines the *jidaigeki* with scenes of *tokusatsu* action. Fukasaku Kinji's *The Green Slime* (*Ganmā Daisan Gō: Uchū Daisakusen*, lit. *Gamma 3: Great Space War*, 1968) is often grouped with *kaijū* films, but is more a space-set *tokusatsu* film with an international cast (funded by MGM). Toei found significant success with *kaijū* on television as the monster boom on the small screen sucked up the cinema audience. Tsuburaya Productions' *kaiki* series (not all episodes feature *kaijū*) *Ultra Q*, first broadcast in 1966, had set the tone for what was to follow, as a kind of *Twilight Zone* in which journalists investigate a series of supernatural events across Japan. The series was followed the same year by *Ultraman*, the first Ultra Brothers series, in which a member of the United Science Patrol, Hayata Shin, is twinned with an alien from the M78 nebula. Hayata can summon the *kyodai hīro* (giant hero) for a short time to battle the week's invading monster (the first series even included a recycled Godzilla costume). Nearly forty series have followed, with film spin-offs, including *Ultraman: The Adventure Begins* (*Urutoraman Yū Esu Ē*, lit. *Ultraman USA*, Ray Patterson and Kusakabe Mitsuo, 1987), a US–Japanese co-produced animated version. *Henshin* (transforming) superhero series have been a staple of Japanese television ever since, with Toei producing their *Kamen Rider* (*Kamen Raidā*) series from 1971 onwards, and *Super Sentai* (*Sūpā Sentai*) from 1975 (it is best known as the basis for Saban's localised *Mighty Morphin Power Rangers* [1993–6]). Tōhō's short-lived *Zone Fighter* (*Ryūsei Ningen Zōn*, lit. *Meteor Human Zone*, 1973) was set in their *kaijū* universe and featured the pantheon of monsters from their films. The growth of regular television programmes helped to pull audiences away from cinema and establish a consistent stream of programming, often on Sunday mornings, that appealed to the core *kaijū* cinema audience. The monster boom on the big screen wound down by the mid-1970s, to be resurrected at the end of the *Shōwa* period with the *Heisei* Godzilla, Mothra and Gamera series. Japanese media production later became subject to the synergies of the media mix (*media mikkusu*) (Steinberg 2012) or Production Committee (*seisakuiinkai*) 'simultaneous mix' (Joo, Denison and Furukawa 2013) systems that integrate a range of branded products, including films, TV series, manga, games, toys and advertising. The breadth of practices at play in contemporary Japanese character franchises, such as Ultraman, Godzilla and *Pokémon*, meant the *kaijū eiga* became subsumed into Japanese cultural production more widely. We'll return to these Japanese titans later, but, in the next chapter, we'll begin to look at the spread of transnational variants of the *kaijū* film.

## Notes

1. *Gojira* shared several cast members with its stablemates: Shimura Takashi and Nakajima Haruo (who played the monster) in Kurosawa's epic, and Hirata Akihiko in the Inagaki film.
2. In *The Mysterians*, the burrowing robot is named Mogera, from the Japanese word for mole (*mogura*), but in the *Heisei* era this becomes an acronym for 'Mobile Operation Godzilla Universal Expert Robot Aero-Type' in the English translation for *Godzilla vs. SpaceGodzilla* (*Gojira tai Supēsugojira*, Yamashita Kensho, 1994).
3. *Tokusatsu* is the Japanese word for special effects and is regularly used to refer to particular kinds of effects used in *kaijū* and *henshin* (transformation) genres, particularly suitmation and miniatures.
4. This refers to the movie universe, since more monsters have crossed over in other media, such as in the novel *Gojira Kaijū Mokushiroku* (*Monster Apocalypse*) by Oki Takeshi, which recounts the build-up to the events of the first anime film *Godzilla: Planet of the Monsters* (*Gojira Kaijū Wakusei*, Shizuno Kobun and Seshita Hiroyuki, 2017).
5. Religion became a recurring aspect of some *kaijū* movies, particularly *Mothra*, where the narrative resolves outside a church in Rolisica's New Kirk City, a thinly veiled New York stand-in where the collective spirit of those hiding at the church can help the protagonists recognise the symbol that will pacify Mothra's assault on the city to rescue the *Shobijin*, the two miniature faeries kidnapped from Bikini Island.
6. Other accounts have claimed it was an island rather than a cloud (Macias 2020, 7).
7. *Zatōichi: On the Road, Zatōichi kenka-tabi, 1963; Adventures of Zatōichi, Zatōichi sekisho-yaburi, 1964; Zatōichi's Cane Sword, Zatōichi tekka-tabi, 1967; Zatōichi and the Fugitives, Zatōichi hatashijō, 1968; Zatōichi and the*

One-Armed Swordsman, Shin Zatōichi: Yabure! Tōjin-ken, 1971; Zatōichi's Conspiracy, Shin Zatōichi monogatari: Kasama no chimatsuri, 1973.
8. Yōkai Monsters: 100 Monsters, Yōkai Hyaku Monogatari, 1968; Yōkai Monsters: Along with Ghosts, Tōkaidō obake dōchū, 1969. The third film, Yōkai Monsters: Spook Warfare (Yōkai Daisensō, lit. The Great Yōkai War, Yoshiyuki Kuroda, 1968), was a major influence on Miike Takashi's Yōkai Daisensō, released in 2005.
9. Misumi was one of Daiei's most prolific and reliable directors (Gatto and Mes 2005). In addition to Shaka (1961), Misumi was also a regular director of chambara for Daiei and other companies following Daiei's first collapse. He directed the first Zatōichi film, Zatōichi monogatari (1962), and five more in the series, as well as the majority of the Lone Wolf and Cub series (four of the six films in 1972 and 1973, for Tōhō) and the first Hanzo the Razor (Goyōkiba) film starring and independently produced by Katsu Shintaro in 1972.
10. In his commentary for the Arrow Films release of the trilogy, Jonathan Clements (2020) remarks that the religious concept in the film is unusually western in its monotheistic god. The central concept is much less divine natural kami than it is individually Abrahamic.
11. Daiei relied on FEPA to finance all but two of the Gamera films produced until the company's collapse in 1971. Tōhō never used the scheme to fund their kaijū films, since the interest rate of the loans was on a par with that of their bonds (Tanikawa 2020).
12. Okada is best known for his work with Alain Resnais, Hiroshima mon amour (1959), and with Teshigahara Hiroshi, Woman in the Dunes (Suna no Onna, lit. Sand Woman, 1964).
13. Neal moved to Japan as a student and had a short-lived career as an actor, almost exclusively in science-fiction films, before returning to acting nearly fifty years later.
14. The monster was named following a public competition.
15. Kawakami had previously worked with Tsuburaya at Tōhō during the war, before leaving to join Shōchiku's special effects department.
16. Taiyozoku films took their name from a term applied to a disillusioned post-war generation of prosperous, nihilistic youth. The films were sexy and violent, depicting rabble-rousing youngsters who rejected the values of their parents' generation.

CHAPTER 3

# Exchanging Monsters: Korean *Kaijū*

*Gojira* quickly established the *kaijū* film as an attractive film genre. The film's success, and that of its sequels and imitators, cemented trends for *kaijū* not just in Japan, but globally. Producers had already borrowed elements from *King Kong* to develop their own variants, but once defined, the *kaijū* film spread more generally. This chapter thus continues to look at how the *kaijū* film developed via cultural flow and transnational connections. While the previous chapters have sought to make a case for the *kaijū* film as a popular national cinema genre reliant upon transnational influences and networks, this chapter steps outside Japan to look at how the *kaijū* film became adopted in other countries. Initially, we'll explore East Asian variants and the ways in which *kaijū* were imitated regionally in a few guises. Our case study will almost exclusively be of films produced in South and North Korea, to look at the ways in which genrification (to use Rick Altman's [1999] term) occurs in supranational spaces but is grounded in local production (as Elena Oliete-Aldea, Beatriz Oria and Juan A. Tarancón argue in the Introduction to *Global Genres, Local Films* [2016]). The South Korean film *Yongary: Monster from the Deep* (*Taegoesu Yonggari*, lit. *Great Beast Yongary,* Kim Kidŏk, 1967) closely mimics the Godzilla structure, with a child protagonist and a dancing monster. Yet it has a tenuous basis in local mythology. This is, however, unlike other regional *kaijū* films, such as the North Korean *Pulgasari* (Shin Sang-ok, 1985) or the Thai *Garuda* (*Paksa wayu*, Monthon Arayangkoon, 2004), both of which draw more explicitly on myths to different ends (especially in the case of *Pulgasari*). Others, such as Hong Kong's *The Mighty Peking Man* or South Korea's *A\*P\*E*, are more exploitative attempts to capitalise on the release of popular films, particularly the 1976 remake of *King Kong* (by John Guillermin), and as such we'll consider them in a later chapter under the heading of Kongsploitation.

While elements of these films have been attributed to shared global anxieties and concerns (particularly by Jason Barr, who argues this is a defining facet of the *kaijū* film), the approach taken here is closer to Iain Robert Smith's identification of a meme-like quality in the ways that unofficial remakes in transnational cinema adopt tropes and aspects of Hollywood cinema. Smith polemically locates Hollywood at the centre of global cinematic culture, something that is challenged by this study, where cultural flows are less into or out of the west but often situated within and around Tokyo more generally.

Lines of cultural flow and the mobility of personnel and technology have repeatedly enabled the *kaijū* film to spread across borders. Japanese directors and special effects technicians were often outsourced to neighbouring countries (and the US) to work on *tokusatsu*-style films, from Taiwan to Hong Kong to North and South Korea. While we are perhaps now more used to a more level playing field in terms of effects production, as many countries become home to effects houses through the implementation of tax breaks and the accessibility of digital technology, this wasn't always the case. Therefore, lines of regional flow helped enable the passage of *kaijū* effects from one country to another. Instead of focusing on the films discussed in this chapter, we might have considered films such as *War God* (*Zhànshén*, Chan Hung-man, 1974) or *The Founding of Ming Dynasty* (*Zhū hóngwǔ*, Hsu Da Chuan, 1971), two Taiwanese films that had special effects directed by Takano Koichi, whose work include dozens of *Ultraman* episodes and the *Monkey* (*Saiyûki*) TV show. We could also have considered *The Super Inframan* (*Zhōngguó chāorén*, lit. *Chinese Superman*, Shan Hua, 1975), a production by Hong Kong studio Shaw Brothers that adopted the *henshin* genre, with 'Brucesploitation'[1] stars Danny Lee and Bruce Le, and effects by Japanese personnel. Or we could have discussed the Chinese *Monster Hunt* films (*Zhuō yāo jì*, Hui Raman, 2015 and 2018), the enormously successful adaptations of *Liaozhai zhiyi* (*Strange Tales from a Chinese Studio*) that correspond to *yōkai* as well as *kaijū*. Thai films *Garuda*, based on the Buddhist myths of golden-winged eagles, or the Tsuburaya collaboration with Chaiyo Productions *The 6 Ultra Brothers vs. the Monster Army* (*Urutora Roku Kyōdai tai Kaijū Gundan*, Tōjō Shohei, Sompote Sands, 1974, but unreleased until 1979) would also have fitted under the same umbrella, as would the Hindi films *Gogola* and *Aadi Yug* (Tatieni Prasad, 1978), the latter a caveman film that recycles several minutes from the end of *Frankenstein Conquers the World*. While the focus could shift to different nations and to exploring the connections between different countries and film industries, it would simply produce a list rather than a more detailed exploration of the principles of cultural flow and regional mobility at work in the *kaijū eiga*'s history.

## The *Kaijū* Meme

Smith's *The Hollywood Meme: Transnational Adaptations in World Cinema* (2017) discusses the ways in which filmmakers in countries such as Turkey, India and the Philippines have adopted and adapted cultural material from Hollywood. Smith reworks Richard Dawkins' concept of the genetic meme: 'a unit of culture which spreads and replicates' (31), adapting itself to its new environment as it does so. Studies of adaptation and remakes, Smith argues, have too long focused on core principles of fidelity (to an 'original'). We've all become more used to the conventional form of digital memes that circulate online – digital images and video borrowed, adapted, repurposed and shared through social media – which, for Smith, demonstrate the ways in which the concept of the meme is invested with human agency. This is the key difference from Dawkins' biological memetics, where mutation and transmission are generally automatic. Dawkins does discuss cultural memes in *The Selfish Gene* (1976), but his examples are generally institutions, such as marriage, or reproduced texts that aren't consciously reproduced, such as ear-worm songs that stick in our heads. Smith allots much more agency to film producers, whose contributions to cinema are active engagements with cultural artefacts.

In so doing, Smith references 'Parody and Marginality: The Case of Brazilian Cinema', an article by Robert Stam and João Luiz Vieira (1990) about a Brazilian soft-core porn parody of *Jaws* (Steven Spielberg, 1975) entitled *Codfish* (*Bacalhau*, 1975), and, appropriately for our purposes, *Costinha e o King Mong* (Alcino Diniz, 1977), a lampoon of the first remake of *King Kong*. Stam and Vieira argue that both films actively highlight the transgressive power of the carnivalesque, following Mikhail Bakhtin in *Rabelais and His World* (1984), that has the power to resist – albeit temporarily – oppressive, dominant ideology. Through this lens, Stam and Vieira view parody as a legitimate tool with which to resist the power of domination in a neocolonial context: it 'is well suited to the needs of the oppressed and powerless', rearticulating 'the force of dominant discourse' in subversive ways, to resist that discourse rather than imitate and therefore to be dominated by it (1990, 84). Colonialist oppression can be challenged through transgression and mockery, but the carnivalesque normally quickly reverts to the status quo, while what Homi K. Bhabha (1990) described as 'colonial mimicry' is often the default, where colonial tropes are adopted uncritically in a way that promises inclusion but is a continued form of oppression: internalised denigration.

As globalisation tends to be considered a form of Americanisation, it resembles neocolonialism, an economic rather than military form of occupation. In *Bacalhau,* Stam and Vieira see no 'devastating critique of the shallow factitiousness ultimately conveyed by the increasingly sophisticated mimesis of contemporary dominant cinema' (1990, 95), only the film's 'uncritical admiration' of the 'foreign model' (93). For them, it slips into mimicry, a desire to *be* rather than to oppose the dominant discourse. In response to Stam and Vieira, though, Smith argues that, while their argument 'is certainly politically attractive', viewing appropriations of Hollywood through a blunt focus on dominance and resistance 'can actually neglect the much more ambivalent nature of many of these borrowings' (2017, 27). Smith illustrates his model of the meme-like transmission of cultural material by drawing on Miriam Hansen's concept of vernacular modernism, 'a transnational and translatable resonance' playing 'a key role in mediating competing cultural discourses on modernity and modernization, because it articulated, multiplied, and globalized a particular historical experience' rather than because it created 'universal templates' (1999, 67). Thus, the work of Smith and Hansen can help us understand how Hollywood films contribute to standardisation not simply in their adoption by world cinemas, but in how they become distributed and localised and help to negotiate the experience of multiple modernities. However, as we'll consider in this chapter, the global centre of *kaijū* film production, while it relies on Hollywood for its origins, is Japan. That this centre sits away from Hollywood is an important consideration in thinking about the distinctiveness of the *kaijū* film as a model for interrogating the transnational development of a genre. Erb (2009) stated that *Gojira* represents a vision of how Hollywood films are used globally (thereby pre-empting Smith's work), and we now turn to consider how the tropes from those films are themselves used globally.

Global adaptations of Hollywood films, in Smith's work, demonstrate how these offer a proliferation of memes, which can be a whole film (we can perhaps see *King Kong* as the meme on which *Gojira* is based, although this may be too simplistic a view), which can then be broken into smaller memes (such as the rampaging giant creature in the city, from the 1920s onwards), units that can subsequently be adopted, adapted, reworked and localised. Smith's model helps us understand Hollywood as a giant catalogue of memes that make up the film industry, and the ways in which American cinema's influence is disseminated and recognised globally. Micro-level analysis can therefore help us understand how individual memes – such as a character or an extract from a musical score – are spread and adapted:

> This allows for a comparative model to be developed that maps the proliferation of a meme from one context, and then traces how it spreads and mutates as it travels to other contexts. In this way, the model helps us to consider which memes are flourishing in which locations, how they are being adapted for local (or indeed global) audiences, and to what purpose. (Smith 2017, 32)

Smith's bottom line is that 'scholarship on world cinema tends to neglect the transnational influence of Hollywood', and the discipline 'needs to address this interrelationship in order to better interrogate the complex cultural dynamics underpinning the transnational circulation of cinema' (3). Our goal in this chapter is to explore just such interrelationships, to consider how the *kaijū* film steps away from its Japanese roots to become a global subgenre. Japan stands in for Hollywood in this regard, although Japan's film industry might be seen as an intermediary for indigenised Hollywood memes, which are then further adapted by other filmmakers.

Genres have a meme-like quality, as Oliete-Aldea et al. have also shown. Their blueprints develop through adoption, reworking and innovation, and the *kaijū eiga* is no different. Yet, as Smith argues, the concept of the Hollywood meme helps us to understand how images, or memes, that originate in Hollywood can become adapted for local and global use. The comparative approach taken in this book is very much influenced by Smith's model to understand how the adoption, adaption and spread of the transnational *kaijū eiga*

> can tell us a great deal about the way texts circulate internationally and the specific circumstances in which they are received and reworked. Rather than see the global circulation of Hollywood in terms of blanket Americanisation, . . . a more nuanced model of cultural exchange . . . pays attention to the tensions and ambivalences in these processes of globalisation. These borrowings should be understood less through the prism of cultural domination and resistance than through the lens of agency and creativity. (Smith 2017, 148)

Through this chapter, we'll look at the agency and creativity of filmmakers whose work has progressed the *kaijū* film from a popular Japanese national film product, one very much predicated on export and international exposure for Japanese film companies, to a more globalised pattern of production and circulation. As with the development of the Japanese form of the *kaijū eiga*, transnational *kaijū* cinema relies on interrelated processes of exploitation, appropriation and adaptation. It further relies on elements of transnational collaboration: the co-ordination of personnel across different countries, co-production and localisation of different elements of the subgenre's conception.

## *Kaijū* Head West

Many genres have spread globally, but there are few that rely upon what Vivian P. Y. Lee has termed 'intergeneric and intertextual dialogues' (2015, 147) that go beyond the mimicry of Hollywood genres to produce their own variants. We've seen so far that such dialogue has helped develop the nascent form of the *kaijū* film, but the transnational and transregional spread of the *kaijū eiga* has relied upon processes that have been well explored in relation to the Western. Termed by André Bazin 'the American film *par excellence*' (1972, 143), the Western has been subject to relatively broad cultural spread. Via what were once dismissed as 'cheap opportunistic imitations' (Frayling 2006, 121) of a genre 'assumed to have "cultural roots" in American society' (27), the Western has, as Austin Fisher has argued, developed globally through processes of 'negotiation and cultural blending' (2011, 2). Like *Gojira*'s emergence from post-nuclear trauma and national disaster, the Western has deep national roots, but has become subject to cultural flow, adoption and appropriation by filmmakers (and distributors) across the world. As Lee explains, the Western appears in 'augmented and hybridized forms in the global mediascape, [with] intertwined processes of generic cross-breeding in postmodern film cultures and cross-cultural critical reception' (2015, 147). Just as Derendorf (Maser Patrol 2017) questioned the 'cultural roots' of 'foreign' *kaijū (gaijū)* films, we must acknowledge that similar dialogue, blending and hybridity have occurred as *kaijū* tropes have spread and been mimicked and reworked by the agency and creativity of filmmakers. This is at the core of the *kaijū eiga*'s standing as a transnational genre. Yet, unlike the Western, its centre ('roots' is too simplistic a term) is closely associated with Japan, and not Hollywood. That's not to say the *kaijū eiga* doesn't have a connection with American cinema, but the form that came to circulate globally originated from Japanese culture. We see what Dina Iordanova, David Martin-Jones and Belén Vidal have argued, in the Introduction to *Cinema at the Periphery*, is a 'relationship between center and periphery [that] is no longer necessarily a straightforward, hierarchical one, where the center seeks to subsume its margins', but one where multiple centres and margins are involved in a continual dialogue (2010, 6–7).

Throughout the chapter we'll consider the shifting relationships between centre and margins, and how these have changed historically.

In terms of the historical development of the *kaijū* film outside Japan, it makes sense to consider how, in the US, *kaijū* films developed alongside Japanese studios' production. We've already considered some elements of co-production, but we'll come back to this in the next chapter, when we look more at how American distributors helped turned *kaijū* films into exploitation films. Instead, this chapter takes a geographical approach, since cultural flow is perhaps best understood geographically through the overlaps, connections and relationships between nations, in centre–margins relationships. This approach can help bring into focus areas of hierarchy and imbalance in cultural power. It is also a way to consider the impact of soft power. Since Japan's government provided support for the *kaijū eiga* precisely because it was of international interest, its articulation of soft power is inherent. Douglas McGray's well-known identification of Japan's shift towards a cultural economy built on 'gross national cool' (2002) is highly relevant to how those products become articulated through the borrowings of other national film industries in their own *kaijū* films. Figures such as Godzilla and Ultraman factor prominently in accounts of Japanese soft power, not just in films, but in toys, comics, TV series and other ancillary products. However, it's with the films that we're concerned here, as producers respond both to Japan's growing cultural power and to how this might be exploited locally and internationally, since other Asian variants of the *Gojira* format were attractive to international distributors.

## *Kaijū* on the Korean Peninsula

*Yongary* wasn't the first South Korean *kaijū* film, but it is perhaps the one best known from this period, largely because it is the only one still widely in circulation. The first recognised monster film produced in South Korea was *Songdomalnyeoneui Boolgasari* (Kim Myeong-jae), released in 1962. Boolgasari (normally romanised as Pulgasari, as with the more famous North Korean adaptation of the myth) is a metal-eating monster in Korean legend. No footage from the film is currently extant, but a 2008 exhibition by the Korean Film Archive brought a new focus to this lost film, more for its poor critical reception than its success. On initial release, it was dismissed as 'technically immature' in relation to its better-known American and Japanese rivals – it was essentially scorned as a Korean version of *King Kong* (Lee 2008). By 1967, the monster boom in Japan was in full swing and *kaijū* films were rampaging across the world. *Yongary* was released just two months after another South Korean monster film, *Space Monster Wangmagwi* (*Woojoogoein wangmagwi*,

Hyeok-jinn Gwon, 1967). This is another lamented 'lost' *kaijū* film, with no existing home cinema or wide festival exhibition since its original release. Two prints are held in the Korean Film Archive (KFA), but a release has long been delayed due to copyright holders' reported lack of interest in releasing the film. The film is only sporadically exhibited publicly. Its legendary status has been inflated by the relative dearth of South Korean monster films since the early 1960s, with few receiving international release, while persistent online rumours suggest it holds the record for the highest number of extras ever assembled for a film shoot. Wangmagwi is an alien-controlled, city-smashing, humanoid monster, sometimes confused with a gorilla. Peirse and Martin refer to it simply as 'a rampaging, wedding-crashing, city-destroying alien beast' (2013, 5). It has similarities with *King Kong*, as the monster kidnaps a bride, in traditional outfit, from her wedding, and carries her through the city. The film seems destined to be an object of fascination for *kaijū* fans in the absence of a wide release outside limited festivals.

*Yongary* shares some features with *Wangmagwi*, both as a 'lost' film and in terms of plotting and sensibility. The existing version in circulation remains the American International TV English-dubbed version. All that exists of the original Korean version is a 48-minute excerpt that was first screened at the KFA monster movie retrospective but hasn't been included in the 200-plus films that the KFA distributed via their YouTube channel. The film is therefore much better known than its forebears, but it is more in the mould of Japanese *kaijū* films and thus evidences fairly overt forms of transnational blending. Constantin Film, a regular distributor of *kaijū* films in Germany, felt the similarities with Godzilla were so overt that they released the film with the title *Godzilla's Todespranke* (*Godzilla's Hand of Death*, an exploitative title that sounds more appropriate for a kung fu film than a *kaijū* one). What is perhaps more surprising about the appropriation of the Godzilla formula and image[2] is that, due to long-held resentment following Japan's brutal occupation of the Korean peninsula between 1910 and 1945, Japanese cultural products were banned in South Korea until 1998 (Peirse and Martin 2013, 3). Despite the ban, long-standing underground networks imported Japanese culture into South Korea. However, one of the key ways in which local producers can circumvent the absence of another country's popular culture is to appropriate and remake those works. The production of *kaijū* movies is one way in which such a ban can be sidestepped. Dimitris Eleftheriotis has pointed out that such forms can often be pushed to one side in considerations of national cinema: hybrid forms such as 'co-productions, adaptations, or texts that clearly engage with foreign forms' are often considered 'too complicated or too contaminating of the hegemonic understanding of the "national" as "essential" or "pure"' (2006, 226). *Yongary* helps us to reflect on how a range of national, regional and international factors impact our understanding of hybrid forms.

Daniel Martin notes the film is 'shamelessly' drawn from the *Gojira* model, yet deeply resonant of core themes of the emerging Korean horror cinema (2014, 427). He argues the monster shares sympathetic traits with the *wonhon* (avenging female ghost) and has melodramatic moments expressing *han*, 'a deeply seated Korean experience of oppression and unrequited resentment born of generations of struggle' (Robinson 2005, 27). Chung-kang Kim has argued that the film's 'transnational cultural nexus' represents a collision of a number of local and regional discourses that define the production and ideological content (Kim 2018, 399). At one end of the scale is the film's production. Japanese *kaijū* films, like most Japanese cultural products, were banned in South Korea at the time of the film's conception. The producers, like those of *Wangmagmi*, were required to apply for special permission to develop the film, such was state control of the film industry at the time. Kim explains that the film's government deliberation record stated that the film should "not include anything that violates national security issues"' (405). The Motion Picture Law ensured that South Korean films were under the sway of government policy. Science-fiction films, as Kim explains, played a key role in the dissemination of positive messages about Park Chung-Hee's government's science and technology policies. Scientific education was a prime goal for the South Korean government, and this is strongly reflected in *Yongary*. Science-fiction also played an important role in communicating anti-Communist messages, as propaganda films were routinely exhibited in South Korean cinemas: 'Since science-fiction films were intended for children, it is more likely that the theater was viewed as an anticommunist educational space' (406).

The permission to produce films in a typically Japanese genre was granted, while the production itself was more problematic, since it was a co-production. The development of a *kaijū* film was largely motivated by popular director Kim Kidŏk's Far East Entertainment (Keukdong Heungup) and the shift of government policy towards family entertainment films rather than didactic social realism (Ryfle and Kim 2016). Kim places the film's text in relation to 'the two most significant political events in 1960s South Korea[:] the 1964 decision to send Korean troops to Vietnam and the 1965 normalization of diplomatic ties with former colonial occupier Japan' (Kim 2018, 401). The treaty that restored relations between South Korea and Japan had taken two decades to negotiate and led to the payment of substantial reparations by Japan. The Normalization Act led to massive public protests, but this allowed Kim's company to collaborate with Japanese filmmakers on the production (Kim 2018). Toei were engaged to produce the special effects, and a team including seasoned effects personnel Suzuki Akira, Murase Keizō and Yagi Masao, the original designer of the Gamera suit, were allowed to enter South Korea to work on the film. The Japanese company later assumed the role of distributor and sales representative for the film, which enabled it to be sold globally, perhaps further speeding the cause of its mistaken national identity.

*Yongary* exhibits a strong degree of transnational dialogue and hybridity. Its origins demonstrate very specific cross-border relationships. Conditions provided by the Normalization Act and resumption of relations between South Korea and Japan enabled co-production flows, but cultural exchange determined the form of the film itself. *Yongary* develops the anti-nuclear text of the *kaijū* film, and maps this onto specifically South Korean concerns. As Kim explains:

> In *Yonggari*, the centrality of the images of a developed South Korean nation, heroic (male) scientists, young boys as future scientists, and ideas of national safety and prosperity reinforce the positive 'socio-technological' imagination stimulating the utopian impulse of the national people. (Kim 2018, 400)

The film is set in a fictional Republic of Korea, with a developed space programme (South Korea had no space programme to speak of in the 1960s), prosperity (in scenes alongside the monster's rampage, some citizens flee Seoul while others decadently party), while advanced scientific development enables Koreans to fight back against the monster (Figure 3.1). As the Kino Lorber DVD release's audio commentary makes clear, there are no western faces in this film at all (Ryfle and Kim 2016). As discussed in the previous chapter, Japanese producers had gone to extreme lengths to cast western performers in their films (even if those faces didn't belong to actors but to the children of ex-pat American businesspeople or military personnel stationed in Japan). While this was often a consequence of transnational co-production, *Yongary* makes no such concession. This monster is fought off solely by Korean citizens with Korean science. One area where Toei's co-production did have influence was in the casting of eight-year-old Lee Kwang-ho, who plays Yoo Young (which became the more Japanese-sounding 'Icho' in the dubbed version), the youngster who forges a close affinity with the monster. The character develops as a combination of the ideal South Korean

**Figure 3.1** *Yongary, Monster from the Deep* imagines a futuristic and self-reliant Republic of Korea (MGM)

viewer, the inquisitive scientific genius, the boys' adventure story protagonist and the core audience member for Japanese *kaijū* films.

The plot of *Yongary* resurrects the shadow of nuclear destruction, an event that, as Kim notes, killed a great number of 'colonially subjugated' Koreans in Japan in 1945, and had only just begun to be discussed publicly at the time of the film's release (2018, 414). Scenes of the monster rampage also evoke the national memory of the Korean and Vietnam Wars. The film begins with a wedding, of South Korea's most notable astronaut. His honeymoon is swiftly cut short to investigate a dangerous nuclear test (in the Middle East in the dubbed version, but attributed to China in the original script), which leads to an earthquake that spells impending danger for the Korean peninsula. The sacrifice of the heroic male (and to some degree his new wife in this Confucian focus on the prominence of the masculine) to the national cause is significant in the film's promotion of nationalist scientific discourses. National duty comes before personal happiness, as it does for the film's protagonist, the scientist Ko Il-woo (Oh Young-il), and his disgruntled girlfriend, Soon-a (Nam Jeong-im). The earthquake begins to head straight for the 38th parallel, the circle of latitude that divides North and South Korea. A photographer witnesses the quake destroying the ground in Hwanghae, and a photographer captures an image of a giant monster in the rupture near P'anmunjŏm, the location of the signature of the Armistice Agreement at the end of the Korean War. That the monster emerges from the location of the fissure between North and South is highly significant, as it comes above ground at the very location of the country's division. This split in the ground and the resulting monster metaphorically reflects decades-old wounds of division and resentment, one reason why Martin would see the monster as invested with *han*. That Yoo comes to empathise with rather than fear the monster is highly significant in this regard. Just as Godzilla was an ambivalent reflection of both Japanese trauma and guilt about those who didn't return, Yongary is similarly ambivalent, reflecting Otherness in the form of Communist nuclear tests, the menace to the North but as a sympathetic victim of oppression and division. The monster heads south towards Seoul, and, as in *Gojira*, attacks a series of recognisable landmarks, including the imposing imperial-era Japanese General Government Building (Figure 3.2). Just as Godzilla destroyed the Diet building in Tokyo, Yongary destroys the seat of South Korean government at the time, a double criticism of Japanese colonial rule and the dictatorship of Park's government. With Yoo's help, the military and Il-woo find a way of defeating the petrol-guzzling monster. This extends the good/bad scientific ambivalence of the *kaijū* movie: the only way to defeat the consequences of bad science is through good science.

The final point of discussion, though, is about the role of Yoo in the film. While Yoo is the 'boy genius', as Kim calls him, he shares a significant moment of affinity with the monster. In one of the most bizarre scenes in 1960s *kaijū* cinema, Yoo witnesses Yongary dancing to a surf guitar version of 'Arirang'. The song is a Korean folk song, appearing twice on UNESCO's list of intangible cultural heritage, once for the South and once for the North. Atkins discusses how 'Arirang' became a nationalist rallying cry: 'Japanese colonial presence thus gave "Arirang" its special resonance for articulating the *han* (indignant sorrow) that many Koreans consider to be a national trait' (Atkins 2007, 647). Again, we can make a connection between Yongary and *han* as a shared sorrow

**Figure 3.2** Yongary destroys the seat of colonial government in Seoul (MGM)

of colonial oppression (the monster's destruction of an iconic colonial building is heroic), but the dancing to 'Arirang' connects Yongary with both the Korean people (through Yoo) and their culture (Figure 3.3). This connection is apparent in the film's final moments, when the monster is defeated. In the extant version, Yoo expresses remorse for Yongary's death; it was just an animal in search of food, and its destruction was inevitable. Yet, in the original version, it's implied that Yongary hasn't died, but will be shot into space (à la Gamera), something Kim discusses as 'Korea's desire to make this native monster a fantastic otherworldly symbol of potential world peace rather than simply destroy it for its inassimilable difference ' (2018, 413). The monster is treated as a sympathetic victim, one whose death need not be inevitable, but which hints at a broader role for the creature, as was reserved for Japan's giant monsters. Yongary's dance also reflects a moment in the Godzilla film *Invasion of Astro-Monster*. After defeating King Ghidorah, Godzilla dances what is known as *shē* (シェー), a reference to a popular contemporary manga series, Akatsuka Fujio's *Osomatsu-kun* (1962–9), and a trend derived from one of its characters (Iyami) (it has also become a popular meme).

This first detailed example demonstrates how transnational dialogue and the appropriation and negotiation of generic content have helped develop the form of the *kaijū* film. The national–transnational nexus helps to demonstrate how a transnational genre like the *kaijū eiga* derives from the interplay of local, regional and international discourses, from the highly specific (South Korean cultural and political policy) to the generic (the 'shameless' borrowing of the Godzilla template translated into a local frame), but with a clear vision of the promotion of national

**Figure 3.3** The monster dances with Yoo to 'Arirang', the traditional national song (MGM)

discourses on the global stage (the *kaijū* film as export product). Since the release of these two films at the height of the monster boom in the 1960s, production of *kaijū* films in South Korea has been sporadic.

As a lengthy entry on the Maser Patrol blog about South Korean special effects production demonstrates (Maser Patrol 2021), Japanese and global trends were regularly translated into local productions. The blog details a range of *tokusatsu, henshin* and *kaijū* productions that seemingly circumvented the ban on Japanese cultural productions through processes of hybridity and remaking. The blog's author, Kevin Derendorf, points to a 'fast-and-loose approach to intellectual property' that marks several of the properties discussed in the article. But, as Smith argues in the case of Turkish cinema, global approaches to copyright can be significantly different:

> international treaties on copyright protection tend to serve the purposes of those who are exporters of content rather than those who are primarily importing content from elsewhere. In the case of 1970s Turkey, a net-importer of such assets, the incentive was not there to expand copyright protection to the media texts entering the country and this contributed to the cultural climate in which *Turist Ömer Uzay Yolunda* was able to replicate much of the *Star Trek* episode. (2017, 87)

The case of *Turist Ömer Uzay Yolunda* (*Tourist Omer in Star Trek*, 1974), a virtual remake, with lifted titles and music, of *Star Trek*'s first episode ('The Man Trap', 1966), is relevant here, since it demonstrates 'how comparative analysis of transnational adaptation can tell us a great deal about the way texts circulate internationally and the specific circumstances in which they are received and reworked' (Smith 2017, 228–9). The ban on Japanese cultural products in South Korea until the 1990s helps us understand how cultural trends, rather than being unknown, are adopted, transculturated and reworked through local lenses. Arjun Appadurai refers to these lines of cultural flow as *mediascapes*, the means by which images of the world can be disseminated and produced, as well as the images created by such technologies across a range of genres, and *ideoscapes*, where those images service ideologies of nation or resistances to such (Appadurai 1990). As an 'official' (since unofficial networks existed to share Japanese products) non-importer of cultural products, South Korea tended to receive such products through processes of transculturation. *Yongary* and *Wangmagwi* are early variants of this, as are other examples on Maser Patrol's list. Hence, the shamelessness of their cultural borrowing can be understood not as a 'fast-and-loose' approach to intellectual property, but through the unequal lines of cultural power and regional hierarchies that help to explain such borrowings and repurposing.

The Maser Patrol blog was posted in response to the first American release of the South Korean *kaijū* movie *War of the God Monsters* (*Bicheongoesu*, normally translated as *The Undead Beast*, but released in Japan as *Hiten Kaijū*, literally *The Flying Monster*, and often known on bootleg video as *Flying Dragon Attacks*, Kim Jeong-yong, 1984). Kim Jeong-yong had previously been a director of Korean and co-produced Korean–Hong Kong martial arts and 'Brucesploitation' cinema, whose *War of the God Monsters* has been considered the only South Korean *kaijū eiga* of the 1980s. The film's story is fairly basic. A journalist, Kang, sets out to find the reclusive scientist Dr Kim, whose theories of resurrected dinosaurs have led him to disappear in search of evidence of their existence. Kang poses as Kim's housekeeper, and she bonds with his daughter, whose mother has died. The scientist finds evidence – a recent un-fossilised skeleton, giant eggs, humungous footprints on the beach – that prove the existence of the dinosaurs. He theorises that they might have been frozen, like primitive humans or goldfish, in ice and then reanimated as the oceans warmed. The film is lightly environmental in its motivations for the return of giant creatures from long ago. This connects it with existing aspects of the *kaijū* film. As Rhoads and McCorkle argue, the *kaijū* film is fundamentally one concerned with green politics: 'The Godzilla and Gamera franchises of the early 1970s both emphasized the desperate state of Japan's environment, especially its seas and sea life' (Rhoads and McCorkle 2018, 111). While *War of the God Monsters* makes little sustained comment on environmental politics in the vein of *Godzilla vs. Hedorah* (*Gojira tai Hedora*, Banno Yoshimitsu 1971) or *Gamera vs. Zigra* (*Gamera tai Shinkai Kaijū Jigura*, lit. *Gamera vs. Deep-sea monster Zigra*, Yuasa Noriaki 1971), it offers a plot motivation that maps environmental concerns onto a Korean context.[3] A brief stock footage sequence of ice breaking apart and melting contextualises the environmental themes motivating the narrative. Like Japan, South Korea experienced rapid modernisation and industrialisation in the second half of the twentieth century, leading to similar concerns about environmental impact in both countries. The South Korean motto of 'faster and faster' came to be reassessed in the 1980s and 1990s when the impacts of industrial pollution were being understood. It was only in 1980 that the country's constitution was updated to give citizens the right to a clean and pollution-free environment (Cho 1999).

While this accounts for how *ideoscapes* help to contextualise the flow of political context from country to country, it doesn't account for the unusual nature of the film, which emphasises how cultural flow can problematise copyright and demonstrate how material is used across borders. Throughout *War of the God Monsters*, we witness giant monsters attacking cities, oil refineries and tankers and being attacked by defence forces. What's perhaps surprising about the film, though, is that almost all the special effects footage is recycled from Japanese television or one Taiwanese film (with special effects by Japanese filmmakers). This explains why characters never interact with the monster action, beyond a few reactions. Most of the material comes from various *Ultraman* series, *Fireman* (*Faiyāman*, 1973), another Tsuburaya production, and the Taiwanese film *The Founding of Ming Dynasty* the monster effects for which were by Tsuburaya's company.[4] SRS Cinema's 2021 release in the US circumvented the difficulties of releasing such copyrighted content with consent from Tsuburaya Productions to distribute it intact (previously it had been considered 'lost'). The processes mirror those discussed by Kukhee Choo in terms of Korean animation. Choo argues that the history of Korean animation is problematised by accusations of plagiarism. She contends that Korean animators were exposed to Japanese productions as animators from Japan outsourced elements of production to the Korean peninsula from the 1950s onwards. This was something that helped some productions overcome the ban on Japanese products by being designated as 'Korean'. Choo sees what she describes as a 'hyperbolic nationalism' overwriting the Japanese productions, as a form of overcoming the historical colonisation of Korea rather than the desire to mimic the coloniser. She says that where Korean animators were accused of plagiarism, 'criticisms fail to take into account the multiple processes, layers, and directions of globalization which produce media that transcend spatial, textual, and cultural boundaries' (2014, 158). Such processes and layers help to account for how *kaijū* films were transculturated in South Korea, not just with what we might see as 'hyperbolic nationalism' in the fantastical space age ROK of *Yongary*, but also with the palimpsestic nature of *War of the God Monsters'* reuse of Japanese *tokusatsu*. Smith (2017) also uses the metaphor of the palimpsest to talk about how Turkish filmmakers 'overwrote' *Star Trek* with their own parodic take on foreign cultural production. Kim's film reflects Choo's observation about the 'patchwork' nature of some South Korean cultural production, where Japanese imagery is borrowed and reworked in a nationalist context. *War of the God Monsters* perhaps doesn't evidence a strongly nationalistic text, although it does share a sense of *han* in the broken and exiled family at the core of the story. Yet its adoption of Japanese imagery, including monsters such as Verokron (part sea monster, part coral) and Pestar (an oil-consuming starfish), evidences how cultural borrowing can continue to compensate for the absence of popular culture output in a different national context. However, this adoption also demonstrates the statelessness of Japanese *mukokuseki*: the material can simply by reworked in a different context. Thus, while local variations are highly contingent on historical and national circumstances, the underlying generic material is open to adaptation and thereby able to be subsumed by processes of cultural flow. This restates the core argument of this book, namely that the *kaijū eiga* is fundamentally transnational in that it is at once specifically national but simultaneously impacted by global flows related to a series of processes that transcend, as Choo points out, a range of borders and boundaries.

## Kim Jong-Il's *Kaijū*

Currently, it makes sense chronologically to step across the Korean Demilitarized Zone to consider one of the most infamous *kaijū* films of all time, the North Korean *Pulgasari* (*Boolgasari*, Shin Sang-ok, 1985). The best-known and most-seen film produced by the North Korean (Democratic People's Republic of Korea, DPRK) regime, *Pulgasari* has a relatively well-known backstory. It was the last film produced by Shin following his kidnapping at Kim Jong-Il's orders. Schooled in Tokyo towards the end of Japanese colonial rule, Shin rose post-liberation through the ranks to become one of South Korea's most notable and iconic directors. The head of his own studio, across the late 1950s and 1960s Shin produced a series of quality melodramas that, as Steven Chung puts it, 'became synonymous with the postwar Korean imagination', such as *Romance Papa* (*Romaenseǔ ppappa*, 1960) and *The Houseguest and My Mother* (*Sarangbang sonnim kwa ŏmŏni*, 1961) (Chung 2014). Shin's career waned during the 1970s, not only alongside the general decline of the wider film industry in South Korea, but also in the face of growing government censorship and restrictions from the Park regime that led to the withdrawal of Shin's licence to film (Chung 2014). In 1978, Shin disappeared in Hong Kong, reportedly in search of his ex-wife Choi Eun-hee, who had been reported missing. Both had been kidnapped by North Korean special forces, with the express goal of helping Kim Jong-Il, a recognised film obsessive, develop the stagnant North Korean film industry to become a productive source of propaganda films in service of the regime's socialist ideology. As Paul Fischer describes in his book *A Kim Jong-Il Production: The Incredibly True Story of North Korea and the Most Audacious Kidnapping in History* (2015), the DPRK authorities reportedly tortured and imprisoned them both in labour camps. However,

Fischer suggests that once Shin was able to rediscover his passion for filmmaking, he and Choi remarried and settled into a comfortable life in the North. They, in Chung's terms, 'defected back' to the South in 1986 after a trip to Vienna for a film festival. Shin worked once again in the South Korean and American film industries, but with little of his previous success.

*Pulgasari* is one of few North Korean films to be shown outside of the secretive regime. This is largely down to its genre, not because of its cultural connections with other *kaijū* films (Kim was reported to be a fan of Godzilla movies) but because of the personnel who worked on the film. As with *Yongary*, Japanese special effects directors and performers visited for the purpose. The monster was performed by Satsuma Kenpachiro. Satsuma was a seasoned *tokusatsu* performer, having played antagonists Hedorah and Gigan opposite Nakajima Haruo in *Shōwa*-era Godzilla films. When Nakajima retired from the Godzilla suit, Satsuma took over for 1984's *Gojira*. He would play Godzilla for the remainder of the *Heisei* series, until Godzilla's 'death' in 1995's *Godzilla vs. Destroyah* (*Gojira tai Desutoroia*, Okawara Takao). Satsuma documented his experiences in his book *North Korea as Seen by Godzilla*. Fifteen special effects personnel from Tōhō – most of the crew who had worked on *The Return of Godzilla* the previous year, including Nakano Teruyoshi, the effects director – were hired to work on the film. Fischer summarises their experience: the crew were told they were being hired for a major Hollywood film shooting in Beijing, but after a few days there, they were flown to Pyongyang and their passports were confiscated. Hampered by repeated power cuts and shortages of kit (everything had to be approved by the ruling Party), the Japanese crew were mainly kept separate from the Korean one, who reportedly stole kit daily (Fischer 2015, 285–6). Fischer describes the results as 'representative of the absurdities and contradictions of North Korean cinema, of Shin himself, and of Kim Jong-Il . . . the sort of terrible classic that is given midnight retrospectives in underground and art-house cinemas around the world' (282). The film has inevitably achieved cult classic status, a source of mockery not just because of the crazy story behind it, but also because of its place within a genre that is itself one of cinema's most cultish. It's harsh to call the film 'terrible' when it stands up to many of its contemporary *kaijū* films, including *War of the God Monsters*; Satsuma was known to joke that it was better received than his first outing as Godzilla.

*Pulgasari* was intended to be Kim Jong-Il's anti-capitalist epic, in service of the DPRK's *Juche* ideology, the quasi-socialist philosophy of independence, economic self-sufficiency and military self-reliance.

The legend of the iron-eating monster originates from the *Koryŏ* era (tenth to fourteenth centuries), its name meaning either 'can't be killed' or 'killed by fire', depending on how it is written (Park 2019, 143). Park refers to the monster as an ambivalent figure, the product of tumultuous political circumstances, 'as both monster and hero' (139) while 'a positive image of Bulgasari delivers an additional context: the "colonized" Korean people's longing to break free from Japanese Imperialism' (143). *Kaijū* have generally been modern inventions, born of atomic nightmares though with reflections of folkloric monsters, so *Pulgasari* is uncommon in the way it evokes folklore. The ambivalence described by Park also translated into the confused political messaging of the film's plot (how intentional this is on the part of the filmmakers has been open to debate, however). Set somewhere in the *Koryŏ* period, the story focuses on a starving rural village. The times are ripe for revolution. Young villagers are fleeing to the mountains to take up the fight against the local governor, who seizes the villagers' pots, pans and farming equipment to smelt into weapons to maintain order in the region. When the villagers resist, many are rounded up and imprisoned. There is a shortage of iron, which the village's blacksmith elder blames on the legend of Pulgasari, the iron-eating monster. Taken captive and on hunger strike, the blacksmith fashions a small figurine of the monster from rice and prays to the heavens that the village be saved. As he dies, the figure glows, as it's passed around the grieving villagers. It magically comes to life in his daughter Ami's sewing box, and swiftly begins to consume needles and pins. The monster starts to grow, eating more and more iron in the process. The blacksmith's apprentice and local firebrand Inde is subsequently convicted for his defiance and sentenced to death. As he is put to the sword, the monster intercedes, taking a bite out of the executioner's sword. Inde escapes. The government capture Pulgasari, but they quickly discover that it can't be killed with conventional weapons, and it breaks free. The villagers meanwhile believe that the beast could be the key to salvation from tyranny. While the government torture the villagers, the monster eludes capture. Following one brutal scene of torture in which a woman is beaten with wooden beams across her legs, the villagers attack the castle in vengeance, and Inde kills the governor, who is fleeing with the outpost's money box. The king swears to smash the resistance, appointing cruel General Fuan to lead his forces. Skirmishes take place in the mountains until the now human-sized monster frightens off some government soldiers who are chasing Ami. Pulgasari begins to fight alongside the revolutionaries on the battlefield, as they win victory after victory against the government forces. The bandits feed the growing creature on the weapons of their defeated enemies. Sensing the monster's weakness government forces kidnap Ami. Pulgasari allows itself to be captured to save her from death. The soldiers imprison the monster and attempt to burn it. But, in fire-red lighting from below, Pulgasari emerges from the pyre, like burning iron, and plunges into a river to cool.

Both sides regroup, while General Fuan hatches another plan to capture the monster in a giant hole (built using forced slave labour). The battle rages, and Pulgasari smashes through buildings (Figure 3.4), unknowingly heading towards the trap. Just in case, though, Fuan has a local priestess perform a ritual to exorcise the spirit of the blacksmith that conjured the monster. Temporarily disoriented, the giant creature walks straight into Fuan's trap and is buried. Its absence allows Fuan to strike back against the revolt, and hang the leaders, including Inde. But Ami promises to fight on. She infiltrates the army's encampment to resurrect the *kaijū*. Fortunately, decadent soldiers are easily distracted with wine. Although her cover is blown, she's able to bring the monster back to life by spilling her blood on its rocky grave. As the resistance fighters bear down on their oppressors with the monster in tow, the government have one final plot to destroy the creature and restore order: huge cannons so destructive they can destroy mountains. But, mockingly, Pulgasari simply swallows the cannonballs and spits them back. The monster smashes the castle and comfortably defeats the government. The now-free villagers are unable to feed Pulgasari enough iron and can't afford to give up their tools to feed the creature (just as they couldn't with their previous rulers),

**Figure 3.4** Fiery Pulgasari attacks the overlords who repress the masses (Korean Film)

and this may threaten the wider peace. Ami lures the monster with the castle's iron bell and, hidden inside it as it is eaten, prays to the creature to disappear and free them. It turns to stone and smashes into rubble. A new, tiny Pulgasari emerges from the wreckage and returns to its spirit, inhabiting the body of Ami, as a tear rolls down her cheek.

As Park mentions, the film 'is definitely a proletarian and pro-revolutionary text' (2019, 149), one that champions the class struggle at the heart of its story, with oppressed people rising up with the monster's help to challenge the corrupt and greed regime. He references other South Korean critics who have seen the film solely through the lens of socialist realism, as a *kaijū* variant on traditionally Communist filmmaking that, in the Soviet Union as well as North Korea, upheld agrarian values and focused on proletarian struggles. As Fischer contends, the film is also open to readings that suggest Shin was resisting the totalitarian regime to mock the very excesses and corruption of Kim Il-sung's DPRK where he was a 'guest'. Chung contests this, that if 'there are slippages in *Pulgasari*, they are not only the sly manipulation of the author but the consequence of the contradictions of Shin's (and Kim Jong Il's) cinematic project' (Chung 2014). Much of this Chung attributes to Shin's overarching populism and interest in cinematic spectacle. Barr meanwhile argues that the ending of the film throws interpretations into 'disarray: is it an indictment or promotion of the North Korean government?' (Barr 2016, 67). Without answering that question, it's possible to see shades of both in the film, as the socialist realist reading is highly attractive given the film's production history, while it's also compelling to understand the film as one that draws meaning from Shin's own personal circumstances (the assumption that he was unhappy making films in North Korea, which Fischer seems to dispute). Barr's argument appears to struggle to place *Pulgasari* within a wider canon of *kaijū* films: he refers to it as 'a bizarre and distorted reflection of popular *kaijū* cinema' (68). It's easy, however, to agree with Barr's point that *Pulgasari* shares much of its DNA with the *Daimajin* movies, with its quasi-religious undertones. The monster is activated by the prayer of central characters, to whom it comes to the rescue from oppressors who would destroy their communities. The ending of the film is also familiar. Having destroyed the evil lords, the monster turns its attention to those who summoned it – it is fully ambivalent – when only the prayer of the righteous will satiate it (even down to the tears). The Korean film even shares the same confused reflection of contemporary religion (*Daimajin*'s very Christian monotheistic take on *kami*) where belief in spirits seems incompatible with Communist atheism (as does the sacrifice of the individual). However, this seems in keeping with North Korean appropriation of folklore, such as the invocation of Mount Paektu as the birthplace of Kim Jong-Il. In terms of the location of *Pulgasari* within a transnational understanding of the *kaijū* film, though, it seems a key example of the localisation of the genre, a mixture of tropes from other *kaijū* films that emphasise lines of influence and cultural flow that are further enabled by the mobility of Japanese special effects technicians, directors and performers. Appadurai refers to the transnational flow of people as *ethnoscapes*: flows of peoples across borders that reflect shifting boundaries that challenge the politics of and relationships between nations: 'tourists, immigrants, refugees, exiles, guestworkers and other moving groups and persons' (1990, 297). These guestworkers help create a unified look for the genre, regardless of its nation of origin. Even if their movement was enabled by deceit, such a passage helps fortify the core suitmation effects techniques within *kaijū* film, just as it enabled the production of *Yongary* and Hong Kong, Taiwanese or Hollywood films.

Park cites a comment from Shin that took an alternative stance on *Pulgasari*'s meaning, one that makes it easier to place the film within a canon of *kaijū* films: 'What I really wanted to deliver was a warning message against the nuclear weapons race, something that could disrupt world peace' (Park 2019, 149). When placed in this context, the film can be seen more clearly as a North Korean version of Godzilla, as it is so often referenced. The peace at the outset of the film is an oppressive one, based on the military might of the oppressive lord, who wants more and more weapons even if it leaves the people of the land destitute. The old blacksmith is angered to see his village manufacturing weapons destined for the bandits in the mountains. His own anger leads to the creation of an effective super-weapon, one that literally eats other weapons, can't be destroyed and will eventually deliver only a perilous peace that will turn the villagers into the very people they've overthrown. Ami's sacrifice mirrors that of Serizawa, whose own monstrosity is taken to the grave to ensure the weapon is never used or seen again. Shin's pacificism echoes Honda's, as well as the Cold War themes of 1984's *Gojira*. It therefore offers a very regional take on the central themes of the *kaijū* film, a product of a filmmaker displaced across borders, and enabled by the importation of talent from Japan. Its subsequent place in *kaijū* legend, and as the only accessible North Korean film, makes it a significant object of scrutiny and cult appreciation, both serious and ironic.

Following his escape from North Korean captivity, Shin's career was never able to reach its former heights. He made several unsuccessful films, in South Korea and in Hollywood. One is of interest, a *kaijū* film that is believed to be a loose remake of his North Korean epic: *Galgameth* (Sean McNamara, 1996), sometimes known as *The Legend* or *Adventures of Galgameth*. Working in Hollywood under the westernised name of Simon Sheen, Shin's career was riding something of a relative high, having produced, directed or executive produced the three follow-ups to *3 Ninja Kids* (John Turtletaub, 1992), a Disney-produced surprise family hit. The three sequels, the first of which was directed by Shin, were produced at Tristar Pictures and none achieved the same success as the first. *Galgameth* is a typical straight-to-video (STV) movie; as Lobato describes STV films, they are normally 'made in [the] interstices of the global film economy, . . . feature one location masquerading (often unsuccessfully) as another, or . . . an incoherent polyphony of accents and costumes' (Lobato 2012, 24). This film received some partial cinema distribution, but was largely released direct to video, through Trimark, and had a TV premiere on the Disney Channel nearly two years later. At a reported cost of nearly $10 million, it was shot on location in Romania (Variety Staff 1995), with a bizarre mixture of American and British accents (not unlike the much bigger-budget *Robin Hood: Prince of Thieves* [Kevin Reynolds, 1991]). It is generally received as a remake of *Pulgasari*. The film's Internet Movie Database and Wikipedia pages both attribute the film's origins to the North Korean film, and this may simply be down to Shin's involvement, since there is no official credited attribution.

*Galgameth* is a children's fantasy film. It takes places in the kingdom of Donnegold, where Prince Davin must summon his courage when the Black Knight, the cat-loving El, poisons his father, King Henryk, takes over the land in the prince's name and oppresses its subjects. Davin can escape and fight back because of Galgameth, the *kaijū* legend that protects his family. The film certainly recycles beats from *Pulgasari*, but some may be more attributable to the Korean folklore behind the film than to a direct remake. The monster is initially brought to life from a figurine. King Henryk explains the legend on his deathbed, and it's implied his soul passes into the monster, just as the old blacksmith's prayers had been answered in the form of the rice sculpture. Galgameth (referred to throughout as Galgy) grows from a small, cute creature – reminiscent of the designs and animatronics from *Teenage Mutant Ninja Turtles* (Steve Barron, 1990) – and, importantly, eats metal (Figure 3.5). The monster is also vulnerable to fire – Davin reminds it that it's 'not fireproof.' Just as in *Pulgasari*, the villains trap the monster and burn it (this time it's in a barn, where they have stored metal to attract the creature). The monster emerges from the flames illuminated by the fire, this time in a CGI

**Figure 3.5** The cute Ninja-Turtle-styled Galgameth spies another meal of delicious metal (Sheen Communications)

effect with patchwork burns beneath its skin. The *mise en scène* seems highly reminiscent of the corresponding scene in *Pulgasari*, although without the cooling off in a stream afterwards (the monster later dies saving Davin from the sea). There is even a moment where Galgameth eats an executioner's axe. The film's climax features a ragtag (again, Robin Hood-style) group of fighters storming the castle with the support of the rampaging destruction of the giant *kaijū*. There are notable differences, however, mostly due to the film's children-friendly template. The morality is much more clear-cut, and there is no conflict between collectivism and individualism. Prince Davin must find the source of his courage and take back his kingdom from the evil El. The monster makes the grand sacrifice to save the protagonists. The coda to *Pulgasari* that resolves the film's themes is very different – there's no sense that Galgameth would need to be destroyed to stop Donnegold taking over neighbouring kingdoms for their metal. The design of the monster in its *kaijū* form is very different from that of the Japanese-designed and -produced Pulgasari suit. Suitmation techniques are still utilised but the monster – played by Doug Jones, who would become synonymous with the monster roles in Guillermo del Toro's films – is much less fearsome, more akin to the *kawaii* Godzilla of the late 1960s, mixed with some of the Gamera-style of the *Turtles* film and given a much longer tail and single horn (not unlike Goliath from the Japanese *Daigoro vs. Goliath* [*Kaijū Daifunsen Daigorō tai Goriasu*, lit. *Great Monster Battle: Daigoro vs. Goliath*, Ijima Toshihiro, 1972]). Internet reviews treat the film as a straight remake of *Pulgasari*, despite the substantial differences, whereas much of this seems attributable to Shin's contribution (he wrote the story and executive produced, although without a screenplay credit). Had Shin not been involved, the film would perhaps have been consigned to history (it is less epic than the North Korean version), although his involvement does illuminate the shared cultural history behind the monster; Galgameth is a clear variant of Korean mythology transplanted into a family-friendly Robin Hood–*Turtles* mash-up without the ambivalent protector–destroyer dimensions of the creature's roots. As an STV transnational co-production, the film does also help shed light on some of the *kaijū* production that would follow, from South Korea and the US, where many *kaijū* films would benefit from transnational co-production and financing. Even specifically national films would be produced with eyes on transnational markets. As such, *Galgameth* provides an interesting stepping stone from what might be seen as the final film in the first phase of *kaijū* production (crossing over with the first *Heisei* Godzilla film) and the trends for transnational co-operation that would come to mark the *kaijū* genre in its low-budget STV and big-budget cinematic variants in the next two-and-a-bit decades.

## *Kaijū* in New Korean Cinema

South Korean society underwent rapid change in the 1980s and 1990s. Park Chung-hee was assassinated in 1979, leading to a period of uncertainty. The June 1987 Movement pushed for democratic reform against the military dictatorship of Chun Doo-hwan, who had taken control of the country in the vacuum left by Park's death. Seoul hosted the Olympics in 1988, before the country joined the United Nations in 1991. The futuristic promises of *Yongary* had never materialised. South Korean cinema developed rapidly following the return to democracy. The directors of the South Korean New Wave engaged with social issues and the realities of life for ordinary citizens (Korean Film Archive n.d.). South Korean cinema had previously been tightly managed by the government through import controls and exhibition quotas. With the liberalisation of imports from Hollywood in the late 1980s, the South Korean film industry began to develop into the one which is more familiar today. *Chaebol*, giant conglomerates such as Samsung, Daewoo and CJ Entertainment, began to develop commercial markets that imported Hollywood-style methods of production, bigger budgets and extended marketing. As Darrell William Davis and Emilie Yueh-yu Yeh point out, this led to local versions of the blockbuster being produced: 'Emphasis on stars, well-defined genres and pre-production marketing [became] important parts of *chaebol* operation' (Davis and Yeh 2008, 14). Chris Berry notes that two films produced at the turn of the century helped define the Korean blockbuster globally: *Shiri* (*Swiri*, Kang Je-gyu, 1999) and *Joint Security Area* (*Kongdonggyŏngbiguyŏk cheiesŭei*, Park Chan-wook, 2000), which both engaged with the ongoing tensions surrounding Korean division and defined the success of the Korean blockbuster, as both out-grossed the record of *Titanic* (James Cameron, 1997) at the South Korean box office (Berry 2003). Just over two decades later, this trend has continued, with the Academy Award success of Bong Joon-ho's *Parasite* (*Kisaengch'ung*, 2019) alongside the continued global triumphs of the *hallyu*, a term that describes the 'Korean Wave', a transmediated and transnational phenomenon of popular culture across Asia and the wider world. Film, television drama and pop music have been at the core of the continued rise of Korean culture and soft power, with 'Hallyu 2.0' exploiting transnational cultural flows through global *mediascapes*, often through social media (Jin and Yoon 2016). The global success of South Korean cinema has been built largely on that of key genres, such as thrillers, horror and social drama. There hasn't been a systematic focus on the production of giant monster movies, although there have been some notable films that we would consider under the heading of transnational genre production. Some of the films produced during this period have very much engaged with the transnational themes of the *kaijū* film, or demonstrate traits of transnational production methods that target globalised markets.

The films of Shim Hyung-Rae perhaps constitute a mini-cycle of their own, either as parodies of *kaijū* films or as serious attempts to produce South Korean blockbusters with international appeal. Shim's career developed as both a performer and director in a comedy series about the innocent stooge Young-gu (a sort of equivalent to Pee-Wee Herman and Jerry Lewis). Young-gu began as a popular TV character before Shim produced several films featuring the character. Many engage with monster tropes. In *Young-gu and Daengchili* (*Young-guwa daengchili*, 1989), Young-gu fights a series of monsters based on Dracula, Frankenstein's monster, Chinese *jiangshi* (hopping vampires) and Korean *wonhon*. *Dragon Tuka* (*Deuraegon Tuka*, 1996) then saw Young-gu sent back to the sixteenth century to help aliens fight off a dragon. Shim revived the character in 2010 in *The Last Godfather* (*Laseuteu Gatpadeo*), which took Young-gu to New York as the illegitimate son of a Mafia don played by Harvey Keitel (Jon Polito and Jason Mewes also appeared in the film). We can already see how the Young-gu series engages with transnational tropes from multiple genres, but for mainly South Korean audiences. The film perhaps most relevant to this argument is *Young-gu and the Dinosaur ZuZu* (*Yeong-gu wa gongnyong Jju-jju Bar*, 1993). The film's target is obvious from its opening frames, as a giant monster circles a city landscape. The monster has the single horned face of Yongary, a nostalgic reference to the old film. The film's plot concerns Young-gu's adventure after he discovers a huge egg in a cave, which effectively hatches into a baby Yongary. Young-gu must keep the creature safe from gangsters and police until the monster's fully grown *kaijū* parent arrives. The typical scenes of rampaging destruction ensue with fairly primitive suitmation effects intercut with a lot of stock footage of military planes. The monster dies outside a simple model of the General Government Building in Seoul, itself smashed by the real Yongary. The action is unusually violent for a *kaijū* film, especially one made for a family audience – the *kaijū*'s death is surprisingly bloody, while the baby monster is repeatedly shot at close range by the police *and* military after seeing its parent killed. Its revival brings a happy ending. As a nostalgic reflection of a South Korean classic, it makes for a strong example of a film derived from the transnational basis of the genre, but largely for local markets. Shim would go on to produce two big *kaijū* films that were much more obviously targeted at transnational markets.

Shim's fully realised remake of *Yongary* (also known as *Reptilian*) was first released in 1999. A version with 'upgraded' effects was released in 2001. At a reported $9.1 million, it was then one of the highest-budgeted films ever produced in South Korea (Berry 2003, 222).[5] Financiers for the film included *chaebol* involvement, with backers such as Hyundai, a range of capital investment firms and local government. The film coincided with the release of Sony's Hollywood version of *Godzilla* (1998), and the marketing of the film made little effort to disguise this. The poster for the film's Cannes marketplace exhibition had the tag line 'Think Bigger', an obvious take-off of the Hollywood blockbuster's 'Size Does Matter' campaign. Perhaps ironically, Sony acquired the US distribution rights, and their release also exploited the similarities with *Godzilla* posters. The title *Reptilian* is embossed on the same glowing green background, while the monster peers through a city street of skyscrapers above the tag line 'Bigger. Badder. Meaner'. This is not where the similarities end. *Yonggary* (the film's normal romanised title has a second 'g', unlike the conventional rendering of the earlier film's title, so the longer title will be used to differentiate between the two) seems conceived to attract international audiences. Perhaps most noticeable in this regard is the film's cast and dialogue, which are principally English-speaking American (there are small amounts of Korean spoken). Its plot relies heavily upon tropes from the 1960s (reflecting Shim's previous nostalgia for the genre), whereby an attempted alien invasion resurrects the long-dead skeleton of Yongary. The skeleton is initially discovered in South-East Asian cave by a group of archaeologists, most of whom are then thought to have been killed in an explosion set off by a mysterious force. The leader of the expedition survives and begins to excavate the fossil. Two years later, *Time* magazine journalists uncover the story and discover a cover-up of an alien attack. This mixture of scientists and journalists as protagonists directly echoes the lead characters from Emmerich's *Godzilla*. The alien invaders bring the creature back to life, killing the unscrupulous palaeontologist who had attempted to hide the bodies of undocumented migrant workers killed by the reanimating remains. Under the aliens' control, the monster fights off the US military and heads towards Los Angeles, where much of the action takes place. Eventually, the military sever the aliens' command over Yongary. With a nuclear strike heading for the city, the now-freed *kaijū* is confronted with a new foe sent by the invaders, Cykor, an electricity-spitting cross between a Tyrannosaurus rex and a crustacean. Yongary decapitates Cykor just in time for the nuclear attack to be avoided. The monster is then captured, sedated and transported to a 'monster island' (Figure 3.6).

The resurrected creature is referred to by Hye Seung Cheung and David Scott Diffrient as 'a palimpsest-like trace of the (cinematic) past', yet they point out that the film is 'indicative of things to come in the increasingly transnationalized sphere of postmillennial cultural production' (Cheung and Diffrient 2015, 159). For them, it is not the largely American cast in the film that mark it as indicative of a growing transnationalism, but its broadening of the sphere of the film's setting, with global cities and the ways in which 'members of disparate social groups come together at a time of *international*, rather than strictly national, crisis' (2015, 159). *Yonggary* is therefore emblematic of a transnational turn in South Korean cinema, along with other blockbusters that had significantly international outlooks. Yet, as Cheung and Diffrient lament, this meant a disjuncture with other, more distinctively South Korean filmmakers, such as Im Kwon-Taek, whom Hye Jean Chung (2009, 50) describes as 'aestheticizing traditional Korean culture', and thus 'the past itself, as a reservoir of historical memories and collective traumas, becomes

**Figure 3.6** The CGI creature is shipped away to its own monster island at the end of *Yonggary* (Zero Nine Entertainment)

secondary to the primary goal of genre diversification and deconstruction, with even the most "allegorical" of genres' (160). It's difficult to see any allegory in *Yonggary*, although the film does reflect *kaijū* themes we've discussed previously, such as the distinctions of good and bad science (as in the palaeontologist who puts fame above the public good) and destructive trauma, although the deflection from countries devasted by war or nuclear bombings to Los Angeles means any potential allegorical reading is deflated. The remake of *Yongary* thus seems more to reflect the developing trends of South Korean cinema than the kind of internal nationalism witnessed in the original version. The white faces, English language and American cities all seem designed to capture the attentions of the international marketplace, although the film was a mild success at home. Even the cultural references in the film refer to current trends in world cinema: Bud Black, the photojournalist, speculates there will be more 'dead bodies than a Tarantino flick', while one of the soldiers in the film remarks, 'compared to this guy, Godzilla is a pussy'. There is also no sense of continuity with the previous *Yongary* film. The mad doctor in the film (who turns out to be trustworthy) explains that Yong-gary (as he pronounces it) is an old South-East Asian legend about a dinosaur that would return to destroy the world. There's no sense that the creature has attacked in the past, unlike many of the Godzilla films that create their own tenuous continuity.

The *Yongary* remake displays many of the hallmarks of some of the production that would come to grace low-budget straight-to-DVD/TV/streaming filmmaking in the subsequent decades, especially the 'mockbusters' produced by The Asylum: cheap CGI effects that don't interact with human characters; lots of expositional dialogue delivered by characters in static locations, such as situation rooms or cars and helicopter cockpits; close-ups to mask locations; and generally slow pacing without a lot of action scenes. Given this is a South Korean attempt seemingly to emulate the Hollywood blockbuster, this problematises the film in some sense as 'colonial mimicry', a trend towards emulating American cinema that Berry notes 'exposes the fallacy of the "level playing field" egalitarianism that underpins the free-trade rhetoric of globalization[, with] the necessary pluralisation of the blockbuster that occurs with the inability to match Hollywood budgets' (2003, 226). Shim's *Yonggary* seems a poor imitation of the Hollywood blockbuster, conceived for global viewers, while pointing ahead to developing trends in South Korean production.

Shim's next film, *Dragon Wars* (*D-War*, 2007), took this further. The film was also set in Los Angeles, where two Imugi, dragons resembling serpents, not unlike the Tōhō *kaijū* Manda or the dragons from the recycled footage in *War of the God Monsters*, appear and face off against one another. Backed by CJ Entertainment, the film was the highest-budgeted film ever produced by a South Korean company. Estimates place the budget anywhere from 30 billion won (around $30 million) to $99 million. Again, an almost entirely American cast was assembled, including Jason Behr, Robert Forster, Elizabeth Peña and Craig Robinson. Like many genre films, it premiered at the American Film Market in search of a distributor. What perhaps marks this film as different from *Yonggary* was its wide release in the US, the first South Korean film to successfully cross over from arthouse to mainstream cinemas, grossing a creditable amount of just under $11 million from a very wide and short release (Box Office Mojo 2021c). The film was a major success at the South Korean box office, however, with $55 million of its $75 million global figure grossed in its home country. The film's success was helped in some part by Shim's past roles as Young-gu, but also by a coda to the South Korean version in which Shim explains his struggles producing the film while depicted in front of the Hollywood sign, defiant, with 'Arirang' playing in the background (Lee 2011). The film blends national folklore with transnational production in ways that have been explored more than once in this chapter, from *Galgameth* onwards, this time with a budget that rivals the mid-range for a Hollywood blockbuster; although, despite this, the film was typically received poorly outside its home country. Chung explains that the film's exploitation of a transnational imagination and negation of national specificity was problematic when placed alongside its nationalism: she identifies how a 'tension between national essentialism and transnational aspirations that conflicts global media texts was glaringly apparent in both the film and the surrounding discourse, most notably in Shim's contradictory endeavors to simultaneously hide and highlight, erase and exploit the idea of "Korean-ness" in *D-War*' (Chung 2009, 50).

I want to finish this case study by referring to a South Korean film that perhaps best emphasises the transnational dimensions of the *kaijū* film in East Asia, even if its creator downplayed the film's relationship with the genre more broadly: Bong Joon-ho's *The Host*. Chung connects the film with *D-War* and 'how, through the visualization of a transnational space in the textual realm, the two monster films most successfully accomplish the deterritorialization that contemporary media strive for in the era of global mobility' (2009, 53). Likewise, Cheung and Diffrient argue that 'Bong's paradoxical investment in and rejection of the historical project is representative of broader patterns in South Korean cultural production over the past ten years' (Cheung and Diffrient 2015, 150). Nikki Lee suggests that the film is symptomatic of 'the localized globalization of the Korean film industry supported by a nationalistic ideological discourse' (Lee 2011, 46). Lee refers to both *The Host* and *D-War* as 'localized global movies', where local strategies for production merge with global and transnational approaches to content and a Hollywood-style approach to funding, marketing and distribution. Yet Lee doesn't agree with critics who see the adoption of Hollywood styles of filmmaking as creating a de-westernised system: 'the production of highly successful Korean blockbusters like *The Host* has not de-Westernized the domestic film industry so much as it has reorganized it into a localized pseudo-Hollywood system' (Lee 2011, 61). The proximity of *The Host* to the *kaijū* film is perhaps less obvious than in *D-War* and *Yonggary*, given the film's focus on the family drama at its heart instead of monster-smashing action. Lee notes that local posters for the film played up these dimensions rather than its generic content, which was more the focus of international marketing; the latter used films such as *Jaws* and *Jurassic Park* to stabilise pre-readings of the film, as was typical for imported East Asian cinema at the time, the peak of the Asia Extreme movement (Martin 2009, Rawle 2014, Shin 2008). Once more this speaks to the regional and international globalisation and localisation of monster movie memes, where the presence of the giant monster invites readings of the film along the blurring of national and transnational tropes. Bong distanced his film from the monster movie in interviews, telling *Indiewire* that there is 'no monster or creature film tradition in South Korea, so there are prejudices against genre films' (Indiewire 2007). In the press notes for the US Magnolia release, Bong mentions:

> When I first brought up the story of this film, people seems [*sic*] confused about the scale of the monster. Many thought of giant monsters like Godzilla, which in fact it's the size of Alien [Ridley Scott, 1979]. From a bigger perspective, JAWS is also a monster film. The monster in THE HOST is also a biological mutation. At any rate, I don't think there are any similar texts. (Magnolia Pictures 2006)

The push away from connections with previous *kaijū* films, especially in the lack of a name for the monster and in the absence of anthropomorphic qualities (it is a mutated marine creature), leaves the film open to multiple interpretations. Its inclusion here, however, is based on how it does rearticulate key aspects of *kaijū* traditions. Many commentators connected the film with the limited monster traditions in South Korean filmmaking, from *Yongary* and its imitation of Japanese films to Shim's pictures, given their historical proximity, and therefore it speaks to many aspects of the *kaijū* meme, albeit in the localised-globalised dimension discussed by Lee, who points out that the film was '[n]oted for its "messy" qualities, [and therefore . . .] invites multiple readings' (Lee 2011, 55). The film is at once: a family drama, as a dim-witted, lazy father attempts to rescue his daughter from the monster's lair; a metaphorical discussion of US-South Korean relations and collective national trauma; and, viewed from the remove of fifteen years during the Covid-19 pandemic, an infection outbreak film, replete with conspiracies and cover-ups. This makes sense given the film's proximity to the 2003–4 SARS (severe acute respiratory syndrome) outbreak. While South Korea reported no SARS infections, the outbreak led to significant changes in the ways in which the country managed public health (Cho 2020). The threat of a virus is used to cover up the monster's presence in the river: surgical masks become endemic around the city. At one point, some commuters wait for a bus at the side of the road. One man begins to cough, while the rest of the group backs away from him. He pulls down his mask and spits into the gutter, right before a bus speeds by and soaks them all. Looking back at the film, and from a western perspective, such images become much more relatable.

The film focuses on the Park family. The father, Hee-bong, runs a snack concession (*maejŏm*) alongside the Han river. His son, Gang-du (Bong regular Song Kang-ho), ineffectively helps out, eating customers' food and stealing small change, alongside his daughter, Hyun-seo

(Go Ah-sung). Gang-du's siblings are similarly flawed. Sister Nam-joo (Bae Doona) is a national-level competitive archer, whose hesitations cause her to fail to reach her potential, while brother Nam-il (Park Hae-il) is a heavy drinker who's failed to establish a career after graduating from university. The family are drawn into the events when a huge creature emerges from the river and attacks the crowds gathered there. Gang-du is a witness to this, throwing a beer can into the river to taunt the monster. In the ensuing chaos, Hyun-seo is taken by the creature when the fleeing Gang-du takes the hand of the wrong girl. Hyun-seo is presumed dead, along with the rest of the victims of the attack. At a mass funeral, where the family publicly show their excessive grief together, the American military arrives and begins to quarantine anyone who has had contact with the creature, including Gang-du, whose face was covered in the monster's blood while trying to fight it. A call from Hyun-seo's mobile phone alerts Gang-du to her survival, and the family escape from the hospital with the help of gangsters who extort all of Hee-bong's credit cards in return. Meanwhile, two homeless boys break into the abandoned food stall and are themselves abducted by the monster. One of the two finds himself in the monster's sewer lair with Hyun-seo. After more run-ins with the monster, and the death of their father, the Park siblings locate Hyun-seo's phone with the help of an old college friend of Nam-il's, who, in enormous amounts of debt, sells them out to the authorities. The government announce plans, along with the US military, to attack the monster using a poisonous chemical called 'Agent Yellow'. The monster is eventually defeated through the efforts of Hyun-seo, who doesn't survive, and the three surviving Parks, alongside a homeless man who helps Nam-il create Molotov cocktails. In the film's final scene, Gang-du and his newly adopted son, in the concession stand, eat together, turning off the TV's broadcast of the Americans' explanation of the events of the film.

In the opening scene of the film, an American military doctor[6] orders a subordinate to pour formaldehyde down the drain and into the water supply from the Han river. This was motivated by a real event (from 2000, which is explicitly the time when the scene occurs in the film), in which Albert McFarland, the most senior civilian employee at the American military morgue in Seoul, ordered two members of staff to pour 192 bottles of formaldehyde down a drain and into the river. McFarland caused further anger by refusing to appear at his trial, only showing up for his appeal. He was initially sentenced to six months in prison, which was later reduced to two years' probation. The court had rejected the US offer of a $4,300 fine (Weaver Hwang Hae-Rym 2005). This immediately activates two strands of the thematic core of the monster film: profligate, irresponsible science, and anti-American sentiment. Later in the film, when the Americans are set to unleash Agent Yellow – a thinly veiled reference to Agent Orange, the toxic herbicide used by American forces during the Vietnam War that left a legacy of physical and mental health conditions in civilians – protesters gather in resistance. Some demand the release of Gang-du, while others demand freedoms from the restrictions in response to the virus seemingly rampaging in the city. This references a tradition of protests in Seoul, from the April Revolution in 1960 to the pro-democracy movement of the 1980s, and in response to the real dumping of chemicals in the river. Nam-il's role in the film as a lapsed revolutionary, along with his friend at the telecoms company who has firmly switched to pro-capitalist beliefs (even though capitalism is crushing him financially), is an important connection to these events, as it critiques both the historical traumas of struggle and the shift towards capitalism, of which the film is also a shining example. It explains too why Nam-il knows how to make a Molotov cocktail.

While these elements of the plot activate the film's main connection with the *kaijū* film, in terms of both narrative motivation and thematically, the title monster is treated not as the star of the movie, but almost as background. *The Chosunilbo* even referred to the film's creature as a McGuffin, an element that kick-starts the plot but plays no active role (Chosunilbo 2006). Indeed, as Cheung and Diffrient point out:

> the common complaint (among some genre enthusiasts as well as general audiences) that monster movies 'take too long' to show the unknowable thing, the hideous creature that serves so many allegorical purposes (in the minds of many critics), is met with a sharp rejoinder in *The Host*, which gives the viewer what it presumably wants – a full-on shot of the monster – a mere fourteen minutes into the narrative. (2015, 172)

Scenes of spectacle play a significant role in the film, namely the monster's two attacks on the riverbank, and its final defeat. Yet the film is unconcerned with the monster as a source of fascination – there's almost no attempt to decipher its origins, other than a short scene where two fishermen look at something (unseen) that they fish out of the water in a cup. The presence of the monster acts more as a device to enable the film's social and political threads to take place: the search for the daughter and Gang-du's maturing (although he turns away from being politically engaged at the end of the film) take centre stage, along with the satirical reflections of national and international issues. This is quite unlike most *kaijū* films, where the main criticism is often the lack of concern for human characters amongst the monster-smashing action. This may of course preclude *The Host* from our discussion at all, since the film fits more with some of Bong's influences than with Godzilla movies. Bong's status as a noted auteur also helped to differentiate *The Host* from other Korean monster movies, such as *Yonggary*, after the success of *Memories of Murder* (*Salinui chueok*) three years previously. But its themes and place between national imaginaries and transnational methods of production[7] sit it comfortably within our discussion of how the *kaijū* film has developed as a distinctively transnational genre (the creature can be called a strange beast, after all). Despite the considerable success of *The Host* and *D-War*, full-on monster films have been slow to develop in South Korea, with Shim's sequel mired in development hell, despite the announcement of a 2017 release through a Chinese co-production deal (Cotter 2020).

What I've attempted to demonstrate in this chapter is the way in which *kaijū* movies have developed as a transnational genre through the 'localised globalisation' of a range of aspects. By focusing on the *kaijū* films produced by South Korean filmmakers, the chapter has explored how the *kaijū* film exhibits global mobility. As Iwabuchi (2002) argues, transculturation occurs when 'foreign' products are appropriated, hybridised and indigenised. This is enabled partly by the odourless nature of Japanese cultural products that allows them to be remade, reworked, adapted or localised through several different processes. Here, we've seen how that is through imitation (in *Yongary*), the co-optation of stock footage (in *War of the God Monsters*), appropriation (as in *Pulgasari*) or indigenisation of the generic narrative templates or thematic core of the *kaijū* film with local mythology, political discourse or cultural policy. Given the colonial history between Korea and Japan, this is made more problematic, especially when we consider that for a long time Japanese culture was banned in South Korea, meaning the only means of appropriation was through 'unofficial' means. We'll continue to consider this more closely in a global context in the next chapter, as we look more broadly at the globalisation of the *kaijū* film beyond regional contexts.

## Notes

1. This term refers to a wave of production following Bruce Lee's death in 1973. Many films were produced starring Lee lookalikes in an attempt to exploit his popularity.

2. *Yongary* translates somewhere close to 'dragonfish', a combination of dragon and a reference to Boolgasari, which is itself an appropriate description of Tōhō's giant beast.
3. SRS Cinema's subtitle translation is much more explicit in connecting the environmental concerns with contemporary language regarding climate change.
4. The climactic battle with a white ape is recycled at the beginning of another Taiwanese film, *The Fairy and the Devil* (*Guan shi yin yu Hai long wang*, Chiang Tai, 1982), along with music from the *Star Trek* films, while it also appears with almost no context in the South Korean martial arts film *Son of the Dragon King* (*Yongwang samtaeja*, Choi Dong-joon, 1977), which ends with the same footage of serpent dragons that is included at the end of *War of the God Monsters*. That film is very similar to another Taiwanese film, known internationally as *Sea God and Ghosts*, but translating closer to *Third Son of Dragon King* (*Long wang san tai zi*, Chin Sheng-En, Chung Fu-Wen, 1977), an identical title to that of the Korean version.
5. Tsutsui quotes a figure of $13.5 million (2004, 197).
6. The doctor is played by Scott Wilson, an actor best known for his role as Hershel in *The Walking Dead* (2010–22). Bong cast the actor on the basis of his role in Patty Jenkins' Aileen Wuornos biopic, *Monster* (2003), which, perhaps, ironically, was the film that meant *Gwoemul* became *The Host* for international release, instead of having a more literal translation.
7. Unlike *Yonggary*, where Shim's own company produced the special effects, *The Host*'s monster effects were a collaboration with New Zealand's Weta Workshop and The Orphanage in the US, and therefore fitted the global (that is, Hollywood) standards of effects at the time much more.

CHAPTER 4

# Distributing *Kaijū*: Localisation and Exploitation

Harry and Michael Medved's *The Fifty Worst Movies of All Time* (1979) was one of the first popular books devoted to bad films. Their list of 'wretched films' and 'embarrassing disasters' covers everything from big-budget failures (like *Lost Horizon* [Charles Jarrott, 1973]) to pretentious art cinema (including Alain Resnais's *Last Year at Marienbad* [*L'Année dernière à Marienbad*, 1961]). The Medveds' list also devotes space to 'hackneyed and ridiculous film formulas', noting that 'no book on the worst films could be complete without a jungle movie, Japanese horror epic, a singing-cowboy saga, a violent blaxploitation films and a spaghetti Western' (11). Their chosen *kaijū* film is *Godzilla vs. the Smog Monster* (*Gojira tai Hedora*, 1971).[1] In their introduction, the Medveds mention that 'foreign' films are beyond the scope of their investigation, and that unreleased or low-budget cinemas make comparisons with Hollywood standards either impossible or unfair. The *kaijū* film is fair game, however, although the Medveds don't mention that the version they're referencing was both altered and dubbed by AIP. The 'immortal dialogue' from the film was inserted by AIP, rather than using the international version provided by Tōhō. The *kaijū* film is dismissed as shlock: 'To ensure consistent quality, each of [its] new creations was presented with atrocious acting, sloppy direction, farfetched scripts, execrable music, amateurish photography, laughable sets, and last but not least, ludicrous monsters' (93). While *Godzilla vs. Hedorah* represents the intensifying crisis in the Japanese film industry at the time, many of the criticisms directed at the film are the result of the decisions of American distributors, who regularly transformed *kaijū* films, through dubbing, use of library music and re-editing. Many of these decisions helped transform the *kaijū* film into the 'bad object' of the Medveds' book, as well as allowing the genre to become the subject of cult fascination. There are many sites and online articles, videos and podcasts devoted to documenting the changes made to *kaijū* films by global distributors, from inserting new English-speaking characters to retitling for release to fit with pre-existing content or properties. As I argue here, such changes played an instrumental role in turning examples of popular national cinema into global exploitation film.

So far, I've explored how the *kaijū* film's local and regional variants have shared concerns but are grounded in specifically local thematic or industrial discourses. Some of these have emphasised problematic national, colonial or deep-seated historical relationships that have an impact on the forms that those films take when giant, large or strange monsters smash into locally determined interpretations. This has taken the form of imitation, borrowing, appropriation or even more straightforward forms of recycling, such as the reuse of effects footage. In the next few chapters, we'll begin to look at how those tropes crossed to the west, into Europe and the United States particularly. Whereas we've seen, to use Erb's words, 'questions of international uses of Hollywood films' (2009, 19), we'll invert this to see Hollywood (or westernised) uses of international films.

A recent NBC News article goes right to the heart of the dynamic at play in the global circulation of *kaijū* films, in the United States in particular. Its title speaks volumes: '"Godzilla" Was a Metaphor for Hiroshima, and Hollywood Whitewashed It' (Yam 2020). Written to coincide with the seventy-fifth anniversary of the atomic bombing in August 1945, and in the wake of the Black Lives Matter protests following the murder of George Floyd in Minneapolis in May 2020, the article argues that 'Hollywood took the Japanese concept and scrubbed it of its political message before presenting it to American audiences to deflect from the U.S. decision to drop the bombs.' We've already looked in some depth at national trauma in *Gojira*, and its revision to the emerging giant monster film that became its originary text. As Yam contends here, there is an explicit argument regarding a 'Hollywood' that seeks to deflect from American culpability 'to deny its traumatic history in Japan'. This dynamic of cultural power and colonial history underlies the transformation of *Gojira* into *Godzilla, King of the Monsters!*, especially when phrased in terms of political racial discourse (whitewashing has become a recurring argument around remakes and uses of Japanese intellectual property in American cinema), yet there are other processes at play in the global circulation of *kaijū* films, especially those from Japan. As we've already seen, government funding for film exports and co-productions with filmmakers from America ensured a global platform for the *kaijū* film that didn't necessarily emerge for other genres less designed for export. This included elements of complicit whitewashing and internalised Orientalism that produced films for global and national markets. Even where choices made by filmmakers to edit, dub or reshoot films reveal imbalances in cultural power, the success of *Godzilla, King of the Monsters!* and subsequent Tōhō productions ensured a regular flow of *kaijū* films into the international marketplace, and recurring forms of localisation that turned a big-budget commercial genre in Japan into forms of exploitation films.

Hence, this chapter looks at the ways in which the *kaijū* genre developed in global circulation. Unlike other forms of national cinema, such as those in realist or modernist traditions, the *kaijū* film has never been held in significant critical esteem, as the Medveds demonstrate. The chapter examines how distributors were key to the ways in which this popular national genre cinema entered transnational circulation. The chapter also engages with the ways in which transnational genres are subject to appropriation and localisation through distribution and co-production that problematise further the association of the genre with definable national origins and mythologies. Following principles of exploitation cinema defined by Eric Schaefer, the chapter explores the ways in which popular national cinema becomes a transnational exploitation cinema. Principally, this examines the ways in which films in the 1950s, 1960s and beyond were retitled, edited, dubbed and marketed by distributors across Europe and the US. This focuses on the work of several companies who were involved in the marketing and distribution of *kaijū* films, such as Embassy (who released *Godzilla, King of the Monsters!*), AIP (who released many Godzilla and other *kaijū* movies in a variety of forms) and New World (who released *Godzilla 1985* as a follow-up to *Godzilla, King of the Monsters!*). We'll also briefly consider the circulation of *kaijū* films in countries such as Spain, Italy and Germany where *kaijū* films were routinely distributed under different titles.

## National Cinema: Quality and Trash

The study of national cinemas has long been associated with the concept of auteur-produced art cinema. Paul Willeman's article 'The National Revisited' (2006) posits that the only viable national cinema is one that is marginal, crtically charged, countercultural and struggling against popular multinational cinemas reliant on major capitalist markets. For this to be the case, we must firstly understand an 'enclosed' nation with stable and closed borders, impervious to the culture of other nations. As we've already seen, the *kaijū* film is 'impure' (Higson 2006), a hybrid format derived from the interactions of nationally specific histories and concepts, and where the 'use of international films' became reflective of popular national trends. Higson reminds us that 'borders are always leaky and there is considerable degree of movement across them' (2006, 19). Previous chapters have considered how personnel, capital, ideas and films themselves have crossed borders easily to emphasise the local–global nexus (Smith 2016) that helps define transnational cinema. Nevertheless, it's difficult to see the *kaijū* film as emphasising a 'quality' cinema that defines a site of cultural struggle. Stephen Crofts has argued that '[i]n the context of the relations of unequal economic and cultural exchange obtaining between Hollywood and (other) national cinemas, the generation and/or survival of indigenous genres is a gauge of the strength and dynamism of a national cinema' (2006, 55–6). It's questionable whether the *kaijū eiga* consitutes a fully 'indigenous genre' given its cultural origins, but its non-Anglophone loanword name suggests the generation and circulation of a genre that has become synonymous with many visions of Japan. Japanese *kaijū* films have entered global circulation widely, through cinemas as well as television and home video (this is not to mention other ancillary markets, such as merchandising, video games, comics, novels, and fan-produced podcasts and YouTube videos), but generally not in ways that benefit from a Eurocentric *'national cinema effect'*, to use Lim's (2009) term.

As we've already seen, Japanese cinema engaged strongly with globalised production methods when it came to the *kaijū* films of the 1960s. When the industry struggled financially in the face of challenges from other media and pastimes, it turned to government subsidies to finance films intended explicitly for export. This helped support a wave of genre films that relied on 'Hollywood's international domination' (Higson 2002, 133). While that strategy wasn't successful, it demonstrates how aspects of national cinema engage with the popular, while traditional concepts of national cinema, which include both the production of popular genres and how industries interact with national cultural policy, have tended to focus on the production of particular forms of national identity, or a specific type of quality arthouse cinema that resists and challenges, rather than adopting or mimicking popular genres from abroad. So far, we've seen that these aspects of what Ella Shohat and Robert Stam define as 'fields of power, energy, and struggle' (1994, 48) help to define cross-border borrowing and imitation, in either flows from the United States to Japan or from Japan to South Korea, that emphasise the transnational interactions at play in the *kaijū* film.

When it comes to the *kaijū* film, there are degrees of quality. The international release of Honda's original version of *Gojira* in 2004 helped the film overcome the perceptions created by the changes made by distributors that had blighted the *kaijū* film for nearly fifty years. It became lauded as a classic of national cinema, its themes of trauma seen widely, largely for the first time. The film had undergone processes of de- and re-territorialisation (Martin-Jones 2006) that enabled its contemporary national text to be restored. However, this hasn't always been the case with other films in the Godzilla series or for the *kaijū eiga* more generally. Despite serious recent releases from the Criterion Collection and Arrow Films, the *kaijū* film retains its paracinematic assessment as trash cinema. Jeffrey Sconce even included 'Japanese monster movies' in his list of quintessentially paracinematic genres, alongside 'splatterpunk, "mondo" films, sword and sandal epics, Elvis flicks, government hygiene films . . . beach-party musicals, and just about every other historical manifestation of exploitation cinema from juvenile delinquency documentaries to soft-core pornography' (Sconce 1995, 372). Paracinematic tastes directly challenge the formation of cinematic cultures, of the preferences for particular types of aesthetic conventions. Sconce describes paracinema as 'a direct challenge to the values of aesthete film culture and a general affront to the "refined" sensibility of the parent taste culture' (376). Paracinema, for Sconce, is a 'shadow realm', a parallel world to the high art of the exalted auteurs who inhabit the high cultural capital of arthouses. When Sconce mentions that '[t]he films are unwatchable for most mainstream viewers, and consequently have assumed an exalted status among the "hardcore" badfilm faction of paracinematic culture', he might be discussing the *kaijū eiga* (390). When, in his introduction to the collection *Sleaze Artists: Cinema at the Margins of Taste, Style and Politics*, Sconce argues that the fact that '"sleazy," "trashy," and just downright "bad" lie outside the borders of normative film practice is not surprising', he offers a conundrum for our purposes in the notion of 'normative practice' (2007, 5–6). By framing national cinema within conventional discourses of a normalising Eurocentric art cinema practice in this chapter, I've tried to complicate how we might think about the products of a popular national cinema when they are filtered through distribution systems that transform the films into something Other than the assumed norms of artistic production. As many studies of cult cinema practices have shown, discourses of Otherness are key to positioning the abnormality of cult texts – they sit outside the borders of what is considered 'good taste' and somewhere between appreciation and mockery (Mathijs and Sexton 2011, Sexton 2016, Smith 2013). Honda's original has been canonised as a classic of national cinema. It is now lauded for its creative and timely evocation of shared national trauma, an evocation made possible by the development of certain conditions within the Japanese film industry at the time in relation to occupation and the limits of public discourse.

But what of a developing series of films marked by their declining budgets, the emphatic difference in special effects technology, or their being marketed more and more at children? These factors help position the films further from the assumed norms of conventional film practice. The cultural status of the *kaijū eiga* has been, at least in the west, determined largely through the practices of film distributors rather than of film producers. Ramon Lobato and Mark Ryan's paper 'Rethinking Genre Studies through Distribution Analysis: Issues in International Horror Movie Circuits' calls for a new approach to consider how film studies thinks about how distribution plays a key role in shaping genre development. These authors contend that many industrial studies of distribution have failed to consider how the activity of distributors helps shape understanding and development of genres. 'Distribution analysis', they argue, 'can help to foreground some of the thoroughly material constraints that enable and constrain generic change, allowing a retheorization of genre as something more than a semiotic compact between producer and audience or the end-product of sublimated social desire' (Lobato and Ryan 2011, 189). Explorations of the work of distributors can help us see the historical shaping of genres and the ways in which the specific conditions of the recirculation of films, some of which are decided prior to a film's production, can demonstrate the contexts by which cultural patterns of classification are moulded. Firstly, 'distribution shapes genre through its capacity to circulate or withhold individual texts and groups of texts' (192). Distributors decide what is available and which texts are subject to a moratorium (in an official sense, as many films are distributed through unofficial channels, a 'shadow economy' in Lobato's terms [2012]). Crucially for our purposes here, distributors also make decisions on which media films are distributed through, and this plays a vital role in how films are viewed. For many viewers, the *kaijū eiga* is strongly associated with television, not cinema. Secondly, distributors make decisions concerning how films circulate, how long for, on how many screens, exhibition windows, 'leaks', previews and so on. Thus, the 'availability and cultural prominence of generic "ingredients" is contingent upon effective distribution' (2011, 192). However, our discussion of such ingredients must factor in the decisions made by distributors to prepare non-American films for their markets, thereby ingraining key attributes behind the *kaijū eiga*: dubbing, re-editing, retitling, the insertion of new scenes and western faces. These are key factors behind the genre's paracinematic standing, and crucially involve decisions made around distribution. As much as they constitute a practice of avoiding American culpability for raising Godzilla up from the depths, they certainly remake the films in ways assumed palatable for American consumers. In the process, they turn the products of popular cinema – generally Japanese popular cinema – into exploitation films.

The term that eventually emerged for this is localisation, a practice very familiar to many viewers and fans. In some regards, this whole book is about localisation. We've already encountered processes of global localisation such as remaking, appropriating, borrowing, adaptation, and the development of local discourses in the *kaijū eiga*. But in this chapter, we'll engage with perhaps more familiar processes of localisation: dubbing, re-editing, retitling and reframing of narratives. As such, it's of benefit to take a little time to explore of the issues surrounding localisation. Abé Mark Nornes, in *Cinema Babel: Translating Global Cinema* (2007), discusses how globalisation has intensified practices of translation amid the circulation of film: 'The big picture presents us with a vast number of prints trafficking the planet, moving through a system that networks, rationalizes, and homogenizes, but inevitably works with products marked by foreignness – marking that can either help or hinder circulation' (233). Homogenisation is an impact factor here: while some elements of exotic Otherness are considered helpful (Higson 2006), others are not, and therefore are often overwritten, removed or replaced to create a more 'knowable' text. Dubbing, for instance, is denounced by Nornes 'as the lowest form of translation'. In a dubbed version, a film's 'foreign language is completely extracted, replaced with sameness' (219). Localisation therefore enables an 'exotic' text to be interpreted through local frames of reference, 'translated into a local idiom' in Andrew Higson's terms (Higson 2006, 19). As many scholars have shown in studies of anime and video games, the assumptions made by producers are often problematic and lead to lukewarm reception by fans (Ruh 2010, Roedder 2014, Denison 2015, Carlson and Corliss 2011).

Ruh discusses a highly relevant example for our purposes here: *Battle of the Planets* (1978). It is relevant for two reasons. Firstly, it displays some of the marks of localisation that had already become common for *kaijū* films. *Battle of the Planets* was a localised version of the anime series *Science Ninja Team Gatchaman* (*Kagaku ninjatai Gatchaman*, 1972–4), imported in the wake of the success of *Star Wars* (George Lucas, 1977). New stories were created for the localised show, which wasn't in any way a faithful translation of the concept or dialogue featured in the original version of the show. *Gatchaman* was a *henshin* show about a series of ninjas, whose signature martial arts styles resembled birds, to battle environmentally wasteful capitalist terrorists. *Battle of the Planets* retained none of this backstory. Instead, the Science Ninja Team became G-Force, five teenagers tasked with protecting the world from the evil Zoltar, commander of the forces of planet Spectra. New narrative framing was created with the robots 7-Zark-7 (an obvious R2-D2 clone), and robot dog 1-Rover-1, who would help to explain each week's episode. Episodes were rescored, and violence and potentially adult content toned down for Saturday morning syndication. This pattern relies heavily on what had taken place in *kaijū* films from *Godzilla, King of the Monsters!* onwards: not only were imported products modelled on previously released ones, but also, as Ruh points out, many of those local variants were produced in the wake of the success of globally circulated films, and therefore were already closely related before they were exported and reworked (Ruh 2010, 34). The second relevant factor is the involvement of Sandy Frank. Frank was a notable television producer and distributor, whose high-profile shows included a revival of gameshow *Name that Tune* (1984–5) and a syndicated version of *The Dating Game* (1973–4). Frank acquired *Gatchaman* following the success of *Star Wars*, having reportedly encountered the show prior to this. His company invested '\$5 million . . . acquiring the rights, commissioning new animation, editing, dubbing, and rescoring' in *Battle of the Planets* (Ruh 2010, 35), which was successfully syndicated until the mid-1980s, after which it was replaced by more authentic localised versions (it didn't appear in its original version subtitled until the early twenty-first century). In the mid-1980s, Frank acquired the rights to several of the *Gamera* films from Daiei, which were redubbed for syndicated release. Despite his previous experience of localising Japanese media with *Battle of the Planets*, Frank's versions of the five Gamera films were more faithful than the American International TV versions released in the 1960s and 1970s. His adaptations were largely uncut, but with new dubs. These were released on video and it's through this connection that the films fell into the public domain and became staples of *Mystery Science Theater 3000*. A localisation strategy such as that of *Battle of the Planets* is largely the default for many *kaijū* films, a consequence of the perceived need to familiarise generic content for international distribution (it's worth noting that many dubs of globally distributed *kaijū* films were produced by Japanese studios, often in Hong Kong, in preparation for international distribution, although companies like AIP often chose to produce their own dubs).

Iain Robert Smith has argued that models of 'localization that frame . . . cross-cultural adaptations as primarily "local" versions of "global" texts misrepresent... the complex and contradictory ways texts are actually adopted across borders' (Smith 2016, 38). Smith is here discussing the adaptation of Arthur Conan Doyle's Sherlock Holmes into the Italian-Japanese anime *Sherlock Hound* (1984–5) and the 'complex and intersecting nexus of global and local forces that complicate any straightforward model of localization'. Andrea Esser has also argued that audiences' preferences are more diverse than previously theorised, and therefore earlier concepts of 'cultural discount' and 'cultural proximity' are problematised by viewers whose tastes are shaped by encounters with a broad range of global media: 'They are inevitably diverse, manifold, and fluid, and this is true even for each individual viewer':

> Cult film fan communities and gaming and other YouTube communities forming around global popular culture create such networks across state borders without thinking – a sign of everyday, 'banal cosmopolitanism' and of the intensification of popular culture's 'cosmopolitanization'..., networks where place and space are disconnected; networks that are multiple, diverse, complex and highly fluid. (Esser 2016, 27)

Our opening example demonstrates how localisation can be a problematic process, where the removal or downplaying of nationally specific elements leads to a negative result. Yet the localisation of the *kaijū eiga*, something which begins with the production of films in Japan and elsewhere, often for export, is already more complex, and demonstrate how 'local' industries interact with a global and national nexus where outward- and inward-looking forces mingle. Esser's points about audiences are also highly relevant here, given the cultification of the *kaijū* film and the sharing of films and histories that takes place in many videos, podcasts and blogs. *Kaijū* fans are active collectors of different versions and localisations of media that play an important role in the global fandom around *kaijū*. In localising the *kaijū* film, many global and local forces come into play, in the reworking and adaptations taking place, and in how those variations circulate. While some of these undoubtedly fall under the umbrella of Americanisation, other aspects are emphasised that heighten the transnational–national dimensions of the genre. One of the more significant effects of the localisation of *kaijū* films was to turn them into a form of the exploitation film.

## Popular Cinema to Exploitation Film

There is something inherently exploitative about popular cinema. Hunter's comments about the difficulty of unravelling popular cinema and exploitation cinema are highly pertinent (Hunter 2013, 24). It's certainly possible to argue that the practices of Japanese studios in the 1960s were exploitative. Once Tōhō's *Godzilla* films showed the way, other studios followed in their attempts to produce imitations and variations that would meet with similar (especially global) success. We've seen too how producers outside Japan attempted to capitalise on that success by developing their own versions of the *kaijū* film. Yet this doesn't explain how *kaijū* films became exploitation films. The exploitation film is distinct from practices of exploitation. As Eric Shaefer defines the form in *'Bold! Daring! Shocking! True!' A History of Exploitation Films, 1919–1959*, exploitation films were generally low-budget, independently produced and exhibited films that relied on shocking or sensational (often taboo) content (Schaefer 1999, 4–6). Schaefer also mentions that exploitation films tended to exist in multiple forms, were 'fluid, ever changing', and could exist in different versions, often with different titles. Until the mid-1980s, and even beyond, international distributors tended to transform *kaijū* films into exploitation films. It was the 1990s before *kaijū* films were picked up by major distributors, largely down to the production of the first US *Godzilla*, which saw the *Heisei* Godzilla series released on DVD by Sony.

Many decisions were taken by distributors that enabled the *kaijū* film to become an exploitation, and television syndication, staple. For instance, the Eros Films quad poster for the British release of *Godzilla, King of the Monsters!* demonstrates how the film's marketing adopted some of the appeals of the exploitation film that Schaefer describes: it has an 'adults only' designation (rated X), an emphasis on visual spectacle and a focus on a heterosexual couple (there are no Asian faces on the poster – everyone is Caucasian). We'll come to how independent producers and distributors played a key role soon, but other factors, along with the continuing existence of the different cuts of other *kaijū* films, also tend to speak to the nature of the exploitation film. Later Godzilla films circulated in multiple forms, with different names: for instance, 1974's *Godzilla vs. MechaGodzilla* (*Gojira tai Mechagojira*, Fukuda Jun) was released first by Cinema Shares (run by former MGM and UPA sales manager Mel Maron) as *Godzilla vs. The Bionic Monster*; this proved too similar (in true exploitation fashion) to *The Bionic Woman* TV show, so it became *Godzilla vs. the Cosmic Monster*. The film now generally circulates under its original title. New World released an uncut VHS version under its translated title in 1988. However, later releases reverted to the Cinema Shares title (including a 1994 UAV release that featured a still from *Godzilla vs. Megalon* [*Gojira tai Megaro*, Fukuda, 1973] on the reverse cover, with Godzilla and Jet Jaguar shaking hands[2]).

Many other films were also subject to changing titles and versions. *Gojira, Ebira, Mosura Nankai no Daikettō* (lit. *Godzilla, Ebirah, Mothra Great Battle in the South Seas*, Fukuda Jun, 1967), originally planned as a Tōhō co-production with American company Rankin-Bass to promote their *King Kong Show* cartoon (1966–9, co-produced with Toei) (Ryfle 1998, 135),[3] was first syndicated to television, with some minor amendments, including to the music, and dubbed, as *Godzilla vs. the Sea Monster*. The film also had a limited theatrical release by Continental Pictures as *Ebirah, Horror of the Deep*, a title by which the film is still known today (a Kraken DVD release uses both titles on its cover). In Germany, the film was released as *Frankenstein and the Monster from the Seas* (*Frankenstein und die Ungeheuer aus dem Meer*), and several other *kaijū* films were renamed using the Frankenstein title, including *King Kong Escapes* as *King Kong: Frankensteins Sohn* (*King Kong: Son of Frankenstein*) and *Godzilla vs. Hedorah* as *Frankensteins Kampf gegen die Teufelmonster* (*Frankenstein's Fight against the Devil Monster*), while the German title for *Frankenstein Conquers the World*, *Frankenstein: Der Schrecken mit dem Affengesicht*, translates literally as *Frankenstein: The Horror with the Monkey Face*. Tsutsui has also noted this phenomenon, alongside such retitling as the Italian release of *Destroy all Monsters* (*Kaijū Sōshingeki*, lit. *Monster Total Advance*, Honda, 1968) as *Il Ritorno di Gorgo* (*The Return of Gorgo*) (Tsutsui 2004, 194). The picture is more confusing than this: *Destroy all Monsters* was released as *Gli Eredi di King Kong* (*The Heirs of King Kong*). *All Monsters Attack* (*Gojira Minira Gabara Ōru Kaijū Daishingeki*, lit. *Godzilla, Miniya, and Gabara: All Monsters Attack*, AKA *Godzilla's Revenge*, Honda, 1969) was released as *Il Ritorno di Gorgo*, although a DVD cover also gives its title as *Son of Godzilla, Part Two*. *Godzilla vs. Megalon* was infamously released in Spain as *Gorgo y Superman se Citan en Tokio* (*Gorgo and Superman Fight in Tokyo*) with Jet Jaguar referred to throughout the dubbed track as Superman (subsequent releases have also retained the title and the dub, but refer to Jet Jaguar by name on the box cover). The Spanish distributor had changed the title to capitalise upon similarities with another Japanese character, *Super Giant* (*Sûpâ jaiantsu*, *Starman* in America and *Spaceman* in other parts of Europe), who was renamed *Superman* for Spanish release. In some sense this emphasises the multilayered nature of cultural flows, where a character influenced by DC Comics' Superman finds it way internationally to sharing that name as well, just as *Super Inframan* became *Chinese Superman*, complete with the superhero's logo on its poster. In Germany, *Godzilla vs. Megalon* became *King-Kong: Dämonen aus dem Weltall* (*King Kong: Demons from Outer Space*).

This kind of messy retitling has become the subject of online mockery, but it also demonstrates the standing of the films globally as exploitation films, with producers and distributors taking advantage of global, and more local, trends to position films in their markets.

## Long Live the King

Steve Ryfle has shown how *Godzilla, King of the Monsters!* emerged from Hollywood's 'exploitation-movie madness' (Ryfle 1998, 51), as small-time film distributor Edmund Goldman optioned the film and TV rights to Tōhō's hit for $25,000. Goldman was a foreign distributor of American films for East Asia, so he enlisted the help of Harold Ross and Richard Kay, independent producers (working as Jewell Enterprises), who contracted Joseph E. Levine's Embassy Pictures, with whom they had worked on a previous film, to finance revisions and distribute the film through Trans World Releasing. Editor and occasional director Terry O. Morse was hired to rework Tōhō's version – now known as *King of the Monsters!* to play up its relationship with *King Kong* – for the American market. Trans World's marketing even told the world that the film would 'Out-Monster' the giant ape (Ryfle 1998, 53). Such a brief history (the story is well told by Ryfle through interviews with many of the participants) immediately emphasises the exploitation roots of the localisation of Godzilla in Schaefer's terms: the role of independent production, the low-budget methods ($100,000 was reportedly spent on the film), and the sensationalised marketing (right down to the exclamation mark in the film's new title). The film they produced would become the default version for most of the next fifty years until the original version resurfaced. Embassy's version was even subtitled and successfully released in Japan by Tōhō (despite its incoherent reordering of Japanese dialogue).

The Embassy/Trans World version begins with the same pounding thunder as Tōhō's original, over black, before fading up to the sea upon which the *Eiko-maru* first encounters the monster. The sea bubbles as we hear the creature's shriek for the first time. The film's title zooms onto the screen. Gone is the sedate opening of the original. There is no 'Godzilla March', and we jump straight into the middle of the action, after Godzilla's first attack, tracking across devastation. A voiceover, in English, explains: 'This is Tokyo, once a city of six million people: what has happened here was caused by a force which, up until a few days ago, was entirely beyond the scope of Man's imagination.' Tokyo is described as a 'smouldering memorial to the unknown'. We cut to a destroyed office to find our new main character, Steve Martin (played by Raymond Burr, who would later find fame as a TV star in legal and police procedurals, just two years after his role as the murdering husband in Hitchcock's *Rear Window* [1954]), buried beneath the rubble. Martin is the foreign correspondent for United World News, his 'social call' stopover in Tokyo turned into the 'living hell of another world'. Martin is treated by Emiko in the aftermath of Godzilla's Tokyo attack, her head turned away from camera to conveniently disguise the body double and dubbing. Martin flashes back to recount the story of the *Eiko-maru*, and his visit to catch up with old friend Serizawa. Upon his arrival in Tokyo, Martin finds Serizawa delayed by a field trip, and is detained for questioning by the security forces, which gives him a helpful sidekick through whom to translate the Japanese dialogue. The plot is streamlined – the core romantic triangle between Emiko, Serizawa and Ogata is edited significantly, with two scenes fully removed, and another trimmed. The impact on citizens in Tokyo is minimised, with the scene on the train where commuters discuss their nuclear trauma cut, as are shots of frightened people in Godzilla's first attack, in favour of a focus on Martin. Young Shinkichi's role in the film is trimmed to provide space for Martin's reactions, and the journalist pushes Emiko to make the decision to reveal Serizawa's Oxygen Destroyer (the closest his character gets to taking an active role). Godzilla's stated height is increased, by two and a half times.

Many changes to the film reorder action or trim for pacing. But the key change is one to the ending. Yamane's final speech about the fear of another Godzilla is cut and replaced with more voiceover from Martin: 'The menace was gone ... so was a great man. But the whole world could wake up and live again.' This is a major shift in morality from the original. Yamane's concerned pacifism is replaced with closure. Godzilla has been defeated and the world is safe. This shift reflects a core distinction in the horror film. Robin Wood, in his seminal article 'An Introduction to the American Horror Film', distinguished between the progressive and reactionary wings of the classic horror film, into which the two versions of the first Godzilla films fit comfortably. The negative progressive film is more apocalyptic in Wood's thinking. The repressed returns, as Igarashi also mentioned, but its recognition signals 'ideology's disintegration'. While the ending of *Gojira* is perhaps not that pessimistic, it highlights the ways in which nuclear trauma's return (or the return of the war dead) signals a shift in contemporary thinking. Yet the transformation of the film shifts its politics (the source of accusations of whitewashing, even though Japaneseness is not fully erased in the film). For Wood, the reactionary horror film positions its monster as evil, inhuman and unsympathetic, and ultimately to defeat it is to completely neutralise the threat it poses socially and politically (Wood 1985, 215–16). Martin's unambiguous claims (Figure 4.1) to victory at the end of the film signal a very definitive shift in the film's politics that might make it sit more comfortably with American variants of the science-fiction atomic monster film. The monster still meets its defeat in the Japanese cut of the film, but Yamane's warning emphasises the ongoing trauma of apocalyptic nuclear attack.

Tsutsui points to how 'Americanization thus rendered *Gojira* a standard monster-on-the-loose action film, radiation a gimmick rather than moral crisis, and Godzilla firmly recast in the inoffensive tradition of American atomic-age science-fiction' (2004, 41). Donald Richie simply said it was *Gojira* with 'all of the good stuff' removed (Richie 2001, 267). Martin acts as a narrative focaliser for American viewers. He plays a big role in the film, but generally at a remove, often in the background of scenes, listening or having things explained to him. Consequently, the film keeps a surprising amount of its Japanese dialogue (although Japanese text in newspaper headlines is cut), often explained by Martin's liberally used voiceover. Yamane's testimony about the possible causes is untranslated (during which he says 'Gojira' before the creature is named by the Odo Island residents in the film), as is the dialogue of the Odo islanders. Additional Japanese dialogue is added when Martin investigates Odo Island (Figure 4.2). Security officer Tomo Iwanaga (the character shares its name with the actor who played it, part-time actor and insurance seller Frank Iwanaga) acts as an intermediary to allow

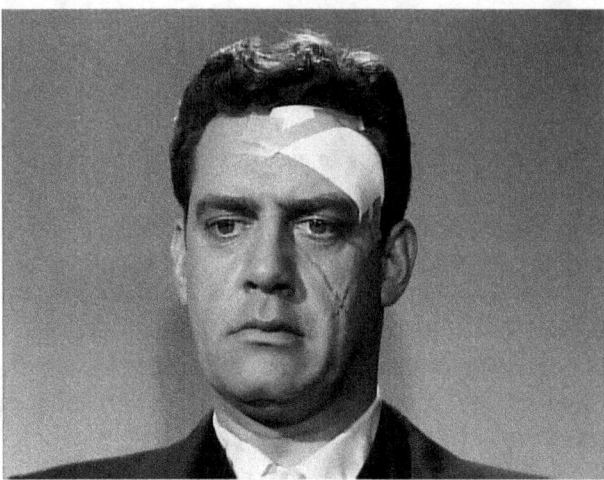

**Figure 4.1.** Martin watches on from an obvious studio background whilst witnessing Godzilla's demise at sea (Tōhō)

**Figure 4.2** Steve Martin is inserted into Odo Island ritual as Tomo Iwanaga translates in *Godzilla, King of the Monsters!* (Tōhō)

Martin to observe, explain and understand, as Iwanaga translates. The act of watching – most of Martin's scenes are static, at the back of other onlookers or talking to the main characters from the film – reinforces the documentary aspects of Honda's filming, something that is clear in the Odo Island section of the film. If acts of dubbing reinforce sameness, the retention of Japanese dialogue from the original, and new scenes featuring the awkward Japanese of Asian-American actors, means the film is marked by cultural difference, since traces of the original are retained. This is accidental on the part of the filmmakers, however. There was no attempt to implicate difference in the text, just to save money. Burr filmed all his scenes in a single, albeit very long, day, and the dubbing was recorded in just five hours (Ryfle 1998, 54). The remaining Japanese dialogue – and the essentialist Japaneseness of the text – is an accidental side effect of the exploitation tactics of the producers to shape the new version as quickly and, above all, cheaply as possible.

Many territories (such as Mexico, Poland) released the localised American version in dubbed versions, sometimes with differing titles. In Spain, it was known as *Japon Bajo el Terror del Monstruo* (*Japan *under the Terror of the Monster*). However, other distributors produced their own edits. There are currently six known versions of *Gojira/ Godzilla, King of the Monsters!*, including the original and Embassy/ Trans World versions (Wikizilla 2021). The existence of some of these versions demonstrates some of the complexities of globalisation. As Smith argues (2016), localisation can evidence more than simply the essentialist national characteristics of the localising country. The *kaijū* film, as I've argued, displays a high degree of hybridity and the localisations of the original film continue to highlight such cultural blending and exchange. The existence of multiple versions (or rumours of their existence in fandoms) points to the activities of exploitation producers whose licensing or sub-licensing of already localised films led to the circulation of different versions, or, in the digital era, the legends of such films. The latter is evidenced by the legend of the Filipino film *Tokyo 1960* (Teodorico C. Santos, 1957). A poster for the film was uncovered from the collection of a blog devoted to Philippine (or Pinoy) cinema (Santos 2008). The blog points to the existence of a small cycle of late 1950s Pinoy films that appear to echo films from the US and Japan. The poster for *Tokyo 1960* depicts Godzilla, train in mouth, above the faces of its three stars: Tessie Quintana, Eddie Del Mar and Zaldy Zshornack. Santos, a prolific director of genre films, is credited as director and Cirio H. Santiago (another Filipino film industry veteran) as executive producer. No Japanese names are included in the credits, although the film's poster boasts 'Giant Monster Blasts Tokyo' and that it was 'filmed in Tokyo, Japan'. Little else is known about the film's plot, but we might briefly consider the evidence of the film's existence through the lens of Iain Robert Smith's exploration of Philippine cultural borrowing. Filipino filmmakers were prolific in the mid-to-late twentieth century, producing hundreds of genre movies that Smith argues have received only minor consideration in studies of the cinema of the Philippines. 'Many of these films were imitations of imported films and were heavily criticised for their low budgets, blatant commercialism and appeal to what was referred to as "bakya crowds"' (Smith 2017, 80). Smith argues that 'the hybrid nature of these popular Philippine films could potentially offer us an invaluable insight into the intricate processes of cultural globalisation . . . [although] the hybrid forms of Philippine popular cinema came to be situated as a capitulation to American influence and a betrayal of Philippine national heritage' (82). However, given the difficulties and political turmoil of the 1970s under Ferdinand Marcos' rule, we can only speculate how *Tokyo 1960* relates to this schema of 'local agency and creativity', since the film remains lost. Fans imagine the work as a

*King of the Monsters!*-style localisation with Filipino actors playing the roles of Raymond Burr and Iwanaga, or it may simply be a direct remake reusing the special effects from Honda's version (this theory may understand the film through a postcolonial understanding of Philippine–Japanese relations following the latter's invasion during the Second World War). Smith's argument helps us position an attractive argument for cultural borrowing in Filipino cinema that supports fan theories, but until the film resurfaces, it's impossible for it to be anything other than speculative.

German and French distributors produced their own versions of *Gojira*. The French version was a reworked American cut. Retitled *Godzilla: Le Monstre de L'Ocean Pacifique* (*Godzilla: The Monster from the Pacific Ocean*), the film begins with the creature's name in katakana, only upside down. The French version circulated until fairly recently on VHS, with a running time of ninety minutes. Taking into account the PAL format's 4 per cent speed-up, it makes the film approximately two minutes shorter than the Japanese version but over ten minutes longer than *King of the Monsters!* This is largely down to its unusual combination of both versions. The opening of the film cuts the flashforward and narration device, beginning with Godzilla's attack on the fishing boat. Martin enters the film later. Some elements of the Emiko–Ogata romance have been reinstated for an unusual mix of Martin's observer role and a more conventional romantic narrative. All dialogue has been translated into French in this version, even where it is out of continuity (as we've seen, Yamane names the creature before it's named in the narrative, something the American version glosses over). This effects the complete erasure of Japanese identity, something that is usually attributed to the American release.

German releases of *kaijū* films were often notorious for their exploitative retitling of the films, even though few changes were made to the films themselves. For the purposes of the original, however, Germany was one of the very few territories where the film was released without the involvement of Transworld and Embassy. The German release, by Atrium and Lehmacher Filmverleih, was surprisingly faithful to the original. Although it was dubbed into German, with some fidelity, the running time was cut by around twelve minutes, through the removal of dialogue scenes. All the destructive action scenes are left intact. Scenes in the Diet building with Yamane and several of the scenes involving Emiko, Serizawa and Ogata are trimmed or removed. The trimmed version is more 'knowable' in its appeal to a specific audience – the sensational aspects of the film are emphasised above the emotional and political drama. This is arguably a more 'whitewashed' version than the

American one, and certainly one more appealing to concepts of exploitation, where films routinely circulated with different running times, according to Schaefer (1999), but often with their 'best bits' intact. VHS copies of the French and German versions are now fairly rare – *King of the Monsters!* has remained in circulation and become the authoritative localised version of the film, and there is considerable affection for it from fans who grew up with it as the only version of the original film.

## *Cozzilla*

The final localised version of *Gojira* that I want to consider is generally considered the most bizarre: Luigi Cozzi's 1977 *Godzilla*, although the film is better known as *Cozzilla*.[4] Cozzi was an Italian distributor, producer, director and writer whose partnership with Dario Argento on *Four Flies on Grey Velvet* (*4 Mosche di Velluto Grigio*, 1971) and *The Five Days* (*Le Cinque Giornate*, 1973) made him a noted name in 1970s Italian exploitation cinema. He also built a reputation as a director whose work wasn't afraid to capitalise on popular trends. *Starcrash* (1978) is a shameless *Star Wars* rip-off, with robots, camp costumes, David Hasselhoff, Hammer star Caroline Munro, and Christopher Plummer as 'Emperor of the First Circles of the Universe', which has been referred to as 'submental' (Hoffman 2020). Cozzi's version of *Hercules* (1983) is an updated version of the Steve Reeves-starring 1958 peplum film with Lou Ferrigno (TV's Incredible Hulk), released the year after Dino De Laurentiis's *Conan the Barbarian* (John Milius, 1982) with Arnold Schwarzenegger. Such tactics are characteristic of the Italian film market at the time. As Mikel Koven argues:

> Italian exploitation cinema has always been characterised by cycles of imitations and down right rip-offs of other European and American films. A film will emerge that seems to take the national box-office, or at least to receive the media's attention, and then very quickly, often before the original has reached the Italian cinema screens itself, a whole slew of imitators emerge. (Koven 2004, 19–20)

Cozzi's version of *Godzilla* was timed, like other imitators, to coincide with the release of the *King Kong* remake. He confessed in an interview that he had initially tried to obtain the rights to Lourié's *Gorgo* instead, but found the rights owners asked for too much money (DeSentis 2009). This is perhaps logical, since *Gorgo*'s narrative, in which a monster is taken to London by an opportunistic fisherman who sells the creature to a circus, is more closely modelled on *King Kong* than *Gojira*. Moreover, as previously mentioned, Godzilla had been renamed

Gorgo for the release of *All Monsters Attack* in Italy.⁵ *Son of Godzilla* (*Il Figlio di Godzilla*) had been released in 1976 under the title *Il Ritorno di Gorgo* (*All Monsters Attack* also circulated under this title), largely because the same distributor held the rights to both films. Cozzi then attempted to license the original *Gojira* from Tōhō but claimed they would only allow the rights to *Godzilla, King of the Monsters!* The filmmaker therefore started modernising the Italian version, *Godzilla: Il Rei dei Mostri*, recycling its Italian dubbing. To satisfy the demands of the contemporary market in Italy, he set about transforming the film.

Koven's study of the Italian *giallo* (yellow) film (detective thrillers, named after the colour of novels' spines) defines it as vernacular cinema:

> Vernacular cinema . . . is largely formulaic cinema: it relies heavily on preexisting formulas that . . . transform the movie theatre into a social space for a variety of activities, while still enabling the film text in question to be comprehensible . . . Formulaic narratives enable the story to be followed undemandingly. In addition, due to vernacular cinema's tendency to function as an 'attraction' – to draw the vernacular audiences' attention back onto the screen – narrative functions as merely a framework on which hang the spectacle sequences of violence, sex, and graphic gore. (Koven 2006, 37)

In this context, vernacular cinema encompasses the low-brow activities of the producer-distributor, to emphasise, above all, the appeals of sensational content, and the rejection of the high-brow tendencies that are often lauded as central to trends for national and 'foreign' cinemas through the lens of auteurist art cinema. Also, Koven notes, vernacular pertains to processes of localisation, normally through linguistic or artistic processes. *Cozzilla* sits comfortably as an example of vernacular cinema in this context.

This version stands apart from the other ones. While it conforms with other variants through its geographical and cultural localisation, it is also historically localised, and therefore updates to the expectations of 1970s Italian exploitation cinema. It is colourised and lengthened, and its impact is ramped up using new footage, music and sound effects. Hence, in the terms of the vernacular cinema laid out by Koven, *Cozzilla* is an 'attraction', a sensationalised address to spectators, as in early cinema (Gunning 2006). Cozzi said he was 'trying to give an "up-to-date" and more violent look to the old 1954 movie, considering that it was going to be re-released theatrically in the second half of the seventies when the audience's tastes had obviously changed a lot' (DeSentis 2009). Using his experience and assets as a distributor, Cozzi was able to bulk out the film with effects shots from some of the films to which he owned distribution rights: this included scenes of a crash from *The Train* (John Frankenheimer, 1964) and some carnage from British science-fiction film *The Day the Earth Caught Fire* (Val Guest, 1961). Two *kaijū* movies were used for some extra spectacle, which Cozzi described as 'tributes', with the shark tussling with the octopus from *The Beast from 20,000 Fathoms* and convicts being consumed by a flood from *Godzilla Raids Again*, both from Cozzi's 16-mm collection. While some of these aspects speak to the perceived expectations of audiences in 1970s Italy, they also speak to more complex processes of localisation as a range of different filmmaking standards are brought together to produce a composite work of Japanese, American, British and Italian cinema, filtered through the vernacular processes of pre-existing formulas and locally set standards of both Italian and Hollywood cinemas. That *Cozzilla* is also a localised version of an already localised product (albeit one that hadn't erased the original Japaneseness of the text, even though it had challenged its coherence[6]) puts it at a double remove from *Gojira*.

Several other factors have led to *Cozzilla* becoming known as a 'lurid tie-dye version' (Glaser 2019). Firstly, the reputation of the film has been built by its inaccessibility (in the same way that the Filipino version has gained traction as a 'lost film'). When Cozzi licensed the American version from Tōhō, they stipulated that the film would return to its original owners once Cozzi was finished with it. Tōhō have never released the film. It remains locked in their vault. Bootlegs do circulate, but the film is generally unseen, even by many hardcore *kaijū* fans. Secondly, some of Cozzi's updating introduced elements that were either deemed 'trippy' or, as Ed Glaser puts it, in 'lousy taste'. In terms of the latter, Cozzi introduced an opening prologue of nearly four minutes made up of stock footage of the real Hiroshima bombing (Figure 4.3). An opening caption unambiguously connects the film with its themes: 'Hiroshima, 6 Agosto [August] 1945'. Once the film begins, we're told the action takes place on 6 August 1954, a hardly subtle link to emphasise Godzilla's metaphorical reflections. It opens on the approaching *Enola Gay* (although it is stock footage of a different B-52 bomber), followed by overhead shots of Hiroshima, calm and unassuming. Stock footage of an atomic explosion follows, under loud and lengthy sound effects, before a montage of aerial shots of the ruined city and even optical close-ups of charred bodies in the rubble. The length of the sequence makes it difficult to watch. The tone of the music, a pulsating techno track by Vince Tempera (credited as Magnetic System, alongside Fabio Frizzi and Franco Bixio, who managed Argento's band Goblin), also seems at odds with the tone of the sequence. Initially, there is just a dance beat under the shots

Figure 4.3 Cozzi cut real footage of the devastation from the nuclear bombings to preface *Cozzilla* (Tōhō)

of the approaching plane, while the track breaks out into a synth beat like that composed by Frizzi for Lucio Fulci's *Zombi 2* (AKA *Zombie Flesh Eaters*, 1979). The opening sequence breaks into the credits with a snippet of music from the opening of *King of the Monsters!* and the credits play over wind noise, interspersed with the monster's roar and crashing footsteps. The bassy music and ramped-up sound effects were consciously conceived for the Futursound system Cozzi used for the film; this was largely a knock-off version of Sensurround, the Universal Studios-developed process that added more impact to spectacular sounds effects (first used for *Earthquake* [Mark Robson] in 1974). Cozzi later confirmed that the film was most successful in theatres that had Sensurround systems (DeSentis 2009). The film's credits call it an 'incredible vibrating effect' (*incredibili effetti vibratori*).

The film itself is relatively straightforwardly translated from the American version. Events follow roughly the same pattern, but impacts are generally sensationalised. Godzilla's second attack on fishing vessels is padded out with stock footage of military vessels exploding. The sequence with the storm on Odo Island is much more significantly developed, with animated lightning flashes and stock footage of storm damage. Curiously, this has the effect of lessening Godzilla's impact, making the storm much less ambiguously the act of the monster. Godzilla's roar is also much less audible in this sequence than it is in the other versions.

In addition, Cozzi has reordered the scenes, so this is after Martin has asked Yamane to accompany him to the Island, but we don't see Yamane's first testimony at the Diet with the Odo Islanders, or his first appearance in *King of the Monsters!* when he names the monster before it is named on Odo Island.

The film's most memorable effects relate to its colourisation. Using a process called 'Spectrorama 70' (a name Cozzi said he used in a William Castle-style piece of self-promotion [DeSentis 2009]), the film was colourised (perhaps a generous term for this) using stop-motion photography and coloured gels. The film was photographed frame-by-frame with coloured overlays, roughly corresponding to what is on screen, so blue for sky, red/orange for fire and so on, although most of the film remains in black and white (the credits even promote this when they say it's a version of a black-and-white film). When Godzilla first attacks Tokyo, it is a dazzling kaleidoscope of colour. Godzilla's atomic breath is sometimes bright orange. The explosions (of which there are many, from the original and the stock footage) produce strobe effects with bright flashes of colour. The Spectrorama colouring struggles throughout the film: at times it's possible to see there are right-angled shapes over the image, and the process has difficulty with camera movement. But this perhaps adds to the attractional nature of the sequences – they are sensational and spectacular (even for effects overwriting action sequences that are already spectacular in nature). It's impossible to watch *Cozzilla* and ignore the interventions of Cozzi and his collaborators. As a piece of vernacular cinema specific to this period of Italian cinema, the localisation of *Godzilla, King of the Monsters!* functions to promote the actions of the producer-distributor, and draws attention to its violence, lurid colourisation and at times aggressive editing (Figure 4.4). Given it was produced at such a remove from the original film, it updates the film's own exploitation tactics to those of the era, one of few localisations that have done so. Esser (2016) ask which audience the localisation is for; the answer is clear to see in this version. Levine and Morse's work translated *Gojira* back to the norms of the American monster, from which the film was already localised, while *Cozzilla* intentionally transformed *King of the Monsters!* to fit the appeals of Italian exploitation cinema of the 1970s. As such, it has become an oddity given its effective burial by Tōhō. Part of this intrigue was heightened by the film poster's appearance on the cover of the first issue of *Fangoria* through a connection of Cozzi's. It helped turn the film into a little-seen legend for fans of Godzilla, at least prior to the internet age. That place is now taken by the lost Filipino version.

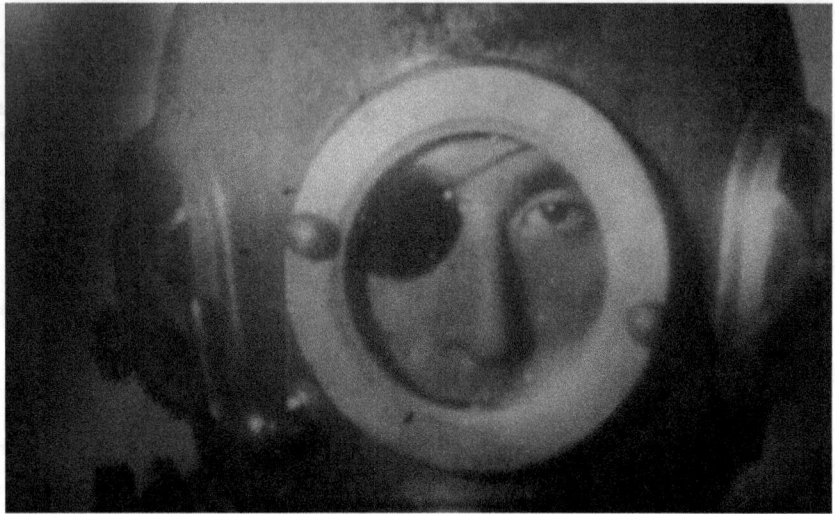

**Figure 4.4** Before unleashing the Oxygen Destroyer, Serizawa watches a shark and octopus fight in *Cozzilla*, a scene lifted from *The Beast from 20,000 Fathoms* (Tōhō)

## The Return of Steve Martin

*Godzilla, King of the Monsters!* set the template for the localisation of *kaijū* films for decades to come. *Half Human* underwent one of the most substantial transformations. New framing scenes were filmed with John Carradine as 'Dr John Rayburn, Anthropologist' (as the credits name him) narrating almost the entire film. Unlike Morse's additions, Carradine's character doesn't interact with the main narrative at all. Trimmed by over half an hour, to little over sixty minutes' running time, the film credits almost none of the original crew at the start (there are only credits for producers Tanaka and Sakamoto Minoru). The final card of the film states that 'segments of this picture depicting Japanese people and locales were written and filmed in Japan. Special credit is due the artists and technicians there who contributed so much to the authenticity of this production.' Most of the Japanese crew are credited following this (with customary errors of transcription, 'Eigi [*sic*] Tsuburaya', and 'Inoshiro Honda'). All the film's Japanese dialogue is removed. None of the characters speak for themselves – it's always narrated by Carradine. This allows the film to retain the *tokusatsu* effects sequences and avoid the plotting. Most of the monster's sequences are kept intact to highlight the spectacle and sensation. Scenes from the original version take place with almost no diegetic sound effects; there are some footsteps, screaming or a fire burning, but otherwise just music (although not the score from

Honda's version). This is quite at odds with the static and talky scenes of Carradine and his colleagues pontificating about anthropological theories and the work of 'Dr Tanaka' in Japan. Again, this fits with exploitation tactics. This version was prepared and released by Distributors Corporation of America (DCA) in 1957 as a 'terror-iffic' double bill with *The Monster from Green Hell*, a giant atomic monster movie in the vein of *Them!* substituting wasps for ants, directed by Kenneth G. Crane, who also directed the English-language inserts for *Half Human*. DCA were an importer of foreign films – one of their early releases was Henri-Georges Clouzot's *The Wages of Fear* (*Le Salaire de la Peur*, 1953) – but their final releases were exploitation genre fare, including *Plan 9 from Outer Space* (Edward D. Wood Jr, 1959). The *Half Human* poster mirrors the whiteness of the posters for *Godzilla*, the monster enlarged to *kaijū* size holding a partially naked white woman in its hand, à la *King Kong*. The pressbook (DCA Productions 2016) for the release promotes it as a '*special* exploitation show!' It suggests exhibitors create a jungle exhibit in their lobby ('steamship lines, your public library and travel agencies can supply you with astonishing facts about the African jungle') or 'Street Bally' with costumes and masks from 'local novelty stores' to meet the monsters face to face. Shaefer mentions that distributors like DCA (and American International) were not strictly exploitation distributors in the classical sense, but more traditionally in the B-picture mould. They were often closer in budget to B-movie levels, but their embrace of the emerging teenage market moved them closer to exploitation models, in that 'their advertising promised more than the films actually delivered' (Schaefer 1999, 330–1). This seems quite a fitting description of DCA's version of *Half Human*. Due to Tōhō's own moratorium on the film's circulation, it remains the version most available after VHS releases, and now online.

The sequel to *Gojira* was perhaps mystifyingly released under the title *Gigantis, the Fire Monster* by Warner Bros. For reasons that have never been fully explained (Ryfle 1998, Myrtdi 2011), Warners changed the name of the monster from Godzilla to present the illusion of an all-new spectacle (not for any legal reasons, as Ryfle points out has often been assumed). The film was padded out with stock footage, trims made, music replaced with library scores, and a dub that introduced a voiceover and corny translation. *The History Vortex*, a site run by *G-Fan* co-founders John Roberto and Robert Biondi, contend that Gigantis 'will stand as a prime example on [*sic*] how intelligent, entertaining Japanese fantasy films were ruined by the process of Americanization' (Myrtdi 2011). *King Kong vs. Godzilla* is perhaps the most reviled of American localisations, the plot transformed from a satire of Japanese consumerism into a version with little subtext, as American producers added around twenty minutes of new footage and made a series of cuts and reorderings (including replacing the original score with library music).[7] Until the last ten years, this has been the version of the film that circulated outside Japan, before the new release of all the Godzilla *Shōwa* films from the Criterion Collection following a German DVD release in 2013. Godzilla wasn't the only monster localised. DCA produced a version of *Rodan*, and Gamera's first film was reworked by Harris Associates as *Gammera the Invincible*. Lots of scenes of soldiers and politicians discussing the threat were added, as well as a TV show debate between scholars that descends into an argument. While Arrow Films released this version on Blu-ray in 2020, it had fallen out of circulation when Sandy Frank acquired the rights to the originals and produced new dub tracks for the first four *Gamera* films. Dubbing and re-editing continued to contribute to the reviled critical standing of *kaijū* films, but later films were less impacted by such radical localisations.

As discussed in Chapter 2, co-production became a more effective means of localising content through the embedding of material into the fabric of the film, such as American stars, Caucasian children, English dialogue and western cultural material. This began as early as the aborted co-production of *Varan the Unbelievable*, which itself was released in a version with new narrative framing. Transnational contact zones, as we have seen, became more visible within the Japanese and American versions of the films. UPA, AIP and Rankin-Bass became more engaged in the production of the films, and, while this led to some changes, such as the ending of *Frankenstein Conquers the World* or the music in *All Monsters Attack*, fewer were made to the films. Even so, this has not been without controversy for some fans. As Kalat notes (1997, 99), AIP's release of *Destroy All Monsters* made relatively few changes, namely some alterations to music and trims to some shots, and the addition of new opening and end credits. The main change AIP made was with the creation of a new dub track, produced by Titan Productions in New York. Tōhō had, as they often did, produced an English dub from Frontier Enterprises in Tokyo that was included in international sales. But AIP were unimpressed with the Tōhō dub. In subsequent years, the subtitled and international dub have become the versions in circulation. However, fans continue to express their nostalgia for the versions they watched as children, and this led to a fan-driven effort to fully restore the AIP version, based on the HD transfer from a Media Blasters Blu-ray release, combined with elements from VHS and DVD releases

(Red Menace 2016). Thus, while it seems easy and compelling to critique the bad localisations and attribute their continuing success to paracinematic factors, it's important to note that fans don't always want authenticity. There is a strong nostalgic pull towards the localised versions as well as the 'original' editions, hence the recreations of this and *Godzilla 1985*.

Following a series of celebrations, festivals and reissues, Godzilla was back in the big time in Japan in the early 1980s, just in time for the thirtieth anniversary (Kalat 1997). Popular re-releases had led to excited campaigns to relaunch the film series (the booming market for Godzilla merchandise and spin-offs had also helped). Tanaka was ready to produce another film in the series, as were Tōhō. Although Honda and Ifukube declined to be involved, Tanaka aimed to return the series to its serious anti-nuclear roots. Hashimoto Kōji would eventually direct, having been an assistant director on earlier *kaijū* films, despite coming off the back of a major flop with environmental science-fiction blockbuster *Sayonara Jupiter* (1984). Nakano returned as special effects director, ensuring continuity with the previous entries in the *Shōwa* series. Although titled simply *Gojira*, it was intended as a direct sequel to Honda's 1954 version, even though the resurrection of the monster is never explained. It received a limited international release as *The Return of Godzilla*, albeit not in the US. It is a serious film, directed with a stern vision by Hashimoto. The film recasts Godzilla not as the friendly protector of Japan, but as the fearsome nuclear devastator of its first film appearance.

The creature's return from the depths prompts a stand-off between the US and the Soviet Union with Japan right in the middle. The 1980s was a time of tension between the US and Japan, particularly in economic terms. The ascendancy of the Japanese economy, prior to the collapse of the bubble in 1989, was seen as a threat to US global hegemony. As Andrew C. McKevitt explains, US media was filled with 'yellow peril' narratives as Japanese consumer products flooded the American market, in a 'shock of the global'. This was aligned with a stagnant Cold War, isolated protests over military bases or sales of military technology to the Soviets aside (McKevitt 2017, 20). Japanese economic power seemed to provide, at that moment, a reversal of conventional flows of globalisation. Whereas the mid-twentieth century had seen globalisation take shape as Americanisation, McKevitt presents the flow into the US *from* Japan, a reversal of traditional theories of globalisation. 'Cultural power mattered too' (24), as McKevitt mentions, something central to the purposes of this book. Godzilla returned into a changing power dynamic between the two superpowers, with Japan in between. Without getting into too much depth here, the *Heisei* series of Godzilla films (as well as the returns of Gamera and Mothra to their own series) instituted a new cycle of national films, less concerned with visible marks of globalisation and more with modern Japan. In the eight years Godzilla was off the screen, there were attempts to produce new films, including Saperstein's proposal for *Godzilla vs. Gargantua*, and an attempted all-American version directed by *Friday the 13th*'s (1980) Steve Miner, *Godzilla: King of the Monsters in 3D*. But Tanaka's vision was reported as being a film 'strictly for domestic consumption' (Ryfle 1998, 223). When the film was a reasonable but not stunning (given its reported budget), success, Tōhō turned to the international market to increase their profits.

By the mid-1980s, UPA, AIP and Rankin-Bass were defunct, bought out or about to be. Former AIP producer and exploitation legend Roger Corman had founded New World Pictures in 1970, enabling him to continue his low-budget production methods. Corman had sold the company in 1983 to a pair of lawyers who aimed to model it on rising Hollywood companies such as Orion. Tōhō had reportedly been asking $5 million for the international rights to *The Return of Godzilla* but struggled to find a buyer. New World eventually acquired the rights for $500,000. Ryfle reports that this was then supported with $200,000 for production and $2.5 million for prints and advertising costs. The film became *Godzilla 1985*, in reference to *Frankenstein 1970* (Howard W. Koch, 1958) (Ryfle 1998, 237). New World made a major assumption about the audience they were localising the film for, and initially conceived it as a spoof, with Leslie Nielsen as star. When Lorne Greene was suggested, the producers turned to Raymond Burr, and decided to resurrect Steve Martin. This time, however, the film would make no effort to integrate Burr into the diegesis of the film. Martin spends his time in the film watching from a war room. And, because of the famous comedian Steve Martin, he's simply called Mr Martin this time round (although he does have a book called *Cairo via Tokyo* on his desk, a nod to the journey taken on his first appearance). Again, all of Burr's scenes were shot in a single day.

The reworking of *Godzilla 1985* seems to act as a culmination of decades of assumptions and critical opinions of 'cheesy' and 'campy' Godzilla films. It reads like a text conscious of its own reception and is almost a meta-text about processes of localisation, assumptions about audience and paracinematic pleasures. This occurred right from the marketing campaign for the film. It was promoted as campy excess, the voiceover in the trailer telling us that Godzilla's 'acting technique was revolutionary. His presence . . . overwhelming. He possessed more raw talent than any performer of his generation . . . Now he is back. And he's more magnificent, more glamorous, more devastating than ever.'

The trailer's voiceover echoes some of the Medveds' ironic criticism of Godzilla films:

> Godzilla has long been a favorite Japanese leading man. His riveting performance in *Godzilla Versus the Smog Monster* ranks among his best. To register anger he throws his arms about, wiggles his hips, stomps his feet, and makes obscene hand gestures to the smog monster. In addition to his natural charm, Godzilla has the advantage of a jazzy nightclub band that plays his theme music. (Medved and Medved 1979, 91)

By tapping into the cult reception of previous Godzilla films, the trailer playfully and ironically mocks the tradition into which it fits. It's consistent with contemporary theories of postmodern referentiality and parody. Indeed, Linda Hutcheon might have been thinking about *Godzilla 1985* when she called postmodern parody an 'ironically recontextualized echoing of the forms of the past' (Hutcheon 1986, 203). Contemporaneous with the production of *Godzilla 1985*, postmodernism revelled in nostalgic references to past media texts. For Fredric Jameson, it was 'blank parody', an impulse towards reference without an ulterior critical motive (Jameson 1991). However, the positioning of ironic texts is typical of cult film, where there is a double coded impulse towards simultaneous celebration and mockery (Smith 2013).

*The Return of Godzilla* is a very serious film. Its tone is one important reason why *Godzilla 1985* seems such an irreverent localisation. The plot focuses predominantly on a journalist named Maki Gorō (Tanaka Ken) who discovers a wrecked ship while sailing. He investigates and is attacked by a giant sea louse. A sole survivor, Okumura Hiroshi (Takuma Shin), saves him. Maki helps Okumura identify the real culprit: Godzilla. After Maki's account of the incident is suppressed, he's encouraged to meet with Professor Hayashida (Natsuki Yosuke), a research scientist whose parents were killed by Godzilla in 1954 (the previous fourteen films have been retconned so that this is a direct sequel to the original). Maki discovers that Okumura's sister, Naoko (Sawaguchi Yasuko), works with Hayashida, and that she doesn't know Okumura is still alive. Meanwhile, a Soviet submarine is attacked in the Pacific. The Soviets suspect the Americans and threaten to retaliate. The Japanese government has no option but to go public with the knowledge of the monster's return after thirty years. The creature comes ashore and attacks the Ihama nuclear plant in Shizuoka. The attack allows Hayashida to notice that Godzilla is distracted by a flock of birds and that a primordial area of its brain may help them to lead it to Mount Mihara, where a triggered volcanic eruption might be able to kill the *kaijū*. The Japanese government finds itself stuck between the American and Soviet envoys. Both of them want to use nuclear strikes to kill Godzilla. The Japanese prime minister faces a moral dilemma, but ultimately decides to stick with the three pillars of the Treaty on the Non-Proliferation of Nuclear Weapons signed in 1968. A Russian cargo ship in Tokyo Bay is primed to launch the missile, then aborted. Godzilla is spotted nearing Tokyo Bay and proceeds, just as in 1954, to attack the city and head for Shinjuku, where the creature faces the government's new weapon, Super X, armed with cadmium rockets. Despite the best efforts of a Soviet sailor, the cargo ship is scuttled by the monster attack and the Soviet weapon is launched. Hayashida, Maki and Naoko are trapped inside a building while the battle takes place outside. Okumura arrives in a helicopter, but is able only to rescue Hayashida, who is taken to Mount Mihara with the device that will lead Godzilla there. Maki and Naoko must escape for themselves. Godzilla is knocked unconscious by Super X's attacks and falls into a building. A US missile destroys the Soviet missile, but the resulting explosion and electrical pulse knock out communications and down Super X. They also revive Godzilla. Once the monster has defeated its military enemies, crushing Super X with a skyscraper, it's attracted to Oshima, where it's lured into the erupting volcano. The credits roll over the creature's exploding tomb.

The American version introduced multiple revisions. Watched side by side, it's noticeable how much pacier the re-edited version is. Many sequences are compressed, and scene transitions are often trimmed. For instance, the sequence in which the Japanese prime minister reveals Godzilla's return to the public with Okumura's testimony is significantly trimmed, as are many of the scenes featuring Hayashida, Maki and Naoko: we don't see much of them attempting to escape a building when anti-earthquake measures are triggered, and the final scenes with Maki and Naoko's developing romance are largely removed. This echoes the minimising of the Emiko, Ogata and Serizawa triangle in *Godzilla, King of the Monsters!* New World also brought more focus to the Soviet–US–Japan conflicts in their version. The two envoys are introduced much earlier in the film, and the discussions about nuclear weapons are raised prior to Godzilla's first attack on the Japanese mainland. The moral arguments about Japanese uses of nuclear weapons are removed altogether, and the anti-nuclear stance of the Japanese government is made much clearer. The attack on the Soviet submarine happens earlier in the film, while the subtitled dialogue no longer speculates that the Americans are behind the attack. Scenes on the Soviet cargo ship also frame the evil of the Soviets, as the first scene shows the Soviet captain keeping their 'options open' to use their missile, while during Godzilla's Tokyo Bay attack the skipper struggles to launch the missile, not to stop it launching, as in the original version. Some shots are reordered. When Godzilla attacks Tokyo, scenes from Shinjuku are moved forward to show people fleeing from the monster's footsteps (despite no people in the preceding shots), and footage from the government briefing about the return of Godzilla is used for an evacuation notice that makes Tokyo look like a totalitarian state, with the massive face of the prime minister on a giant screen. There is also much more liberal use of music in *Godzilla 1985*; there is no music in the original Soviet submarine attack scene, while there is in the American version. The soundtrack leaves no Japanese language in the film – all characters are dubbed with strong American accents, with some comic dialogue. (A scene with a homeless man is played for laughs in both versions, but the English dialogue replaces the man's taunt about Godzilla acting like a big shot having just arrived in 'town', when the original dialogue specifically mentions the monster's arrival in Shinjuku, the aspirational cultural and commercial centre of Tokyo.[8])

We could thus level similar accusations at *Godzilla 1985* to those levelled at *Godzilla, King of the Monsters!* American culpability has been downplayed and the impact of trauma and US occupation has been sidestepped, particularly the arguments around Japanese nuclear weapons. But what most strongly links the films is the presence of Burr. He appears in fewer scenes than before. At the film's outset, he seems to sense the return of the monster while sitting at his desk. He's brought in by the American forces to advise on the incident. However, he plays less of a role in this version than he did before, when at least he had agency in encouraging Emiko to reveal Serizawa's weapon. This time round, he watches on a screen and acts as an explainer for what happened in the past – the film even cuts in some shots from the opening of *Godzilla, King of the Monsters!* showing the devastation of the aftermath of Godzilla's attack. Mr Martin also repeatedly warns of the difficulties of killing the monster and that it isn't really dead when it topples over. Burr's performance is tonally at odds with others in the American scenes. His seriousness is maintained throughout (his tone matches that of the performances in Hashimoto's version), but he clashes with the two main American characters: General Goodhoe (played by Warren J. Kemmerling, a former Marine who specialised in military characters) and Major McDonough (Travis Swords). Goodhoe arrives in the film straight from the golf course, still wearing his spikes. When Godzilla falls, McDonough refers to the monster as 'Wonder Lizard'. The tone fits with some aspects of the dubbing, particularly when the homeless man tells Godzilla, 'Let's do lunch sometime!' Burr's dialogue is portentous. He tells Goodhoe: 'Godzilla's like a hurricane or a tidal wave. We must approach him as we would a force of nature. We must understand him. Deal with him. Perhaps, even, try to communicate with him. And, just for the record, 30 years ago they never found any corpse.'[9] Again, the final word goes to Mr Martin:

> Nature has a way sometimes of reminding man of just how small he is. She occasionally throws up the terrible offspring of our pride and carelessness to remind us of how puny we really are in the face of a tornado, an earthquake or a Godzilla. The reckless ambitions of man are often dwarfed by their dangerous consequences. For now, Godzilla – that strangely innocent and tragic monster – has gone to earth. Whether he returns or not or is never again seen by human eyes, the things he has taught us remain.

There is no corresponding voiceover ending in the Japanese version; the credits merely roll as Hayashida looks on after Godzilla is trapped in the volcano. The meaning of the monster in this sequel, in either version, is more confused. Godzilla is a returning menace, more a memory than a specific articulation of nuclear anxiety or a metaphor for the bomb itself. The monster finds itself trapped within the contemporary Cold War nuclear tensions, and the film draws much more on transnational relationships than previous films to discuss Japan's place within the Cold War. Godzilla is neither tragic nor innocent, as Martin pontificates. It is more animalistic and less mythic than presented in the original *Gojira*.

Both versions play with nostalgia, but in different ways. *The Return of Godzilla* recontextualises the monster, after years of it being children's friendly protector, as a frightening destroyer (apart from *Gojira* and *Shin Gojira*, this is the only film where Godzilla has no *kaijū* foe), framed within the discourses of mid-1980s Japanese prosperity (a confident Japan) but stuck between its two neighbouring superpowers. Likewise, *Godzilla 1985* evokes the nostalgic memory of localised Godzilla movies, familiar from Creature Double Features on TV, with their cheesy dubbing and white faces. But it also creates a simplified and Americanised morality. There is no debate for Japan in this version about ending the commitment to the three pillars of non-proliferation, and the villainous Russians (a trope of mid-1980s American action cinema) reframe the core conflict in the film.

There is one more important aspect of the localisation, though. In one earlier scene, Goodhoe is briefed on the action after being so rudely interrupted on the golf course. Framed perfectly in the middle of the shot is a Dr Pepper vending machine. When Mr Martin's grandson is playing with his *kaijū* toys as the military comes calling, there is a Dr Pepper can on the floor. At the end of the film, when Godzilla heads to Oshima island, we cut to a shot of the American characters, tracking left from McDonough to Martin. McDonough is drinking a can of Dr Pepper (Figure 4.5). This last one is the most overt of placements for the drinks brand. While Japanese production committee methods of media content creation are not immune to such overt production placement, the manner of this final shot is particularly incredible and not necessarily in keeping with the tone of much of the film. When New World licensed the film from Tōhō, Dr Pepper had already signed their own deal with the studio to use Godzilla in their marketing (Kalat 1997). Dr Pepper provided funding for the new scenes with the proviso they would feature product placement, while Dr Pepper's Godzilla-starring TV and radio commercials would reciprocally promote *Godzilla 1985*. As products of late capitalism, the blurring of commerce and ironic localisation help heighten the meta-textual aspects of *Godzilla 1985*, as an ironic blending of past features of localised films and Americanised Cold War themes.

Unlike *Godzilla, King of the Monsters!*, *Godzilla 1985* has generally fallen out of official circulation. Tōhō have never released this version and there are rights issues with the recycled music from Canadian science-fiction film *Def-Con 4* (Paul Donovan, 1985, also released by New World) in the Soviet submarine scene. It was the last Japanese *kaijū* film localised in this fashion. None of the subsequent *Heisei* or Millennium

**Figure 4.5** Major McDonough enjoys a refreshing piece of product placement at a high point of tension in *Godzilla 1985* (Tōhō)

series films, in any franchises, received any tinkering other than dubbing or subtitling. Some films retained the nostalgic effect of cheap forms of dubbing (some releases have used Tōhō's Hong Kong-produced dubs, others their own). *Godzilla 2000* (*Gojira Nisen: Mireniamu*, Okawara Takao, 1999), the first film in the Millennium series, received a particularly ironic dub. In Sony's dub, characters speak in Asian-accented English, using phrases such as 'Gott in Himmel!' and 'Great Caesar's ghost!' that self-consciously and nostalgically emphasise the paracinematic appeal of the dubbed track. Such nostalgic references underline the pleasures of the localised versions of Japanese *kaijū* films that, for many fans, are intrinsic to the experience of the films.

*Godzilla 1985* was a moderate success on cinema release, but it was a major hit for New World on VHS. As Kalat notes (1997, 171), the film took a bashing from critics on its initial run, for its ironic dubbing, with the background of the decades of accumulated reputation from dubbed, re-edited and campy appropriation of *kaijū* films. Even though the film grossed just $4.1 million at the US box office, it was, after an advertising blitz, one of New World's most successful releases once the VHS edition was factored in (Ryfle 1998, 242). The VHS version of the film also included, as cinema prints had, *Bambi Meets Godzilla* (Marv Newland, 1969), a short lasting approximately 100 seconds (mostly credits) in which a fawn grazes peacefully, only to be stamped flat by a giant lizard's foot. Rossini's pastoral William Tell overture gives way to a half-speed discord from the end of The Beatles' 'A Day in a Life' when Godzilla's foot smashes down. In the next chapter, we'll continue to look at how *kaijū* films went on moving further west, and how subsequent productions have revisited the imagination of disaster.

## Notes

1. The Medveds list the film with its American release date of 1972.
2. The website Toho Kingdom (2014) has collected a broad range of international VHS box art for a host of Tōhō's films.
3. Rankin-Bass and Tōhō produced *King Kong Escapes* instead, turning this film into a Godzilla movie.
4. It's signed as this at the end of the film, and was reportedly one of Cozzi's nicknames.
5. The film's poster depicts a giant claw emerging from the sea to attack an aircraft carrier, which is not something that actually happens in the film. This was also the poster for *Gorgo*'s release in Italy. This doesn't happen in that film either.

6. Yamane's first testimony is missing from *Cozzilla*. It moves more quickly to Odo Island.
7. A detailed breakdown of the differences between the two versions can be found online (Muck47 2013).
8. In the Japanese version, it's really the only joke in the whole film. Even the homeless man's death is played seriously.
9. This is the only explanation in either version of how the monster from the first film could have returned.

CHAPTER 5

# 'Paul Bunyan Never Fought Rodan'

In *The Simpsons* episode 'Simpsons Tall Tales' (S12E21), the family find themselves on a freight train to Delaware after Homer loses his temper refusing to pay an airport tax. They meet a singing hobo who tells three stories portmanteau style. The first features Homer as Paul Bunyan, the legendary American folk hero who grows too big for his home town. In the story, after being cast out, Bunyan and his ox Babe fight Rodan. Lisa corrects the hobo, saying that this isn't part of the tale. A post-credits sequence in the *Rick and Morty* episode 'Gotron Jerrysis Rickvangelion' (S5E07)[1] makes a similar reference to *kaijū* culture. We cut to another universe, where a group of young bugs are at school. They're training for a mission to travel to another universe to tell the people there about the cure for AIDS. One of the bugs asks if the portal they'll travel through might remove all their clothes and make them giant and impossible to understand (the instructor responds, 'It's not like interdimensional travel strips us of our clothes and makes us screaming monsters. Or, maybe it does, impossible to know'). Naturally, this is exactly what happens, and the *kaijū*-sized bug is destroyed by the military while subtitled 'Buginese' wonders, 'My clothes . . . Where'd they go?' These two examples demonstrate how engrained references to *kaijū* are in western culture, particularly in American media, the second largest market for *kaijū* films after Japan. In this chapter, we'll continue to look at how western cultures localised *kaijū* tropes (or memes) through the production of variants of *kaijū* movies.

Western *kaijū* media ranges from parody, as in the two examples above, to homage, such as 'The Zillo Beast' episodes of *Star Wars: The Clone Wars* (S02E18 and E19). The Zillo Beast is an obvious nod to Godzilla, a giant reptilian creature that rampages across Coruscant after being brought there for scientific testing. The Beast returned in a one-shot Marvel comic, 'The Age of Resistance' (2019), in which Kylo Ren tackles a giant beast worshipped by the Bethany, a Wookiee-like warrior race. Marvel are no strangers to *kaijū* stories. Their *Godzilla: King of the Monsters* series ran for twenty-four issues between 1977 and 1979. It built the monster into the Marvel universe, running into S.H.I.E.L.D. and various superheroes, including Avengers, but for licensing reasons, Godzilla never fought any of their foes from Tōhō's *Shōwa* series.

But we're more concerned here with appropriations of *kaijū* than simply adaptations. Marvel's late-1970s *Star Wars* run included a cycle in which Han Solo and Chewbacca fight the Behemoth, summoned by a shaman who conjures the giant monster during a battle between moisture farmers and bandits (issue 9, 1979). The Behemoth is another giant reptile with mythic proportions, eventually defeated by a lightsabre (issue 10, 1979).[2] In 2019, smart-mouthed mercenary Deadpool became the king of the monsters on Monsteropolis (a renamed Staten Island), fighting off Avengers, a Kraken, wannabe kings and monster hunter Elsa Bloodstone, herself fresh from battling *kaijū* in *Monsters Unleashed* (2017–18) alongside Kid Kaiju (Kei Kawade), a teenager able to summon monsters by drawing them. These series sit alongside Marvel's *Ultraman* run (2020–2). In 2016, Todd Ziller joined the Avengers universe, a super-solider in the vein of Captain America. After being subjected to medical experimentation, Ziller transformed into a giant lizard with the Stars and Stripes on its chest and took on the name of American Kaiju. There is a proliferation of Anglophone *kaijū* comics, including not only IDW's *Godzilla* comics but also independent ones such as *Kaijumax*, by Zander Cannon (2016–21), or the Lovecraft-inspired *Monstress*, by Marjorie Liu (2015–present), both of which draw on giant monster motifs. A wide range of *kaijū* novels exists, particularly in English and German, from fanfiction to Marc Jacobson's metaphysical *Gojiro* (1991), about the exploits of an accidentally famous irradiated reptile and his *hibakusha* best friend near the time of their mutually agreed suicide pact. This is in addition to the Hanna-Barbera *Godzilla* cartoons (1978) featuring Godzooky, the *kaijū* Scrappy Doo. Hanna-Barbera also collaborated with Tsuburaya Productions on an English-language animated Ultraman film, *Ultraman: The Adventure Begins*, a pilot that never developed into a series. What such examples demonstrate is the breadth of the adoption of giant monster memes in western media, some of which are official licensed adaptations, others inspired by Japanese films and media, often using the loanword *kaijū*.

In many regards, this looks ahead to our next chapter on the cycle of *kaijū* films produced by Legendary Entertainment, but this chapter will explore more broadly how the genre has been adopted and adapted by (mostly) western producers. This will help us continue to explore elements of cultural flow along global lines as the west reappropriated *kaijū* films. We've already seen how Japanese producers used the templates developed by American producers, especially in response to *King Kong*, but this also enables us to complicate issues of appropriation. In the previous chapter, we saw how accusations of whitewashing have been levelled at the American distributors of *Godzilla, King of the Monsters!* for their reworking of the narrative and especially for the avoidance of American culpability for the bombings that metaphorically created Godzilla. However, we also saw that there were more complex forces at play in the various ways in which the film was adapted into local contexts. In this chapter, we'll continue this exploration. In some sense, it's compelling to argue that the (re-)westernisation of the *kaijū eiga* represents a form of neocolonialist appropriation, that the power of Hollywood to adopt and adapt global formulas rides roughshod over the creativity, ingenuity and ultimately cultural specificity of a genre that became synonymous with Japan. But, as we've discussed already, the *kaijū* film is a modern rather than traditional form, and, as such, a product of media globalisation. Tōhō, their competitor studios and the Japanese government helped develop the *kaijū* film as an export product, so it's difficult to see globalisation simply as Americanisation in this context. The *kaijū* film continues to be highly adaptable to different national contexts and engages with transnational themes and lines of cultural flow. Even though most of those flows do head towards Hollywood in a hierarchised fashion, the western *kaijū* film has, until the last two decades, tended to be one that sat in low-budget and exploitation fields, cultivating the disreputable perception of the genre, something that continues in associations with 'mockbusters'. Hence, we'll consider tropes of monster movies as a key part of straight-to-video and online markets, exploring low-cultural fare such as that produced by The Asylum, like *Atlantic Rim* (Jared Cohn, 2013), *Sharknado* (Anthony C. Ferrante, 2013), *Mega Shark versus Mecha Shark* (Emile Edwin Smith, 2014), *Monster Island* (Mark Atkins, 2019) and *Ape vs. Monster* (Daniel Lusko, 2021). Finally, the chapter will discuss probably the most developed cycle of films in the global flow of *kaijū* movies: the films that Raphael Raphael terms 'the bad Kongs' (Raphael 2016, 207) and the many rip-offs and parodies of the original giant ape film. In so doing, the chapter will examine how, in Raphael's terms, the *kaijū* film demonstrates 'its resistance to national borders and generic ones . . . as a spectacular site for a global conversation about power, and resisting power' (206). But first we'll consider some of the ramifications for global cultural power.

## Appropriation, Borrowing, Exchange

The distinction between *kaijū* and *gaijū* raised in Chapter 1 from the Maser Patrol blog (Maser Patrol 2017) hints at questions of cultural power. While it is in some sense a question of translation or localisation, it also raises issues concerning the moral and ethical dimensions of borrowing culture across borders. Cultural blending and hybridity help to stress how different nations make sense of the intangible culture of another nation, either by interpreting it in particular ways or by shaping it into more 'local' forms. The overlapping spaces between cultures and nations are also not neutral. Cultural contact zones (Pratt 1991) bring challenges in terms of national, colonial and neocolonial relationships. Scars can be deep, and we've seen particularly how the contact zone between Japan and South Korea produced *kaijū* films through contact zones that mapped both Koreas, Japan and the United States. The relationships were fundamentally uneven, with military, economic and cultural dimensions relating to colonial and historical connections. In Chapter 4, localisation was viewed as a problematic process that partially or fully overwrote national texts, hence the 'whitewashing' argument. But it does beg the question of how producers of *kaijū* films benefited or lost out in terms of those relationships. Were Japanese producers losing out when their films were licensed to overseas distributors who altered them? Was harm done when they were adapted? Perhaps not in a commercial sense, since the financial bottom line was upheld, but where producers were assumed to be making a cultural expression, auteurs like Honda might be seen as harmed because their vision is compromised. The *kaijū* film doesn't necessarily conform with most concepts of art cinema,[3] hence it was seen as more ephemeral, but it is still assumed by many commentators to be essentially a national mode of communication (Anderson 2006, Blouin 2013, Deamer 2014, Noriega 1987, Yomota 2007).

In many regards, this concerns aspects of cultural appropriation. As mainstream culture becomes more attuned to inclusion and diversity, cultural appropriation has become a regular cultural battleground covering everything from fashion to hairstyles to food and art. In a blog post for *The Hollywood Reporter* (2018), Marc Bernardin criticised Wes Anderson's *Isle of Dogs* (2018) for treating Japanese 'culture a bit like wallpaper', with the story focusing on a series of dogs, all voiced by white North American actors, while Japanese characters are subtitled or translated – essentially relegated to the background. This isn't a million miles away from *Godzilla, King of the Monsters!* While that film kept elements of the Japaneseness of the text, it pushed it into the background, behind Raymond Burr and the Asian-American actors who acted as translators. Bernardin accuses Anderson's reverent adoption of Japanese signifiers of being 'fetishized exoticism' that treats 'culture like some kind of Vegas buffet'. Bernardin uses a personal anecdote to frame the issue:

> I grew up on a steady diet of Godzilla movies – as a kid born in New York in the 1970s, my viewing habits were a constant rotation of giant monster flicks, syndicated kung fu movies and *Star Wars* knockoffs. When I finally got to write my first comic book, it was called *Monster Attack Network* and it was about, among other things, a Pacific Island paradise that was routinely beset by giant monsters. I understood the metaphor behind Godzilla and why it is so specifically Japanese – the internalized guilt of the only country to have been subject to nuclear bombings is haunted by a monster fueled by atomic fire, one that would destroy Japanese cities over and over and over again. When I co-wrote that comic book in 2004, with Adam Freeman, I didn't give a second thought as to whether I should tell this story, one that has so many signifiers from a culture that wasn't my own. I just thought it was fun.

Bernardin concludes by saying he'd write the story again, but with a Pacific Islander as the protagonist rather than 'a beefy white guy'. This poses an important question for our discussion and for where the limits of cultural appropriation lie: is it the figure of the monster and its attendant metaphorical purpose? Is it the setting? Or the characters? Or the casting? In an obvious reference to Guillermo del Toro and *Pacific Rim*, Bernardin asks, 'If I'm, say, a Mexican filmmaker who loves giant robots and giant monsters, do I have to present myself to an anime gatekeeper for permission?'

In their Introduction to *Borrowed Power: Essays on Cultural Appropriation*, Bruce Ziff and Pratima V. Rao discuss cultural appropriation as 'a multidimensional phenomenon' (1997, 1). Since we're discussing elements of culture, we're referring to a combination of intangible ideas and rituals. UNESCO's list of intangible Japanese cultural heritage includes examples such as Kabuki and Nôgaku theatres, Washi, the craft of producing hand-made paper, Kumiodori, Okinawan musical theatre and Ainu dance (UNESCO 2021). There is therefore a distinction between traditional cultural heritage, which often draws from diverse ethnic groups within and across nations, and commercial products like films. As Ziff and Rao argue, cultural appropriation arises from contact between culture and peoples, associated with 'commonly held notions of authorship' (4), where the origins of 'works' can be found in the work of individuals (or collectives). They draw on Barthes' notion of the writerly text, namely that cultural products are 'tissues of quotations' and therefore not connected to individuals in a traditional sense (Barthes 1978). Creative acts 'blend, merge and synthesize' from a range of sources (Ziff and Rao 1997, 4–5). As the title of their book emphasises, such processes are inherently about power, and the political argument about who can control intangible culture: 'Politics is generally about power', they argue, 'who gets to control the processes for allocating scarce resources. In the context of cultural appropriation, the resources at issue are the many and varied forms of cultural production, expression, and creation' (7). Bernardin's example fits with these acts in some sense, as an appropriation of motifs from a Japanese cultural text, embedded within a western cultural imaginary, resulting in the erasure of cultural difference and the ascendance of the white male protagonist. Ziff and Rao attest to such processes when they argue that 'appropriation erodes or degrades cultural identity and therefore threatens diversity' (10). Bernardin's writing therefore does suggest some cultural harm, with cultural diversity overwritten in favour of the tropes of genre.

In terms developed by Henry Jenkins, Bernardin's reflection demonstrates a shift from 'textual poaching' to 'pop cosmopolitanism'. First mooted in Jenkins' book *Textual Poachers: Television Fans and Participatory Culture*, the concept of textual poaching, developed from Michel de Certeau's work, is an active engagement with popular texts: 'Fans construct their cultural and social identity through borrowing and inflecting mass culture images, articulating concerns which often go unvoiced within the dominant media' (Jenkins 1992, 23). Importantly, Jenkins argues that fans are often in a marginal position socially and economically, frequently for reasons of their identity, and thus 'actively struggle with and against the meanings imposed upon them by their borrowed material' (33). Bernardin's question about del Toro suggests a different form of appropriation, where the filmmaker has the full resources of a Hollywood studio behind them, while more marginal works, such as *Monstress*, don't, and reinterpret the original works within feminist frameworks. Jenkins' subsequent reinterpretation of the concept of appropriative poaching as pop cosmopolitanism suggests a greater awareness of how mass-produced texts engage with cultural difference: he argues that the term 'refers to the ways that the transcultural flows of popular culture inspire new forms of global consciousness and cultural competency' (Jenkins 2004, 117). Importantly for our purposes here, Jenkins makes a distinction between top-down corporate forms of convergence – major media conglomerates with multinational interests, such as Universal or Dalian Wanda – and bottom-up grassroots movements, in which engaged consumers can impact the media they consume. Jenkins discusses a key example of convergence that blends Asian pop culture references with western traditions: *The Matrix* (the Wachowskis, 1999), which mixes elements of martial arts films with manga-inspired imagery and references to anime. He argues that it is an example of

> corporate hybridity [that] depend[s] on consumers with the kinds of cultural competencies that could only originate in the context of global convergence, requiring not simply knowledge of Asian popular culture but an understanding of its similarities and differences with parallel traditions in the West. (2004, 132)

Pop cosmopolitanism therefore helps us situate cultural appropriation within a larger media ecology of blending and hybrid cultural acts by producers and audiences.

Throughout this book, we've seen how *kaijū* media have been developed, produced, reworked or circulated through processes of localisation, hybridity, blending and cultural flow. As we turn to look more closely at how the west reappropriated the *kaijū* film, this raises questions about the cultural ownership of the genre, with its Japanese name, association with national trauma and a story of modernisation and economic development in the broader context of Japan's cross-border relationships. Ethically, does such appropriation constitute cultural harm? The processes of localisation we looked at in the last chapter certainly contributed to stereotypes and clichés around Japanese media that have persisted for decades. And, as negotiated cultural appropriation is 'always dogged by questions of power and post-colonial inequalities' (Young and Brunk 2009, 7), it would be naïve to assume there weren't imbalances in the flow of content and ideas from one country to another. But, as many people have shown, cultural borrowing is often endemic, especially in global exploitation cinema. The term 'borrowing' suggests a more benign process of sharing and reciprocal relationships of cultural exchange, itself a more equal-sounding term.

Adaptations that are also appropriations abound in low-budget genre cinema. I. Q. Hunter has argued that exploitation cinema tends to resist conventional fidelity-to-source forms of adaptation and fits more closely with intertextual models. He argues that 'exploitation is a minor, left-handed form of adaptation; . . . it is adaptation's shadowy Other (as exploitation is also mainstream cinema's) -- because *all* adaptation, by a certain way of thinking, is exploitation' (Hunter 2009, 10). Hunter examines how Jawsploitation, a cycle of imitation that originates not just with *Jaws* but with the 1950s monster-on-the-loose cycles, including *Godzilla, King of the Monsters!* (2009, 16–17), developed across waves of imitation, parody and soft-core eroticism to bigger-budget versions decades later. Although it's difficult to claim *Jaws* as a *kaijū* film (the monster is neither strange nor big enough and doesn't smash cities), this emphasises an important function of the appropriation of *kaijū* films globally. In some sense, they do represent Erb's (2009) point regarding the uses of Hollywood movies internationally, and that all *kaijū* films, including *Gojira*, might represent a mode of Kongsploitation. As such forms of exploitation, cultural appropriation may illuminate cultural relationships, but given the attention that global imitations of the *kaijū* film focused on Japan, the cultural harm may not be so significant, especially as Japanese studios benefited from the commercial exploitation of the films. But, just as there is a 'trickle-up' effect of exploitation into the Hollywood studio system (Clover 1992, 20, cited by Hunter 2009, 20), so the *kaijū* film has eventually become part of Hollywood's convergent strategy of developing 'network narratives', to borrow Chuck Tryon's (2009) reuse of David Bordwell's (2012) term. Power might therefore be felt more keenly when major conglomerates become involved. Jenkins' top-down model of convergence is thus more tangible, even where films may exhibit *The Matrix*'s 'corporate hybridity'. Cultural appropriation may therefore be seen in a more negative light in this regard, as we step from Hollywood's 'shadowy Other' into the mainstream.

## European *Kaijū*

Perhaps appropriately, given its place within global exploitation cinema, the *kaijū* film is often primarily concerned with aspects of exploitation, showmanship and the consequences of irresponsible, regularly colonial, power. As Jason Barr points out, in reference to *King Kong* and other films reflecting nature/culture binaries, 'exploitation of the island or the culture therefore leads to the punishment or destruction of "civilization," which often is horribly unequipped to stop the destruction until entire cities are leveled' (Barr 2016, 50). This narrative template is determined very early in the cycle of giant-monsters-on-the-rampage films, from *The Lost World* onwards. This is unsurprising, given that *kaijū* films tended to originate from colonial or neocolonial nations: the United States, Japan and, in this next section, the United Kingdom.

In the late 1950s and early 1960s, Britain produced a short sequence of what we can identify as *kaijū* films. Hammer's *The Quatermass Xperiment* (Val Guest, 1955, *The Creeping Unknown* on its American release) and *Quatermass 2* (Val Guest, 1957, *Enemy from Space* in America) are lightly connected to the genre, with the latter especially concerning a giant alien threat. *Quatermass 2* concludes with a scene in which huge gelatinous blobs burst out of their 200-foot-tall domes and smash the buildings around them. These films share *kaijū*'s focus on urban destruction and Cold War paranoia, but, along with *X: The Unknown*, they differ in important ways from Japanese and American counterparts. Peter Hutchings puts this down to an indifferent attitude to Otherness that the creatures represent. While the films focus on things, blobs and objects (in Hutchings' words), they are:

> contrasted with American 1950s SF where if the monsters were not assigned to a particular planet (usually Mars, the *red* planet) then they were implicitly seen as stemming from a communist society (either Russia or China). While American 1950s monsters tended to be signalled as completely Other within the context of extreme social 'normalcy', the monsters in the corresponding British films are shown as Other quite simply because the films do not seem to be able to specify exactly what they are or where they come from. (1993, 42)

This is an important distinction. In *kaijū* films, we almost always know the origins of the creature, even if we don't always understand how they got that big. In *Gojira*, we know the creature is a radiation-mutated dinosaur; Mothra is a goddess from Bikini Island; Hedorah caused by pollution; Biollante a rose mutated by contact with Godzilla's DNA. There is often little ambiguity about the origins of the monster. Despite the appearance of Bernard Quatermass himself (Brian Donlevy) in Harris Associate's version of *Gamera*, the Hammer films' connection with the *kaijū* film is fairly loose.

The short cycle of British *kaijū* films following the *Quatermass* films do share, as Barr suggests, the origins of creatures in Other places, and their exploitation is an important element of the films. Three are important for our purposes here: *Behemoth the Sea Monster* (1959, *The Giant Behemoth* on its US release), *Gorgo* (1961) and *Konga*. We'll return to *Konga* later as, its title makes clear, an example of Kongsploitation. *Behemoth* and *Gorgo*, though, are both giant sea monster stories, and directed by Eugène Lourié, who had directed *The Beast from 20,000 Fathoms*. Now, if the core of our argument is how the *kaijū* film has been appropriated, it's difficult to make this case here. These films relate directly to the origins of the genre, so, while they might have transformed in the wake of the release of *Godzilla, King of the Monsters!*, it's hard to see the film originating from 'borrowed' material. Lourié's authorship essentially protects the films from such an accusation. Like Honda, Lourié is one of the key architects of the *kaijū* film.[4] *Behemoth* is largely a retread of *The Beast*. The director referred to it as a 'second edition' (Lourié 1985, 242). Radiation leads to the death of a Cornish fisherman along with that of many tons of fish. As the fisherman dies, he utters a creature's name. After a similar event on a farm in Essex, it's surmised the creature will head for London, which, of course, it does. Famous landmarks are destroyed, until the monster falls from Tower Bridge into the Thames. *Gorgo* also concludes with a rampage in London that smashes well-known tourist sites (Figure 5.1). The plot, modelled on *King Kong*, has a salvage boat encountering a mythic monster, 'Orga, the sea spirit'. The unscrupulous captain captures the monster and then sells it to a circus in London; they name it Gorgo, a shortening of 'gorgon'. Eventually, Gorgo's mother arrives to save its offspring, smashing across London with the military unable to stop it, before it's able to reunite with the child and return to the sea. Gorgo's narrative strongly prefigures the plot of *Gappa*, where it's a baby *kaijū* that is captured, experimented upon and exhibited before parents come to the rescue. This helps us emphasise further lines of cultural flow, where localised ideas move from country to country, are remodelled and adapted, before moving on to further distribution.

Ian Conrich has explored how these films draw on factors common to many British horror films of the time where 'remote coastal and island communities' are threatened at the outset, before the action moves to the metropolis for its main spectacle: 'these close-knit communities, with their customs and regional language (in *Gorgo* the villagers speak

**Figure 5.1** Gorgo revisits a London landmark familiar from the inception of the *kaijū* film (Blair & Associates)

Gaelic to exclude the strangers), functioned as rustic, hermetic and distant places in the fantasies of the many British film companies based in cosmopolitan London' (Conrich 1999, 91). When Professor Bickford and Steve Karnes from the Atomic Energy Commission first meet the Cornish fishermen in *Behemoth*, the men are standoffish and suspicious of the city folk, although more open once they determine that the city types aren't from the press. The film has direct reflections of *Gojira*, given the origins of the monster along the shore of a remote community and the impact on fishing (it's on the beach rather than just at sea, though), and in Karnes' lecture that opens the film, one attending scientist draws comparisons with incidents in Japan where 'boatloads of fish' were destroyed by atomic testing. It seems an obvious reference to the *Daigo Fukuryū Maru* incident that motivated the plot of the Japanese film, a key point of cultural exchange between the films.

Conrich does connect these films (which he calls 'colossal creature' rather than *kaijū* films) with the *Quatermass* ones but notes that Britain had only been 'threatened sporadically' before the late 1950s (1999, 88). These exploitation films, he argues, were products of a crisis of hegemony in Britain, motivated by the Second World War and the decline of the British Empire. The scenes of destruction and devastation in London are reminiscent of images from the war: as Conrich argues, 'the British films recycle the audio and visual signifiers of the trauma of the Blitz' (97). The monsters' destruction of both mundane and famous sights in London echoes previous *kaijū* films, where identifiable landmarks are recreated in miniature only to be spectacularly destroyed, their moment in the sun brief, cameos to delight the audience (this book has already mentioned several, from Japanese and South Korean films, seemingly created in irony or as political commentary). British films' development of *kaijū* motifs, like other examples, fit with contemporary discourses or crises, representations of previous traumas or fantasies about the restoration of national ascendancy. The employment of British scientific and military ingenuity or power is actually celebrated in the films. Whereas the Japan Self-Defense Forces were repeatedly presented as pathetically unable to stand up to the threat of the giant monsters, British forces mobilised here are a powerful reflection of the state's strength: 'Britain under threat is still protected by the powers of an immutable state. Regardless of the period's crisis of hegemony, the Britain of the films depends on and trusts authority' (97). Britain was a waning superpower in the aftermath of the Second World War. The imperial power was in decline, and, as Conrich notes, the Suez crisis of 1956 had shown an impotent British state – something that is fantastically overcome in the narratives of both films, where the British military are empowered, despite being unable to overcome the monsters in *Gorgo*. *Behemoth* reflects both Blitz-era imagery and the collective spirit of swift military action (Figure 5.2). After the monster attacks the Woolwich ferry, the army is deployed, and we see scenes of calm evacuations with complicit and unpanicked citizens before a short montage of shots of empty streets. One shot appears to depict the area of Vauxhall and its gasholder near the Oval cricket ground; it shows a deserted residential street that already echoes the remaining scars of the Second World War bombings. Once the monster comes ashore, however, panic ensues and the radiation emanating from it leaves soldiers burned and charred in shots that echo images of bodies from Hiroshima, an event referenced earlier in the film.

This short-lived cycle of British *kaijū* production raises some questions about the place of *kaijū* films in British culture. These two films have strong connections with the distributors who brought *kaijū* films to Britain in the late 1950s. *Behemoth* was initially developed by Eros Films (American Film Institute 2019). Eros were a small independent distributor run by Phil and Sid Hyams, two former cinema operators whose company was reportedly a helpful contact when larger distributors were unwilling to work with producers (McFarlane and Slide 2014, 233). Kevin Heffernan describes Eros as a 'specialist in imports, quote program features, youth pictures, and X-Certificate horror films such as *The Trollenberg Terror* and *Fiend without a Face* (both 1958)' (Heffernan

**Figure 5.2** A still-Blitz-scarred London is attacked by the Giant Behemoth (Warner Bros.)

2017, 116–17). In 1956, Eros had released the X-rated *Godzilla, King of the Monsters!* (in a double bill with the previously unseen Universal horror *House of Dracula* [Erle C. Kenton, 1945]) and later released *Gigantis, the Fire Monster* (with a child-friendlier A-rating, alongside the less appropriate Italian film *The Nights of Lucrecia Borgia* [as *Nights of Temptation*, Sergio Grieco, 1959]). Eros also released *Half Human* in British cinemas, alongside *The Man Without a Body* (Charles Saunders, W. Lee Wilder, 1958).[5] As Heffernan describes it, the Eros slate was largely in line with American exploitation producers' formula for sensational marketing and X-certification to promote films, as television began to eat into cinema's audience (Johnston 2014). Eros submitted the film to the BBFC twice – as the British Board of Film Classification's (2021) records show: it was submitted in January 1959 and received an X-certificate, only to be reclassified four days later as an A when trimmed by two minutes and retitled *Behemoth the Sea Monster*. The film would become regarded as a 'quickie horror movie' noted for its Willis O'Brien-produced special effects (albeit on a low budget), but remains largely a remake of *The Beast from 20,000 Fathoms*, which even Lourié described as 'plagiarizing myself' (Lourié 1985, 242), from the concept to plotting and even the design of the monster.

Gorgo meanwhile was originally intended to destroy Australia. Maurice King, according to one of the film's producers, complained 'there are no monuments in Australia, and besides, who cares if a monster destroys Australia?' Instead, they switched focus to Paris, since no massive monster film had ever destroyed the City of Light, unlike Tokyo or New York. Because of an English source of funding, the target switched to London (Warren 2017).[6] Maurice and his brothers, Herman and Frank, were Jewish American New Yorkers, originally Kozinsky, who built their California business, after numerous menial jobs, through their ownership of over 19,000 slot machines. They reportedly entered the film industry to spite Cecil B. DeMille after a deal had gone badly. From 1941 onwards, they produced and distributed a series of films, many of which were produced with blacklisted personnel (including *Gorgo*, co-written by Daniel James, who had also worked on *Behemoth* with Lourié). The King brothers had a reputation for being difficult, and this alienated many big-name stars and producers, who refused to work with them. But they were also savvy marketers and would name racehorses after their soon-to-be-released films (García 2019, 100–1). Like Eros, King Brothers had form releasing *kaijū* films, having produced an Americanised version of *Rodan* that was especially successful on its initial release by DCA. Sensing an opportunity, the brothers produced their own, approaching Lourié. The director tried to take the film in a different, more humanist direction than his previous monster movies, endeavouring to avoid scenes of carnage and to let the monster survive. Lourié got his wish for the latter, but the producers ensured plenty of destruction (Warren 2017). Unlike in *Behemoth*, where the monster is just seen walking around Westminster, *Gorgo*'s mother destroys a series of landmarks in the area: Big Ben and the Palace of Westminster, and Tower Bridge. Also, unlike Lourié's previous *kaijū* films, *Gorgo* utilised suitmation techniques rather than stop-motion, as a budget-saving measure (Warren 2017), but this helps connect the film more strongly with its Japanese contemporaries. Nevertheless, the film is largely an updating of the *King Kong* template, where a monster is snatched from its primitive locale (Nara [an anagram of the real Aran] Island is more rurally Othered than it is primitive) and taken to the big city, where chaos ensues. *Gorgo*'s twist, the entrance of the even bigger maternal monster, differentiates it from earlier films, as does the absence of atomic radiation, something that links most of the *kaijū* films that preceded it.

The King Brothers' involvement and Eros Film's production of *Behemoth* ensured a continuing trend for producer-distributors to entwine foreign and locally produced *kaijū* films. Exploitation or B-movie producers in both cases tested the terrain with successful distribution of reworked *kaijū* films before appropriating the material for their own productions. Into this mix we can also throw another European *kaijū* film, *Reptilicus*, a co-production between AIP and Danish studio Saga. Produced by Sidney Pink, through his deal with AIP, the film was shot in dual language versions, Pink directing the English version, and Poul Bang (brother to the Bang & Olufsen founder, Peter) the Danish. Unlike many previous dual language films, such as *Dracula* (Tod Browning/ George Melford, 1931), where cast and crew would alternate between day and night shifts, *Reptilicus* was shot alternately set-up by set-up (Warren 2017). This dual language process is largely unknown in *kaijū* films, with dubbing preferred (although the film also dubs its Danish cast). Nornes points out that multilanguage versions (MLVs) were largely a European phenomenon, with most early talkie MLVs produced in Germany. They were not common in the US, where accents were often an issue, but dubbing became a low-cost alternative to MLVs. Nornes also notes how dubbing was preferred by fascist governments in Spain, Italy and Germany in the 1930s as a means of standardising speech and as an insular method of naturalising films' language (Nornes 2007). In terms of its ability to translate genre and standardise formats, dubbing became a preference. Therefore, *Reptilicus* is unique, and highly transnational. The film also casts noted Danish stars, such as Dirch Passer, a famous comedian, who plays a janitor. The Danish version has more scenes featuring him than the American cut, including a musical interlude. Casts are slightly different in the two as well, with Bodil Miller playing Connie Miller, a UNESCO representative, in the Danish version while Marla Behrens plays the role in the American one.[7]

*Reptilicus* tells the story of a group of miners in Lapland who uncover a section of a frozen tail that regenerates into a giant serpent with wings (but all scenes of the monster flying were removed from the American version). Warren calls this perhaps 'the most unconvincing monster in the history of motion pictures', ludicrously vomiting 'green poison' (2017). The film has generally been perceived as one of the worst *kaijū* films ever made. In fact, AIP even refused to release Pink's original cut. Samuel Arkoff reportedly called it 'virtually unreleasable' (Craig 2019, 304), and sued Pink for non-performance of 'contracted production activities agreed upon' (Warren 2017). AIP dubbed the Danish performances in the film (which were already in English), and worked with screenwriter Ib Melchior to rework the film, including the removal of some special effects shots. While the film goes down in history as a risible example of the *kaijū* genre, its character as an MLV does make it stand out in this exploration of the transnational basis of the *kaijū* film. It reflects the growing trends for transnationalism and figures of globalisation across *kaijū* films at the time. It also continues to demonstrate how the work of distribution companies would appropriate global tropes, or memes, into their own production or co-production, and evidences further signs of cross-border flow and connections that are key to the form.

## Hollywood *Kaijū*

It is only relatively recently that *kaijū* films have been produced by Hollywood studios. It's important here that we continue to make distinctions between different sectors of the American film industry. Major Hollywood studios have been involved with the *kaijū* film: RKO, Warner Bros., Universal and Columbia are our most relevant examples. But then there are many independent and exploitation producers that have been responsible for production of what we can identify as *kaijū* films in American cinema. Apart from RKO's *King Kong*, Hollywood has produced relatively few identifiable *kaijū* films. *The Beast from 20,000 Fathoms* and *King Kong* (1976) were both produced independently,[8] but distributed by studios. Major Hollywood studios have produced dinosaur films, from 20th Century Fox's 1960 version of *The Lost World* (Irwin Allen) and the Hammer–Warner co-production *One Million Years B.C.* (Don Chaffey, 1966) to Warner's *The Valley of Gwangi* (which repurposed some models from the previous film). AIP's *The Land that Time Forgot* (Kevin Connor, 1974) was an exploitation adaptation. These regularly intersect with personnel associated with *kaijū* films, particularly Willis O'Brien and Ray Harryhausen, and adopt some elements of the nature/culture dichotomy that motivates many *kaijū* narratives. Like *King Kong*, they are generally expedition narratives, crossing a threshold into an Othered unknown space, where creatures lurk, and not all of the members of the expedition make their way back to civilisation.

Perhaps, as Barr has also noted, the most significant motivating factor for Hollywood production of *kaijū* films has been *Jurassic Park*. Spielberg's film foregrounds the classic spectacle associated with the *kaijū* film. The scene in which the protagonists encounter the Brachiosaurus for the first time is overtly structured to highlight acts of looking. Grant's (Sam Neill) first glimpse of the creature is more reaction than point of view. The camera quickly tracks in to him seated in the back of jeep; he clumsily takes off his hat, but the camera cuts closer to his face as he stands. He awkwardly struggles to remove his sunglasses. He moves his hand down and places it on Sattler's (Laura Dern) head, distracting her from a leaf, and turns her towards the same direction off screen. Her mouth drops open, agog, and she now stands to look at whatever is just off camera. It's only then that we cut to the reverse-shot of what they're looking at. The impact of the spectacle is performed by the two actors, an emotional cue for the audience to respond. But it's difficult to see it as a comfortable fit with the *kaijū* film, since the dinosaurs are more animalistic, less anthropomorphised than would be typical of Godzilla and their ilk. Core themes, such as fears of genetic engineering, good science vs. bad (capitalist) science and Promethean meddling with godlike powers ('life finds a way') do connect with *kaijū* films, especially the 1990s Mothra trilogy and 1989's *Godzilla vs. Biollante*. Such themes have a basis too in Shelley's *Frankenstein: or, The Modern Prometheus* (1818), which has also provided source material for *kaijū* films. They all connect with a contemporary zeitgeist around technology and environmentalism. In *Dinosaurs Ever Evolving: The Changing Face of Prehistoric Animals in Popular Culture* (2016), Allen A. Debus makes a distinction between dino-anthropomorphism, especially in *kaijū* films, and the 'traditional life-through-time paleoimagery' (9) that speaks to contemporary fears of modernity. While there is some overlap between the two, the dinosaur film and the *kaijū* film, as contemporaries, tread different pathways through spectacle, destruction and modern fears. Like the *kaijū* film, the dinosaur film is best described as a hybrid subgenre, connecting parts of the science-fiction and horror films.

Genres develop core themes and narrative templates that are open to hybridisation. Yet, as Joyce E. Boss argues, 'recognizable instances of hybridity – in characters, genres, texts, and such – call our attention to larger unresolved social issues involving identity and power' (2006, 104). She argues that distinctions of hybridity become useless unless they are rooted in discussions of identity and transnational power. All texts are hybrid to some degree. Producers don't work in a vacuum, and therefore adopt and adapt ideas from works around them. This has been an important element of our discussion so far. Given discussions of cultural appropriation throughout this chapter, distinctions of cultural power through co-optation and hybridisation are highly relevant. The local dimensions of genre production allow texts to 'speak to' concerns that matter to the people closest to the work and those affected by the circumstances that are discussed. Hollywood's development of a thread of production that integrates or reworks those concerns relies on its global power and ascendancy in most national cinema markets. Thus, notions of hybridity help to speak more directly to how Hollywood appropriated the *kaijū* film. *The Lost World: Jurassic Park* (1997), as its title suggests, evidences the co-optation of the *kaijū* formula into the franchise's structure. The final act of the film, when a male T. rex is brought to the mainland park in San Diego, reflects the narrative of the first giant-monster-on-the-loose film in 1925. While this demonstrates the influence of *The Lost World*, the presence of an injured infant T. rex that the male is motivated to rescue brings the film into proximity with *Gorgo* and *Gappa*, as does its happy ending, with the reunited family of dinosaurs back on the island. The arrival of the ship in San Diego, however, has shades of the *Demeter*'s arrival in Whitby in Stoker's *Dracula* (1897), with the crew all killed by the monster and the hull smashing into the docks. The T. rex as vampire in this instance conflates the threat of the ancient with the modern fears of rampant capitalism (almost overcoming the irony of New Hollywood blockbusters as rampant capitalism). In terms of cultural power, this example is less about the cultural origins of the material than the commercial impact. The year 1997 was one of Japan's strongest at the domestic box office, with Japanese films, led by *Princess Mononoke* (*Mononoke-hime*, Miyazaki Hayao), accounting for 41.5 per cent of the market (Motion Picture Producers Association of Japan 2021), despite the success of *Titanic*, which at the time was the highest-grossing film ever in Japan. What is significant here is less the global impact of a *Jurassic Park–kaijū* fusion than what its dino-mania inspired.

When *Jurassic Park* was released in 1993, work was already under way on an American version of *Godzilla* at Columbia Tristar. As meticulous research by Keith Aiken (2015) and Steve Ryfle (1998) has shown, the Columbia *Godzilla* was in development for a long time. In a deal originally brokered by Henry Saperstein of UPA, who had played a key role in licensing the monster in the US, Columbia bought remake rights from Tōhō, who provided a seventy-five-page memo documenting what could and couldn't be done with the monster (Aiken 2015). The film had a script written by Ted Elliott and Terry Rossio (later writers of the *Shrek* and *Pirates of the Caribbean* films), and producers had sounded out big-name directors to take it on. While the stalled project had signed Jan de Bont, best known for *Speed* (1994), up-and-coming German filmmaker Roland Emmerich, who eventually directed, had initially been approached to direct, but declined at that point: "'I was never a big Godzilla fan," acknowledged Emmerich. "They were just the weekend matinees you saw as a kid, like Hercules films and the really bad Italian westerns. You'd go with all your friends and just laugh'" (Aiken 2015). Emmerich's comments here highlight the association between *kaijū* films and exploitation cinema, aspects that were reportedly difficult for the film's producers to overcome, the cheesy and campy presentation of giant monsters from Japan having been created by the work of distributors, just as German and Italian exploitation producers and distributors have created waves of films in other genres.

*Jurassic Park* made dinosaur movies hot again. The closest a major Hollywood studio had come to producing a *kaijū* film by that time was *Clash of the Titans* (Desmond Davis, 1981), with the human-like Kraken, a sea creature from Norse myth that was previously depicted as a huge octopus, but given a more humanoid form by Harryhausen as a massive four-armed lizard. The 2010 remake (Louis Leterrier) ups the spectacle but retains the Harryhausen-style design of the monster. The Kraken found its way onto the poster as well, as a key selling point of the film's release.[9] But, in 1993, the conditions seemed right to develop an American Godzilla film, with name recognition ready for a market filled with pre-sold properties. Nike had also licensed the monster for their 'Godzilla vs. Charles Barkley' series of commercials, where Barkley challenged the rampaging *kaijū* to a game of one-on-one basketball.[10] The commercials helped return the monster to the public consciousness in the same way the Dr Pepper commercials had done in 1985. Tōhō's blessing extended to the production of a trailer that accompanied their own film,

*Godzilla vs. MechaGodzilla* (*Gojira tai Mekagojira*, known internationally as *Godzilla vs. MechaGodzilla 2*, Okawara Takao, 1993), promising 'Dynamic Hollywood Film Making' for the 'All New Godzilla American Version'. They even planned to retire their own Godzilla films after five entries in the *Heisei* series.[11] De Bont's *Godzilla* went deep into pre-production, the stage where filmmaking becomes more concrete. Monster designs and storyboards were produced, but the studio was worried about the cost of such an effects-heavy film (Aiken 2015). The project eventually passed to Emmerich and partner Dean Devlin, stepping back from their disparaging comments about the Japanese films, and on a roll from the enormously successful *Independence Day*. They set about redesigning the *kaijū*; 'animal, not monster' was their mantra (Aiken 2015), and the film had a massive blitz of publicity and merchandising tie-ins in the run-up to its release. Following the success of *Independence Day*'s famous White House-destroying Super Bowl commercial, *Godzilla* was spectacularly teased on prints of *Men in Black* (Barry Sonnenfeld, 1997). In the teaser, we visit the New York Natural History Museum, where a school group are being shown the 'colossal' T. rex fossil, and a list of its traits is read out. The building starts to shake, with booms, tremors and dust falling from the ceiling, until a giant lizard foot smashes through the roof and squashes the dinosaur (Figure 5.3). It moves away, the huge tail swishing across the gaping hole in the roof. 'Guess who's coming to town' the caption reads, as Godzilla's trademark roar sounds over the film's title. It's an obvious roast of *Jurassic Park*'s signature monster,

**Figure 5.3** Emmerich's monster makes a statement in the teaser trailer by crushing the puny T. rex from *Jurassic Park* (Sony)

but also a forerunner of the 'Size Does Matter' campaign (this was not the campaign for the Japanese market, which knew exactly how big the creature was already). The film itself says a great deal about cross-border co-optation and the ways in which globalised material demonstrates more traditional forms of Americanisation, despite its transnational crew, cast and material.

Emmerich's *Godzilla* was a major creative failure, returning a small profit, despite the scale of its marketing and wide release (3,310 screens in the US). As Aiken points out, the pre-release tracking in Japan suggested a hit on the scale of *Titanic* and *Princess Mononoke*. The film's release there mirrored the domestic release, beginning with a big weekend, but plummeted during the second week. It was replaced at the top of the box office by the first *Pokémon* film. Fans refused to acknowledge the creature as Godzilla – it was a sleek, fast-moving lizard, an iguana mutated by French nuclear tests. And far too easily destroyed. The creature is now known as GINO (Godzilla In Name Only), or Zilla (*jira*), as Tōhō re-copyrighted the monster once Sony's rights lapsed, and it featured in *Godzilla: Final Wars* (*Gojira Fainaru Uōzu*, Kitamura Ryuhei, 2004), the fiftieth-anniversary celebration film that brought together all of Tōhō's *kaijū*. Zilla fights the 'real' Godzilla in Sydney, only to be swiftly dumped onto the Opera House and obliterated by atomic fire (Emmerich and Devlin chose not to give their giant iguana atomic breath – it only breathes fire). The fight doesn't even last a minute. It's easy to read the sequence as a comment about appropriation and the negative consequences of overwriting 'the national' with globalised and jingoistic Americanism. But, as Aaron Kerner argues, the shift to a sleek, shiny body for Godzilla is problematic in its disconnection from Japanese trauma and the metaphorical Gojira, with its keloid scars indicating it as *hibakusha*. The suitmation style, for Kerner, is a necessary part of the national body in *Gojira*: the rubber suit's design is redolent in a way that the CGI monster is not. 'Gojira's "force"', Lerner mentions, is not just 'that which permits the monster to destroy an urban center, but rather as the emotional charge associated with working through trauma' (Lerner 2006, 117). It is a common criticism of transnational remakes that the remake 'overwrites' the national specificity of the original, appropriated text. However, '[t]he notion of an inherently Japanese text', as Smith and Verevis discuss in their collection on transnational remakes, has been exposed as 'itself problematic and somewhat essentialist' (2017, 2). Lines of cultural flow, as we've heard so far, are more complex, and producers are more open to adapting global ideas than simply those of the culture surrounding them. Much of this book has discussed more positive or collaborative modes of cultural exchange or borrowing that have led to new forms of expression through the colossal monsters in the *kaijū eiga*, yet the Emmerich *Godzilla* tends to demonstrate negative forms of cultural exchange, especially where the text appears to disparage its source material.

The interpolation of the monster into the American blockbuster situates it as more of a dinosaur film than a *kaijū* film, even though it attempts to reframe the origins of the Japanese series. Across 1995 and early 1996, France tested six nuclear devices in the South Pacific. While the Americans hadn't conducted nuclear testing since 1992, the legacy of the 1954 Castle Bravo tests is writ large across the Godzilla series. But, to update the series, Emmerich and Devlin make the French nuclear tests the source of the monster's mutation. This is confirmed right from the beginning of the film's opening titles, with footage of nuclear tests, signs in French, and the innocent iguana that will become the victim of the fallout. We therefore return to questions of 'whitewashing'. The sidestepping of American culpability in the creation of the monster echoes the argument about the same avoidance in *Godzilla, King of the Monsters!* It is the ascendancy of American military might that solves the problem here, rather than causes it. Whereas the *kaijū* film had generally seen decades of failures by the military to kill the cinematic beasts, the monster in Emmerich's iteration is surprisingly easily defeated, not once but twice, by the US military. At the film's midpoint Godzilla is presumed dead after being hit by several torpedoes from a submarine, and the monster is then killed at the end by the US Air Force after being trapped on the Brooklyn Bridge. New York is damaged and military vehicles blown up as the monster slithers its way around the city, but in the end, it doesn't take too much to kill the creature. This is quite a deviation from the core text of the *kaijū* film, where the military are often impotent to destroy the monsters (it normally takes other monsters to kill the monsters). The nature/civilisation dichotomy is usually tipped towards nature, because it is the hubris and promethean impulses of humanity that bring about the monsters. Chon Noriega's point about the internalised Otherness of the monster, at once both us and them in Japanese terms (Noriega 1987), simply doesn't translate into the Otherness of GINO. This beast is an Other from elsewhere, a signifier of foreignness that signals no return of the repressed, just a giant opponent to be returned to the depths. Its simplistic anti-nuclear message is projected outward, rather than simultaneously inward and outward. That said, the ending of the film, with the opening of the remaining egg in Madison Square Gardens, does echo Yamane's warning that others will come, but it's not framed within a statement about denuclearisation. With the ending of the Cold War, this argument was perhaps passé, and the triumphalism of *Independence Day*, itself a pastiche of 1950s alien invasion films, comes to the fore. Hence, the arguments surrounding Americanisation and appropriation homogenising cultural difference and threatening diversity are highly attractive in the case of this remake.

When approaching the film as a remake, however, it's important to contextualise how remakes are an acknowledged form of intertextuality. Texts are constructed through a range of strategies that recontextualise pre-existing material. In Chapter 1, *Gojira* was itself considered a remake of *The Beast from 20,000 Fathoms*, although framed via a Japanese cultural imaginary that reflected on (or exploited) national trauma. The accusation of cultural appropriation here is problematised further by Japanese victimhood expressed through the original film. Paradoxically, as the *kaijū* film becomes more global it becomes further associated with Japan. Thus, when the cultural power of Hollywood is articulated through such a form, it becomes problematic. However, we also must acknowledge that Emmerich's *Godzilla* is perhaps more a remake of *The Beast* than it is a remake of *Gojira*. The brand-name recognition of the monster and its official licensing from Tōhō aside, the narrative template is more reminiscent of Lourié's film than Honda's. A giant monster is roused by nuclear explosions. It attacks boats and heads directly to New York. It rampages through the city causing huge damage. Attempts to kill the monster fail, until it's trapped in a famous landmark and destroyed. Such a simple narrative outline perhaps fits many *kaijū* films, but Emmerich's version, which was significantly different from the one De Bont developed, evokes the memory of *The Beast*, the creature just as animalistic as the Rhedosaurus. Its proximity to *Jurassic Park* is also inescapable. Once Godzilla has been defeated for the first time, the action switches to the stadium, where the main characters encounter dozens of Godzilla's babies hatching from eggs. It's impossible to watch without thinking about the Velociraptor sequences of Spielberg's films, or of a familiar science-fiction film like *Aliens* (James Cameron, 1986), where the threat is less about the scale of the monster than their volume. While *kaijū* films haven't been averse to junior monsters, from Gorgo to Gappa, and even to younger Godzillas, Miniya and Godzilla Junior,[12] the spectacle is qualitatively different in these scenes from conventional *kaijū* films. The blending of different sources emphasises the intertextual web or references in the films, only one of which is *Gojira*.

*Godzilla* is highly typical of transnational Hollywood films of the late twentieth/early twenty-first century. Shaw's overview of transnational emphases (2013b) highlights several relevant aspects for our purposes here. Drawing on Andrew Higson's problematisation of national cinema constructs, Shaw responds to his comments about the 'leaky borders' of transnational cinema that challenges the essentialism of national cinema effects, and 'injects meaning into [the] emerging field' (2013b, 51). While no longer an emerging discipline, transnational cinema studies has established a vocabulary for discussing how cultural formations straddle borders and boundaries. Shaw's terminological intervention, a development from the editorial that launched the *Transnational Cinema* (now *Screens*) journal (Shaw and De La Garza 2010, De La Garza, Doughty and Shaw 2019), helps us discuss how films like *Godzilla* develop along transnational lines, as well as how they engage with transnational cultural meaning. Firstly, *Godzilla* is a film undoubtedly enabled by transnational capital relating to production, distribution and exhibition. Shaw notes that this 'assume[s] hegemonic power structures that favour Hollywood's domination of many film markets' (52–3). While Hollywood is generally not considered to be an American national cinema, Shaw's assumption is partly enabled through an awareness of Hollywood's transnational ownership and capitalisation, partly a consequence of its dominance in international markets. *Godzilla* was produced by Columbia Tristar, a combined entity owned by Sony, the Japanese technology producer (the company has been known simply as Sony Pictures Entertainment Motion Picture Group since 2013). Sony's deal with Tōhō to license the character for the film (and its spin-off animated series) also relies on cross-border trade and finance.

Border crossing is explicit in the film as one that takes place across 'multiple locations', where locations 'are used for their narrative potential rather than to make serious social commentary' (55). Although the film was generally shot across the United States, from Hawaii to New York, the monster travels from French Polynesia via Panama and Jamaica, where giant footprints and skin samples turn up. After the scuttling of a Japanese cannery ship, the survivors are taken to Tahiti, where the French secret service question them. There's also a short sequence set near Chernobyl. But, in line with Shaw's comments, these aren't used in a way that critiques the impact of nuclear testing on local communities; they are backdrops for the growing enigma around the monster and its journey to America. The film was also produced by a transnational cast and crew, 'physical embodiments of cultural exchange' (60), with a German director (Emmerich) and French star Jean Reno. The Japanese characters in the film are mostly played by Asian-American actors of a range of different ethnicities: Japanese-American Lloyd Kino (formerly

Kinoshita), Chinese-American Al Leong and Hawaiian Clyde Kusatsu, as well as Japanese actor Masaya Katô. This is a problematic inclusion in the film, the impact on the Japanese ship harking back to the opening of *Gojira*, but there's little sensitivity in the casting. The scene plays a key narrative role, when the sole survivor is asked by Reno's mysterious secret service operative what he saw: 'Gojira'. When the tape of the revelation is leaked to aspiring journalist Audrey (Maria Pitillo), it is broadcast by Charles Caiman, the unscrupulous and abusive anchor for whom she works (Harry Shearer),[13] who mishears the name as 'Godzilla'. 'It's Gojira, you moron!' Audrey screams at the TV across a crowded bar. The translation is a clumsy justification of the transliterated name. Naming the creature in this way is ironic, with the American stupidly mishearing, but it also evokes some of the politics of cultural exchange in which the American appropriation renames and reclassifies 'the thing' without reverence for the source. It seems a signifier of a more literal Americanisation alongside what takes place within the film.

*Godzilla* (1998) highlights negative impacts of globalisation and transnationalism. As Hollywood becomes more transnational (of which more in the next chapter), there is a greater engagement with themes of border crossing as well as the impact of transnational capital, not just in the *kaijū* film but more broadly. In her book on Hollywood remakes of French films, Lucy Mazdon challenges the essentialist national assumption of the perceived inferiority of remakes of classic French art films. She argues that the relationship between remake and original demonstrates 'the varying forms of exchange and interaction which identify the remake process'. Whereas reception can often prioritise notions of the 'national' as a core concept, 'tropes of intertextuality and the hybrid nature of the products of an increasingly globalised cinema industry undermine national identities' (Mazdon 2000, 67). *Godzilla* exhibits some of the concepts of exchange that challenge the essentialism of the original in translation, where those aspects are interpolated into a more globalised framework. While this often leads to 'condemnation of the remake as an act of violence against the "national" culture' (88), the either/or isn't always so simple. Emmerich's film attempts to retain some 'Japaneseness' (the opening attack on the cannery ship and the old Japanese man's naming of the monster), yet cultural exchange places tropes into an ongoing cycle of borrowing, adaptation and recycling, in and out of different national contexts. *Godzilla* is perhaps better thought of as a signifier of transnational intertextuality than as a remake (as the 2014 film of the same name might also be considered): an adaptation that engages with culturally specific aspects of the text.

Emmerich's *Godzilla* didn't necessarily create a wave of new *kaijū* films from Hollywood. Sony's rights to the property lapsed, while Tōhō rebooted their franchise in Japan. Subsequent spectacle-laden blockbusters have engaged with giant monsters, although sporadically in the first decade of the twenty-first century. As transmedia franchises became the flavour of the moment, *kaijū* films searched for their place in that market. As we'll see in the next chapter, 2014's *Godzilla* took time to develop from the boom for East Asian film remakes during the noughties. *Cloverfield*, as Steffen Hantke has argued, 'signals more clearly than any other film of its kind a return to the films that, in retrospect, have come to define American science-fiction and horror cinema during the 1950s' (2010, 239). Hantke argues that *Cloverfield* sidesteps the camp and irony that had marked earlier blockbusters nostalgic for the classic mid-century science-fiction creature feature, with 'the dropping of the hip hyper-ironic pose that looks back at 1950s science-fiction and sees only camp' (238). *Cloverfield* also reframes the traumatic origins of the *kaijū* film, this time born of the horror of 11 September 2001. For Hantke, the film is pure allegory, on a sublime level: 'In opting for the use of the giant creature premise, *Cloverfield* assumes that, in a manner of speaking, everybody "always already knows what happened on 9/11"' (247). As many contemporary reviewers and scholars have noted, *Cloverfield* is an overt metaphor for the events of 9/11, shot in a style that emphasises the citizen journalism that marked, accidentally, so much of the coverage of the attacks. In this way, *Cloverfield* avoids the tongue-in-cheek tone of *Godzilla*, and cuts through the disreputable perception of *kaijū* films. It is serious in tone and relies more on the generic elements of horror that are often less central to *kaijū* films than their family-friendly science-fiction. The film was released at the time of popular found footage films, following in the wake of *The Last Broadcast* (Stefan Avalos and Lance Weiler, 1998), the monstrously successful *The Blair Witch Project* (Daniel Myrick and Eduardo Sánchez, 1999), *The Last Horror Movie* (Julian Richards, 2005) and *Paranormal Activity* (Oren Peli, 2007). As Steven Pile has commented, Cloverfield 'looked like *Blair Witch* meets *Godzilla*, set in New York' (Pile 2011, 289).

According to J. J. Abrams, the film's producer, *Cloverfield* was conceived during a visit to Japan while promoting another film. He said he visited a toy store full of Godzilla toys and thought, 'We need our own monster.' The inspiration was explicitly to adapt the *kaijū* formula for American audiences: 'King Kong is just adorable and Godzilla is a charming monster. I love Godzilla but I wanted something that was just insane and intense' (Movies Online 2008). *Cloverfield* restages *kaijū*-related trauma within an American framework. It opens with blank titles, white on black: 'Document #USGX-8810-B467/Digital SD Card/Multiple Sightings of Case Designate/"Cloverfield"'. On the next, 'Camera Retrieved at Incident Site "US-447"/Area Formerly Known As "Central Park"'. The slides are watermarked 'Property of the U.S. Government/Do Not Duplicate'. There is a rolling time code at the bottom. This signifies both the inevitability of the traumatic destruction of a New York landmark and the 'foundness' of the footage, an artefact and document of the monster's rampage. The story follows Rob (Michael Stahl-David) as he prepares to leave for Japan (a clear generic connection) to take up a new job. Initial footage on the SD card is of Rob waking up with Beth (Odette Yustman) in her father's upper Midtown apartment. We see them enjoying a day out together across New York and Coney Island. We cut back to this repeatedly throughout the film. The bulk of the film takes place on a single evening; Rob's brother is throwing a surprise party for him. Hud (T. J. Miller) is tasked with recording testimonials for Rob, thereby justifying the rolling camera during the attack. Rob and Beth argue – it's clear some time has passed since the earlier scenes on the card – and she leaves with her date. The party is then interrupted by a supposed earthquake and power cut. The TV reports an attack on a boat near Liberty Island (another recurring generic narrative point) before explosions and debris can be seen outside the apartment's windows. This is perhaps the first point of confluence with citizen journalism from 9/11, the accidental filming of the first plane striking the North Tower, and reactions to the event. Video such as this played repeatedly on television across the reporting of the events. The partygoers head outside and find panic. The head of the Statue of Liberty smashes down the street around them before they witness the Woolworth Building collapse. Waves of dust flood the streets, and Rob, Jason, Jason's girlfriend Lily (Jessica Lucas) and Marlena (Lizzy Caplan), along with the ever-filming Hud, attempt to take shelter in a nearby bodega. Again, this forms a point of familiarity from footage of 9/11, the collapse of the buildings sending clouds of dust throughout lower Manhattan, and the video testimonials from witnesses of the dust blocking the light outside windows. The group then try to evacuate the island, across the Brooklyn Bridge, but it's destroyed by the monster's tail, killing Jason. Rob learns of Beth's survival, but she's trapped in the apartment we saw at the beginning. The group head against the evacuation to rescue her, finding themselves amid the military's battle with the creature (in some sense the overall story is like that of Emmerich's *Godzilla*, but we witness the events through the lens of ordinary citizens rather than politicians, the military and their advisors). They try to bypass the fighting by going into the subway, but they're attacked by the smaller creatures that have fallen from the monster. Marlena is bitten, becomes ill and eventually explodes while the military try to treat her. Rob, Lily and Hud are then able to pass into Midtown while the army prep their bombing of the creature in 'Operation Hammer Down'. It provides a time lock for the final act, with just fifteen minutes to rescue Beth. They find her in the apartment building, crossing from the skyscraper next door, which has toppled against it. Although she's injured, they take her to the evacuation point. Lily leaves unharmed in the first helicopter, but the rest of the group are pulled down by the creature after it reaches out of the debris and hits their helicopter as it takes off. Our protagonists survive. Hud finds the camera, but the monster kills him. Rob and Beth take shelter under a bridge while the final act of the bombing destroys the city. They make their peace before being buried in rubble to the sounds of the monster's screams.

With its lower budget (approximately $30 million) and innovative viral marketing campaign, *Cloverfield* provides something of a corrective to the bloated *Godzilla*. By staging the events at the level of the ground, rather than with the focus on the display of rampage and destruction, the film is much more concerned with reflecting personal trauma. While the monster metaphorically evokes the 9/11 attack, the found footage format foregrounds the realism of the impact of the events. The highly mobile handheld frame means the monster attacks tend to be seen as snippets rather than lingering spectacle. As Pile notes:

> The camera's ability to see is drastically limited by the ability of the person holding the camera to work it. The ability is not simply technical, it is also experiential: people's perception and comprehension lag behind the unfolding events, and the camera lags behind the people. These lessons *Cloverfield* learned from 9/11. They were not the only ones. (Pile 2011, 292)

Neil McRobert refers to it as 'the definitive post-9/11 horror film' for its depictions of 'the horror of the real' and continuity with the epistemological concerns of gothic texts (2015, 146). Emanuelle Wessels, however, is much more critical of this, mentioning that *Cloverfield* 'incorporated the aesthetic of 9/11 footage, as well as the practices and actions of those who documented it, into a mainstream, commercial motion picture' (Wessels 2011, 77–8). Along with its lack of diversity (with the exception of Jessica Lucas, most of the main cast are white, and we see African-Americans looting a drug store during the attack), Wessels is critical of the exploitation of the events in a major Hollywood motion picture: 'What do you think? Is it another terrorist attack?' one character asks. Emmerich's *Godzilla* had suggested that the monster's destruction is the worst attack in the city since the 1993 bombing of the World Trade Centre, when a group of Islamic terrorists detonated a van full of explosives in one of the underground parking garages, killing six people. In *Cloverfield*, there's no direct comparison, just the inevitability of the attack, while the *mise en scène* reminds viewers of the reporting from the day. Pile has noted how reception of the film praised the effects and tension, but often emphasised its exploitative metaphorical references to 9/11 (it must be 'tasteless or dumb', in Pile's conclusion [2011, 298]). This is not unlike the reception of *Gojira* in 1954, in which the proximity of the film to trauma was a regular criticism. For Pile, this emphasises the uncanny nature of *Cloverfield*, in Freudian terms; that is, its ability to evoke a return of past repressions that transfer into compulsions to repeat. Clover's monstrous metaphor makes it a 'pure' expression of the *kaijū* genre – it has elements of science-fiction (in the film's final moments, we return to a happy instant in the video, and see a tiny speck splash into the water in the background) blended with horror (the found footage style and the smaller monsters that attack in the sewers). That it evokes the obsessions with trauma and disaster noted by Sontag (2009) and Napier (1993) make it a clear example of how transnational genres can hybridise local and global, the endless cycle of creolisation described by Altman (1999).

*Cloverfield*'s sequels were much less concerned with the *kaijū* elements of the story than with the universe the first film furnished. The first sequel, *10 Cloverfield Lane* (Dan Trachtenberg, 2016), is more of a conventional horror film, in the vein of *Misery* (Rob Reiner, 1990). We get a sense that the monster attacks have become more widespread. Our protagonist, Michelle (Mary Elizabeth Wanstead), escapes New Orleans, only to find herself taken hostage by Howard (John Goodman). Howard tells her the air outside is poisoned and that they must remain underground, where there is a third resident, Emmet (John Gallagher Jr). Howard becomes more controlling, and it's apparent he's not as benign as he seemed and may have run Michelle's car off the road to imprison her. She eventually escapes to find the air clean, but an alien spacecraft hovering outside. The *Cloverfield* sequel had initially developed from a script entitled *The Cellar*, which took place outside the Cloververse. *10 Cloverfield Lane* was shot in secret before being revealed as a sequel to *Cloverfield* (Sullivan 2016). The sequel evolves the universe of the first film but doesn't really feature much in the way of *kaijū* action. The third film (directed by Julius Onah) was revealed during the 2018 Super

Bowl and released directly to Netflix. The Cloverfield Paradox of the title is the impact of a particle accelerator that opens portals to parallel universes and ultimately leads to the incident at the end of the first film, when a capsule from a space station lands in the sea, followed by a giant monster. It too developed from a spec script, entitled *The God Particle*, written by Oren Uziel, which was adapted to fit the Cloververse (Chitwood 2017) and provide some form of closure to the enigma of the first film. *Cloverfield*'s expanded universe also included an Augmented Reality Game that proved background for the film's events before these were developed in the third film. The ARG used several websites to cover the events of the monster's first attack at the Atlantic mining platform Chuai Station, owned by the Tagruato corporation. The events were framed through an activist group, TIDO Wave, whose blogs documented the events at the platform and a missing member of the group. Some of the events alongside the ARG were documented in a tie-in manga, *Cloverfield/KISHIN* (*Kurōbāfirudo/KISHIN*, 2008), released only in Japan on Kadokawa's website, and never officially translated (although it has been translated by fans). Of the Cloververse's transmediation, including the fan-prosumer competition to create mini-documents of their own, Wessels comments:

> *Cloverfield*'s spectators are hailed as active, labouring agents, working to tutor themselves in proper rituals of subject formation as an extension of the security apparatus, working to build a trans-media, trans-discursive bridge that extends the *Cloverfield* narrative by explicitly linking it to the 9/11 attacks while producing surplus value for the original media product. (Wessels 2011, 81)

Wessels' Marxist take on fandom's activity here illuminates part of the appeal of *Cloverfield* for fans: it is participatory, and the producers' playfulness in denying glimpses of coming entries to the film series feeds the anticipation around subsequent entries in the series. Extensions of the Cloververse, relying on multiple genres to supplement the underlying science-fiction conceit, play with nationally specific discourses. The existence of the Japan-only manga further teases fans denied access to the work in translation (again, fan labour fills the gap), but that it was Japanese further illuminates the relationships at play in cross-Pacific exchange between the US and Japan in the construction of a transnational genre.

Post-*Cloverfield*, a more socially conscious *kaijū* film emerges, engaging with other contemporary discourses in US society. Edwards' *Monsters* was a British production, backed by the independent company Vertigo Films. The director mentioned in interviews that, as a film student, he had fantasised about a *Jurassic Park* film that had taken place in suburbia. As the idea developed, it became a found footage film, but *Cloverfield* beat him to it. Then the release of *District 9* (Neill Blomkamp, 2009), a monster movie without the scope of a *kaijū* film, disrupted its development into a war film. Instead, it became set on the US–Mexican border (Lambie 2010). As an independent film, *Monsters* might be said to sit closer to other trends in indie film than to the *kaijū* film, especially given the background role played by the giant alien creatures in the film. With what has been termed 'smart cinema' by Jeffrey Sconce (2002) and Claire Perkins (2013), the film shares a sensibility with other independently produced films, where there is often a focus on post-youth cultures and '"adulthood" is not automatically achieved with age' (Perkins 2013, 9–10). In *Monsters*, this is shown in the infantilisation of the daughter of a rich industrialist and a photographer's struggles with his own fatherhood. The film is also a border narrative, concerning the journey undertaken by two individuals to reach the United States border, and (presumed) civilisation and freedom. One is the privileged daughter of a wealthy publisher, Sam (Whitney Able), whose father sends photojournalist Andrew (Scoot McNairy) to retrieve her after she's been injured during an alien attack. The aliens have arrived on Earth, we're told in the opening moments of the film, after a NASA probe encountered life in space and crash-landed in northern Mexico, creating a huge 'Infected Zone' where the American military have engaged the monsters in open warfare. Andrew must transport Sam back through the Infected Zone and cross the border into the United States. This is a journey undertaken by thousands of migrants every year in real life, and Edwards' film engages strongly with elements of filmmaking reminiscent of other border films, such as *Babel* (Alejandro González Iñárritu, 2006) and *Sin Nombre* (Cary Jôji Fukunaga, 2009) or *In This World* (Michael Winterbottom, 2002), a docudrama about two Afghan migrants attempting to cross Europe that Edwards cited as a key influence (Lambie 2010). We therefore find similarities between this monster film and the migrant border-crossing narratives described by Isolina Ballesteros in her book *Immigration Cinema in the New Europe*:

> the journey is determined by the characters' desperate need to reach the ultimate goal, and their movement across open space is curtailed by visible and invisible borders and thus not necessarily liberating, as it usually carries with it fears of being captured or deported, suffocating inside a vehicle, dehydrating in the desert, or drowning at sea, among other hazards. Border-crossing films are often adaptations of the outlaw road movie, in which characters are on the road out of necessity rather than choice; they are fugitives escaping from oppression, persecution, or

economic disadvantage whose liberation depends on the success of their flight, their survival, and their arrival at their destination. (Ballesteros 2015, 179)

Celestino Deleyto is unambiguous about the film's narrative in this regard: '*Monsters* is a border film: one in which the borderlands become the privileged space to meditate on people's place in our globalized world and on the urgency but also the ingrained ambiguities of a cosmopolitan ethics' (Deleyto 2020, 334). While *Monsters* doesn't focus on the place of the dispossessed in the Global South, the narrative allows a space for the two central characters to reflect on their own privilege as they become the ones threatened by their passage through the borderlands. Roger Luckhurst, who criticises the simplistic reading of the film as a metaphor for US imperialism, argues that the film 'explores a very different and very contemporary logic of the border, conceived not as a line to be transgressed, a boundary crossed, a self that is punctured or menaced by a monstrous other, but as a volume that weirdly expands, enfolds and entwines identities in a wholly new way' (Luckhurst 2020, 279). The Infected Zone is not imagined as a borderline or boundary to be crossed. Throughout the film we're encouraged to see it as a space. At one point we see the Zone on a map, a wide strip across the north of Mexico up to the Texas, California and Arizona borders. This becomes a liminal space for Sam and Andrew. When within the Infected Zone, Kirk Combe argues, '[Andrew] and Sam, after all, are *without* the hegemonic order' (Combe 2015, 1020). While outside, as a consequence of the American war with the aliens, Sam and Andrew have space to reflect on their own identities as privileged cosmopolitan border crossers.

As Deleyto points out, *Monsters* 'blends the realist, the documentary, and the analogic with the digital and the science-fictional' (Deleyto 2020, 327). Its largely handheld docudrama style is reminiscent of the film's influences. It opens with a familiar scene: a green-tinted night shoot-out between American forces and a huge monster. Part insect, part Cthulhu-style squid-tentacle monster, the creature looms high above a billboard. The troops locate male and female survivors of the attack and engage the creature. One of the soldiers hums 'Ride of the Valkyries' ('That's my theme song'), not only an obvious nod to *Apocalypse Now* (Francis Ford Coppola, 1979) and the triumphalism of Colonel Kilgore's surfing Calvary, but also an underlying reference to the film's source material, Joseph Conrad's 1899 novella *Heart of Darkness*, about a river journey into colonial Africa by an ivory trader. The intertextual connection foreshadows the dangerous riverboat journey undertaken by the protagonists in *Monsters*, heading into an imperially controlled zone.

The first parts of the film have a documentary feel: many scenes were improvised and, apart from the two American leads, roles were played by locals from the Latin American countries across which the film was shot. Andrew travels to a Mexican hospital, where he's been ordered to collect Sam (her father refers to her as his 'little girl' when he talks to her).We're not told what kind of publication her father is involved in, but Andrew explains that it will pay $50,000 for a picture of a child killed by an alien attack, but nothing for a happy one (he says he 'documents tragedy'). First, they travel by train to try to get to the coast, but the tracks are damaged. They then pay $5,000 each for tickets on a ferry to the coast, knowing that if they can't get out in forty-eight hours, they'll be stuck for six months. Andrew and Sam both have sad lives at home; Sam an unhappy relationship with her fiancé and Andrew with his ex and estranged son. As they pass through areas of Mexico towards the Infected Zone, they interact with locals: those who have been impacted by the war between the Americans and the aliens, the dispossessed individuals and children who bear the brunt of the cost of globalisation. Andrew plays football with some children in front of a giant mural depicting airstrikes on a monster. It begins to become clear that the monsters of the title are not the alien *kaijū*, but the foreign imperial force trying to fight the creatures.

Andrew and Sam begin to bond, and the film takes on dimensions of the romcom road movie, Deleyto (2020, 336–7) also notes, especially *It Happened One Night* (Frank Capra, 1934), another film in which a runaway heiress is taken on a journey by a cynical journalist. They enjoy a night of drinking together but are robbed after Andrew sleeps with a local, who takes their tickets, money and passports while Andrew and Sam argue outside. They find they have no option but to travel into the Infected Zone. The journey towards the Zone is structured through signposts that count down the distance; the signs suggest more danger the closer they get, with the need for gas masks. After they lose their tickets, they procure travel through the black market. Sam uses her engagement ring to pay the man who arranges their passage. Posing as aid workers (which Sam actually seems to be), they are smuggled into the Infected Zone. The armed guards transporting them tell them the creatures are generally benign, and that the attacks from the Americans make them mad. We see one creature in the river tussling with a downed fighter jet, taking no interest in the passing boat. The guards also explain the 'infection', showing the American pair luminescent growths on the trees that gestate the creature's young. The Infected Zone seems more like an arbitrary war zone than a source of disease and infestation. That the aliens were brought to Earth by a NASA probe is ironic – this isn't an invasion. The creatures are accidental visitors, peaceful until provoked. They are Other, but not the aggressive invaders the Americans portray them as. Deleyto suggests the creatures have a kinship with the dispossessed Mexican victims of the war: 'One would not be surprised if the monsters could speak Spanish, too' (Deleyto 2020, 335). But, after an accidental meeting with migrating creatures, the team guiding Andrew and Sam are killed, and Andrew has his chance to take the picture that would make him $50,000. He declines and covers the body of the deceased child, coming to see the war as more than his opportunity for fortune and glory, achieving empathy with those truly impacted by the colonial war being fought by the American troops.

Sam and Andrew finally make it to the border and see the Trumpesque wall from the top of a Mayan temple, a relic of a past civilisation, looking on at the most modern of structures. 'That's the biggest man-made structure I've ever seen', Andrew says. Stunned, Sam replies, 'It's like the seventh wonder.' *Monsters* was released six years before Trump's election, when much of the US–Mexico border was already a wall, yet this still seems prophetic when one looks back, especially in the context of discourses surrounding immigration in the preceding years. The two protagonists cross the border into Texas. The wall is open and the gate unguarded. They find the border towns destroyed, uninhabited but for a single, crazed old lady. The political metaphor is obvious: '*Monsters* envisions that equally inevitable moment when American homeland security finally fails, when our economic and cultural walls are breached', as Combe puts it (2015, 1012). The protagonists eventually reach a gas station, where they can find food and shelter. They relax and call their former partners. When a creature arrives, its tentacles stretch into the store and it appears to draw energy from the television, which is playing footage of the destruction in the country. Sam turns off the power and the creature leaves, before another arrives and the two seem to procreate, sharing the energy drawn from the TV. It forms an analogy with Sam and Andrew, who finally kiss. The creatures move away, their energy reacting with the clouds, triggering lightning. Just at this point, the cavalry arrives, humming 'Ride of the Valkyries', and we come to realise that the film has been non-linear, and the male and female from the start of the film were Sam and Andrew: thus, 'Sam comes to harm, and likely is killed, only when she arrives *back home*, that is, on the *American* side of the border. *Home* no longer *is* safe' (Combe 2015, 1026).

What's perhaps telling about these two low(er)-budget films is that they're much less concerned with 'monster smash' action, often having just glimpses of the monsters, than with the social echoes and metaphors of the impact on individuals. They take place from the ground up, rather than from above and zooming into the action underfoot. In so doing, the films engage more clearly with the politics of the transnational. The Infection Zone in *Monsters* becomes a threshold space for Sam and Andrew to experience the Otherness shared with monsters and the dispossessed people who live near or strive for the border. The space helps them deconstruct their identities as white middle- or upper-class individuals. As an infantilised woman, Sam is struggling with a literal form of patriarchy in the shape of her father, while Andrew presents himself as a cynical capitalist at the beginning of the film, there to document, nothing else. The creatures are innocent victims, their spectacle more sublime than destructive. As a *kaijū* film, it lacks the emphasis on destruction, although there is plenty, and the constant fighters overheard are a reminder of the war's ever-present threat and the ongoing surveillance of the border region. Throughout this book, we've considered how borders are leaky, culturally, politically and for people, and *Monsters* encapsulates those themes – the border isn't a neat line here, as Luckhurst also argues: 'It's an ever growing space, spanning different countries and drawing more and more people into its territory, by force or by accident.' Luckhurst says that these monsters are 'unreadable' and 'morph beyond the hermeneutic confidence inspired by the tool kit of monster theory' (2020, 286), but this has been core to the 'strange beasts' of the *kaijū* film. They are not conventionally gothic in this regard, and their existence as boundary crossers is less to do with the identity of the monster than with the zones they bring meaning to. Discourses of nation remain at the core of the giant monster film, their anxieties, worries and traumas, and *Monsters* is simply more conscious in critique, rather than straightforward allegory, of national anxieties. Its resonances with Trump-era immigration hysteria emphasise the colonial American fear of being Other at home, something the aliens bring with them, but something Americans have taken with them to other countries.

The *Monsters* sequel, *Dark Continent* (Tom Green, 2014), makes this even more explicit. It largely retreads the first film's themes about learning that the threat lies not with the conventional Other but closer to home. Its story follows a group of soldiers, all from deprived backgrounds in Detroit, who ship out to an Infected Zone in the Middle East. They are sent on a mission to recover a group of soldiers taken captive by a group of insurgents. In the course of events, the friends die one by one, never from contact with the creatures, and the main character comes to empathise with the local population. The film largely transplants the original into the war film, in a critical vein shared with *Three Kings* (Spike Jonze, 1999). Once more, it engages with American colonialism and its impact on dispossessed populations. The Infected Zone is again a space of transformation for the protagonist. Even when a gigantic monster emerges from underground in the final moments of the film, it's clear the monster is less of a threat than the foreign policy of the United States. If we frame this within a *kaijū* meme, it shows how the meme can be appropriated for critical purposes to engage with questions of foreign policy (it's telling these were British films made about America, rather than American films), and they bring transnational themes into focus through the adaptation of *kaijū* iconography.

One final film to mention here is Spanish director Nacho Vigalondo's *Colossal* (2016). This independently produced film tells the story of Gloria (Anne Hathaway), a young woman who discovers that she is in control of a giant reptilian monster that is causing havoc in Seoul. Gloria is a struggling writer whose alcohol abuse fuels her destructive behaviour. After a relationship breaks down and she's thrown out of her New York apartment, she's forced to move back in with her parents in New Hampshire. Her behaviour becomes more erratic as she falls back into old patterns at home. At the same time, the *kaijū* begins to attack Seoul in a seemingly unrelated occurrence. Gloria comes to realise that when she walks across a particular playground, the monster appears and she's able to control it. The main conflict in the film is between Gloria and her childhood friend, Oscar (Jason Sudeikis), a bar-owner whose offer of a bartending job enables Gloria's drinking. Oscar's manipulative toxic masculinity is the ultimate subject of the film, as his jealousy and rage at Gloria's escape from small-town life and relationships with other men fuel the *kaijū* battles in Seoul. A flashback shows us how Oscar, in a characteristic jealous fury, once destroyed Gloria's model of Seoul in the very playground from where she is able to manifest the *kaijū*. Oscar's own toy robot enables him to manifest as a giant robot and battle Gloria's Godzilla-like monster. She eventually travels to South Korea to make the *kaijū* appear in the playground at home and destroys Oscar while he projects his own automaton from there.

One review referred to *Colossal* as '*Pacific Rim* meets *Winter's Bone*' (De Semlyen 2017). It blends the interpersonal drama of the 'quirky' indie film with the spectacle of the *kaijū* film. While it doesn't explore traditional concepts of the *kaijū* film – it focuses on personal rather than shared national trauma – the appropriation of the *kaijū* meme is a highly conscious intertextual element in the film. So self-conscious was its borrowing that Tōhō sued the production company while they were attempting to finance the film (Siegemund-Broka 2015). Tōhō accused Vigalondo of attempting to produce an unauthorised Godzilla film, which later resulted in the film shifting the location for its *kaijū* scenes from Tokyo to another East Asian capital. The film is highly revealing of the flexibility of the *kaijū* meme as it uses the tropes of the giant monster film to create a metaphorical backdrop for the conflicts being played out in the realist world of the film. However, its border crossing is largely arbitrary, unlike the examples mentioned above, as a consequence of its intertextuality. As many reviews pointed out, it focuses on the very human dramas that are seen as secondary in the *kaijū* film. It stands out as an oddity in the transnational *kaijū* canon, a giant monster film in miniature that projects the massive emotions of its main characters onto the biggest canvas imaginable. *Kaijū* destruction becomes a metaphor for personal self-destruction and the harmful manipulations of toxic masculinity. In promoting the film, Hathaway and Sudeikis spoke about how the cast discussed men's rights activism, alt-right movements and Gamergate, the misogynistic campaign against women in the video games industry, to inform their characters. As Vigalondo phrased it, the 'men who act like monsters, they don't always look like monsters from the very beginning' (Buchanan 2016). In its engagement with gender in this way, it is perhaps the *kaijū* film that most exemplifies gothic tendencies to explore the monstrosity of identity.

## *Kaijū* Mockbusters

In the next chapter, we'll return to more recent films that draw on *kaijū* conventions, but for now I want to return to exploitation cycles. While Hollywood or major independent companies have embraced the *kaijū* film as a major source of spectacle, cycles of exploitation have continued to welcome giant monsters as a staple of their production cycles. A mockbuster, as described by M. Keith Booker, is a 'low-budget, quickly made knockoff of a major theatrical film that is expected to achieve blockbuster status' (Booker 2020, 293). Mockbusters form an extension of the exploitation market. Whereas classic exploitation markets capitalised on already successful films, such as the waves following the first *King Kong* and *Gojira* films, mockbusters tend to pre-empt the release of blockbuster films; in industrial terms, '"high-concept" pictures that will have "drafting opportunities,"'[for mockbusters to] play off bigger better-known movies in the marketplace' (Block 2015). The drafting metaphor is best considered through the analogy of a racing car sitting in the slipstream behind a faster car, dragged along. Mockbusters will generally capitalise on the known aspects of bigger films, such as titles, poster design and iconography. But the key aspect of the 'drafting opportunity' is to beat the bigger film to market, with a release date in the days running up to the release of the blockbuster that ensures the mockbuster benefits from the marketing of the bigger film. This therefore enables the mockbuster to appear as the bigger film, which gives it one of its biggest audiences: those who buy the film, often in supermarkets, by accident on DVD. Yet the films also attract cult audiences, ironically as 'so-bad-they're-good' films. The clean, TV and family-friendly nature of the films also attracts audiences put off by the salacious content of the big screen equivalent (TV Tropes n.d.). The Asylum, a major American producer of mockbusters, or 'off-brand B movies' (Katz 2013), has claimed never to have made a loss on a film. While *Battleship* (Peter Berg, 2012) grossed just $65 million domestically against a $200 million budget (and equivalent release costs), The Asylum's version, *American Warships* (Thunder Levin, 2012), reportedly doubled its investment on a £250,000 budget (Katz 2013). For The Asylum in particular, *kaijū* films have proven a sustainable part of their output: not just their mockbusters, but more traditional exploitation films, shark and monster films that capitalise on other existing tropes. A brief list demonstrates this: *King of the Lost World* was their version of *King Kong* (2005); *Monster* (2008) was a found footage film set in Tokyo released three days before *Cloverfield*; *Pacific Rim* became *Atlantic Rim* (2013); *Megalodon* was an obvious rip-off of *The Meg* (Jon Turtletaub, 2018); *Atlantic Rim*'s sequel was *Resurrection* rather than *Uprising*; *Monster Island* was released alongside *Godzilla: King of the Monsters*; *Godzilla vs. Kong* became *Ape vs. Monster*. As Ramon Lobato has argued, the production of such films calls into question the originality of genre tropes in the first place. While brand recognition draws attention to the studio ownership of property, the gleaning of such codes from genre challenges the proprietary claims of Hollywood studios. Furthermore, 'Hollywood has freely pilfered textual content from Asian cinemas whilst waging rhetorical war against copyright infringement' (2012, 81), and therefore further appropriation is problematised by Hollywood's borrowing of the material in the first place.

The Asylum are far from the first company to produce low-budget straight-to-video *kaijū* films. While they are perhaps the most successful, and most current, they follow from other companies. Full Moon Entertainment are the direct-to-video producer and distributor behind long-running series including *Puppet Master*, a series of fourteen films (1989–present) about demonic puppets, and *Trancers* (1984–2002), originated in Full Moon's previous incarnation as Empire Pictures. In the mid-to-late 1990s, Full Moon, under an imprint called Monster Island Entertainment, produced two *kaijū* films amongst the dino-mania that spawned Emmerich's *Godzilla* and the popularity of *Power Rangers*: the two were *Zarkorr! The Invader* (Michael Deak, Aaron Osborne, 1996) and *Kraa! The Sea Monster* (Aaron Osborne, Dave Parker, 1998). Both films have the conventional *kaijū* narrative structure, where a giant monster, controlled by alien invaders (echoing the *Power Rangers* influence), smashes buildings and rampages through a miniature environment (Figure 5.4) while 'ordinary' protagonists step up to destroy the monster. The films are obviously low-budget. The plots are borderline incoherent with a series of stock characters (such as the mad hacker in *Kraa!*), and visibly low-budget special effects with little interaction between actors and effects (aside from some compositing at the end of *Zarkorr!*). Perhaps most tellingly exploitational is a moment in *Kraa!* where we suddenly cut to a close-up of the logo from *Godzilla*. A wider shot reveals the billboard on the side of an apartment building. The monster smashes through the building and the logo, taking on Emmerich's film at its own game: size really does matter. What Full Moon's films

**Figure 5.4** *Kraa! The Sea Monster* takes aim at *Godzilla* (1998) as it rampages through a miniature city street (Full Moon Entertainment)

emphasise, in some regard, is the prominence of *kaijū* tropes circulating in American culture at the time, where giant monsters and alien invaders were at the forefront of blockbuster cultures. But these films also emphasise the disposable cultural value of the straight-to-video feature: as Lobato (2012, 36) points out, this 'is not a field of undiscovered gems, but the films' existence does help demonstrate the impact of distribution on demand for production, as a feedback loop.' The production of these and the later Asylum films helps bring into focus the cycles of western *kaijū* film production, from their place within, again in Lobato's terms, a 'shadow economy'. As *kaijū* memes circulate, parallel cycles of production develop alongside major Hollywood blockbusters. While the association between exploitation production and *kaijū eiga* is nothing new, the shadow cycles of the past quarter of a century, accelerating as Hollywood hastens its own production of *kaijū* films, highlights how waves of production and distribution contribute not just to the development of the genre's conventions and iconography, but more broadly how transnational cycles are supported and accelerated by mainstream and parallel production economies. However, this is generally at the expense of the smart nature of many *kaijū* film and their metaphorical engagement with social and political themes, either intentionally or through the absorption of the zeitgeist. There is little cultural worth in many mockbusters, hence their minor place in any cultural history of *kaijū* films. But they help to emphasise the continued transnationalisation of *kaijū* films, as cycles of distribution and production cement the strange beasts within the imaginary of western science-fiction monster films.

Mockbusters and cult exploitation films aren't simply representative of transnational trends in genre movies; they spring forth from transnational markets and resources. As Lobato describes, they 'are usually more likely to be made in [the] interstices of the global film economy, or to feature one location masquerading (often unsuccessfully) as another, or to feature an incoherent polyphony of accents and costumes' (2012, 24). *Monster Island*, for instance, was shot entirely in South Africa with a largely South African cast, aside from marquee stars Eric Roberts and Toshi Toda (after his small role in *Godzilla*). Fan favourite Robert Scott Field, a former Japan-based American baseball player whose place in *kaijū* history was secured with his role as Android M-11 in *Godzilla vs. King Ghidorah* (*Gojira vs. Kingu Gidorâ*, Ōmori Kazuki, 1991), also has a small voice-only role. In the film, the *kaijū* threaten the New Zealand coast, and it's up to the coastguard to save the day. Incoherent stock characters proliferate, including Roberts as a New Zealand Coast Guard officer, in a uniform displaying an Australian flag and with no attempt at a local accent. It fits Lobato's assessment of the straight-to-video format perfectly.

For companies like The Asylum, international distribution is central to their income, alongside television sales: 'Roughly half the money for every Asylum film budget comes from international sales – Europe, China, the Middle East – and those happen at the American Film Market. It's where independent producers like The Asylum gather to unload product on distributors from every country on earth' (Katz 2013). The American Film Market connects production with distribution, where works in progress and development packages raise production revenue through international sales. The prominence of China as a key market for The Asylum's films mirrors the development of the Hollywood *kaijū* film, as we'll see in the next chapter, as the growth of Hollywood's relationship with China has been instrumental in the recent development of this genre, also proving one of its most resilient markets for distribution. Exploitation markets therefore continue to play a key role in the globalisation of the *kaijū* film, in terms of both production and distribution. The mockbusters sit alongside more typical sharksploitation films and series such as *Sharknado* (2013–18), The Asylum's *Mega Shark* films (2009–15), *2-Headed Shark* and its sequels with increasing numbers of shark heads (2012–18) that continue to exploit giant monster tropes. The continuing shadow economy of exploitation films produces a sustainable market for giant monster and *kaijū* films that have capitalised on ongoing trends. As we've seen throughout this book, the exploitation sector has been instrumental in westernising *kaijū eiga*, with forms of localisation that encompass editing, dubbing and remaking, although in their adaptation of giant monsters they often hollow out the social and political dimensions of *kaijū* films that have produced their most enduring variants.

## Kongsploitation

I want to end this chapter by reflecting on perhaps the most sustained cycle of *kaijū* adaptation, often referred to as Kongsploitation. Just as the terms 'Jawsploitation' (Hunter 2009) and 'Brucesploitation' (Bowman 2019) reference respectively the success of *Jaws* and the gap left by the death of Bruce Lee, Kongsploitation imagines a single point of imitation. In many cases, this answers Erb's (2009) point about the uses of *King Kong* by a range of local and global producers. Giant ape films are at the root of the *kaijū eiga*. In many regards, *Gojira* is an example of Kongsploitaiton, probably the most famous outside of the two authorised remakes. However, while many of the films I've explored in this chapter have been giant lizard or dinosaur films, the Kong derivatives form a more widespread set of exploitation films, beginning globally more or less as soon as *King Kong* is released. They speak strongly to the globalisation of the *kaijū* film, long before globalisation was conceptualised.

The term 'Kongsploitation' has come into vogue recently. A quick Google search for the term will reveal a range of recent posts and discussions concerning Kongsploitation, including a Kaiju Transmissions Podcast on the subject (2017). However, previous discussions have used the term 'apesploitation' (Hunter 2005). Whatever term we use, the practice began as soon as *King Kong* was released. As John LeMay documents in *The Big Book of Japanese Giant Monster Movies: The Lost Films* (2019), when Shōchiku distributed *King Kong* in Japan, they released it with a supporting short directed by comedian Saito Torajiro. The film's title was *Wasei Kingu Kongu* (1933). *Wasei* (和製) generally references outside terms or language 'made Japanese', and the title of this film is normally *King Kong Made in Japan*. It reportedly concerns a simple story of a homeless man who, inspired by the success of *King Kong*, develops a stage act in which he destroys miniature props while dressed in an ape suit. The success of his own show enables him to marry his sweetheart, whose father opposes their union due to the man's low status. The film is generally considered lost (LeMay reports it lost in the Hiroshima bombing), but its standing as the first Japanese *kaijū* film is widely repeated online. Likewise, 1938's silent drama *The King Kong That Appeared in Edo* (*Edo ni Arawareta Kingu Kongu*, Kumagai Sōya), produced by Zensho Cinema, a low-budget producer, and released near to King Kong's re-release in Japan, is now a lost film. Reports about the film describe it as a *jidaigeki* in which a trained ape, named King Kong in the film's advertising, is used in a plot to kidnap the daughter of the film's main character. All that remains of the film's existence is a profile in *Kinema Junpō*. Posters for the film depicted the ape as a giant, but this doesn't translate into the film itself (LeMay 2019). Again, this demonstrates how distributors have played an active role in adapting cross-cultural material into local forms, with localised narratives and stars that translate global material. The films have remained in narratives about the *kaijū* film online, as well as works such as LeMay's. This helps point to some of the ways in which fans contribute to a generic canon. Despite the lost status of these two early films, they appear on lists of Japanese *kaijū* films. They exist as important stepping stones in transculturation. Films circulate across borders and are influential for producers, and these ideas become more local in dimension. We could see this as a form of colonial mimicry, or Americanisation, but as we've discussed repeatedly during this book, the role of producers in adapting global material is hugely significant in how transnational forms develop and how they interact with and entangle national and international discourses.

A quick survey of derivatives of *King Kong* produces a wide range of films. This would include not only *Gojira* but also the 'sequels' to the original film: *Son of Kong* (Ernest B. Schoedsack, 1933) and *Mighty Joe Young* (Schoedsack, 1949). *Mighty Joe Young* was remade in 1998 (Ron Underwood), the same year as Emmerich's *Godzilla*, at the height of one of the booms in production of giant monster movies. Scenes with giant apes also featured in 1948's *Lost World–King Kong* mash-up, *Unknown Island* (Jack Bernhard, 1948). Independently produced, it even includes a scene in which a giant gorilla fights a T. rex. The twentieth-anniversary re-release of the original spawned another wave of production, including not only Honda's variation on a theme but also *Half Human*, which undoubtedly trades on *Kong*'s narrative template of a trip into unknown primitive realms and the ape-like creature (it's not the only Kong variant that swaps a yeti for an ape). The British film *Konga* also obviously appropriates the Kong name, and focuses on another story of scientific hubris, in which Michael Gough's botanist character returns from a trip to 'Africa' (this film's Othered native space, its Skull Island or Japanese Alps). The crazed scientist discovers a serum that not only changes his chimpanzee into a gorilla, but also makes it grow to gigantic proportions. The growing ape becomes his assassin before it inevitably rampages through London. This film was another of AIP's runaway productions, co-financed and co-produced with Anglo-Amalgamated, who were able to retain distribution for British imperial locations (Heffernan 2004, 194). Konga also appeared in a series of comics written by Spider-Man co-creator Steve Ditko.

In the early 1960s, Indian company Eagle Films produced *Shikari* (Mohammed Hussain, 1963), a combination of *Kong* and *Dr Cyclops* (1940), both Schoedsack-directed films. *Shikari* is largely based on the narrative formula of *Kong*, in which a circus expedition sets out to capture a legendary monster. But they encounter a mad scientist, Dr Cyclops, whose experiments are attempting to turn village residents into gorillas. Cyclops promises the expedition the giant ape if they will allow him to marry the female member of the group. The giant gorilla eventually arrives to destroy the village, and dies chasing the expedition through the jungle. The film's reported underperformance at the Indian box office was down to one of the regular criticisms of *kaijū* films: too much focus on human characters and not enough on monster destruction (Mondal 2017).

American film *The Mighty Gorga* (David L. Hewitt, 1969) also builds on this meme, starting with the story of a circus owner who sets out to retrieve a giant ape from Africa. He disappears, so his daughter sets out to look for him. They encounter a sort of Lost World, and are attacked by a T. rex, which the ape fights off. They also come across a primitive culture whose people help them. But, this time, as with other variants on the Kong template, the ape doesn't come to the city, either dying in the wilderness or being left alone. Presumably for budget reasons.

De Laurentiis' remake of *King Kong* sent Kong rip-offs into overdrive, with American–South Korean co-production *A\*P\*E*, Japanese–Hong Kong collaboration *The Mighty Peking Man*, German–British softcore parody *Queen Kong*, Brazilian *Costinha e o King Mong* and the Italian–Canadian *Yeti: Giant of the 20th Century* all released in the year or so around the big-budget release. The following year saw French–Italian film *Bye Bye Monkey* (*Ciao Maschio*, Marco Ferreri, 1978), starring Gerard Depardieu and Marcelo Mastroianni, in which the body of a giant ape is found on a beach in New York with a live infant ape in its hand. Ferreri's film uses the *kaijū* iconography as background to explore bourgeois values within a dystopian New York. The film, whose title translates more literally as 'Goodbye Masculinity', tied for the Grand Prix at the 1978 Cannes Film Festival (with *The Shout* [Jerzy Skolimowski]). It challenges conventional gender stereotypes, with Depardieu's character mocked and belittled by the feminist theatre group for whom he works as a stagehand. Rumours abound online that the ape in the film is the body of King Kong, while even its IMDb synopsis calls it a 'corpse' (Internet Movie Database n.d.). When Mastroianni's Luigi, an artist, first lays eyes on the creature, he's struck by its beauty as a 'sculpture'. The film's *mise en scène* strikingly frames the ape in the foreground with the World Trade Center, the scene of the cinematic creature's demise, towering in the background. The ape becomes an absurd piece of detritus, as if left to rot on the beach by De Laurentiis' crew. Later in the film, only the head remains. The chimpanzee wrapped in its hand becomes Depardieu's son (named Cornelius, in reference to the character from *Planet of the Apes*), a means through which the film investigates masculinity. The baby Kong is eventually consumed by rats, while Depardieu's real son outlives him. As Hunter mentions regarding Jawsploitation, 'the meme is probably a useful metaphor' (Hunter 2009, 22), and this is largely the case here. Each of these films capitalises on the Kong meme, whether giant destructive apes or reinterpreting the Eighth Wonder of the World into a metaphysical object symbolising simulacra in a decaying postmodern culture.

Raphael refers to *King Kong* as a 'chronotope' (following Bakhtin), 'tied to social and economic crisis' (2016, 207). The mid-1970s films discussed here, and by Raphael, draw on the marginalised body of Kong, its 'instability' (209) and critique of power. Running throughout many of the films here, including the 1976 *Kong*, *A*P*E* and *Mighty Peking Man*, are anti-colonial threads that critique both military power (especially *Kong*) and colonial rule (in *Mighty Peking Man*). Raphael understands the most famous moment from *A*P*E*, in which the gorilla (obviously a man in an ape suit rampaging through unconvincing miniatures) gives the finger to the US military (Figure 5.5), in these terms. These are transnational productions, made using cross-border capital and personnel as well as cultural material, in which 'the chronotope of *King Kong* appears to have served, in times of local and national crisis, as spectacular refracted vision of trauma, a charged space in which disparate audiences might imagine, even if only temporarily, the possibility of resistance against power' (216). Perhaps apart from *Yeti*, which substitutes a giant prehistoric man for the ape, there is a distinct strain of anti-Americanism in the reworking of the *Kong* chronotope (or meme, depending on the terminology used).

Erb traces a similar lineage through the *Kong* meme 'as a story of "male trouble" in an effort to highlight the differences between men, as well as shifting historical constructions of masculinity, even within minority or subcultural groups'. Her exploration of camp and black

**Figure 5.5** The monster makes a pejorative statement about the US military in *A*P*E* (Kukje Movies/Lee Ming Film Co./Kino-Lorber)

appropriations (particularly parodies) of Kong, across a range of media, that 'extend forms of identification and desire to those minority viewers too often neglected by the mainstream cinema' (Erb 2009, 207–8) demonstrates the breadth of response to Kong's images of abjection and marginality in opposition to the conventional reading of the film as a racist fantasy. Likewise, Robert Stam and João Luiz Vieira have argued that *Costinha e o King Mong* uses parody as a tool to resist the oppression of neocolonialism, and that parody 'is well suited to the needs of the oppressed and powerless' because it uses 'the force of dominant discourse' contrary to its intended goals, to subvert that discourse rather than to imitate it and therefore to be dominated by it (1990, 84). Such critiques of Kongsploitation films demonstrate how the appropriation of *kaijū* memes has deeper resonances beyond their surface adoption of icons and tropes from the original film. *Kong* looms large over the *kaijū* film as the root of signifiers of crisis, from national trauma to marginalised genders, sexualities and ethnicities, as Raphael, Erb and Stam and Vieira have shown. Kongsploitation therefore need not be, and has not been, simply considered as a reflection of cultural appropriation or as exploitation cinema. As Hunter argues, the 'exploitation film that copies another film, as a short cut to establishing a relationship with an audience, is constrained to play a different intertextual game from a conventional adaptation' (Hunter 2009, 10). Read as a form of adaptation rather than appropriation (or mimicry), the reworking of *Kong*, as meme, chronotope or carnivalesque parody, resists seeing the giant ape's adaptations as simply 'bad Kongs'.

Nevertheless, Kongsploitation films have regularly been received as bad films. *A\*P\*E* occupies a position as perhaps the worst, for its terrible 3D effects, bad acting and poor general effects (especially the obvious toy cows that the ape steps over), although the film itself teeters on parody. A fan overview of *Kong* rip-offs refers to it as '[f]rom start to finish . . . utterly incompetent but never boring' (Roebuck 2020). This list also covers such shadow exploitation productions as *King Dong* (AKA *Lost on Adventure Island*, Yancey Hendrieth, 1984), a pornographic parody that prefigures *Kinky Kong* (John Bacchus, 2006), The Asylum's *King of the Lost World*, the mockbuster version of Peter Jackson's 2005 remake, and the Bangladeshi *Bangla King Kong* (Iftekhar Jahan, 2010), which another fan referred to as feeling 'like it was assembled from the ghosts of a hundred other movies and the dream of making one, a blockbuster version of King Kong unlike any seen before or since' (bandsaboutmovies 2021). Both fan responses allude to the cheap special effects and the implausible sight of the film's female lead singing to the deceased ape at the end. Like many transnational *Kong* adaptations, including *A\*P\*E*, *Bangla King Kong* falls into the 'so bad it's good' category, ongoing objects of fascination for *kaijū* fans that reflect trends in exploitation and genre production. But, as Iain Robert Smith has argued, there are problematic implications to the 'camp engagement' with Kongsploitation, especially by western viewers. 'It is dangerous', he argues:

> to simply treat this camp engagement with 'so bad it's good' cinema as harmless laughter at failed intention or to treat it 'objectively' as if these questions of cultural and ethnic power are not involved. We should keep in mind that these forms of accented cult cinema are shaped by a tension between celebration and mockery of cultural difference. (2019, 713)

While critics such as Erb, Raphael and Stam and Vieira might see such appropriations as positive interventions in cultural discourses, the Othering of such works by viewers and fans emphasises such a tension as Smith discusses here. Given the elements of spectacle at the core of *kaijū* cinema, the question of 'failed intention' and deviations from norms of Hollywood cinema, especially where Jackson's remake takes such a serious stance on the material (Allison 2011), are relevant. As an accented, in Hamid Naficy's terms (2001), cult cinema, such global appropriations of Kong point to problematic dimensions of reception, even where it might be possible to celebrate the resistant discourses of the films themselves. Such adaptations, to use Hunter's terms, help to demonstrate how intertextual reworking of memes combine national and global meaning in a range of ways when considering the exploitation of King Kong. And, with the exception of *Jaws*, no other genre film has spawned as much imitation or exploitation as *King Kong*.

Throughout this chapter, I've attempted to complicate aspects of cultural appropriation in the ways in which *kaijū* films have reworked, adapted or recycled elements of the *kaijū eiga*. Whether we refer to the underlying template as a meme, a chronotope or a discourse, the exploration of westernised *kaijū* media, including aspects of its reception, points to cultural appropriation as lying upon a spectrum. Some forms might be seen as harmful to local producers through the borrowing (or licensing) of national cinema or the ironic reception of imitative films, yet cultural borrowing or exchange, as we've explored throughout this book, can have alternative, shadowy impacts through continuity of generic discourse or resistance to conventional meanings. However, at its core, the *kaijū* film remains emblematic of the relationship between nationally specific cultural meaning and global concerns. As we move into the next chapter, this raises questions about transnational and global industries and their interrelationships. If a film such as video game adaptation *Rampage* represents the culmination of several cycles, with its giant albino gorilla (named George), huge mutated lizard (Lizzie) and monster wolf (Ralph) drawing on different cinematic *kaijū* icons, the big-budget cycle of *kaijū* films produced in the last decade helps us draw conclusions about flows of cultural power towards Hollywood and how the recent production of *kaijū* cinema demonstrates shifting power dynamics in the global film industry.

## Notes

1. This whole episode is an anime-inspired tale of Rick's obsessive attempts to possess every Gotron, a giant mecha combining five different animal robots. Some anime characters kidnap Morty and tell him they're the 'rightful owners' of the robots, 'in a cultural sense': 'What your grandpa did is called appropriation! Not cool, *heugh*!' The episode's title is an overt reference to *Neon Genesis Evangelion* (1995–6), the classic post-apocalyptic anime series about giant human-controlled robots that fight off invading 'Angels'.
2. The story fits into a cycle inspired by Kurosawa's *Seven Samurai*, in which Solo puts together a ragtag band of misfits (including a Don Quixote figure and giant rabbit) to protect the farmers from bandits (issues 8–10).
3. David Bordwell contends that art cinema usually postitions the author as a 'formal component' to determine who is speaking and what that individual is perceived to be trying to say (Bordwell 1999, 719).
4. Lourié was a cosmopolitan filmmaker. Born in Kharkiv, Ukraine, he was forced to flee the Soviet revolution, going to Turkey before reaching Paris in 1921. Most of his work in the film industry was as an assistant director and production designer. He worked with Jean Renoir on some of his most notable films of the 1930s, including *La Grande Illusion* (1937) and *La Règle du Jeu* (1939). He left Europe with Renoir and worked as an art director and designer on films including *The Diary of a Chambermaid* (Renoir, 1946) and *Limelight* (Charles Chaplin, 1952). He continued to work as an art director on his own films, and subsequently on several of Samuel Fuller's films, every episode of the TV show *Kung Fu* (1972–5) and *Krakatoa: East of Java* (Bernard L. Kowalski, 1968). He only directed four films, three of which were instrumental in the development of a transnational *kaijū* cinema. Lourié said his association with *kaijū* movies was 'an albatross around my own neck' which led to many offers to direct giant monster films, 'all of them unbelievably bad' (Lourié 1985, 241), and his autobiography includes a chapter focusing on *The Beast*, but only small references to the other two films.

5. *Monster from Green Hell* was released in a different double bill by Eros, with the Ray Harryhausen effects film *Earth vs. the Flying Saucers* (Fred F. Sears, 1956). For an overview of British releasing of *kaijū* films, see the fan-written article 'Monsters From An Unknown Culture: Godzilla (and friends) in Britain 1957–1980' by Sim Branaghan (2018).
6. In his autobiography, Lourié explains how the project was originally conceived as *Kuru Island* and took place in Tokyo. When the Japanese finance fell through, production moved to London (Lourié 1985, 242).
7. Miller was a rising star prior to *Reptilicus*, a Danish-born actor contracted by Universal, whose career was largely seen to be damaged by her involvement in the monster film, so bad was its reputation (Danish Film Institute n.d.). Behrens (whose name was Marlies rather than Marla) was a former Miss Germany who featured in a few films.
8. The latter's producer, Dino De Laurentiis, was even sued by two major studios after acquiring the remake rights from RKO.
9. Despite Legendary Entertainment being one of the film's producers, and despite the Harryhausen inspiration, the Kraken hasn't been adopted as *kaijū* by fans. On Wikizilla, the Kraken does appear, but not for its *kaijū*-style appearance in *Clash of the Titans*; instead it is there for appearances in *The King Kong Show* (itself closely related to *King Kong Escapes* and *Ebirah*) and as the name of one of the Titans in the novelisation of *Godzilla: King of the Monsters* (Wikizilla n.d.).
10. It was also adapted as a comic.
11. They eventually produced two more, leading to Godzilla's death in *Godzilla vs. Destroyah* [*Gojira tai Desutoroia*, Okawara, 1995], a demise that prepared the way for the monster to finally makes its Hollywood bow.
12. Godzilla Junior was first introduced in *Godzilla vs. MechaGodzilla 2* as *Bebīgojira* (Baby Godzilla), later growing up to replace the deceased Godzilla (*Shinsei Gojira*, Rebirth Godzilla).
13. Two decades pre-#MeToo, the scenes featuring the harassment of Audrey by Caiman are uncomfortable, played close to comedy and normalised in terms of what should be expected in a media industry workplace. Caiman is played as a comic villain but receives no significant retribution for his actions. Audrey is simply able to rise above it.

CHAPTER 6

# Legendary Monsters

The *kaijū eiga* saw a strong global renaissance during the second decade of the twenty-first century. Films like *Love and Monsters* (Michael Matthews, 2020), *Tremors: Shrieker Island* (Don Michael Paul, 2020), *Monster Hunter* (Paul W. S. Anderson, 2021), and *Notzilla* (Mitch Teemley, 2019) have all made the most of trends for giant monster films. This chapter, however, will focus on a cycle of transnational productions, including *Pacific Rim*, its sequel and *The Great Wall* (Zhang Yimou, 2016), that have helped to build global interest in giant monster spectacle. These films, along with the MonsterVerse series, encompassing *Godzilla* (2014), *Kong: Skull Island*, *Godzilla: King of the Monsters* and *Godzilla vs. Kong*, all have a shared production company: Legendary Entertainment. This chapter examines their attempt to create a Marvel-style shared universe for their monster films that resembles aspects of 1960s Tōhō films such as *King Kong vs. Godzilla*, *King Kong Escapes*, and the wider universe implied by the plethora of monsters resident on Monster Island. The manufacturing of a transnational genre in this regard is cyclical, from the sharing of monsters across national borders to the collaboration between Asian and American producers. However, the *kaijū* genre's breakthrough as a mainstream cinematic genre in the west is now more in keeping with modern blockbuster production tactics of transnational co-production, franchising and reliance on CGI spectacle. This chapter explores the networking of the narratives in the MonsterVerse, including its transmedia elements.

Furthermore, this chapter examines the globalising transnational strategies behind the creation of this wave of *kaijū* films. Legendary's deals with Universal and Warner Bros. strongly focused on the development of transmedia properties, alongside Legendary's access to transnational networks, particularly in Asia. The chapter takes a close look at Legendary, who were bought out by Dalian Wanda in 2016. Wanda are a major Chinese conglomerate with interests in property and tourism, and the owners of the world's largest chain of cinemas. The acquisition of Legendary is a major part of their convergent strategy. *The Great Wall* is an important text here, as a film reminiscent of previous transnational blockbusters, such as *Crouching Tiger, Hidden Dragon* (Ang Lee, 2000), with its *wuxia pian* (martial hero) setting crossed with the monster genre. Christina Klein said the earlier film muddied 'the distinction between Hollywood and "foreign" cinema' with 'aesthetic affiliations [that] cross multiple cultural boundaries' (2004, 37). This seems applicable to *The Great Wall* as another 'exemplary instance of transnational cinema', combining different East Asian genres with the casting of western stars. Consequently, the chapter argues that these are globalising tactics, along the lines of those defined by Mette Hjort (2010), to broaden the appeal of the films within and beyond Asian markets, co-ordinated across Legendary's output. There is also a crucial shift in the *kaijū eiga*, away from Japanese cultural influence towards state attempts to promote the growing prominence of Chinese soft power.

## Legendary Entertainment

Founded at the turn of the twenty-first century, Legendary have played a significant role in the development of contemporary transnational Hollywood. They began as an independent finance company, helping to fund and produce some of Hollywood's biggest hits: Christopher Nolan's *Dark Knight* trilogy (2005–12), *Inception* (2010) and the *Hangover* trilogy (2009–13). Partnerships with Warner Bros., and subsequently Universal, allowed the company to develop a slate of franchise movies. With the advent of several Chinese–American agreements, Legendary, and their subsidiary Legendary East, developed a series of films that had substantial appeal for Chinese audiences and secured both investment from Chinese studios and access to Chinese cinemas. Legendary's output often exhibits significant levels of transcultural blending, multicultural casting and, in Mette Hjort's (2010) terms, globalising and modernising transnationalism in accordance with Wanda's overarching company approach. Films such as *Pokémon Detective Pikachu* (Rob Letterman, 2019) and the MonsterVerse series help to demonstrate Legendary's films' attractiveness for both US and global markets, especially in China, where their films earn the bulk of their international box office (in the case of *Godzilla: King of the Monsters*, the figure was 20 per cent more than the domestic gross). Contemporary Hollywood mediates such flows of capital, culture and personnel evidenced both in terms of production and visibly onscreen.

Founded by Thomas Tull, a venture capitalist and comic book fan, Legendary made its first big splash in Hollywood when Warner Bros. announced that together they would co-produce films in 'marquee franchises' (McClintock 2005, 75), *Batman Begins* (Christopher Nolan, 2005) and *Superman Returns* (Bryan Singer, 2006). Tull was supported by a consortium of investors to the tune of half a billion dollars in 2004, including ABRY, Bank of America Capital Investors and AGI Direct Investments. Self-styled 'movie geek' Tull (McClintock 2005, 6) subsequently signed a seven-year deal with Warners to co-produce and co-finance up to forty films (Graser and Abrams 2011). Legendary took on half of the cost of films it co-financed, contributing a 10 per cent distribution fee to Warner Bros. and equal profit sharing (Robehmed 2016). Films produced under the deal were generally big-budget tentpole blockbusters with pre-sold audiences, including comic book adaptations *300* (Zack Snyder, 2006) and *Watchmen* (Zack Snyder, 2009), in addition to Nolan's continuing Batman trilogy (*The Dark Knight*, 2008, and *The Dark Knight Rises*, 2012) and building the DC Cinematic Universe with the Superman reboot *Man of Steel* (Zack Snyder, 2013). The company continued to experience major hits with tentpoles based on existing Warner-owned properties, such as *Inception* (Fleming 2009), quasi-*kaijū* remake *Clash of the Titans* and its sequel, *Wrath of the Titans* (Jonathan Liebesman, 2012). Comedy *The Hangover* (Todd Philips, 2009), which was produced from a spec script by Jon Lucas and Scott Moore that Warner acquired for $2 million and rushed into production before the 2007 Writers Guild of America strike (Garrett 2007), became a significant sleeper hit for the company.

This initial period in Legendary's history established them as a big-hitting Hollywood player, and elevated Tull to the upper echelons of executives. The company prospered by exploiting established properties and trends. As the company moved from finance to production, they faltered for the first time: the Jackie Robinson biopic *42* (Brian Helgeland, 2013)[1] was a moderate critical and commercial success, but Legendary experienced major failures with the Michael Mann-directed *Blackhat* (2015) alongside difficult production[2] *Seventh Son* (Sergei Bodrov, 2014). *Variety* reported that Legendary were pressed to write down the value of both films, diminishing their asset value by, respectively, $90 million (against a $70-million budget) and $85 million ($95-million budget) (Graser 2015). In June 2011, however, Tull announced a new wing of the company, Legendary East, a partnership between Legendary, Chinese studio Huayi Brothers and Kelvin Wu King Shiu, CEO of Hong Kong-based Orange Sky Golden Harvest (OSGH).[3] Established during a Sino-US co-production summit, Legendary East became one of the first Chinese investments in the American film industry; OSGH took a 3 per cent stake in Legendary (for $25 million, which valued the company at around $750 million in 2010). The co-CEO of Huayi Brothers, Wang Zhongjun, noted that the new entity would seek to produce 'wonderful movies with Asian themes and backgrounds'. Tull likewise called the films 'global movies' (Landreth 2011). Legendary East subsequently secured a deal with China Film Co. for around $10 million investment in *Seventh Son* and their *World of Warcraft* adaptation (Duncan Jones, 2016) (McNary 2014a). At the time, this was a breakthrough for both the global interests of Hollywood and the Chinese state. China Film Co., a division of China Film Group, essentially run Chinese cinema as a state-monopoly system. The Chinese market allows imports of just thirty-four foreign films a year. Given their Chinese partnership, Legendary East was able to bypass state control by assuming national film status for their output.

As Klein (2007) has argued, China Film Group and Huayi Brothers have both been influential in facilitating Chinese cinema's expansion into the global marketplace. In her article on Stephen Chow's *Kung Fu Hustle* (*Gongfu*, 2004), Klein demonstrates how the involvement of both companies aided Hong Kong cinema's viability after the 1997 handover to China led to declining film exports and a talent drain from the territory. The participation of the two mainland Chinese studios ensured that Chow's film was granted official Chinese national status, enabling it to circumvent the limits on film imports and navigating its way through state censorship. Klein argues this transformed Hong Kong's film industry, a national cinema without a nation, into a more transnational one: 'a marker of the Chinese film industry's efforts to transform itself from a state-run instrument of education and propaganda into a viable commercial industry' (Klein 2007, 202–3). This highlights multidirectional global flows: 'out of Hollywood (in the form of capital, mode of production, stylistic conventions) into Hong Kong; reverse flows out of Hong Kong . . . into the United States; and regional flows out of Hong Kong (in the form of its film workers and expertise) into China' (204). In the case of the formation of Legendary East, such flows have become more complex, involving movements of capital *into* Hollywood as well as between China and Hong Kong, and of content into China, since these two deals ensured Legendary gained access to the Chinese market in the same way as *Kung Fu Hustle*.

In January 2016, Wanda paid $3.5 billion for Legendary, a surprisingly high sum for a company that had backed a string of major hits but owned no significant intellectual property of their own. Legendary had co-produced or co-financed films in major franchises, including *Batman*, *Superman*, *Jurassic World* and *Godzilla*, but all related IP was owned by Warner Bros. or Universal, or licensed from other companies.[4] When *Forbes* reported on the buyout, the valuation was baffling:

> Disney paid $4.1 billion for Lucasfilm and the mighty Star Wars franchise and another $4 billion for Marvel and a character universe – the Hulk, Thor and Captain America – that collectively is the highest-grossing franchise of all time. What does Wang's $3.5 billion, which includes some $900 million in debt, buy him? . . . Legendary boasts about the content it owns, but there's no way Pacific Rim, along with a small horror movie and three disappointments, can almost equal the value of Star Wars. Not even close. (Robehmed 2016)

Wanda had taken over the AMC cinema chain for $2.6 billion in 2012 and possessed a development portfolio of over a hundred Wanda Plaza shopping and entertainment complexes in China. The Legendary deal meant they now owned one of the biggest stakes by a Chinese business in an American company. A 2015 *New York Times* exposé discovered deep-rooted associations between Wang Jianglin, Wanda's owner and Asia's richest person, and the Chinese Communist Party through ownership of shares by relatives and business associates of high-ranking officials; President Xi Jinping's sister was a major shareholder. The investigation stressed that Wanda's development might have less to do with smart investments (including the bizarre valuation for Legendary) than with state interests extending to the promotion of the nation's soft power on the global stage. A corporate entity like Disney might incidentally promote American soft power, but the Chinese state's intention seems to be geared towards the promotion of positive cultural images related to the country (Forsythe 2015). As the *New York Times* article alleges, this national strategy includes Wanda's media holdings and acquisitions. Besides their buyouts of AMC and Legendary, the company built the world's largest film studio in Qingdao, priced around $8 billion (Dalton 2018). In the words of a former Legendary investor, Wanda's ultimate goal is to become 'a global vertically integrated motion picture company' (Robehmed 2016). The development of facilities, ownership of cinemas and acquisition of a major global production and financing company would place Wanda in the same bracket as Hollywood studios prior to the 1948 Paramount decree. For Wanda, there are no state or legislative barriers to full vertical integration. Such stated intentions fit well with how Hjort describes globalising transnationalism, combining Hollywood production standards with content that blends aspects of national soft power. One of the first productions to shoot at the Qingdao studio complex was *The Great Wall*, its blend of Chinese genre, stars and international outlook tailored to transnational approaches to producing content that appeals to global audiences, while simultaneously promoting positive images of China.

## Marked/Unmarked Transnational Cinema

Transnational concepts envision flows of culture and capital positioned 'below-global/above-national' (Ďurovičová 2010, x) as well as ways in which contact zones help us to move 'beyond any tendency to reduce the centers and peripheries of present-day capitalism to the past familiar binary of cultural imperialism' (Newman 2010, 9). Flows are unequal and continue to demonstrate 'the persistent agency of the state' (Ďurovičová 2010, x). Hjort argues,

> [a]s transnationalism becomes part of the becoming and being of filmmakers, as a core ontological feature, new and important voices become part of the conversation of World Cinema. Far from being a symptom of monocultural convergence linked to the putative imposition of a single (western) standard of filmmaking, the ontological transnationalism of the filmmaker helps to make World Cinema a rich and diverse phenomenon. (Hjort 2019, 65)

Hjort's comment here problematises our conception of a transnational cinema. The 'rich and diverse' voices at the centre of her proposition about transnational solidarity, based on her research with talent development organisation Filmlab Palestine, sit within 'bi- or multi-directional flows' that attempt to ensure the development of transnational networks that might be overwhelmed or hidden by 'uni-directional' flows of people and money. For the purposes of our discussion here we are perhaps less concerned with peripheral or marginal cinemas (Iordanova, Martin-Jones and Vidal 2010), yet cross-border flows remain fundamental to how transnationalism is conceived in relation to our discussion of business conducted across borders and its relationship with representation. The concept of monocultural convergence with standards of filmmaking in the west (for which Hollywood is metonymic) raises challenging questions regarding the increasing prominence of Sino-Hollywood collaboration, as many US-based production and finance companies work to gain access to Chinese markets while, conversely, Chinese companies are looking to invest in Hollywood production. Such transnational connections allow us to examine not only the changing landscape of the contemporary film industry, but also how those relationships are represented textually as film production seeks to diversify its audience and its income streams.

In her earlier, now seminal, article, 'On the Plurality of Cinematic Transnationalisms' (2010), Hjort examines multiple definitions of transnationalism, arguing that the concept of the transnational can become 'shorthand for a series of assumptions about the networked and globalized realities that are those of a contemporary situation', playing 'a strangely homogenizing role'. As she has also discussed more recently, transnationalism is a pluralistic notion, conceptualised (as it had been by Appadurai) along multiple lines of flow, leading to a range of belongings and 'values, some of which are economic, artistic, cultural, social, or political' (2010, 30). Hjort gives us several major taxonomic classes. The first is a binary between marked and unmarked transnationalisms. Films become marked as transnational whenever they resemble 'properties that encourage thinking about transnationality'. Alternatively, 'unmarked' transnational cinema projects generally come into being through cross-border co-operation, often co-production, but their onscreen content is generally more conventionally culturally national (14). Andrew Higson's notion of 'culturally English' cinema is similar: films might be produced by capital and personnel from a range of nations, but tell stories rooted in a single cultural context (2011). Unmarked transnational films are generally financed by international money, and feature multinational casts and crew, but, especially in the case of Hollywood films, their content tends towards notions of 'universality'. For instance, a Legendary film like *Enola Holmes* (Harry Bradbeer, 2020), produced following their Wanda buyout, is very weakly marked as a transnational film. Produced through Legendary alongside star Millie Bobby Brown's PCMA Productions, the film was globally released by Netflix, except in China (Kit 2020). Although it is a product of transnational financing, it features a largely British cast and crew, adapts Sherlock Holmes for a contemporary audience and therefore does not 'encourage thinking about transnationality'. It is, in Higson's terms, culturally English, despite its international origins and distribution. The flows that produced and distributed the film are therefore not significantly evidenced in it. Legendary's *kaijū* films have tended to be more marked in nature, given they evidence not just transnational production but onscreen aspects of cultural exchange, as we'll come to later.

In addition to the marked/unmarked distinction, Hjort identified nine aspects of transnational production: epiphanic; affinitive; milieu-building; opportunistic; cosmopolitan; globalising; auteurist;

modernising; and experimental. The first two are perhaps self-evident, in that they reveal (as an epiphany) shared cross-border belongings (Hjort's work is rooted in Scandinavian cinema and the shared sense of belonging for people from the region's different nations) and affinity, where kinships are revealed despite national differences. Perhaps most relevant for the discussion here are opportunistic, milieu-building, globalising and modernising transnationalisms. Opportunistic and milieu-building transnationalisms refer to two sides of the same coin: opportunistic seeks to capitalise on fortuitous financial conditions on a production-by-production basis, whereas milieu-building involves the creation of sustainable connections between (often marginal) film industries. Hollywood's push towards Sino-US co-production, exploiting the sizeable Chinese market and its projected future growth, does suggest opportunism, just as Hollywood have exploited favourable conditions in other countries through tax breaks, for instance in the United Kingdom or India. But Hollywood is often not specifically interested in developing sustainable employment in those countries or regions (moving on once the tax breaks are removed). However, inward and outward investment between Hollywood and China suggests a growing milieu involving the two countries, and sometimes this means controversies caused by those relationships will be overlooked.[5]

## *Pacific Rim*

Even though it was a pre-Wanda Legendary film, *Pacific Rim* begins to engage with several critical threads through which we can understand the period of Legendary Monsters as symptomatic of several globalising trends. The film presents a clear blending of overt references to *kaijū eiga* built upon Guillermo del Toro's own fandom of Japanese monster movies (Figure 6.1). He explained to *Collider* that the history of *kaijū* films and his own 'enmeshed' engagement with the genre were channelled into the fabric of the film:

> The great thing with the Kaiju genre is that you have your crustacean Kaiju, you have your reptilian Kaiju, you have your insectoid Kaiju. I mean there's room for so much and the idea behind the movie, the idea of how the kaijus [*sic*] were created and why, and how specific they are, makes each monster be completely different. Kaiju, a lot of their character comes defined by the way they look. The Kaiju are almost living weapons, so when you see a Kaiju you know what it does, Hedorah, or if you see Baragon, its [*sic*] echoing a specific type of function, dragon like, or Hedorah looks exactly like what it is, like a giant trash amoeba from outer space [laughs] (Weintraub 2013)

**Figure 6.1** A brief intro to *Pacific Rim* includes a short insert of a Japanese-style TV show (Legendary/Universal)

The references to *kaijū* traditions in the film were meant to be more than a 'postmodern reflection', substituting a different East Asian metropolis, Hong Kong, for Tokyo, to sidestep the 'wink-wink nudge-nudge' moment (Gilchrist 2013). Nevertheless, the borrowing of *kaijū* tropes was obvious when the film was released. *Variety*'s review, noting the risk of 'a non-franchise property, rooted in the Japanese Kaiju tradition that spawned Godzilla among other legends', described it as 'a crushed-metal orgy that plays like an extended 3D episode of "Mighty Morphin Power Rangers" on very expensive acid' (Chang 2013). Its initial release was seen as something of an underperformance, domestic gross only just breaking $100 million, but with a substantially stronger international box office performance, roughly three times that in North America (Box Office Mojo 2021e). This has come to be one of the defining trends of Legendary's monster films. Each has seen an imbalance between domestic and international performance in favour of audiences outside the US and Canada (whereas many major blockbusters are often 50/50 in terms of the domestic/international split). This partly reflects why each film has built upon global and transcultural forms of content and co-operation.

*Pacific Rim* was a thoroughly transnational film helmed by a director whose voice Deborah Shaw has described as 'large, ambitious, and always transnational' (Shaw 2013a, 20). Niamh Thornton has also explored the film's transnationalism, via what she describes as the director's 'geek auteurism':

> Del Toro draws upon shared fields, such as monster movies, which are easily accessible and have their own distinctive geek following, but he also brings his own blend of culturally specific and transnational references that are there as nods to a multiplicity of fellow geeks and nongeeks alike. (Thornton 2014, 137)

Likewise, Keith McDonald and Roger Clark (2014) have contended that del Toro's work should be viewed through lenses of accented cinema, given their use of multiple voices, trauma and separation on top of the director's blend of transnational influences and collaborators. Like many of del Toro's films, *Pacific Rim* straddles multiple national borders in terms of its production and its text. Its cast consisted of actors from Britain (Charlie Hunman, Idris Elba, Burn Gorman), Canada (Diego Klattenhoff, the Chinese-Vietnamese-descended Luu brothers), the US (Ron Perlman, Max Martini), Japan (Rinko Kikuchi) and Spain (Santiago Segura), and it was shot predominantly in Canada. Its story, put simply, is about cross-border co-operation, a ragtag group of soldiers from multiple countries fighting to tackle an outside threat to global safety. As Thornton also argues: 'It is about an international collective. It isn't another film about "America vs. the World"' (Thornton 2014, 137). Based in a 'Shatterdome' in Hong Kong (a base housing giant robots), a cluster of American, Russian, Chinese, Japanese and British personnel fight off space monsters from 'The Breach', an inter-dimensional portal in the depths of the Pacific Ocean. The monsters are referred to as 'kaiju'. As del Toro's comments stress, the creatures draw on *kaijū* lore and his own fandom of *tokusatsu* media. Some of the *kaijū* refer explicitly to creatures in Japanese films. For instance, Knifehead,[6] a huge bipedal creature with an extended sword-like nose, closely resembles the design of Guiron, the antagonist from *Gamera vs. Guiron* (*Gamera Tai Daikaijū Guiron*, Yuasa Noriaki, 1969). Knifehead is one of the first *kaijū* seen in the film, when the protagonist and his brother fight the creature in Alaska.

The story's heart focuses on Jaeger pilot Raleigh Becket (Hunman). Becket and his brother Yancy (Klattenhoff) pilot the Jaeger Gipsy Danger. The Jaegers are colossal humanoid robots in which the pilots' consciousnesses are fused to together, their two brains each controlling one side of the mecha. The concept of mecha, a term not specifically used in the film, although regularly in discourse surrounding it, stems from another Japanese genre, which included series such as *Robotech*

(1985), *Voltron* (1984), *Neon Genesis Evangelion* (*Shin Seiki Evangerion*, 1995–6) and *Gundam* (2000). Rayna Denison has noted how the mecha genre, initially closely related to *shōnen* (young boys) genres, became one of Japan's most successful media imports (Denison 2015). This has led to more mainstream adoption of the term, albeit in different contexts. Steven Spielberg's *A.I. Artificial Intelligence* (2001) used the term 'mecha' to describe its robot characters. Spielberg's adaptation of Ernest Cline's novel *Ready Player One* (2018) also included mecha, specifically the RX-78-2 Gundam, which takes on MechaGodzilla in the climactic showdown, a further point of *kaijū*-related Hollywood borrowing.[7]

*Pacific Rim* capitalises more directly upon aspects of mecha series, especially *Evangelion*, which tells a similar story about giant robot pilots. The Jaegers, named after the German word for 'Hunter', are called upon regularly to fight off the *kaijū* as they emerge from The Breach. At the film's outset, Gipsy Danger fights off Knifehead, but the monster destroys the Jaeger and kills Yancy. Raleigh, plagued by guilt, leaves the pilot programme to wallow in his existential crisis. In the meantime, the war goes badly, the Jaeger programme is defunded, and the remaining personnel relocate to Hong Kong under the command of Stacker Pentecost (Elba). Pentecost is running out of options, with just a few remaining Jaegers under different international commands (US, Russian, Chinese and Australian). He brings Raleigh back to the programme and pairs him with Mako Mori (Kikuchi), Pentecost's adopted daughter whom he rescued from a *kaijū* attack on Tokyo (we see this when she gets lost in the memory while first 'drifting' with Raleigh). After they discover The Breach will only open for *kaijū* DNA, the pilots are able to work together, overcoming their respective family issues, to detonate a nuclear device inside The Breach and close it.

The film's themes are not particularly complex. As del Toro put it: 'Either we get along or we die' (Russo 2013). Del Toro's utopian message is clear: humanity must put aside difference in order to co-operate and survive. Those who put profit above human interests, such as the black-market trader Hannibal Chau (played by del Toro regular Perlman), succumb under such a theme. After a major *kaijū* attack on Hong Kong, Chau is killed when he attempts to harvest the monster's secondary brain and a baby *kaijū* bursts from its mother to devour him, leaving only one of his trademark shoes. Just as Thornton argued, this image of collaboration, across intersectional lines of gender, nationality and ethnicity, is at the core of the film's themes. Yet it wasn't without controversy: an officer from China's People's Liberation Army accused the film of importing propaganda: 'The decisive battle against the monsters was deliberately set in the South China Sea adjacent to Hong Kong . . . The intention was to demonstrate the U.S. commitment to maintaining stability in the Asia-Pacific area and saving mankind' (Coonan 2013). There is perhaps some credibility in such a commentary, given the film's American leads (even though they're mostly played by Brits), but the film's vision of a collaborative future between BRIC (Brazil, Russia, India, China) and adjacent countries (not just the US, but also Australia) envisages a shift in geopolitical relationships.

*Pacific Rim* is a further example of Jenkins' pop cosmopolitanism (2004). The use of *kaijū* as a loanword, as well as the design of the monsters across the extended universe of the films and transmedia spin-offs, make Legendary's series another instance of corporate hybridity. As Thornton summarises, del Toro's own pop cosmopolitanism extends to a wide range of cultural texts, not just the *kaijū* and mecha genres, but also:

> Anton Chekhov's play *The Cherry Orchard* (1904), German romantic artist Casper David Friedrich, sports movies, westerns and action films, anime and other comic book tropes and techniques, fairy tales (in particular with reference to Mako's childhood scenes), Mexican wrestling films, Zoltan Korda's *Jungle Book* (1942), the *Thunderbirds* television series (1965–66), pantomime, Jules Verne's *10,000 Leagues under the Sea* (1870), and Mexican soap operas. (Thornton 2014, 124)

The breadth of borrowings and appropriations of such a range of cultural material, as we've seen, is at the core of the *kaijū* film. It is fundamentally a genre that highlights cross-border flow. Del Toro's own role as *kaijū* fan was foregrounded in the promotion of the film, which was also initially teased at Comicon 2012 alongside Legendary's forthcoming *Godzilla* film, released the year after *Pacific Rim*. His own standing as an exilic and accented filmmaker importantly contributes to how such borrowing is seen more broadly. The film's introduction of the word *kaijū* to a wider audience, as a loanword, adopts a key Japanese signifier of the genre into an English-speaking idiom (it's also used in The Asylum's *Monster Island*, but not in the MonsterVerse series). This wasn't necessarily seen as a universal positive, as a sign of the genre's elevation beyond marginal, exploitative or fan-focused viewing. An article on Film School Rejects, entitled 'How "Pacific Rim" Got Kaiju Wrong', spells out the argument for such borrowing as more negative cultural appropriation. '*Pacific Rim* really screwed up the kaiju', it begins (Sargent 2013). Sargent argues that *kaijū* are 'an important archetype in 20th Century Japanese storytelling' and that calling the monsters in del Toro's films by the Japanese word is 'borderline offensive'. The article references the foundations of the genre, in the trauma of post-nuclear devastation and in the fallout from irresponsible US testing at Bikini Atoll. Sargent argues that the anti-Americanism of the original metaphor in *Gojira* is undermined by *Pacific Rim*'s appropriation (of a word not specifically used to reference Tōhō's movies until later). Such an argument essentialises the motif of the giant monster, itself one borrowed and indigenised repeatedly, in ways we've investigated again and again throughout this book. The question here is about cultural power, on the basis that the Hollywood machine can take and use elements from perceptiby less powerful industries and that such corporate hybridity tramples on 'smaller' cultures. But when we consider how such a transnational film is not a simple ode to American power, the borrowing of a culturally specific term such as *kaijū* can be seen, in Jamie Sexton's terms, as an exoticisation of the original text. Sexton argues that such impulses can reflect a sense of 'cultural superiority' in the cult viewer, to 'exoticize all types of "foreign" culture" in a superficial manner'. For Sexton, the 'otherness residing in these films is considered exotic as it is a marked feature of texts that appeals to cult consumers looking for something different from the mainstream' (Sexton 2016, 9). Del Toro's mainstreaming of the term *kaijū* de-exoticizes the term within the mainstream, and, as Sexton draws on Smith's notion of 'cult cosmopolitanism' (2014) to suggest, that may help bring viewers to the original texts to which such a reading applies. Del Toro's own cult cosmopolitanism is writ large across the text, in the broad range of references listed by Thornton (which she has drawn from the DVD's audio commentary by the director himself), but the film's engagement with transnational tropes and the cultural exchange evidenced in the text is at the heart of its appeal. The film's success in international markets, and relative failure in the US market, are perhaps symptomatic of its corporate hybridity or cult/pop cosmopolitanism, whichever term we use, and the literacy of viewers (which is also alluded to in Sargent's response to the film) is relied upon heavily in such cases. Very few *kaijū* films, from Hollywood or elsewhere, have crossed over at the North American box office, but they have proven successful, especially for Legendary, with international audiences. Hence, the international success of *Pacific Rim*, particularly with Chinese audiences, contributed to the unusual market valuation of Legendary, since the film and its extended universe were its only established IP. Therefore its success globally helped lay the groundwork for Chinese takeover and subsequent productions like *The Great Wall* and the *Pacific Rim* sequel, *Uprising*.

## *The Great Wall*

I've discussed elsewhere how *The Great Wall* was a 'trans-culturally designed' film (Rawle 2021). Coming around the time of the first hook-up between Legendary and Wanda, it was described by Mac Sullivan in *Film Criticism* as 'a new template of formulaic, stamped for approval, Sino-Hollywood co-productions' (Sullivan 2017). Like *Pacific Rim*, it's a film that focuses on cross-border travel and collaboration. It's about two European mercenaries, the Irish William Garin (played by Matt Damon) and Spanish Pero Tovar (Pedro Pascal), travelling in eleventh-century Song Dynasty China. Close to the Great Wall, the pair are attacked by a monster and captured by the Nameless Order. The group, we find, are taxed with battling Tao Tie, monsters that attack every sixty years. Led by Commander Lin (Jing Tian) and Strategist Wang (Andy Lau), the Order stoically defy the monsters' raids. Garin and Tovar plan a break with Sir Ballard (Willem Dafoe), another imprisoned European earning his keep teaching English, but instead work with the Order in their fight against the monsters. The Europeans abandon their pursuit of 'black powder' possessed by the Order, ensuring that individualist goals are set aside to support the collective common good. The film appears explicitly calculated to appeal to global and especially Chinese markets, with a mixture of *wuxia pian* spectacle, bringing together Hollywood stars with both established (Lau, the star of cult success *Infernal Affairs* [*Mou gaan dou*, Andrew Lau and Alan Mak, 2002]) and emerging Chinese stars (Jing, who also starred in two further Legendary productions, *Kong: Skull Island* and *Pacific Rim: Uprising*).

The film's announcement was condemned for its 'whitewashed' casting of Damon: Asian-American actor Constance Wu criticized its 'racist myth that [only a] white man can save the world' (Wong 2016). Damon responded that his role had not been written for an Asian actor, but was always conceived as a white European: 'It wasn't altered because of me in any way', he argued (Pulver 2016). Damon's character is undoubtedly cast as the lead, and presents ingenious solutions and displays heroism, but the narrative is more symptomatic of what Jing Yang, Min Jiao and Jin Zhang term 'East–West interchange' (Yang, Jiao and Zhang 2020, 668). The film's narrative metaphorises its own production from the collaboration between Hollywood and China Film Group that blends Hollywood tropes with those of Chinese cinema. Hence, while there are elements of white saviour to Damon's character, the film goes to some lengths to display the technological superiority of the Nameless Order, with its use of sophisticated (for the time) solutions, such as the black powder (gunpowder, generally held to be a Chinese invention) and hot-air balloons. When the queen monster is finally defeated, it is through the collaborative efforts of Garin and Lin. 'East–West interchange' is also evident in the magnetic stone Garin carries that pacifies a monster and allows them to capture it. But at the core of the film is the East–West interchange of its production, with financing by Legendary and Atlas Entertainment, in co-operation with the state-run China Film Group and Le Vision, a major Chinese distributor. Sullivan's comment about the 'stamped for approval' co-production is emphasised by the film's conscious blending of transcultural elements, but it is inescapable that many of the production's personnel were Hollywood insiders, including screenwriters Tony Gilroy, Max Brooks and Edward Zwick. Even the film's marketing enabled cross-border collaborations, with promotional songs by Wang Leehom, Tan Weiwei and Jane Zhang, and production by Timbaland and members of Maroon 5. *The Great Wall* therefore sees China, in Aynne Kokas' terms, 'moving from the periphery to a more central role' in the global hierarchy of World Cinema, if we see Hollywood as its centre (Kokas 2019, 220).

*The Great Wall* hybridised two core genres, both of which are strongly associated with East Asian cinema: the *wuxia pian* and the monster film. Since the turn of the twenty-first century, the *wuxia pian* film has been China's most significant film export. *Crouching Tiger, Hidden Dragon* brought the genre to global prominence beyond diasporic and fan communities; Darrell William Davis and Emilie Yueh-yu Yeh refer to it as 'a beacon of cultural China' (2008, 25), while Kokas has argued that '[t]he use of popular genres . . . expands visibility' (Kokas 2019, 222). As Kokas and other commentators have mentioned (Hunt 2003, Lau 2007), this strategy expanded after *Crouching Tiger* with *Hero* (*Ying xiong*, Zhang Yimou, 2002), *House of Flying Daggers* (*Shimian maifu*, Zhang Yimou, 2004), *The Emperor and the Assassin* (*Jing Ke ci Qin Wang*, Chen Kaige, 1998) and *Kung Fu Hustle* (Davis and Yeh 2008, 27–8). Kokas sees such blended processes of funding, casting and genre developing a 'particular form of visibility [that] reinforces that national vision transnationally, strengthening Chinese power hierarchies while also reifying the financially-driven power hierarchies that already prevail in Hollywood' (2019, 224). The gearing of production towards globalised transnational outcomes, Kokas argues, is detrimental to the diversity of production in China, where the outward-looking goal for cultural soft power is coupled with a desire for visibility, in Chow's (2007) terms, on the international stage. Films that exploit popular genres globally take precedence over the growth of a distinctively national cinema, with myths of China predominating over films that promote either 'nuanced historical retelling or an incisive cultural critique' (Kokas 2019, 222). However, Chinese audiences have generally favoured locally produced films over Hollywood blockbusters.

*The Great Wall* adopts further elements of the *kaijū* film but adapts these, with multiple monsters and a queen as the main threat, as in *Godzilla* (1998). The Tao Tie in *The Great Wall* were received as a problematic inclusion. Tao Tie is a part of the centuries-old myth of 'the four perils', and thus one of the great evil creatures of Chinese mythology. Its inclusion in *The Great Wall* shifted its basic meaning, of greed or gluttony, to a more standard reflection of the monsters' strength in numbers. As Chinese viewers observed, the monsters in the movie owed more to the design of lizard-like *kaiju* than mythological Tao Tie (Figure 6.2). In the *Shan Hai Jing*, the creature is described as having 'the body of a ram, tiger fangs, eyes under its armpits and human nails. A goat-owl that makes noises like a baby and eats humans' (Birrell 1999, 43). It was felt that the design of the monsters, and their rewritten origins, were a product of the non-Chinese crew who worked on the film, especially the special effects designers in New Zealand's Weta Workshop (Deng 2017). Yang, Jiao and Zhang have demonstrated that a new wave of 'Chinese monster films have adapted Hollywood's generic conventions to local realities. [Yet] *The Great Wall* exemplified a new level of local–global convergence with the ambition to win a place in the international market' (Yang, Jiao and Zhang 2020, 661). The blending of Chinese mythology with what Hjort (2019) defined as of 'a single (western) standard of filmmaking' restates the transnational and transcultural approaches in the film, part appropriation, part conscious blending: 'While the highlight of Tao Tie's allegorical meaning might be associated with a Chinese approach

**Figure 6.2** The very non-traditionally styled Tao Tie queen from *The Great Wall* (Legendary/Universal)

to engage with the monster genre, the adoption of the white saviour narrative signifies the re-invention of the Western paradigm' (Yang, Jiao and Zhang 2020, 659). Like other Sino-US co-productions, *The Great Wall*'s construction of a mythic China and appeal to global genres failed to generate the desired profits or visibility. Despite a blitz on marketing and the promotion of its transnational nature, the film underperformed at the box office in both the US and China, with losses estimated at around $75 million (McClintock 2017).

### *Pacific Rim: Uprising*

Despite the faltering box office of the first *Pacific Rim*, Universal moved forward with a sequel. The first film had been developed as part of Legendary's deal with Warners, but the follow-up fell under the terms of their partnership with Universal (Block and Masters 2013). A sequel was announced for April 2017 (McNary 2014b), but soon postponed, then cancelled, amid rumours of a breakdown in the relationship between Legendary and Universal, reportedly because of the production of *Kong: Skull Island* and the planned MonsterVerse sequels returning Legendary to Warner Bros. (Masters 2015). The sequel was subsequently cancelled, and del Toro left the project. As soon as the Wanda–Legendary deal was announced, there was speculation, fuelled by a social media post by del Toro, that *Pacific Rim* was back on (Chitwood 2016). In February 2016, the project was green-lit once more, with TV showrunner Steven S. DeKnight replacing del Toro (Fleming 2016). Once the film was released, US commentators quickly dubbed it 'China-bait' (Yoshida 2018), drawing attention to its casting of Chinese actors, Mandarin-language scenes, images of Chinese technology, product placement for a range of Chinese brands and some anti-Japanese sentiment.[8]

In contrast to *The Great Wall*, *Pacific Rim: Uprising* emphasises a different form of Chinese modernity. Instead of a mythic *wuxia* story, *Uprising* imagines a futuristic China (of 2035) where Shao Liwen (Jing Tian) runs the Shao corporation that has mass-produced Jaeger drones that threaten the original programme from the first film. A *kaijū*-corrupted Jaeger kills Mako Mori with assistance from Dr Newton Geiszler (Charlie Day), the scientist who mind-merged with the *kaijū* in the first film. Jake Pentecost (John Boyega), Mori's adopted brother, takes the lead in the film, which builds to a giant showdown in Tokyo between the mecha and monsters.[9] The *Pacific Rim* sequel was a more significant shift towards the global centre of filmmaking for China. Many elements of the film suggest it was specifically designed for the

Chinese marketplace, with clear bidirectional flows of both capital and cultural content between China and the US, although such flows appear to favour the former. In addition to Jing, the cast features several Chinese actors, including Zhang Jin (who also starred in *Crouching Tiger*, here credited as Max Zhang), Huang Kaijie (as Wesley Wong), Ji Li, Lan Yingying, Yu Xiaowei and Chen Zitong. *Uprising* was filmed partly at the Qingdao studios, and includes locations around China, from Shanghai (Oriental Pearl TV Tower) to Guangzhou (Canton Tower). The film also features prominent product placement for Chinese brands including online retailer JD.com and a holographic appearance from Tencent's penguin mascot (Figure 6.3), while an early scene features a close-up of bottles of Tsingtao beer in a fridge. Legendary also worked with Xiaomi to produce a *Pacific Rim* suitcase (Iafulla 2018). Overall, a reported fifteen brand-licensing deals with Chinese firms were signed in relation to the production of the film (Week in China 2018). Despite its western writers, director and producers, the film showcases a progressive and technologically advanced China. Its narrative, revolving around Shao's threat to the Jaeger programme, suggests a 'Yellow Peril' motif that reflects the technology trade war between China and the US during Donald Trump's presidency. Even though the Chinese-developed technology is framed as a threat to the western heroes, it plays a positive role in the film's resolution. When Shao takes control of the mini-Jaeger Scrapper in the final scenes, her intervention enables the victory over the mega-*kaijū*. The positive presentation of a modern China echoes the ruling politburo's call for greater cultural exposition: Xi Jinping's New Year address in 2014 stressed the need for greater 'socialist cultural power' to 'enhance the overall cultural strength and competitiveness'

**Figure 6.3** Tencent's Penguin mascot makes an appearance during a *kaijū*–Jaeger battle in *Pacific Rim: Uprising* (Legendary/Universal)

of China (Xi 2014). In demonstrating 'cultural strength and competitiveness' the *Pacific Rim* sequel echoes Hjort's notion of a modernising transnationalism, to showcase a nation's state-of-the-art modernity, and to promote the global competitiveness of an imagined Chinese future in which the country dominates economically and technologically. It transplants themes from *The Great Wall* about Chinese progress into a science-fiction setting.

Like *The Great Wall*, *Pacific Rim: Uprising* failed to materialise as a great success with audiences. Although more conservatively budgeted than its prequel, at a reported $150 million, it grossed just $60 million in North America, and just under $100 million at the Chinese box office, nearly duplicating the performance of its predecessor (Box Office Mojo 2021f). It had initially outperformed *Black Panther* (Ryan Coogler, 2018) in its first weekend on Chinese release, but tumbled following that, with negative audience reception. In the end, *Pacific Rim: Uprising* was the twenty-fifth-highest grossing film of the year in China (just behind *Black Panther*, which was the top-grossing film in America that year), and ahead of another Legendary production, *Skyscraper* (Rawson Marshall Thurber), a Hong Kong-set disaster movie starring Dwayne Johnson. It was outgrossed by several giant monster movies, including *The Meg*, *Rampage* and the Legendary co-financed *Jurassic World: Fallen Kingdom* (J. A. Bayona, 2018). *The Meg* had also benefited from Chinese co-production, star casting and settings. Internationally, *Avengers: Infinity War* (Joe and Anthony Russo) was the highest-grossing film of the year, but in China it was a distant fifth behind four Chinese-produced films: Dante Lam's action epic *Operation Red Sea* (*Hóng Hǎi Xíng Dòng*, 2018), comedy *Detective Chinatown 2* (*Tángrénjiē tàn àn*, Chen Sicheng, 2018), cancer-drug-smuggling comedy *Dying to Survive* (*Wǒ Bú Shì Yào Shén*, Wen Muye, 2018) and *Brewster's Millions*-style football comedy *Hello Mr. Billionaire* (*Xī hóng shì shǒufù*, Fei Yan and Damo Peng, 2018) (Box Office Mojo 2021b). Thus, despite the Wanda–Legendary partnership developing content that is seemingly glocally tailored to specific audiences (Lin 2011), Chinese-produced films have outperformed the 'Hollywood' blockbusters. So, while the progression of Legendary's global transnational strategy is blending elements for glocal hybridity, the shifts of cultural soft power are noticeable in terms of both production and content. Yet, despite the films performing better at the Chinese box office, their western mindset continues to favour cultural norms away from East Asia. China's visibility has been increased for global viewers (even if it is received negatively, as 'China-bait'), but only moderately successful in attracting Chinese audiences.

## Into the MonsterVerse

Legendary are a case study for the ways in which globalisation has reconfigured areas of transnational finance and production. The instances considered in this chapter so far explore how the contact zone between Hollywood's desire to embrace and capitalise upon China's film market and the PRC's wish to export a competitive image of soft power is providing and yet problematising visibility. As Hjort (2010) exemplifies, modernising transnationalism is determined at the level of state policy as a mean of expanding the nation's global soft power. China's desire to develop a policy like that of Japan and South Korea has emphasised analogous aspects, including investment in Hollywood production (akin to Japanese investment in Hollywood studios from the 1980s onwards). However, in the process Hollywood, as in the case of Disney's *Mulan* remake, have had to overlook alleged human rights abuses by the very Chinese authorities they have collaborated with to produce the films. The films have also presented palatable images of a progressive and unified China that fit the rhetoric of the ruling party. The MonsterVerse series continues to emphasise such flows while carrying on Legendary's move from finance company to diversified entertainment production and publishing company, built around a shared narrative universe.

In 2017, Tull stepped down as Legendary CEO, to become 'founding chairman' (Rainey and Lang 2017). Despite the Wanda takeover and further expansion into the Chinese market, the company had been beset by major losses. However, regardless of such setbacks (which included *The Great Wall*), the company had prospered in terms of diversifying their portfolio to include games, TV and publishing (along the lines of Tull's own geekiness). *Pacific Rim* had seen the company attempt to establish a storytelling universe along the lines of the Marvel and DC model, but it is the MonsterVerse series that pulls together a number of these threads more successfully, in its efforts to produce a transmediated convergent narrative space symptomatic of what Derek Johnson defines as 'shifts in industrial imagination' (Johnson 2012, 4). An established pattern for cross-media genre storytelling, serialised narratives adopt the complex storytelling of television while offering fans engagement beyond the pleasure of viewing: 'Although . . . moments of interconnectivity constitute only a handful of scenes in otherwise self-contained films, when subjected to close visual scrutiny, those scenes offer excisable seriality' (7). As we'll discuss, the excisable scenes tease fans and produce online discussion, and such seriality becomes more evident as the MonsterVerse series develops. The first film in the series, *Godzilla*

(2014), displays little in the way of networked narration. Cinematically, the strategy grows more prominent through *Kong: Skull Island* into subsequent entries, with the inclusion of post-credits sequences that tease further episodes.[10] The first film's plot was trailed in a comic book, *Godzilla: Awakening* (2014), released just a week before the film hit cinemas. Written by the film's screenwriter, Max Borenstein, alongside his brother Greg, it introduces one of the film's main characters, the referential Ishirō Serizawa (played in the film by Ken Watanabe), whose name is a combination of director Honda and the sacrificial scientist from the original film. It's framed as a confession by Serizawa's father, who rescues his son from the rubble of Hiroshima on 6 August 1945, witnessing a wispy apparition that he describes as a 'monster summoned by our own monstrosity' (it later turns out to be a giant bat, a Shinomura). In the panels beneath, what looks like a giant reptile swims away from a submerged Torii gate. The story charts several encounters between the *kaijū* in different countries. The other significant introduction in the book is the organisation Monarch, founded by General Douglas MacArthur to investigate the monsters. The choice of MacArthur consciously reconnects the narrative with Japan and the originary trauma of the *kaijū* film. MacArthur witnessed the surrender of Japan in 1945 and was Supreme Commander responsible for overseeing the Allied occupation there. Monarch are the glue of Legendary's transmedia project, tying the films together across time periods. The comic builds to a climax at Bikini Atoll, where Monarch attempt to kill the Shinomura and Gojira (as the creature is named in this episode). This is a reframed event that will be repeatedly referenced in both *Godzilla* (2014) and *Kong: Skull Island*. As the series develops, it begins to shift from a more classical transmedia narrative, with different parts of the story told across different media, to a Marvel-style Cinematic Universe tying Godzilla and Kong together in ways reminiscent of the 1960s (although 2021's encounter between the two bears no resemblance to the 1962 film).

Before the series began to engage with the changing industrial logic of contemporary Hollywood, *Godzilla* (2014) had been a late entry into the early 2000s fashion for Hollywood remakes of East Asian films, particularly horror films. As Gary Xu argued, this fashion for film production 'outsourcing' was a sign of 'East Asia's new status as the world's production center' (Xu 2007, 156). Xu likens the exporting of film development practices, where ideas and narratives are generated and market tested, to the production of consumer electronics, TVs, phones and so on that have been shifted to East Asian manufacturing. Such practices are a creeping sign of Americanisation for Xu as flows of power benefit Hollywood.

Where films such as *Ring* (Hideo Nakata, 1998) seem designed for export, with generic conventions aligning with those of American horror films, Xu sees remake trends erasing the cultural specificity of East Asian cinema: the 'originals' are 'ethnically specific, albeit Hollywoodized, representations, [while] the remakes are completely severed from the original ethnic soil and become solely the product of Hollywood' (155). The original/remake binary, in which the remake is always inferior, has been something that has been repeatedly challenged throughout this book. As we've seen, processes of global flow help produce hybridised representations that are both global and nationally specific. Koichi Iwabuchi, in *Recentering Globalization*, similarly argues that culture is subject to circular processes of relocalisation as it passes across borders, and therefore:

> the age of 'Americanization'[,] in which cross-cultural consumption was predominantly discussed in terms of the production of a sense of 'yearning' for a way of life and ideas of a dominant country, seems to be over. Global cultural power does not disappear but is now highly dispersed. (2002, 45)

Legendary's shift from US company to Sino-American entity helps to position some of these global shifts in power. Remake trends have again and again been challenged in terms of their impact on cultural specificity, flows of industrial power and the postmodern death of originality, but scholars have repeatedly critiqued the essentialist discourses at the heart of the original-good-remake-bad argument (Herbert 2010, Mazdon 2000, Rawle 2014 and 2015, Shin 2012, Smith and Verevis 2017, Verevis 2006, Wada-Marciano 2009, Wee 2010 and 2011).

*Godzilla* (2014) emerged late in this cycle and is emblematic of many of the arguments directed at transnational remakes, although for many reasons it's difficult to call the film a remake, given its lack of modelling on previous narrative templates. Its proximity to the Japanese horror (J-horror) remakes of the 2000s connects it with an industrial cycle, as does the role of Roy Lee, the Hollywood producer. Lee's company, Vertigo Entertainment, played a significant role in the brokering of South-East and East Asian remake rights, and Lee is credited as a producer or executive producer on many Hollywood remakes, including *The Ring* (Gore Verbinski, 2002), *The Grudge* (Shimizu Takashi, 2004), Oscar winner *The Departed* (Martin Scorsese, 2006), *Shutter* (Ochiai Masayuki, 2008), *The Lake House* (Alejandro Agresti, 2006) and *Oldboy* (Spike Lee, 2013). The second American Godzilla film was long in development. Sony's rights to the property lapsed, while Tōhō put their biggest star on hold following their fiftieth anniversary. It was reported in the run-up to the release of *Cloverfield* that *Godzilla vs. Hedorah* director Banno Yoshimitsu had been working on a new 3D Godzilla film and had been seeking to broker finance from Hollywood companies to develop the project (Aiken and Godziszewski n.d.). Banno's deal with Kerner Production eventually interested Legendary, who were attracted to the property. Banno and Lee helped to secure rights from Tōhō for the film, but the latter along with producers Dan Lin and Doug Davison, was fired, leading to an acrimonious court case over credits, rights to any sequels or prequels and guaranteed participation (Patten 2015).

Writer Frank Darabont and director Gareth Edwards both spoke in interviews about how their Godzilla would avoid prevailing perceptions of the monster and earlier films: Darabont mentioned how the creature had become 'Clifford the Big Red Dog in . . . subsequent films' as 'mascot for Japan'. *Godzilla* would avoid 'camp, not have it be campy' and the monster would be 'a terrifying force of nature' (Woerner 2013). Similarly, Edwards mentioned that 'Godzilla is a symbol of nature coming back to put us in our place, to restore the balance' (Newitz 2013) and this quickly set the tone for the series to come, as the films strongly engage with eco-critique, and the Titans (the series avoids the word *kaijū*) become potent symbols of climate change and efforts to 'rebalance' the world. Hence *Godzilla* (2014) reframes the global themes of the *kaijū eiga*. While the film is by no means the first to connect monsters to the hubris of nuclear power or the social and political impacts of pollution, its growing engagement with human impact in the Anthropocene is an aspect of the MonsterVerse films that grows through the subsequent entries. It is Sontag's (2009) 'imagination of disaster' for a new generation. As is made clear in Andrew Smith and William Hughes' collection *EcoGothic* (2013), monstrous narratives are perhaps one of the best ways in which speculative fiction can explore anxieties around ecological issues: gothic narratives engage with environmental concerns through their 'dystopian ecological visions' (4). While I've argued that the *kaijū eiga* cannot be considered fully gothic, there are many intersections with how grotesque bodies are imagined, in size and their impact upon the environment. Whereas that impact has been imagined largely as one upon an urban environment, the shift from *kaijū* to Titans in the Legendary MonsterVerse takes on a particular kind of 'ecological positionality' (Lysgaard, Bengtsson and Laugesen 2019, 14). In *Dark Pedagogy: Education, Horror and the Anthropocene*, Lysgaard, Bengtsson and Laugesen discuss how education can embrace Lovecraftian concepts of horror to draw attention to the impossible, unimaginable threat of ecological disaster. At the root of their thinking is the terrifying ungraspability of monstrousness: 'To be surrounded in an ecology means to be emotionally affected and surrounded by objects that we are not fully aware of... You can hide away from the monstrosities of this world for only so long, but on the other hand there is no way to confront and embody the darkness that is always present as well' (Lysgaard, Bengtsson and Laugesen 2019, 14).

Monster narratives repeatedly imagine the 'darkness' at the margins of our imaginations that is made material in bodies that reflect trauma. This is right at the roots of *kaijū* narratives, as well as of Lovecraft's strange beasts that threaten to destabilise 'normality'. Lysgaard, Bengtsson and Laugesen turn this metaphor to the monstrous reality that confronts humanity in the era of climate disaster: 'We are to "the monstrous real", what the human characters in the world of Lovecraft are to the outer gods and old ones: irrelevant' (25). Godzilla's relentless pursuit of its enemies in Edwards' film illustrates just this in relation to the human characters. Humans and their environment are simply collateral damage. The almost secondary nature of the monster battles in the film – often just out of reach to the audience, framed in darkness, out of shot or behind closed doors – tends to confirm this as well. The human drama is minor, and plays little role in the actual conflict in the film, which is between the monsters battling somewhere else. Whatever the humans do, it makes no difference. The monsters in the MonsterVerse series sit well within *Dark Pedagogy*'s focus on hyperobjects: '*viscous*, impossible to get rid of, they are *massive*, *displaced* in *time* and *place*'. While some *kaijū* are literally viscous (Hedorah), as hyperobjects ('wicked problems' in Lysgaard, Bengtsson and Laugesen's terms) *kaijū* are also literally massive problems to be solved. Their transcendent size stretches far across borders, and time is largely an irrelevance to them: the MUTOs (Massive Unidentified Terrestrial Organisms) that Godzilla battles are only concerned with consumption and procreation, giant metaphors for capitalism. Hyperobjects also 'draw in very different objects in their never-ending reach. They are in other words *monstrous*' (28; emphasis in original). In shifting the imagination of disaster into an ecological frame (something Rhoads and McCorkle [2018] argue has always been the case with the *kaijū* film), the MonsterVerse engages with climate politics and eco-criqitue, especially if we take at face value the staement of its creators that Godzilla becomes a 'force of nature', and therefore continues to mediate nature/culture binaries.

Like *Gojira*, *Godzilla* (2014) has a single point of inspiration for its opening. There is a short scene, set fifteen years before the main events of the story, in which Serizawa and his assistant Dr Graham (Sally Hawkins) investigate a giant fossil in a mine in the Philippines and discover two spores: one dormant, one hatched with a trail of destruction running to the sea. Then we switch to the fictional town of Janjira, a composite of modern and idyllic Japan, overlooked by Mount Fuji. The nuclear power plant there has experienced some unusual tremors. Plant supervisor Joe Brody (Brian Cranston) is sent to investigate, and orders a team, including his wife (Juliette Binoche), into the tunnels to check the reactor. Another tremor leads to the reactor rupturing and Brody must seal the tunnel while the team, and his wife, are inside. The power plant is destroyed. Janjira effectively stands in for Fukushima, the site of the 3/11 meltdown following the Tōhoku earthquake and subsequent tsunami in 2011. The Fukushima Daiichi plant was disabled by the tsunami and all three of its cores melted within three days. The incident was initially assessed as a level 5 accident on the International Nuclear Events Scale, equivalent to that of the Three Mile Island incident in 1979. However, in the following days, it was raised to 7 (major accident) when the released radioactivity was found to be higher than initially thought, and 160,000 people were evacuated from their homes, with, as of April 2021, some 41,000 still displaced (World Nuclear Association 2021). The film relies strongly on the events of the meltdown for its background, but it doesn't engage directly with images of the disaster. The 2016 film *Shin Gojira* draws much more significantly on images associated not just with the meltdown but with the impact of the tsunami more generally. It also frames its narrative as a satirical commentary on the ineffective government response to the disaster.

Edwards' film evokes the evacuated zone when Brody returns to Janjira. The film picks up in 2014 when Brody's son, Ford (Aaron Taylor-Johnson), is informed that his father has been arrested in the quarantine zone. Ford has only just returned to his own family after a tour of duty with the Navy. Joe has become a typical crazed conspiracy theorist who has pushed away his surviving family due to grief at the loss of his wife. He's obsessed that it's no accident and convinces Ford to join him in Janjira to recover material from their own home. When they see a dog in the streets, they understand the site isn't contaminated. They're discovered within the quarantine zone, and naturally they're taken to exactly the place they want to go: the remnants of the nuclear plant. The plant, they learn, has become home to a giant chrysalis emitting huge electromagnetic pulses. Out hatches a giant flying monster (later named a MUTO), which destroys the plant and kills Joe. The Fukushima Daiichi incident, metaphorised in the fictional city, provides a motivating point for the film, but the monstrosity of the incident is in the hyperobject of the MUTO. Whereas *Shin Gojira*, as we'll see in the Conclusion, situates the darkness of the story in the inept and pathetic response of government officials, here that burden is taken by a more metaphorical monstrosity, fantastical rather than mundane. The MUTO, we learn eventually, is communicating with its partner, the other spore, and in search of nuclear material to consume. But the monster in the title is granted another power.

Edwards' vision of Godzilla is not as the nuclear, irradiated creature. The film's Godzilla is more faithful to the look of the Japanese iteration of the monster (certainly more than Emmerich's), but the degree of monstrosity granted the monster is of another order. The 'force of nature' was not, we find out from Serizawa, made by the Bikini Atoll tests, but awoken by it, as the US military were attempting to kill it (as in the events of the comic prequel). This provides a subtle shift in origin for the monster. While the American military remain complicit for rousing the monster, they didn't create it. As such, they don't share responsibility for its actions. As the lore surrounding the Titans emerges across the next few films in the series, the anti-nuclear subtext is minimised to cast the monsters as ancient protectors, whose bodies are irradiated but are restorative rather than destructive. As the world became less radioactive, they entered dormant states, only to be awakened by human activity.

Steve Ryfle has criticised the reworking of *kaijū* lore in the series. Just as there have been many arguments surrounding the whitewashing anti-Americanism of *Godzilla, King of the Monsters!*, *Godzilla 1985* and other American iterations of *kaijū* media, he accuses the film of 'brazen mendacity [in its] revisionism . . . It is not only an affront to the legacy of Honda's *Gojira*, but it relies on the audience's ignorance of and apathy toward history' (Ryfle 2014). The film turns, he argues, 'Honda's anti-war symbol into a spokes-monster for the nuclear status quo, all the while feigning an interest in the legacy of Hiroshima'. Likewise, Tsutsui sees the adoption of the monster as problematic:

> In the 28 films made by Toho, Godzilla is unmistakably identified as one of *ware-ware Nihonjin* (we Japanese): a monster that goes out of his way to protect and defend his adopted home islands. But things are very different in the 2014 version: as Godzilla turns for the sea at the end of the new movie, we briefly see a 24-hour news network feed declaring him 'King of the Monsters -- Savior of Our City.' . . . And although all of the U.S. cities destroyed in the movie are real, the Japanese city ravaged by the earlier stirrings of the MUTOs, the awkwardly named Janjira, is pure fiction. (Tsutsui 2014)

Both critiques here by noted *kaijū* scholars problematise the original/remake dynamic in which national discourses are often overwritten in favour of broader narratives, generally in problematic ways (Tsutsui's comments about the odd choice of a fictional Japanese town are quite pertinent). We might also throw into the mix the Orientalist Serizawa, often talking in quasi-platitudes, the stereotype of the wise *sensei*. Yet Godzilla remains a victim of American military aggression, and the attempts of the US Navy, with Brody in tow, to kill the monsters are largely ineffective. When Admiral Stenz (David Strathairn) orders nuclear warheads to be used to lure the MUTOs[11] to the ocean to kill them, despite Serizawa and Graham's objections, it develops into a narrative thread in which Brody and his team must save San Francisco from their own warhead. The MUTOs intercept a train carrying the warheads. The female eats several and takes the remaining one to the city to build a nest: a Navy team must then parachute into the city to rescue it not from the monsters, but from their own warhead. Irresponsible use of nuclear energy is problematised in the film. Although the resolution is presented ultimately as heroic, it's inescapable that the film presents American military tactics as not just irresponsible but borderline stupid. This isn't unlike Edwards' previous monster film, where the monsters are ultimately accidental migrants persecuted by US foreign policy intervention that exacerbates the situation rather than nullifying it.

Ryfle (2014) also accuses the film of being 'disaster pornography', featuring 'digitally realistic images resembling Fukushima, the Indian Ocean tsunami, Katrina, 9/11', and rebuts Edwards' suggestion that the film is about modern disasters. He sees no commentary and therefore accuses the film of being 'about nothing'. Yet the film's images of monstrosity come to relate to ecological disaster. Godzilla's image is sometimes fused with the landscape. The first glimpses we have of the creature – just the back plates rising from the water – resemble rocks in the landscape. Robin Murray and Joseph Heumann, in *Monstrous Nature: Environment and Horror on the Big Screen*, contend that the film at least partially qualifies as an example of 'monstrous cli-fi' (climate fiction). They quote a *Time* review that describes the film as engaging with not 'so much what humans do to one another but what they do to the earth' (Murray and Heumann 2016, 200). That the film anthropomorphises nature as a means of disturbing human order is beyond argument: the images that evoke natural disasters – the scenes in Hawaii, when Godzilla's emergence creates a tsunami like that of Boxing Day 2004 in the Indian Ocean, or the post-Hurricane-Katrina-like scenes of people sheltering in a sports stadium – focus on familiar images of the human impact of extreme weather events. Edwards' choice to focus away from the monster battles frustrated many viewers, but, like *Monsters*, the film focuses on the human impact of unknowable monstrosity. The nuclear decisions taken by individuals bring monsters, dark reflections of those actions. The film's (and by extension the series') critique of the impact of climate change is never fully settled, and there's certainly no sense of how to resolve the crisis, but its engagement with broader global environmental concerns is clear. *Monsters* offered an apocalyptic outcome for both the individual and the state, but *Godzilla* is clear in its lack of resolution; if a bigger monster exists, there will always be balance. While that threat is anthropomorphised, a key element of eco-cinema for Murray and Heumann, the heroic monster is ultimately indifferent to human suffering. Godzilla might be the saviour of San Francisco, but that salvation is not without massive collateral damage: human society is irrelevant to the monster, as indifferent as climate change is. Whether this is a serious argument that is intentional in the film or simply undone in the triumphant ending (where Brody proves to be a better father than his own, a more typical American patriarchal narrative running through the film) is still up for debate.

*Kong: Skull Island* picks up the narrative forty years earlier, in 1973. The film develops the seriality of the MonsterVerse series, now spun more explicitly around Monarch. The opening titles of *Skull Island* flash forward across the history of the twentieth century towards its end-of-the-Vietnam-War setting (Figure 6.4). The film's depiction of the 1960s and 1970s, including the use of Jefferson Airplane's song 'White Rabbit', has postmodern written all over it. It is in keeping with Fredric Jameson's conception of the nostalgia film as a historic remembrance mediated through texts of the era (Jameson 1991). The film articulates the Monarch narrative; John Goodman's Monarch scientist tells us it was set up in 1946 by General MacArthur to investigate monsters, recounting the narrative outlined in the comic prequel to *Godzilla* (2014). There's something very reminiscent about the images in the opening titles, a kind of déjà vu (which is ironic even for a historical overview), and we're reminded of this later in the film when Goodman confesses that the 1954 Castle Bravo nuclear tests were trying to kill something. The image of

**Figure 6.4** Side-by-side credits from *Godzilla* (2014) and *Kong: Skull Island* help connect its shared universe (Legendary/Warner Bros.)

the ship he shows has claw marks on it rather than signs of the great ape, more like something from the sea or a giant lizard. Watanabe's Serizawa says something very similar in the Godzilla film. Although the Japanese *kaijū* isn't referenced explicitly in this film, the narration and imagery produce a serial effect. If we turn back to the credits of Edwards' film, they're very similar: a fast-forward redacted history of the twentieth century. There are references to Monarch, and some of the images are reused later in *Skull Island*, such as the mushroom cloud and two newspaper reports, both with a partially obscured headline, 'Government Denies Reports of Third Missing . . . '. It's very clear these two films are being constructed as in the same universe, with *Skull Island* a prequel to Edwards' *Godzilla*. These similarities reward repeat viewing, with the convergence of the narratives and of the monsters, and the networked, convergent and transmediated form fully mimicking that of the Marvel Cinematic Universe (MCU). Development and production of *Skull Island* coincided with the second phase of the MCU, between *Avengers* (Joss Whedon, 2012) and *Avengers: Age of Ultron* (Whedon, 2015). Marvel's networked and serialised transmedia narrative, across film, television and comics, set the precedent for such narratives, and the MonsterVerse began to develop similar principles. While the first film entry in the series relied upon transmedia narration across film and publishing, the release of *Skull Island* confirmed the *kaijū* film's return to the crossovers of the 1960s, leading up to *Godzilla vs. Kong*, which had already been announced as being in development by October 2015 (Lesnick 2015).

This seems to follow the shifting imagination of the convergent Hollywood blockbuster very closely, with the MCU as a clear model for the networked seriality of the films, down to the micro-level of repetition and transmediated narration, with Monarch standing in as a replacement for S.H.I.E.L.D. from the Marvel films. This includes the teasing of further entries in post-credits sequences. The MonsterVerse films lack an Agent Coulson figure, an overarching character who ties different parts of the series together. He is the figure Suzanne Scott (2017) refers to as a 'transmedia everyfan', a primary point of identification for audience members across the transmedia experience. In her discussion of Jason Mittel's (2009) notion of forensic fandom, Scott notes that while

> transmedia franchising is often credited with shifting fannish modes of engagement from the margins to the mainstream (thereby purportedly empowering fans), both transmedia franchising and this shift in terminology ultimately benefit an industry attempting to regulate participatory culture en masse. (1051)

This appears to be the case with Legendary's manufacturing of the MonsterVerse. The post-credits sequences tend to reward the experience of 'drillable texts', as Mittel also describes such practices: they become 'magnets for engagement, drawing viewers into story worlds and urging them to drill down to discover more' (Mittell 2009). Drillable texts are much less engaged with prosumer offshoots (of which there are many in *kaijū* media, from podcasts to self-produced examples of *tokusatsu*) and fan participation than with the 'time and energies [involved] in a vertical descent into a text's complexities'. Post-credits sequences are Easter eggs, hidden bits of information that require decoding and deciphering to understand what's coming in the next instalment. They often rely on pre-existing engagement with related texts. So, at the end of *Skull Island*, the post-credits sequence teases the next film. Monarch highlight what they found on *Skull Island*: art depicting a series of monsters, which is shown to the film's main characters, Tom Hiddleston's ex-SAS captain James Conrad, and Brie Larson's photojournalist Mason Weaver (both of whom are recruited by Monarch, but don't return in later films). They're shown sepia images of cave paintings, although not all will have been recognisable for anyone other than fans of the genre. Godzilla is probably the most identifiable; this seems to be followed by a giant pterodactyl against flame (Rodan); a large moth, behind a group of people in the foreground for perspective (Mothra); and a three-headed hydra (King Ghidorah). A final image of Godzilla and Ghidorah fighting teases a possible narrative for the next Godzilla movie, *Godzilla: King of the Monsters* (Figure 6.5). The drillable sequences of transmedia narratives

**Figure 6.5** *Kong: Skull Island's* post-credits sequence teases *Godzilla: King of the Monsters'* return of King Ghidorah (Legendary/Warner Bros.)

create speculation, discussion and explainers online that discuss the possible narrative, effectively marketing the upcoming film.

When *Godzilla: King of the Monsters* was released, it did indeed deliver a face-off between Godzilla, Mothra, Rodan and Ghidorah. Legendary's marketing campaign for the film followed in a similar vein, sharing images of related discoveries, teasing the monsters in the film. The battle to become the titular king delivered much more of what fans had complained was missing in Edwards' film: fights between giant *kaijū*. Indeed, the film plays as much more of a fannish experience, not just with the appearance of further Tōhō *kaijū* and the use of an 'Oxygen Destroyer' to attempt to kill Godzilla, but also with how Bear McCreary's score interpolates Ifukube's classic Godzilla scores. The development of the monsters in the film also employs performance capture in ways that allude to the previous suitmation techniques utilised in the Japanese films. The performances, and that of Nakajima Haruo in particular, brought an embodied sense of physicality to the movement of the monsters. A Tōhō-contracted stunt performer, Nakajima describes in Ryfle's *Japan's Favorite Mon-Star* (1998) how the bulk of the suit made it difficult to walk more than ten metres before falling down (he professes that he was chosen because he could walk the farthest), but the physical ordeal of moving the costume gave a sense of heft and bulk to the character. The digitally animated monsters retain the lower body bulk of the suitmation costumes, as well as the upright posture, echoing the performer in the suit, even though photorealistic animation pays attention to facial expression and musculature that is impossible in the analogue process. When Godzilla was designed for its 2014 iteration, designer Andrew Baker remarked that the process was more to do with developing a realist look that retained the iconicity of the *kaiju*, without the cuteness of the 1970s design: 'If you go too much in one direction, he [*sic*] looks like a dragon; too much in another direction, he looks like a kitty; and too much in a third direction, he looks like a dinosaur.' The final chiselled-cheekbone facial design was influenced by the Skeksis from Jim Henson's *The Dark Crystal* (1982), themselves a combination of performers in suits and animatronics (Murphy 2014). The physicality of the human carriage of the suitmation performers retains a sense of indexicality in the image. Whereas processes such as stop-motion are also indexical processes, the embodiment of bodies onscreen in suitmation (supplemented with in-camera effects such as puppetry and over-cranking) reminds us of the materiality of the image in ways that digitally animated bodies sometimes do not. As Vivian Sobchak argues, digital presence 'can ignore the lived body that not only once imagined its techno-logic but gave it substantial grounding, gravity, and value', while 'devaluing the physically lived body and the concrete materiality of the world' is a slippery slope to oblivion (Sobchack 2004, 162). Grounding and gravity speak strongly here to the very value of the presence of the body in the *kaijū* film's history. The dedication to Nakajima at the end of *Godzilla: King of the Monsters* confirms a commitment, at the very least, to the memory of the body in the monster. Therefore, the design and animation of the monster bodies in *Godzilla: King of the Monsters* speak to a memory of that body, in their designs and in their performances through the motion capture.

The linking of narratives through the cave paintings in *Skull Island* set up the shift in meaning of the *kaijū* towards their being healers of the Earth, as ancient creatures returning to an 'imbalanced' world, effectively to fight climate change. A thread of the plot also concerns a group of eco-terrorists, led by Charles Dance's former British soldier, who work to reawaken the Titans to tackle the impact humans have had on the planet. But this engages even less with images of trauma than Edwards' film. The climate crisis is a backdrop for the action, not critically considered. Peter Travers' *Rolling Stone* review captures reviewers' weariness with the film's human actors and perfunctory narrative:

> a bloated and humorless script, lazy-ass directing . . . and slumming actors who are forced to scream in terror when they're not shoveling tons of mind-numbing exposition. Do you care? Probably not. The chance to see giant monsters go apeshit – a few more are added near the end – is almost worth the price of admission. (Travers 2019)

The post-credits sequence of *King of the Monsters* provides a further forensic element. While images and newspaper articles look ahead to the pending battle between Godzilla and Kong, the final sequence sees Dance's group acquire the decapitated head of King Ghidorah. This seems to foreshadow the use of the monster's organic body to create MechaGodzilla by the Apex Corporation in the next film (the scientist on the project is the son of Ishirō Serizawa, who sacrificed himself in the second Godzilla film). As several explainers (see Jasper 2019) noted at the time, the decapitation of Ghidorah by Godzilla intertextually seemed to refer to a similar act in 1991's *Godzilla vs. King Ghidorah*, an act that leads to MechaKing Ghidorah's arrival from the future to fight Godzilla. Both creatures sink to the bottom of the sea, but the Mecha's remains are used to build a new MechaGodzilla just two years later, in *Godzilla vs. MechaGodzilla 2*. Such a reference provides a further element to forensic fandom for decipherment and discussion online. However, as both

Scott (2017) and Mittell (2009) note, such fandom tends to be composed mostly of male fans and highly masculine in its policing of knowledge, especially online. There seems little evidence in this case to suggest other than that the lines of forensic investigation help to sustain top-down media industry convergence and aid Legendary's creation of a transmedia cinematic universe around *kaijū*. Images of Skull Island even slightly resemble the outline of Monster Island, harking back to previous iterations of the *kaijū* universe.

Further points of reference to previous eras of *kaijū* co-production include elements of casting. But, as with Legendary's previous monster films, these seem to suggest shifting lines of power in the film industry. As she did in *The Great Wall* and *Pacific Rim: Uprising*, Jing Tian appears in *Skull Island*, as a Monarch biologist. This continues the commitment to transnational casting, especially for actors appealing to Asian markets. Zhang Ziyi plays a double role in *Godzilla: King of the Monsters*, as Dr Chen, another Monarch expert, and her twin Dr Ling. Chen mentions during the film that she is a third-generation employee of Monarch, like her mother and grandmother, a highly specific maternal line that connects her with Mothra. When her twin sister is revealed later in the film, it's clear they are the Infant Island *Shobijin* twins who speak on behalf of their goddess Mothra. The concept receives little development in the film, but it hints at their return in future instalments (the lack of post-credits sequence in *Godzilla vs. Kong* makes it difficult to speculate, at the time of writing, whether there will be further instalments). However, *Shobijin* have traditionally been played by Japanese performers since the 1960s, and this is the first time the characters have been played by a Chinese actor (director Dougherty commented it was important for the part to be played by an Asian actor). The death of Watanabe's Serizawa in the same film played into conspiracy theories like those around the demise of Kikuchi's character in *Uprising*, as did the replacement of Japanese actors with Chinese stars to appeal to the PRC market, but this is undermined by Shun Oguri's appearance in *Godzilla vs. Kong*. While global locations are used within all the films, the use of Hong Kong for the final battle in *Godzilla vs. Kong* appears a further Sinicist element, echoing other Legendary productions, such as both *Pacific Rim* films and *Skyscraper*, that utilise Hong Kong and China as settings. Such inclusions continue to underline the status of the *kaijū* film as a transnational genre, in both setting and production. The casting of transnational stars echoes that of Nick Adams or Russ Tamblyn in the days of Japanese government investment in global co-productions, while, from *Mothra* onwards, Japanese *kaijū* films explored cross-border political relationships directly (rather than by implication in *Gojira*).

Legendary Entertainment have capitalised upon *kaijū* trends to promote a globalised strategy that reflects the shifting business models of transnational Hollywood production. While elements of this echo previous strategies by Tōhō and other Japanese studios to appeal to transnational markets and create shared monster universes, the Legendary monster films have become emblematic of Hollywood's shifting focus towards China and transmedia franchising that draws on fan engagement with drillable texts. The company, even before their buyout by a major Chinese company, have also routinely exploited and borrowed cultural material from Asia. In addition to producing films with giant monsters, they have focused on pocket ones as well. *Pokémon Detective Pikachu* was a live-action reimagining of the card game set in Ryme City, a combination of several global cities, including New York and Tokyo. Although it features no significant Chinese casting, no 'China-bait', the film outperformed its predictions in China, with about 20 per cent of its global box office from there.[12] *Godzilla vs. Kong*, despite the Covid-19 pandemic, almost outperformed its prequel at the domestic box office, but again its gross in China outperformed that in the US, by almost double (partly due to more cinemas being open). This shifting of cultural power towards China is symbolic of changes in global culture power and related flows as Chinese soft power exerts greater influence, and Hollywood's desire to access such a large market means it is often willing to overlook alleged human rights abuses. The texts of the film seem to reflect such desires for global visibility on the part of the Chinese state, while the exploitation of Asian material suggests flows back towards East Asia, whereas previous directions of flow had looked westward. In terms of the *kaijū* film's engagement with transnational networks and lines of cultural exchange, as it has done since its inception, the history of the genre helps tell a story about shifting poles of influence and cultural power. Whereas the primary relationship in the production of the *kaijū* films was tipped towards the US from Japan, those lines are now more multidirectional between these three major powers around the Pacific rim.

**Notes**

1. Unlike the tentpole films it was producing with Warner Bros., *42* had a relatively low budget of $40 million, grossing $95 million domestically, but, as with many sport films, it had little international appeal, grossing just

under $2.5 million from a low number of screens. It played in 160 screens in Japan, reflecting baseball's popularity there, but had niche appeal around the world (Box Office Mojo 2021a). This also reflects the declining fortunes of mid-budget films in Hollywood, as discussed by Alisa Perren *in Indie, Inc.: Miramax and the Transformation of Hollywood in the 1990s* (2012).
2. *Seventh Son* was impacted by the end of the relationship between Legendary and Warner Bros. Its production was also affected by the collapse of visual effects studio Rhythm & Hues. The film's release was delayed four times before it opened to largely poor critical reception (Graser 2015).
3. Golden Harvest was the company founded by Raymond Chow that brought Bruce Lee and Jackie Chan to global stardom.
4. Tōhō owns the Godzilla copyright and licenses the monster on a film-by-film basis along with its adversaries.
5. Disney's remake of *Mulan* (Niki Caro, 2020), in collaboration with 'Chinese cultural consultants' to guarantee the film's authenticity (Zhang 2020), became embroiled in at least one scandal following news that it had filmed in the Xinjiang region in north-western China. The area is home to what the Chinese authorities call 're-education camps' in which the Uighur population, a mostly Muslim Turkic ethnic group, has been reported as subject to internment, forced labour and sterilisation. The United States has accused China of widespread human rights abuses and genocide in the region (BBC 2021). The local authority accused of running the camps is thanked in the credits of the film.
6. *Kaijū* are generally not named in the films, but the extended universe around *Pacific Rim*, including comics, games and the spin-off anime series *Pacific Rim: The Black* (Polygon Pictures, 2021), expands the lore around the monsters, giving many names.
7. The novel is more Japan-philic, with appearances from Godzilla (the film includes a T. rex that stands in for Godzilla and plays a referential role in reminding the viewer of Spielberg's role in the *Jurassic Park* films) and Ultraman. The Iron Giant (another Warner Bros. property) stood in for Ultraman when a separate lawsuit meant the makers of the film couldn't obtain the rights to the character at the time of production (Tilly 2018).
8. Some western fans read the death of Kikuchi's Mako Mori as pandering to anti-Japanese sentiment in China by removing a prominent Japanese actor and replacing her with a Chinese star, Jing Tian, as the focus of the film.
9. Elements of the film are reminiscent of the *Transformers* series, which has been hugely successful in China. The addition of a younger protagonist (Cailee Spaeny), the cutely designed home-made Jaeger Scrapper, and the more active role of the Jaeger seemingly as robots rather than giant exoskeletons feel as though the film shares some of the DNA of the *Transformers* films.

10. *Godzilla vs. Kong* currently lacks a post-credits sequence while it awaits the renewal of the licence from Tōhō. This led to speculation it could be the last film in the MonsterVerse.
11. The American government have also thought it a good idea to relocate the surviving MUTO spore to Nevada from the Philippines. Naturally, it breaks free and attacks nearby Las Vegas.
12. Despite a higher production budget, *Godzilla: King of the Monsters* grossed around $70 million less than *Pokémon Detective Pikachu*.

# Conclusion
# The Limiting Imagination of Transnational Monsters

Throughout this book, we've been considering how the global–local nexus has had a determining effect on the composition of the *kaijū* film. The *kaijū eiga* is a form that both benefits from and originates from aspects of globalisation. The very first *kaijū* films all imagined border crossing, as giant monsters were transported across national thresholds, from primitive spaces to the perceived centres of civilisation. From *The Lost World* to *King Kong* to *Gojira*, the films revolved around binaries of nature and culture that invited chaos into the metropoles of the colonial and neocolonial world. Borders were as porous as the thresholds between civilisation and seemingly primitive cultures that worshipped the giant beasts. In their eventual form, *kaijū* were a modern phenomenon, born of atomic nightmares and growing ecological disaster. These core themes of the *kaijū* film were shared as the films transgressed national borders and found relevance in different cultures. *Gojira* set the precedent for how *kaijū* cinema would understand national trauma, often in the reflection of contemporary events that brought monsters with them. The *kaijū* film came to reflect what Aihwa Ong describes, in *Flexible Citizenship: The Cultural Logics of Transnationality* (1999), as a 'condition of cultural interconnectedness and mobility across space' (4). Following its maturation in the 1950s, the *kaijū* film, like many generic movies, exhibited a high degree of mobility. The films travelled in different ways, either subtitled in their original forms, or exploited in vastly compromised ways. In memetic terms, the tropes and conventions of the *kaijū* film also demonstrated their own mobility, borrowed, reworked or grounded in different cultural contexts. The origins of *kaijū* also posed our cultural connectedness, in either the metaphors they evoked, the colonial relationships they reflected, or how such concepts were erased as films crossed from nation to nation. As I mentioned in the Introduction, this book has been all about the connections and flows at play globally in production, distribution, texts and reception that show globalisation in action.

Even though the *kaijū* film evidences the mobility and interconnectedness typical of transnational flows, its name remains inescapably Japanese. *Kaijū eiga* are essentialised time and again as quintessentially Japanese. Commentators regularly accuse western filmmakers of not 'getting' Godzilla or *kaijū* when they make giant monster movies or use the loanword. In *Godzilla FAQ: All That's Left to Know about the King of the Monsters* (2017), Brian Solomon is unequivocal that *Gojira* is the film that started it all, despite previous giant monster films. *Gojira* is undoubtedly the film that gives the *kaijū* film its definitive form, but essentialising its nationality overlooks how or why foreign cinema is important for the shape eventually taken by national cinemas. Many commentators have discussed the influence of American films on *Gojira* in some detail, and this helps explain both the transnational relationships between the US and Japan that have an impact, and the ways in which film producers adapt ideas around their own national identities without slipping into mimicking colonial occupiers. That *Gojira* can be distinctively Japanese in its adaptation of American material evidences how the flows of culture shape films without ignoring how colonial relationships are manifest in such forms. This is also replicated as Japan passes on the *kaijū* film to other nations, as South Korean filmmakers came to adopt and rework *kaijū* memes from their own colonial occupier. The interplay of national and global in the *kaijū* film is a rich narrative of transnational connections and flows, demonstrating how culture moves across borders to take on new forms (in ways not unproblematic) or how generic content helps to promote soft power and shifts in global power. I'm conscious that the book has looked almost exclusively at cinema and only touched lightly on the breadth of *kaijū* content in television, anime and ancillary merchandising, games and toys. A ful consideration of the place of *kaijū* in Japan's media mix (Steinberg 2012) is material enough for another book.

## National *Kaijū*

Having noted the problematic dimensions of essentialising nation in how films develop or take their eventual generic shape, I want to finish by considering several recent threads that highlight, echoing Deborah Shaw (2013b), the continuing relevance of the national within transnational cinema. The fight between Godzilla and Zilla (the rebranded GINO) in *Godzilla: Final Wars* provides a tantalising metaphor for the push and pull between the national and global. Staged as a tussle between the nostalgically suitmation Godzilla and sleek CGI

Hollywood iguana, the anticlimactic mêlée can help us visualise the tensions inherent in dynamics of cultural power. Just six years before, Hollywood, the global hegemonic factory, had disrespected Japan's citizen and cultural icon. Emmerich's film was accused of missing what made Godzilla so beloved, a literal part of Tokyo's skyline in Shinjuku, not just its destroyer. Tourists flock to Tokyo to enjoy studio tours and undertake the monster's original excursion around the city in 1954. Since 2018, Godzilla has graced Tōhō's cinema near Hibiya Park and their own dedicated store in Shinjuku's Marui Annex department store. Zilla's swift demise and obliteration in Sydney's opera house is an attractive metaphor for the reclamation of the national icon and global symbol of Japan. Just as Gary Xu (2007) had argued, we can overstate the significance of global flows and the equitability of such movements of culture and capital. *Kaijū* are modern commodities, not traditional or religious icons, but the dynamics of cultural power are dictated on hierarchical lines, often reflective of previous colonial relationships or wartime animosities. While Japan have successfully rearticulated their economy and cultural image across the second half of the twentieth century, relationships persist and history, even as it fades from living memory, plays a role in national and global narratives. Emmerich's attempt to make the first American Godzilla film, despite drawing on typically transnational film production (for Hollywood), resurrected the image of hierarchical national relationships. The end of GINO was perhaps inevitable, while Edwards' more referential take on the creature was better received, albeit not without its own critics. At the very least, that film's monster has been allowed to play again, not once but twice.

There are attractive arguments to be made about the competition between global and national *kaijū* films. Prior to the fiasco of Emmerich's version, Tōhō had (initially at least) planned not to compete with Sony's Godzilla films. However, while Legendary's monster films have proved moderately successful in the international market (at time of writing, not successful enough to guarantee further entries in the series), Tōhō has also been producing a series of Godzilla media that help us further consider the global–local dimensions of the *kaijū* film. *Shin Gojira* in 2016 was one of the most successful Godzilla films ever, with the most admissions for a Godzilla film since 1962. But the film is impossible to watch without seeing echoes of the original national nightmares embedded in the first film. Whereas Hiroshima and Nagasaki were evoked by that film, this time the 3/11 earthquake and Fukushima nuclear power plant emergency were the basis for the reboot's subtext. The film also makes statements about the relationships between the US and Japan in their efforts to fight the creeping menace of the new Godzilla. In addition, for the first time, ateji, a system of using kanji phonetically, rather than katakana were used to spell out the monster's name (呉爾羅). Katakana is often used to spell out foreign or globalised terms, so this use of language is a break with series continuity.

Anno and Higuchi's film is reflective of the interrelated national-transnational foundation of the *kaijū* film's origins. It is clearly a strongly national film, with its reflections on the images and aftermath of the earthquake and the nuclear disaster at Fukushima, and, despite the lengthy emphasis on the inept political response to the monster crisis, the focus on the restoration of Japanese strength (as opposed to monster fighting action) makes a solely national reading very seductive. The film's popularity in Japan also shouldn't be underestimated here. It was the second-highest-grossing film of 2016 behind *Your Name* (*Kimi no Na wa*, Shinkai Makoto), and won seven Mainichi awards, including picture and director of the year along with a virtual clean sweep of technical awards. 'It has proven easy', Shaw notes, 'to conflate the terms "international", "global", "transregional" and "transnational", while rejecting "national" cinema as somehow no longer relevant' (65). Therefore, *Shin Gojira* might be read as a conservative, protectionist, national cinema's response to such globalised transnational production, despite Tōhō distributing Legendary's MonsterVerse films in Japan.

Shaw goes on to note that:

> It is important to remember that much film production is made for domestic markets, focuses on specifically local issues, and relies on modes of narration that may not appeal to international audiences. Academics and international audiences often have little awareness of large sectors of the world's film production, precisely because it is not transnational. (65)

Godzilla films are *highly* visible culturally, even if they do receive more niche distribution in the west (*Shin Gojira* was released in the US by anime specialists Funimation and in the UK by Manga). The film certainly has more niche appeal than the English-language alternatives, as it has no identifiable stars and very specific references to Japanese politics. It was clear, however, that the timing of *Shin Gojira*'s production deliberately capitalised on the success of Edwards' *Godzilla*, which was the third-highest-grossing foreign film of its year in Japan, grossing 3.2 billion yen (Box Office Mojo 2021d). The film was distributed by Tōhō in July, and, by December, they had announced their own resurgence in Godzilla production. The report on the announcement in *The Hollywood Reporter* quoted a 'Toho staffer' who confirmed that '[t]he licensing contract we have with Legendary places no restrictions on us making domestic versions' (Blair 2014). This is very similar to the deal struck with Sony, but allowed Tōhō to retain rights for Japan, which included the distribution of the film. At the time of writing, though, Japanese Godzilla films, like Legendary's series, are in limbo. The deal with Legendary delayed a sequel to *Shin Gojira*, as Higuchi confirmed at G-FEST in 2017, but Tōhō's plans subsequently changed, leaving the monster frozen in the middle of Tokyo (Stephens 2018).

There are also many echoes of Honda's original film, particularly its relationship with national narratives of trauma and the shared imagination of disaster. *Shin Gojira* revisits the 'notion of disaster' as a core element of Japanese sci-fi. This in many ways returns to a dominant Japanese national narrative through the film's evocation of images from the earthquake and tsunami, and the Fukushima meltdown (see also Kiejziewicz 2017, Yoshimoto 2019). Images from Sendai (directly north of Tokyo) are mirrored in the film, as boats are swept downstream and the ensuing devastation is wrought as the monster emerges from Tokyo Bay and works its way through Kamakura. The US and UN sanction the use of nuclear weapons – another reflection of disaster in the national reading of the film – and, as in *The Return of Godzilla*, leave Japan stuck in the middle facing the worst possible consequences. But, as Napier (1993) argued, the original evoked the secure horror of the restorative narrative closure through 'good' Japanese science in the face of 'bad' American science. The end of this film is left in suspension, the monster frozen and the threat still literally looming. Furthermore, the dimensions of the monster's body reconnect it with foundational themes in the series. Igarashi has discussed the diminishing monstrosity of Godzilla as the series' shifted towards anthropomorphisation, human-like wrestling movements and, ultimately, banality. The body of Godzilla in *Shin Gojira* is less humanistic, but not animalistic. In Igarashi's terms, the 'monster, which [once] both embodie[d] the war deceased and is empowered by United States' nuclear weapons, serves as a grotesque caricature of postwar Japanese–U.S. relations' (2000, 118). The new body of Godzilla certainly seems even more the gross caricature, as it comes ashore first as a sort of giant fish (Figure C.1) and grows larger until it finally resembles the figure more reminiscent of the classic monster. Its monstrosity isn't anthropomorphised at all; the monster is simply a destructive force flooding ashore. As in *The Host*, American science is to blame and the US effect a cover-up (the only American character, who is Japanese-American, is played by an actor who spoke no English, and delivered her

**Figure C.1** The monster comes ashore as a giant slithering mutated fish before taking on the more familiar shape of Godzilla in *Shin Gojira* (Tōhō)

lines phonetically). But ultimately at the heart of the movie is its focus on national political structures, which remakes the original metaphor of the series in contemporary terms.

The satirical core of the narrative criticises the ineffectual response to the disaster, as committee thinking stifles action to fix the massive, looming problem. The ever-more ludicrous names for the committees ('Unidentified Creature Response Special Task Force') and bureaucratic roles (the film's protagonist is promoted to 'Cabinet Minister of State for Special Missions, Giant Unidentified Creature Unified Response Task Force HQ Bureau Chief and Deputy Director') mock the government's response to disaster (this is responsible for its relatively long, drawn-out running time). When the head of government is more concerned about their ramen noodles going soggy than saving the nation, it speaks volumes. The government is also wrong in almost all their assessments of what will happen next. When they conclude it won't come ashore, we quickly cut to the monster ashore. The comedic thread behind the monster action seems to articulate a more specifically national concern in the narrative. As much as we may also see the film as part of Tōhō's own globalising transnational strategy (or even an opportunistic one), it reaffirms the significance of the national within the transnational matrix. Lobato and Ryan's (2011) point about the important role of nationally specific content for international distribution is highly relevant. The specifically national narrative does not preclude *Shin Gojira* from crossing over to transnational markets. In fact, it has helped the film gain traction and reputation (at G-FEST in 2018, the film was voted fans' second favourite, behind *Gojira*).

It is an attractive argument to suggest that Tōhō's decision to reboot the series in Japan was an attempt to reclaim Godzilla as a national icon in response to the growing transnationalism of the Legendary series. Cameos by directors Hara Kazuo, Tsukamoto Shinya and Ogata Akira also connect it literally with a national cinema. Furthermore, that the film's title can be understood as 'new' or 'true' or 'god' or 'evolution' led to speculation that Tōhō were making a statement about who really owned the monster. The two series seem to sit comfortably side by side, however, and Tōhō benefits from the existence of both, even though it might be tempting to see Hollywood stifling Japanese cinema through the deal with Legendary. Then, in November 2017, Tōhō Animation released *Godzilla: Planet of the Monsters*, in collaboration with Polygon Pictures, and later distributed globally by Netflix. This was the first anime Godzilla, despite the earlier western cartoons and cameos in other anime. The film was released in Japan as *Godzilla* (not *Gojira*): *Kaiju wakusei*, and Netflix initially referred to the film simply as *Godzilla*. It tells the story of a ship of refugees from Earth 20,000 years after Godzilla had made the planet uninhabitable. The film's protagonist, Saraki, convinces the ship's command to return to Earth rather than settle on the planet chosen for colonisation. They find Godzilla has fundamentally changed the planet's atmosphere. They kill a smaller, infant Godzilla, only to discover the original monster, now 300 metres tall, is still alive. This film was followed by two sequels: *Godzilla: City on the Edge of Battle* (*Godzilla: Kessen Kidō Zōshoku Toshi*, Shizuno Kōbun and Seshita Hiroyuki, 2018) and *Godzilla: The Planet Eater* (*Godzilla: Hoshi o Kū Mono*, Shizuno Kōbun and Seshita Hiroyuki, 2018). In 2021, a new anime series, *Godzilla Singular Point* (*Gojira Shingyura Pointo*), debuted, also on Netflix. It focuses on two engineers from a 'do-it-all' factory who investigate a mysterious radio broadcast playing an old song. It leads them and graduate student Mei into a mystery involving the bones of what appears to be Godzilla, flocks of Rodans attacking around the world, and Anguirus, Mandas and Kumongas fighting the band of detectives. The three protagonists are joined by their boss, Gorō (a recurring name in Godzilla films, shared with the characters who discover Godzilla in *Shin Gojira* and *Return of Godzilla*), and his robot, Jet Jaguar (not quite the one from *Megalon*, but similar). The new Godzilla media features nostalgic returns from familiar monsters, as well as continuing to provide new merchandise streams for Tōhō. *Singular Point* merchandise includes a series of plush versions of Mei's cat AI 'Pelops II' and plush Jet Jaguars. They confirm the giant monster's continued place in the media mix.

The oppositional argument between national and transnational or global cinemas has long been attractive, as we've discussed elsewhere in the book. But this assumes that the shift towards national cinema concepts is entirely new, whereas there has always been an intensely national thread in many *kaijū* films. We've considered very broadly the themes that have been supranational in nature (and therefore adaptable), but other elements have remained local by nature. Such examples help us understand that as transnational threads become identifiable (since film companies desire an international reach for their products), national or local aspects are not completely erased, although they might not be immediately apparent to global viewers. This is part of the difficulty for a researcher looking at transnational emphases. In seeking connections, we might overlook specifically local details that a more detailed study of *kaijū* cinema as national cinema might dwell upon in more detail or with a more specific frame of reference. It is undoubtedly one of the drawbacks of methodologies to exploring transnational cinema (and behind Shaw's consideration of national cinema as part of that matrix) that, in considering how transnational film has become, we might produce impoverished studies of different national cinemas. This might be for a variety of reasons, from limitations of language to cultural positioning or simply because, in chasing connections, we overlook the specifics of a text's articulation of nation. I'm conscious this might be why *Heisei* Godzilla, Mothra and Gamera series have not been mentioned in this book as much as *Shōwa* films have been, since the *Heisei* series were subjected to less localisation, were distributed less widely outside Japan and were often highly local in their content. For instance, the appearance of the Fukuoka Dome in the *Heisei* film *Gamera: Guardian of the Universe* (*Gamera: Daikaijū Kūchū Kessen*, Kaneko Shusuke, 1995) might attest to this. The Fukuoka Dome (now the PayPay Dome) is the world's largest geodesic dome and home to the local baseball team. In the film, the dome, completed just before the film's production, is used in an attempt to capture the three Gyaos that have attacked a village on an island in the East China Sea. The dome's retractable roof is used as a key plot point and the building is presented as a technical marvel and source of national pride. Similarly, the cameo of Matsui Hideki in *Godzilla vs. MechaGodzilla 2* might go unnoticed. Matsui was a baseball superstar in Japan, nicknamed 'Godzilla', and signed for the New York Yankees the year after the film was released. His cameo is unsubtle, even if viewers aren't aware of the player's face. He's introduced with a massive close-up of his number 55 Yomiuri Giants shirt. He precedes to hit a homer when the baseball camp he's running with kids is interrupted by the military transporting the mecha Kiryu (the sequence lasts barely thirty seconds). Such references are intensely 'local' in dimension even if the broader cultural material demonstrates transnational influence and has international appeal, as well as promoting the achievements of the nation on a global stage. Into this matrix we might also throw Sono Sion's lovingly nostalgic *Love & Peace* (2015), with its own giant turtle, or the return of Guilala in Kawasaki Minoru's *Monster X Strikes Back: Attack the G8 Summit* (*Girara no Gyakushū: Tōyako Samitto Kiki Ippatsu*, lit. *Guilala's Counterattack: Lake Toya Summit Crisis*, 2008). Kawasaki's later films *Daikaijū Mono* (2016) and *Monster Seafood Wars* (*San Daikaijū Gurume*, lit. *Three Giant Monsters Gourmet*, 2020) revisit the low-budget *tokusatsu* of his earlier films *The Calamari Wrestler* (*Ika resuraa*, 2004) and *Executive Koala* (*Koara kachô*, 2005), and have achieved only niche distribution outside Japan. Such examples help to situate the limits of transnational investigations. In exploring the interconnectedness of global culture, such intensely local works may slip by or simply be too difficult to include in taking the overarching approach, as I have done in this book. While Netflix have continued to bring other *kaijū* media to an international audience, other films remain more limited in their engagement with or access to transnational distribution networks. However, fans have never been put off by the difficulty of accessing such work.

## Nostalgia and Fandom

The final element I want to briefly consider is medium-specific nostalgia in the memories of the *kaijū* film's global circulation. The films are often considered not cinematic but televisual, and viewers regularly articulate memories of the films through the experience of watching them on television. This and *Mystery Science Theater 3000* are recurring factors in recollections of many of the films and play a role in their reception. The success of the New World VHS release of *Godzilla 1985* emphasised the films' association with the small screen rather than the big one, something perhaps partly rectified in the past decade. In the 1960s, *kaijū* films became part of the insatiable appetite for films on syndicated television. As Kevin Heffernan (2004) has shown, the early 1960s were a boom time for exploitation distributors, especially AIP, who licensed almost their entire back catalogue to finance ongoing production. They formed American International Television (AI-TV) in 1964. Other companies, such as Screen Gems, the television wing of Columbia, and UPA were involved in the distribution of *kaijū* films, both theatrically and on television. Foreign as well as domestically produced horror and science-fiction films were in high demand, often for late-night screening, and, as Heffernan points outs, were valuable for their colour and almost entirely dubbed. In fact, the growth of television meant that features began to bypass theatrical distribution altogether: 'The demand for features became so acute and distribution of them so profitable that by 1963 many of the international pictures released to television were so-called orphans, which had never received theatrical runs in the United States' (Heffernan 2004, 227). After the theatrical release of *Godzilla vs. the Thing* (*Godzilla vs. Mothra*, Honda) in 1964, most of AIP's Tōhō acquisitions were handled by AI-TV. This included *Attack of the Mushroom People* (*Matango*, Honda, 1963), *War of the Monsters* (the first Gamera sequel), *Majin, the Monster of Terror* (the first *Daimajin* film) and *Yongary, Monster from the Deep*. This, and other packages by distributors, allowed *kaijū* films to enter wide circulation, especially as the growth of UHF stations fed the demand for features released to syndication, leading to an increase in creature features and double feature slots in many cities (230).

Localised versions have become central to perceptions of *kaijū* films for audiences. David Church, in *Grindhouse Nostalgia: Memory, Home Video and Exploitation Film Fandom*, explores how central home media such as television, and especially VHS, were to the growth of medium-specific nostalgia. As previously discussed, the work of distributors in re-editing, dubbing, titling and circulating *kaijū* films turned them into exploitation cinema for the purposes of global circulation. Audiences and fans regularly express memories of, share and comment on localised phenomena, whether video of dubbed versions, VHS covers or comparisons between versions. Yet perceptions of the *kaijū eiga* are generally defined by what Church calls 'video-mediation'. Video-mediation, Church argues, plays a significant nostalgic role in memories of exploitation films. As he points out, 'technological frameworks can allow specific films to serve as objects of textual nostalgia and vehicles for contextual nostalgia associated with uneven historical terrain' (Church 2016, 244). Therefore, '[t]echnologies of film distribution may have reciprocally influential effects upon perceptions of audiences' (247). Audiences for Godzilla films regularly articulate memories about having seen the films at drive-ins, on television or later on DVD, but in the case of *Godzilla vs. Megalon*, there is a repeated reference to one source of mediated nostalgia: *MST3K*. Church comments that *MST3K* regularly became central to many fans' recollections of cult films, such as *The Touch of Satan* (Don Henderson, 1971) (2016, 1–3). *MST3K* became a recurring memory for these viewers commenting on the Internet Movie Database (there were very minor references to the film's prime-time NBC premiere, which was introduced by John Belushi dressed in a Godzilla costume). Godzilla films featured twice on *MST3K* (*Megalon* along with *Godzilla vs. the Sea Monster*), although neither episode is available on home video due to licensing issues (the *Megalon* episode was available but removed from a subsequent release). Gamera also became a staple of *MST3K* with five *Shōwa* series films making appearances (Figure C.2). This was down to Sandy Frank Entertainment. Hence the giant turtle became something of a recurring joke on the show. The work of distributors therefore ensures the films remain within an exploitation and ironic framework that promotes the 'badness' of localisation, and the nostalgic memories of viewers who have grown up with the films. Nevertheless, for *kaijū* fans, the films remain the subject of ongoing affection that runs much deeper. As Jenkins mentions, 'fans and consumers are also producing their own vernacular theories of globalization, their own understandings of the role Asian content plays in American cultural life, their own explanations for why this material is becoming so accessible to

**Figure C.2** *MST3K* established Gamera as a recurring gag after Sandy Frank's catalogue enabled the show to riff on multiple *Gamera* films (Daiei/Best Brains/KTMA-TV)

them' (Jenkins 2004, 134). The wide range of *kaijū* fan publishing, discussion, online sharing and scholarship has contributed to such understandings of the place of *kaijū,* in American culture in particular. From a scholarly perspective, *kaijū* fandom demands a much more systematic study than I have space for here, so these final observations about the importance of types of nostalgia in memories of monsters are an invitation for further research to consider this transcultural fandom (Chin and Morimoto 2013).

# References

Aiken, Keith (2015), '*Godzilla* Unmade: The History of Jan De Bont's Unproduced TriStar Film', *SciFiJapan*, 10 May. Accessed 3 September 2021. https://www.scifijapan.com/godzilla-toho/godzilla-unmade-the-history-of-jan-de-bonts-unproduced-tristar-film-part-1.

Aiken, Keith, and Ed Godziszewski (n.d.), 'The Long Evolution of *GODZILLA 3-D*', *SciFiJapan*. Accessed 30 September 2021. https://www.scifijapan.com/godzilla-toho/the-long-evolution-of-godzilla-3-d.

Aiken, Keith, Elizabeth Ellis and Alicia Ashby (n.d), '*DAIMAJIN KANON*: The Complete Series Guide'*, SciFiJapan*. Accessed 25 May 2021. https://www.scifijapan.com/kaiju-monsters/daimajin-kanon-the-complete-series-guide.

Allison, Tanine (2011), 'More than a Man in a Monkey Suit: Andy Serkis, Motion Capture, and Digital Realism', *Quarterly Review of Film and Video* (28): 325–41. Accessed 14 February 2020. doi:10.1080/10509208.2010.500947.

Altman, Rick (1984), 'A Semantic/Syntactic Approach to Film Genre', *Cinema Journal* 23 (3): 6–18.

Altman, Rick (1999), *Film/Genre.* London: British Film Institute.

American Film Institute (2019), 'AFI Catalog: *The Giant Behemoth*', American Film Institute. Accessed 31 August 2021. https://catalog.afi.com/Catalog/moviedetails/52893.

Anderson, Joseph L., and Donald Richie (1959), *The Japanese Film: Art and Industry.* Rutland and Tokyo: Charles E. Tuttle.

Anderson, Mark (2006), 'Mobilizing *Gojira*: Mourning Modernity as Monstrosity', in *In Godzilla's Footsteps: Japanese Pop Culture Icons on the Global Stage*, eds William M. Tsutsui and Michiko Ito, 21–40. New York and Basingstoke: Palgrave Macmillan.

Andrew, Dudley (2011), 'An Atlas of World Cinema', in *Critical Visions in Film Theory: Classic and Contemporary Readings*, eds Timothy Corrigan, Patricia White and Meta Mazaj, 999–1010. Boston and New York: Bedford/St Martin's.

Appadurai, Arjun (1990), 'Disjuncture and Difference in the Global Cultural Economy', *Theory, Culture & Society* 7 (2): 295–310.

# REFERENCES

Atkins, E. Taylor (2007), 'The Dual Career of "Arirang": The Korean Resistance Anthem that Became a Japanese Pop Hit', *The Journal of Asian Studies* 66 (3): 645–87.

Bakhtin, Mikhail (1984), *Rabelais and His World*. Translated by Hélène Iswolsky. Bloomington: Indiana University Press.

Baldwin, James, and Sugitani Daisui (1909), 'Rare Myth (Girisha Shinwa)', National Diet Library Digital Collections. Accessed 19 June 2020. doi:10.11501/814828.

Ballesteros, Isolina (2015), *Immigration Cinema in the New Europe*. Bristol and Chicago: Intellect.

bandsaboutmovies (2021), 'Son of Kaiju Day Marathon: *Banglar King Kong* (2010)', *B&S About Movies,* 31 March. Accessed 20 September 2021. https://bandsaboutmovies.com/2021/03/31/son-of-kaiju-day-marathon-banglar-king-kong-2010/.

Barr, Jason (2016), *The Kaiju Film: A Critical Study of Cinema's Biggest Monsters*. Jefferson: McFarland.

Barthes, Roland (1978), 'Death of the Author', in *Image-Music-Text* by Roland Barthes, ed. Stephen Heath, translated by Stephen Heath, 142–8. London: Fontana.

Bazin, André (1972), 'The Western: Or the American Film *Par Excellence*', in *What is Cinema?* Vol. 2, ed. Hugh Gray, translated by Hugh Gray, 140–8. Berkeley: University of California Press.

BBC (2021), 'Who Are the Uighurs and Why Is the US Accusing China of Genocide?', *BBC News*, 9 February. Accessed 9 February 2021. https://www.bbc.co.uk/news/world-asia-china-22278037.

Bergfelder, Tim (2005), 'The Nation Vanishes: European Co-Productions and Popular Genre Formula in the 1950s and 1960s', in *Cinema and Nation*, eds Mette Hjort and Scott Mackenzie, 131–42. London: Routledge.

Berghahn, Daniela, and Claudia Sternberg (2010), 'Locating Migrant and Diasporic Cinema', in *European Cinema in Motion: Migrant and Diasporic Film in Contemporary Europe*, eds Daniela Berghahn and Claudia Sternberg, 12–49. London: Palgrave Macmillan.

Bernardin, Marc (2018), 'Wes Anderson's "Isle of Dogs": Is Cultural Appropriation Hollywood's Next Big Battleground?', *The Hollywood Reporter*, 29 March. Accessed 25 August 2021. https://www.hollywoodreporter.com/movies/movie-news/isle-dogs-is-cultural-appropriation-hollywoods-next-big-battleground-1098228/.

Berry, Chris (2003), '"What's Big About the Big Film?" "De-Westernizing" the Blockbuster in Korea and China', in *Movie Blockbusters*, ed. Julian Stringer, 217–29. London and New York: Routledge.

Bhabha, Homi K. (1990), *Nation and Narration*. London: Routledge.

Birrell, Anne, ed. (1999), *The Classic of Mountains and Seas*. Translated by Anne Birrell. London and New York: Penguin.

Blair, Gavin J. (2014), 'Japan's Toho to Produce New "Godzilla" for 2016, First in 12 Years', *The Hollywood Reporter*, 7 December. Accessed 17 October 2021. https://www.hollywoodreporter.com/news/general-news/japans-toho-produce-new-godzilla-754751/.

Block, Alex Ben (2015), '"Sharknado" Producer Asylum to Distribute a Dozen Movies through Cinedigm', *The Hollywood Reporter*, 5 February. Accessed 16 September 2021. https://www.hollywoodreporter.com/news/general-news/sharknado-producer-asylum-distribute-a-dozen-movies-cinedigm-770657/.

Block, Alex Ben, and Kim Masters (2013), 'Legendary Entertainment Finds New Home at NBC Universal', *The Hollywood Reporter*, 9 July. Accessed 9 February 2021. https://www.hollywoodreporter.com/news/legendary-entertainment-finds-new-home-579935.

Blouin, Michael J. (2013), *Japan and the Cosmopolitan Gothic: Specters of Modernity*. New York: Palgrave Macmillan.

Boddy, William (1985), 'The Studios Move into Prime Time: Hollywood and the Television Industry in the 1950s', *Cinema Journal* 24 (4): 23–37. doi:10.2307/1224894.

Booker, M. Keith (2020), *Historical Dictionary of Science Fiction Cinema*. Lanham: Rowman & Littlefield.

Bordwell, David (1999), '"The Art Cinema as a Mode of Film Practice."', in *Film Theory and Criticism: Introductory Readings*, by eds Leo Braudy and Marshall Cohen, 716–724. New York: Oxford University Press.

Bordwell, David (2012), *Poetics of Cinema*. London: Routledge.

Borenstein, Max, and Greg Borenstein (2014), *Godzilla: Awakening*. Burbank: Legendary.

Boss, Joyce E. (2006), 'Hybridity and Negotiated Identity in Japanese Popular Culture', in *In Godzilla"s Footsteps: Japanese Pop Culture Icons on the Global Stage*, eds William M. Tsutsui and Michiko Ito. New York and Basingstoke: Palgrave Macmillan.

Botting, Fred (2014), *Gothic*. 2nd edn. Abingdon and New York: Routledge.

Bowman, Paul (2019), 'Game of Text: Bruce Lee's Media Legacies', *Global Media and China* 4 (3): 325–38.

Box Office Mojo (2021a), '*42*', *Box Office Mojo*, 4 February. Accessed 4 February 2021. https://www.boxofficemojo.com/title/tt0453562/?ref_=bo_rl_ti.

Box Office Mojo (2021b), 'Chinese Box Office for 2018', *Box Office Mojo*, 11 February. Accessed 11 February 2021. https://www.boxofficemojo.com/year/2018/?area=CN&grossesOption=calendarGrosses.

Box Office Mojo (2021c), '*Dragon Wars: D-War* (2007)', *Box Office Mojo*, 5 August. Accessed 5 August 2021. https://www.boxofficemojo.com/release/rl1263437313/weekly/?ref_=bo_rl_tab#tabs.

Box Office Mojo (2021d), 'Japanese Box Office for 2014', *Box Office Mojo*, 17 October. Accessed 17 October 2021. https://www.boxofficemojo.com/year/2014/?area=JP.

Box Office Mojo (2021e), '*Pacific Rim*', *Box Office Mojo*, 11 February. Accessed 11 February 2021. https://www.boxofficemojo.com/title/tt1663662/?ref_=bo_rl_ti.
Box Office Mojo (2021f), '*Pacific Rim: Uprising*', *Box Office Mojo*, 11 February. Accessed 11 February 2021. https://www.boxofficemojo.com/title/tt2557478/?ref_=bo_rl_ti.
Branaghan, Sim (2018), 'Monsters from an Unknown Culture: Godzilla (and Friends) in Britain 1957–1980', *SMGuariento.com*, May–June. Accessed 31 August 2021. http://www.smguariento.com/monsters-from-an-unknown-culture-godzilla-and-friends-in-britain-1957–1980-by-sim-branaghan-part-1/.
British Board of Film Classification (2021), '*The Giant Behemoth*', British Board of Film Classification, 31 August. Accessed 31 August 2021. https://www.bbfc.co.uk/release/the-giant-behemoth-q29sbgvjdglvbjpwwc0yntg4mde.
Broderick, Mick, ed. (1996), *Hibakusha Cinema: Hiroshima, Nagasaki and the Nuclear Image in Japanese Film*. Abingdon and New York: Routledge.
Brothers, Peter H. (2015), *Atomic Dreams and the Nuclear Nightmare: The Making of Godzilla*. Seattle: CreateSpace Books.
Buchanan, Kyle (2016), 'How Anne Hathaway's Monster Movie *Colossal* Is Informed by Gamergate and the Alt-Right', *Vulture*, 14 September. Accessed 15 December 2021. https://www.vulture.com/2016/09/colossal-anne-hathaway-movie-gamergate-alt-right.html.
Carlson, Rebecca, and Jonathan Corliss (2011), 'Imagined Commodities: Video Game Localization and Mythologies of Cultural Difference', *Games and Culture* 6 (1): 61–82.
Chang, Justin (2013), 'Film Review: "Pacific Rim"', *Variety*, 7 July. Accessed 26 September 2021. https://variety.com/2013/film/reviews/film-review-pacific-rim-1200535260/.
Cheung, Hye Seung, and David Scott Diffrient (2015), *Movie Migrations: Transnational Genre Flows and South Korean Cinema*. New Brunswick, NJ: Rutgers University Press.
Chin, Bertha, and Lori Hitchcock Morimoto (2013), 'Towards a Theory of Transcultural Fandom', *Participations* 10 (1): 92–108.
Chitwood, Adam (2016), 'Legendary Acquired by China's Wanda for $3.5 Billion; Hope for "Pacific Rim 2"?', *Collider*, 11 January. Accessed 11 February 2021. https://collider.com/legendary-china-wanda-pacific-rim-2/.
Chitwood, Adam (2017), 'Exclusive: "God Particle" Writer Oren Uziel on How the Film Became a *Cloverfield* Movie', *Collider*, 17 May. Accessed 9 September 2021. https://collider.com/god-particle-cloverfield-movie-details-oren-uziel/.
Cho, Hae-Wol (2020), 'Effectiveness for the Response to COVID-19: The MERS Outbreak Containment Procedures', *Osong Public Health and Research Perspectives* 11 (1): 1–2. doi:https://doi.org/10.24171/j.phrp.2020.11.1.01.
Cho, Hong Sik (1999), 'An Overview of Korean Environmental Law', *Environmental Law* 29 (3): 501–14. https://www.jstor.org/stable/43266912.

Choo, Kukhee (2014), 'Hyperbolic Nationalism: South Korea's Shadow Animation Industry', *Mechademia: Second Arc* 9: 144–62. doi:doi.org/10.5749/mech.9.2014.0144.

Chosunilbo (2006), 'U.S. Army Keeping Close Eye on Han River Monster', *The Chosunilbo*, 11 August. Accessed 6 August 2021. http://english.chosun.com/site/data/html_dir/2006/08/11/2006081161014.html.

Chow, Rey (2007), *Sentimental Fabulations, Contemporary Chinese Films: Attachment in the Age of Global Visibility*. New York: Columbia University Press.

Chung, Hye Jean (2009), 'The Host and D-War: Complex Intersections of National Imaginings and Transnational Aspirations', *Spectator* 29 (2): 48–56.

Chung, Steven (2014), *Split Screen Korea: Shin Sang-ok and Postwar Cinema*. Minneapolis: University of Minnesota Press.

Church, David (2016), *Grindhouse Nostalgia: Memory, Home Video and Exploitation Film Fandom*. Edinburgh: Edinburgh University Press.

Clements, Jonathan (2020), 'Audio Commentary', *Daimajin*. Blu-ray. London: Arrow Films.

Clover, Carol (1992), *Men, Women and Chainsaws: Gender in the Modern Horror Film*. Princeton and Oxford: Princeton University Press.

Cohen, Jeffrey Jerome (1996), 'Monster Culture (Seven Theses)', in *Monster Theory: Reading Culture*, ed. Jeffrey Jerome Cohen, 3–25. Minneapolis: University of Minnesota Press.

Cohen, Jeffrey Jerome (1999), *Of Giants: Sex, Monsters, and the Middle Ages*. Minneapolis: University of Minnesota Press.

Combe, Kirk (2015), 'Homeland Insecurity: Macho Globalization and Alien Blowback in *Monsters*', *The Journal of Popular Culture* 48 (5): 1010–29.

Conrich, Ian (1999), 'Trashing London: The British Colossal Creature Film and Fantasies of Mass Destruction', in *British Science Fiction Cinema*, ed. I. Q. Hunter, 88–98. London and New York: Routledge.

Coonan, Clifford (2013), 'Chinese PLA Officer Tells Troops "Pacific Rim" Is Hollywood Propaganda', *The Hollywood Reporter*, 27 August. Accessed 11 February 2021. https://www.hollywoodreporter.com/news/chinese-pla-officer-tells-troops-615091.

Cotter, Padraig (2020), '*D-War: Mysteries of the Dragon* Updates: Is The Sequel Still Happening?', *Screen Rant*, 7 November. Accessed 6 August 2021. https://screenrant.com/d-war-mysteries-dragon-movie-updates-release-date-story/.

Craig, Rob (2019), *American International Pictures: A Comprehensive Filmography*. Jefferson: McFarland.

Crandol, Michael (2019), 'Godzilla vs. Dracula: Hammer Horror Films in Japan', *Cinephile* 13 (1): 18–23.

Crofts, Stephen (2006), 'Reconceptualising National Cinema/s', in *Theorising National Cinema*, eds Valentina Vitali and Paul Willemen, 44–58. London: British Film Institute.

Dalton, Ben (2018), 'China's Dalian Wanda opens $7.9bn Studio Complex', *Screen Daily*, 30 April. Accessed 9 February 2021. https://www.screendaily.com/news/chinas-dalian-wanda-opens-79bn-studio-complex-/5128692.article.

Danish Film Institute (n.d.), 'Bodil Miller', Danish Film Institute. Accessed 31 August 2021. https://www.dfi.dk/viden-om-film/filmdatabasen/person/bodil-miller.

Davis, Darrell William, and Emilie Yueh-yu Yeh (2008), *East Asian Screen Industries*. London: British Film Institute.

Dawkins, Richard (1976), *The Selfish Gene*. Oxford and New York: Oxford University Press.

DCA Productions (2016), '*Monster from Green Hell* and *Half Human* Double Bill Pressbook', *Zombo's Closet*, 11 April. Accessed 19 August 2021. https://www.zomboscloset.com/zombos_closet_of_horror_b/2016/04/monster-from-green-hell-and-half-human-double-bill.html.

De La Garza, Armida, Ruth Doughty and Deborah Shaw (2019), 'From Transnational Cinemas to Transnational Screens', *Transnational Screens* 10 (1): i–vi. doi:10.1080/25785273.2019.1660067.

De Semlyen, Nick (2017), '*Colossal* Review', *Empire*, 15 May. Accessed 15 December 2021. https://www.empireonline.com/movies/reviews/colossal-review.

Deamer, David (2014), *Deleuze, Japanese Cinema and the Atom Bomb*. New York and London: Bloomsbury.

Debus, Allen A. (2016), *Dinosaurs Ever Evolving: The Changing Face of Prehistoric Animals in Popular Culture*. Jefferson: McFarland.

Deleyto, Celestino (2020), 'Wonderland: The Digital and the Cosmopolitan at the Borderlands in *Monsters*', *New Review of Film and Television Studies* 18 (3): 325–44.

Deng, Zhangyu (2017), 'Hit and Myth: The Movie Monsters Lost in Translation', *China Daily.com.cn*, 8 January. Accessed 11 February 2021. https://www.chinadaily.com.cn/kindle/2017–01/08/content_27892971.htm.

Denison, Rayna (2015), *Anime: A Critical Introduction*. London and New York: Bloomsbury.

Derendorf, Kevin (2018), *Kaiju for Hipsters: 101 'Alternative' Giant Monster Movies*. n.p.: Maser Press.

DeSentis, John (2009), 'Talking *Cozzilla*: An Interview with Italian Godzilla Director Luigi Cozzi', *SciFiJapan*, April. Accessed 17 August 2021. https://www.scifijapan.com/godzilla-toho/talking-cozzilla-an-interview-with-italian-godzilla-director-luigi-cozzi.

Ďurovičová, Nataša (2010), 'Preface', in *World Cinemas, Transnational Perspectives*, eds Nataša Ďurovičová and Kathleen Newman, ix–xv. London and New York: Routledge.

Eco, Umberto (1986), '*Casablanca*: Cult Movies and Intertextual Collage', in *Faith in Fakes: Travels in Hyperreality* by Umberto Eco, translated by William Weaver, 197–211. Reading: Vintage.

Eleftheriotis, Dimitris (2006), 'Turkish National Cinema', in *Asian Cinemas: A Reader & Guide* eds Dimitris Eleftheriotis and Gary Needham, 220–8. Edinburgh: Edinburgh University Press.

Erb, Cynthia (2009), *Tracking King Kong: A Hollywood Icon in World Culture*. 2nd edn. Detroit: Wayne State University Press.

Esser, Andrea (2016), 'Defining "the Local" in Localization or "Adapting for Whom?"', in *Media Across Borders: Localising TV, Film and Video Games*, eds Andrea Esser, Miguel Á. Bernal-Merino and Iain Robert Smith, 19–33. New York: Routledge.

Fischer, Paul (2015), *A Kim Jong-Il Production: The Incredibly True Story of North Korea and the Most Audacious Kidnapping in History*. London: Viking.

Fisher, Austin (2011), *Radical Frontiers in the Spaghetti Western: Politics, Violence and Popular Italian Cinema*. London and New York: I. B. Tauris.

Fleming, Michael (2009), 'Nolan Tackles "Inception" for WB', *Variety*, 11 February. Accessed 4 February 2021. https://variety.com/2009/film/features/nolan-tackles-inception-for-wb-1117999988/.

Fleming Jr., Mike (2016), '"Spartacus" Creator Steven S. DeKnight to Direct "Pacific Rim 2"', *Deadline*, 23 February. Accessed 11 February 2021. https://deadline.com/2016/02/pacific-rim-2-directed-by-steven-deknight-spartacus-creator-legendary-pictures-guillermo-del-toro-1201708221/.

Forsythe, Michael (2015), 'Wang Jianlin, a Billionaire at the Intersection of Business and Power in China', *The New York Times*, 28 April. Accessed 9 February 2021. https://www.nytimes.com/2015/04/29/world/asia/wang-jianlin-abillionaire-at-the-intersection-of-business-and-power-in-china.html.

Foster, Michael Dylan (2015), *The Book of Yokai: Mysterious Creatures of Japanese Folklore*. Oakland: University of California Press.

Frayling, Christopher (2006), *Spaghetti Westerns: Cowboys and Europeans from Karl May to Sergio Leone*. London and New York: I. B. Tauris.

Fujiki, Hideaki, and Alastair Phillips (2020), 'Japanese Cinema and its Multiple Perspectives', in *The Japanese Cinema Book*, eds Hideaki Fujiki, and Alastair Phillips, 1–22. London: British Film Institute.

Galbraith, Stuart (2008), *The Toho Studios Story: A History and Complete Filmography*. Lanham: Scarecrow Press.

García, Frank (2019), 'Recovering the Chicano Social Problem Film: Racial Consciousness, Rita Moreno, and the Historiography of *The Ring* (1952)', *Black Camera* 11: 89–122.

Garrett, Diane (2007), 'Pitches Flying as Labor Fears Loom', *Variety*, 5 October. Accessed 4 February 2021. https://variety.com/2007/more/news/pitches-flying-as-labor-fears-loom-1117973472/.

Gatto, Robin, and Tom Mes (2005), 'Remembering Kenji Misumi', *Midnight Eye*, 24 October. Accessed 25 May 2021. http://www.midnighteye.com/features/remembering-kenji-misumi/.

Gerow, Aaron (2006), 'Wrestling with Godzilla: Intertextuality, Childish Spectatorship, and the National Body', in *In Godzilla's Footsteps: Japanese Pop Cultures Icons on the Global Stage*, eds William M. Tsutsui and Michiko Ito, 63–81. New York: Palgrave Macmillan. Accessed 18 February 2020. http://works.bepress.com/aarongerow/28/.

Gilchrist, Todd (2013), 'Guillermo del Toro Interview: The "Pacific Rim"! Director Talks Creating the Ultimate Summer Blockbuster', Screen Crush, 11 July. Accessed 26 September 2021. https://screencrush.com/guillermo-del-toro-interview/.

Glaser, Ed (2019), '*Cozzilla*! The True Story of the Colorized Godzilla | 2015 Presentation', YouTube, 13 July. Accessed 18 August 2021. https://www.youtube.com/watch?v=F-L3LyS946o.

Graser, Marc (2015), 'Legendary Stumbles with Big Writedowns on "Seventh Son", "Blackhat"', *Variety*, 4 February. Accessed 4 February 2021. https://variety.com/2015/film/news/legendary-stumbles-with-writedowns-on-seventh-son-blackhat-exclusive-1201423728/.

Graser, Marc, and Rachel Abrams (2011), 'Legendary Pictures Eyes New Credit Line', *Variety*, 15 April. Accessed 4 February 2021. https://variety.com/2011/film/news/legendary-pictures-eyes-new-credit-line-1118035532/.

Gunning, Tom (2006), 'The Cinema of Attraction[s]: Early Film, Its Spectator and the Avant-Garde', in *The Cinema of Attractions Reloaded*, ed. Wanda Strauven, 381–8. Amsterdam: Amsterdam University Press.

Halberstam, Jack (1995), *Skin Shows: Gothic Horror and the Technology of Monsters*. Durham, NC: Duke University Press.

Hall, Stuart (1996), 'When Was the Post-Colonial? Thinking at the Limit', in *The Post-Colonial Question: Common Skies, Divided Horizons*, eds Iain Chambers and Lidia Curti, 242–60. London and New York: Routledge.

Hansen, Miriam (1999), 'The Mass Production of the Senses: Classical Cinema as Vernacular Modernism', *Modernism/Modernity* 6 (2): 59–77. Accessed 21 June 2016. https://muse.jhu.edu/article/23266.

Hantke, Steffen (2010), 'The Return of the Giant Creature: *Cloverfield* and Political Opposition to the War on Terror', *Extrapolation* 51 (2): 235–57.

Heffernan, Kevin (2004), *Ghouls, Gimmicks, and Gold: Horror Films and the American Movie Business, 1953–1968*. Durham, NC and London: Duke University Press.

Heffernan, Kevin (2017), 'A's, B's, Quickies, Orphans, and Nasties: Horror Films in the Context of Distribution and Exhibition', in *A Companion to the Horror Film*, ed. Harry M. Benshoff, 109–29. Malden: Wiley-Blackwell.

Herbert, Daniel (2010), 'Circulations: Technology and Discourse in *The Ring'*, in *Second Takes: Critical Approaches to the Film Sequel*, eds Carolyn Jess-Cooke and Constantine Verevis, 153–70. Albany: State University of New York Press.

Higson, Andrew (2002), 'The Concept of National Cinema', in *The European Cinema Reader*, ed. Catherine Fowler, 132–42. London: Routledge.

Higson, Andrew (2006), 'The Limiting Imagination of National Cinema', in *Transnational Cinema: A Film Reader*, eds Elizabeth Ezra and Terry Rowden, 15–25. Abingdon and New York: Routledge.

Higson, Andrew (2011), *Film England: Culturally English Filmmaking Since the 1990s*. London and New York: I. B. Tauris.

Hjort, Mette (2010), 'On the Plurality of Cinematic Transnationalism', in *World Cinemas, Transnational Perspectives*, eds Nataša Ďurovičová and Kathleen Newman, 12–33. London and New York: Routledge.

Hjort, Mette (2019), 'The Ontological Transnationalism of the Filmmaker: Solidarity-Based Talent Development across Borders', *Transnational Screens* 10 (1): 53–68. doi:10.1080/25785273.2019.1583807.

Hoffman, Jordan (2020), 'My Streaming Gem: Why You Should Watch *Starcrash*', *The Guardian*, 13 April. Accessed 17 August 2021. https://www.theguardian.com/film/2020/apr/13/starcrash-david-hasselhoff-film-amazon-prime.

Hunt, Leon (2003), *Kung Fu Cult Masters: From Bruce Lee to Crouching Tiger*. London and New York: Wallflower.

Hunter, I. Q. (2005), 'The Irrational Enlargement of Queen Kong', *Film International* 3 (3): 42–9.

Hunter, I. Q. (2009), 'Exploitation as Adaptation', in *Cultural Borrowings: Appropriation, Reworking, Transformation*, ed. Iain Robert Smith, 8–33. Nottingham: Scope: An Online Journal of Film and Television Studies.

Hunter, I. Q. (2013), *British Trash Cinema*. London: British Film Institute.

Hutcheon, Linda (1986), 'The Politics of Postmodernism: Parody and History', *Cultural Critique* 179–207.

Hutchings, Peter (1993), *Hammer and Beyond: The British Horror Film*. Manchester: Manchester University Press.

Iafulla, Emanuele (2018), 'For Manga Lovers Here Is the 90 Minutes "Pacific Rim" Suitcase by Xiaomi', *Xiaomi Today*, 13 March. Accessed 11 February 2021. https://en.xiaomitoday.it/per-gli-amanti-dei-manga-ecco-la-valigia-90-minutes-pacific-rim.html.

Igarashi, Yoshikuni (2000), *Bodies of Memory: Narratives of War in Postwar Japanese Culture, 1945–1970*. Princeton: Princeton University Press.

Indiewire (2007), 'Indiewire Interview: "The Host" Director Bong Joon-ho', *Indiewire*, 13 March. Accessed 6 August 2021. https://www.indiewire.com/2007/03/indiewire-interview-the-host-director-bong-joon-ho-74982/.

Internet Movie Database (n.d.), '*Bye Bye Monkey (1978)*', Internet Movie Database. Accessed 20 September 2021. https://www.imdb.com/title/tt0075848/.

Iordanova, Dina, David Martin-Jones and Belén Vidal (2010), 'Introduction: A Peripheral View of World Cinema', in *Cinema at the Periphery*, eds Dina Iordanova, David Martin-Jones and Belén Vidal, 1–19. Detroit: Wayne State University Press.

Iwabuchi, Koichi (2002), *Recentering Globalization: Popular Culture and Japanese Transnationalism*. Durham, NC and London: Duke University Press.

Jameson, Fredric (1991), *Postmodernism, or the Cultural Logic of Late Modernism*. London: Verso.

Jasper, Gavin (2019), '*Godzilla: King of the Monsters*: Post-Credits Scene Explained', *Den of Geek*, 3 June. Accessed 1 October 2021. https://www.denofgeek.com/movies/godzilla-king-of-the-monsters-post-credits-scene-explained/.

Jenkins, Henry (1992), *Textual Poachers: Television Fans and Participatory Culture*. London: Routledge.

Jenkins, Henry (2004), 'Pop Cosmopolitanism: Mapping Cultural Flows in an Age of Media', in *Globalization: Culture and Education in the New Millennium*, eds Marcelo M. Suárez-Orozco and Desirée Baolian Qin-Hilliard, 114–40. Berkeley: University of California Press.

Jin, Dal Yong, and Kyong Yoon (2016), 'The Social Mediascape of Transnational Korean Pop Culture: Hallyu 2.0 as Spreadable Media Practice', *New Media & Society* 1277–92. doi:https://doi.org/10.1177/1461444814554895.

Johnson, Derek (2012), 'Cinematic Destiny: Marvel Studios and the Trade Stories of Industrial Convergence', *Cinema Journal* 52 (1): 1–24.

Johnston, Derek (2014), 'Invaders, Launchpads, and Hybrids: The Importance of Transmediality in British Science Fiction Film in the 1950s', in *The Liverpool Companion to World Science Fiction Film*, ed. Sonja Fritzsche, 89–103. Liverpool: Liverpool University Press.

Joo, Woojeong, Rayna Denison and Hiroko Furukawa (2013), 'Manga Movies Project Report 1: Transmedia Japanese Franchising', Manga Movies Project. Accessed 10 October 2016. http://d284f45nftegze.cloudfront.net/RLDenison/MANGA%20MOVIES%20PROJECT%20REPORT%201%20TRANSMEDIA%20FRANCHISING%20.pdf.

Kaiju Transmissions Podcast (2017), 'Kongsploitation: King Kong Knock-Offs!', *The Kaiju Transmissions Podcast*, 27 February. Accessed 16 September 2021. https://kaijutransmissions.podbean.com/e/kongsploitation-king-kong-knock-offs/.

Kalat, David (1997), *A Critical History and Filmography of Toho's Godzilla Series*. Jefferson and London: McFarland.

Katz, David (2013), 'From Asylum, the People Who Brought You (a Movie Kinda Sorta Like) Pacific Rim', *GQ*, 11 July. Accessed 16 September 2021. https://www.gq.com/story/sharknado-atlantic-rim-pacific-rim-asylum-movie-spoof.

Kiejziewicz, Agnieszka (2017), 'The Nuclear Technology Debate Returns: Narratives about Nuclear Power in Post-Fukushima Japanese Films', *Trans-Missions: The Journal of Film and Media Studies* 2 (1): 117–31.

Kim, Chung-kang (2018), 'Monstrous Science: *The Great Monster Yonggari* (1967) and Cold War Science in 1960s South Korea', *Journal of Korean Studies* 23 (2): 397–421.

Kit, Borys (2020), 'Netflix Picks Up Millie Bobby Brown's "Enola Holmes" from Legendary', *The Hollywood Reporter*, 21 April. Accessed

23 September 2021. https://www.hollywoodreporter.com/movies/movie-news/netflix-picks-up-millie-bobby-browns-enola-holmes-1291066/.

Kitaura, Hiroyuki (2020), 'The Studio System: The Japanese Studio System Revisited', in *The Japanese Cinema Book*, eds Hideaki Fujiki and Alastair Phillips, 109–25. London: British Film Institute.

Klein, Christina (2004), '*Crouching Tiger, Hidden Dragon*: A Diasporic Reading', *Cinema Journal* 43 (4): 18–42.

Klein, Christina (2007), '*Kung Fu Hustle*: Transnational Production and the Global Chinese-Language Film', *Journal of Chinese Cinemas* 1 (3): 189–208.

Kokas, Aynne (2019), 'Producing Global China: *The Great Wall* and Hollywood's Cultivation of the PRC's Global Vision', *Journal of Chinese Cinemas* 13 (3): 215–27. doi:10.1080/17508061.2019.1678485.

Korean Film Archive (n.d.), 'Korean New Wave: 1987–1996', Korean Film Archive. Accessed 5 August 2021. https://artsandculture.google.com/exhibit/korean-new-wave-korean-film-archive/wQzbiZh6?hl=en.

Koven, Mikel J. (2004), '"The Film You Are about to See Is Based on Documented Fact": Italian Nazi Sexploitation Cinema', in *Alternative Europe: Eurotrash and Exploitation Cinema since 1945*, eds Ernest Mathijs and Xavier Mendik, 19–31. London: Wallflower.

Koven, Mikel J. (2006), *La Dolce Morte: Vernacular Cinema and the Italian Giallo Film*. Lanham: Scarecrow Press.

Lambie, Ryan (2010), 'Gareth Edwards Interview: On Making Monsters, Meeting Quentin Tarantino and More', Den of Geek, 29 November. Accessed 9 September 2021. https://www.denofgeek.com/movies/gareth-edwards-interview-on-making-monsters-meeting-quentin-tarantino-and-more/.

Landreth, Jonathan (2011), 'Legendary to Co-Produce "Global" Pics with China's Huayi, Warner to Distribute', *The Hollywood Reporter*, 9 June. Accessed 4 February 2021. https://www.hollywoodreporter.com/news/legendary-produce-global-pics-chinas-196390.

Lau, Jenny Kwok Wah (2007), '*Hero*: China's Response to Hollywood Globalization', *Jump Cut: A Review of Contemporary Media* 49. Accessed 7 June 2016. http://www.ejumpcut.org/archive/jc49.2007/Lau-Hero/index.html.

Lee, Nikki J. Y. (2011), 'Localized Globalization and a Monster National: *The Host* and the South Korean Film Industry', *Cinema Journal* 50 (3): 45–61.

Lee, Sangjoon (2016), 'Dracula, Vampires, and Kung Fu Fighters: *The Legend of the Seven Golden Vampires* and Transnational Horror Co-Production in 1970s Hong Kong', in *Transnational Horror Cinema: Bodies of Excess and the Global Grotesque*, eds Sophia Siddique and Raphael Raphael, 65–80. London: Palgrave Macmillan.

Lee, Vivian P. Y. (2015), 'Staging the "Wild Wild East": Decoding the Western in East Asian Films', in *The Post-2000 Film Western: Contexts, Transnationality, Hybridity*, eds Marek Paryz and John R. Leo, 147–64. London and New York: Palgrave Macmillan.

Lee, Youngjin (2008), '"Encyclopedia of Monsters: A Korean Monster is Coming" to be held at the Korea Film Archive from July 29 to August 5', Cine21, 29 July. Accessed 10 June 2021. http://www.cine21.com/news/view/?mag_id=52373.

Lees, J. D. (2006), 'What is a Kaiju?', *G-Fan* 78: 68–72.

LeMay, John (2017), *The Big Book of Japanese Giant Monster Movies, Volume 1: 1954–1982*. 2nd edn. n.p.: Bicep Books.

LeMay, John (2018), 'Unbelievable! The Secret Origins of Varan', *G-Fan* 119: 20–3.

LeMay, John (2019), *The Big Book of Japanese Giant Monster Movies: The Lost Films*. Roswell: Bicep Books.

Lerner, Aaron (2006), '*Gojira* vs *Godzilla*: Catastrophic Allegories', in *Ritual and Event: Interdisciplinary Perspectives*, ed. Mark Franko, 109–24. London and New York: Routledge.

Lesnick, Silas (2015), 'It's Official! *Godzilla vs Kong* Arrives in 2020', ComingSoon.net, 14 October. Accessed 1 October 2021. https://www.comingsoon.net/movies/news/622605-godzilla-vs-kong-2020.

Lim, Bliss Cua (2009), *Translating Time: Cinema, the Fantastic, and Temporal Critique*. Durham, NC: Duke University Press.

Lin, Feng (2011), 'Glocalizing Stardom: Internet Publicity and the Construction of Chow Yun-Fat's Transnational Stardom', *Transnational Cinemas* 2 (1): 73–91.

Lobato, Ramon (2012), *Shadow Economies of Cinema: Mapping Informal Film Distribution*. London: British Film Institute.

Lobato, Ramon, and Mark David Ryan (2011), 'Rethinking Genre Studies through Distribution Analysis: Issues in International Horror Movie Circuits', *New Review of Film and Television Studies* 9 (2): 188–203.

Lourié, Eugene (1985), *My Work in Films*. San Diego, New York and London: Harcourt Brace Jovanovich.

Luckhurst, Roger (2020), 'After Monster Theory? Gareth Edwards's *Monsters*', *Science Fiction Film and Television* 13 (2): 269–90.

Lysgaard, Jonas Andreasen, Stefan Bengtsson and Martin Hauberg-Lund Laugesen (2019), *Dark Pedagogy: Education, Horror and the Anthropocene*. Cham: Palgrave Macmillan.

Macias, Patrick (2020), 'A History of Gamera', in *Gamera*, ed. Arrow Films, 5–33. London: Arrow Films.

Magnolia Pictures (2006), '*The Host* Press Notes and Director's Interview', SciFiJapan. Accessed 6 August 2021. https://www.scifijapan.com/kaiju-monsters/the-host-press-notes-and-directors-interview#Q&A.

Martin, Daniel (2009), 'Japan's *Blair Witch*: Restraint, Maturity, and Generic Canons in the British Critical Reception of *Ring*', *Cinema Journal* 48 (3): 35–51.

Martin, Daniel (2014), 'South Korean Horror Cinema', in *A Companion to the Horror Film*, ed. Harry M. Benshoff, 423–41. Malden: Wiley.

Martin-Jones, David (2006), *Deleuze, Cinema and National Identity: Narratie Time in National Contexts*. Edinburgh: Edinburgh University Press.

Maser Patrol (2017), '怪獣 or 外獣? (Kaiju or Gaiju?)', Maser Patrol, 8 January. Accessed 28 July 2020. https://maserpatrol.wordpress.com/2017/01/08/怪獣-or-外獣-kaiju-or-gaiju/.

Maser Patrol (2021), 'Old School Special Effects with Seoul', Maser Patrol, 1 April. Accessed 2 August 2021. https://maserpatrol.wordpress.com/2021/04/01/old-school-special-effects-with-seoul.

Masters, Kim (2015), 'Hollywood Gorilla Warfare: It's Universal vs. Legendary Over "Kong: Skull Island" (and Who Says "Thank You")', *The Hollywood Reporter*, 16 September. Accessed 11 February 2021. https://www.hollywoodreporter.com/news/hollywood-gorilla-warfare-s-universal-823715.

Mathijs, Ernest, and Jamie Sexton (2011), *Cult Cinema: An Introduction*. Malden: Wiley-Blackwell.

Mazdon, Lucy (2000), *Encore Hollywood: Remaking French Cinema*. London: British Film Institute.

McClintock, Pamela (2005), 'A Tull Order to Fill', *Variety*, 21–7 November: 6, 75.

McClintock, Pamela (2017), 'Matt Damon's "The Great Wall" to Lose $75 Million; Future U.S.–China Productions in Doubt', *The Hollywood Reporter*, 2 March. Accessed 11 February 2021. https://www.hollywoodreporter.com/news/what-great-walls-box-office-flop-will-cost-studios-981602.

McDonald, Keith, and Roger Clark (2014), *Guillermo del Toro: Film as Alchemic Art*. New York and London: Bloomsbury.

McFarlane, Brian, and Anthony Slide (2014), *The Encyclopedia of British Film*. 4th edn. Manchester: Manchester University Press.

McGray, Douglas (2002), 'Japan's Gross National Cool', *Foreign Policy*, 1 May: 44–54. Accessed 26 July 2016. http://foreignpolicy.com/2009/11/11/japans-gross-national-cool/.

McKenna, A. T. (2016), *Showman of the Screen: Joseph E. Levine and his Revolutions in Film Promotion*. Lexington: University of Kentucky Press.

McKevitt, Andrew C. (2017), *Consuming Japan: Popular Culture and the Globalizing of 1980s America*. Chapel Hill: University of North Carolina Press.

McNary, Dave (2014a), 'Legendary's "Warcraft," "Seventh Son" Secure Chinese Investment', *Variety*, 14 April. Accessed 4 February 2021. https://variety.com/2014/film/asia/legendarys-warcraft-seventh-son-secure-chinese-investment-1201157030/.

McNary, Dave (2014b), '"Pacific Rim 2" Confirmed for April 7, 2017, Release', *Variety*, 26 June. Accessed 11 February 2021. https://variety.com/2014/film/news/pacific-rim-2-confirmed-for-april-7–2017-release-1201251654/.

McRobert, Neil (2015), 'Mimesis of Media: Found Footage Cinema and the Horror of the Real', *Gothic Studies* 17 (2): 137–50.

McRoy, Jay (2008), *Nightmare Japan: Contemporary Japanese Horror Cinema*. Amsterdam and New York: Rodopi.

Medved, Harry, and Michael Medved (1979), *The Fifty Worst Movies of All Time (and How They Got That Way)*. London: Angus & Robertson.

Meikle, Denis, and Christopher T. Koetting (2009), *A History of Horrors: The Rise and Fall of the House of Hammer.* Lanham: Scarecrow Press.

Milner, David (2020), 'Interview with Noriaki Yuasa', in *Gamera*, ed. Arrow Films, 35–45. London: Arrow Films.

Mittell, Jason (2009), 'Forensic Fandom and the Drillable Text', *Spreadable Media*. Accessed 1 October 2021. http://spreadablemedia.org/essays/mittell/index.html#.YVcObprMKUk.

Mondal, Sayantan (2017), 'King Kong, Born in the USA and Happily Adopted the World Over, Including by India', *Scroll.in*, 7 May. Accessed 16 September 2021. https://scroll.in/reel/831104/king-kong-born-in-the-usa-and-happily-adopted-the-world-over-including-by-india.

Motion Picture Producers Association of Japan (2021), 'Statistics of Film Industry', Motion Picture Producers Association of Japan, 31 August. Accessed 31 August 2021. http://www.eiren.org/statistics_e/index.html.

Movies Online (2008), 'JJ Abrams talks *CloverField*', MoviesOnline, 18 February. Accessed 9 September 2021. http://www.moviesonline.ca/movienews_12553.html.

Muck47 (2013), '*King Kong vs Godzilla*', Movie Censorship, 10 June. Accessed 19 August 2021. https://www.movie-censorship.com/report.php?ID=404045.

Murphy, Mekado (2014), 'Face-Lift? Well, You Still Look Like Hell', *The New York Times*, 9 May. Accessed 17 February 2020. https://www.nytimes.com/2014/05/11/movies/godzilla-in-his-many-incarnations.html?_r=1.

Murray, Robin L., and Joseph K. Heumann (2016), *Monstrous Nature: Environment and Horror on the Big Screen*. Lincoln, NE and London: University of Nebraska Press.

Myrtdi (2011), 'Godzilla in America: A Critical Comparison between the Japanese and American Versions of the Godzilla Films', *History Vortex*, 13 November. Accessed 19 August 2021. https://www.historyvortex.org/GodzillaAmerica2.html.

Naficy, Hamid (2001), *An Accented Cinema: Exilic and Diasporic Filmmaking*. Princeton: Princeton University Press.

Nakagawa, Masayuki (1874), 'Taisei Public Opinion (Taisei Zesetsu), Vol. 3', National Diet Digital Library. Accessed 19 June 2020. doi:10.11501/761320.

Naono, Akiko (2019), 'The Origins of "Hibakusha" as a Scientific and Political Classification of the Survivor', *Japanese Studies* 39 (3): 333–52. doi:https://doi.org/10.1080/10371397.2019.1654854.

Napier, Susan J. (1993), 'Panic Sites: The Japanese Imagination of Disaster from *Godzilla* to *Akira*', *The Journal of Japanese Studies* 19 (2): 327–51.

Newitz, Annalee (2013), 'Godzilla Director Gareth Edwards Explains the Symbolism of Kaiju', Gizmodo, 25 July. Accessed 30 September 2021. https://gizmodo.com/godzilla-director-gareth-edwards-explains-the-symbolism-902734240.

Newman, Kathleen (2010), 'Notes on Transnational Film Theory: Decentered Subjectivity, Decentered Capitalism', in *World Cinemas, Transnational Perspectives*, eds Nataša Ďurovičová and Kathleen Newman, 3–11. London and New York: Routledge.

Noriega, Chon (1987), 'Godzilla and the Japanese Nightmare: When "Them!" Is U.S.', *Cinema Journal* 27 (1): 63–77.

Nornes, Abé Mark (2007), *Cinema Babel: Translating Global Cinema*. Minneapolis and London: University of Minnesota Press.

Oliete-Aldea, Elena, Beatriz Oria and Juan A. Tarancón (2016), 'Introduction: Questions of Transnationalism and Genre', in *Global Genres, Local Films: The Transnational Dimension of Spanish Cinema*, eds Elena Oliete-Aldea, Beatriz Oria and Juan A. Tarancón, 1–15. New York and London: Bloomsbury.

Ong, Aihwa (1999), *Flexible Citizenship: The Cultural Logics of Transnationality*. Durham, NC and London: Duke University Press.

O'Regan, Tom (1999), 'Cultural Exchange', in *A Companion to Film Theory*, eds Toby Miller and Robert Stam, 262–94. Oxford: Blackwell.

Park, Jungman (2019), 'Born of Two Koreas, of Human Blood: Monstrosity and the Discourse of Humanity and Pacifism in the Film *Bulgasari*', *Kritika Kultura* (33/34): 136–55. doi:http://dx.doi.org/10.13185/KK2020.03307.

Patten, Dominic (2015), '"Godzilla" Battle Settled Between Legendary & Tossed Producers', *Deadline*, 4 June. Accessed 30 September 2021. https://deadline.com/2015/06/godzilla-lawsuit-setlement-legendary-roy-lee-dan-lin-doug-davison-1201438039/.

Peirse, Alison and Daniel Martin (2013), 'Introduction', in *Korean Horror Cinema*, eds Alison Peirse and Daniel Martin, 1–20. Edinburgh: Edinburgh University Press.

Perkins, Claire (2013), *American Smart Cinema*. Edinburgh: Edinburgh University Press.

Perren, Alisa (2012), *Indie, Inc.: Miramax and the Transformation of Hollywood in the 1990s*. Austin: University of Texas Press.

Pile, Steven (2011), 'Intensities of Feeling: *Cloverfield*, the Uncanny, and the Always Near Collapse of the City', in *The New Blackwell Companion to the City*, eds Gary Bridge and Sophie Watson, 288–303. Malden: Wiley-Blackwell.

Pratt, Mary Louise (1991), 'Arts of the Contact Zone', *Profession* 33–40. http://www.jstor.org/stable/25595469.

Pulver, Andrew (2016), 'Matt Damon on *Great Wall* Whitewashing: "I Didn't Take Role from Chinese Actor"', *The Guardian*, 7 December. Accessed 11 February 2021. https://www.theguardian.com/film/2016/dec/07/matt-damon-on-great-wall-whitewashing-i-didnt-take-role-from-chinese-actor.

Ragone, August (2009), 'Frankenstein vs. the Giant Devilfish: Or "Pardon Me, Your Tentacles Are in My Soup!"', August Ragone, 3 May. Accessed 18 May 2021. http://augustragone.blogspot.com/2009/05/frankenstein-vs-giant-devilfish-or.html.

Rainey, James, and Brent Lang (2017), 'Legendary Entertainment CEO Thomas Tull Exiting', *Variety*, 17 January. Accessed 12 February 2021. https://variety.com/2017/film/news/legendary-entertainment-ceo-thomas-tull-exiting-1201961882/.

Raphael, Raphael (2016), 'Planet Kong: Transnational Flows of King Kong (1933) in Japan and East Asia', in *Transnational Horror Cinema: Bodies of Excess and the Global Grotesque*, eds Sophia Siddique and Raphael Raphael, 205–20. London: Palgrave Macmillan.

Rawle, Steven (2014), 'The Ultimate Super-Happy-Zombie-Romance-Murder-Mystery-Family-Comedy-Karaoke-Disaster-Movie-Part-Animated-Remake-All-Singing-All-Dancing-Musical-Spectacular-Extravaganza: Miike Takashi's The Happiness of the Katakuris as "Cult" Hybrid', in *Screening the Undead: Vampires and Zombies in Film and Television*, eds Leon Hunt, Sharon Lockyer and Milly Williamson, 208–32. London: I. B. Tauris.

Rawle, Steven (2015), 'Ringing *One Missed Call*: Franchising, Transnational Flows and Genre Production', *East Asian Journal of Popular Culture* 1 (1): 97–112.

Rawle, Steven (2021), 'Globalizing Legendary Entertainment: Transnational Finance Meets Transculturality', in *Transcultural Images in Hollywood Cinema: Debates on Migration, Identity, and Finance* eds Uğur Baloğlu and Yıldız Derya Birincioğlu, 9–32. Lanham: Lexington.

Red Menace (2016), '*Destroy All Monsters*: AIP HD Reconstruction (Released)', Original Trilogy.com, 11 August. Accessed 19 August 2021. https://originaltrilogy.com/topic/Destroy-All-Monsters-AIP-HD-Reconstruction-Released/id/51171.

Rhoads, Sean, and Brooke McCorkle (2018), *Japan's Green Monsters: Environmental Commentary in Kaiju Cinema*. Jefferson: McFarland.

Richie, Donald (2001), *A Hundred Years of Japanese Films: A Concise History, with a Selective Guide to DVDs and Videos*. Tokyo: Kodansha.

Robehmed, Natalie (2016), 'Box Office Billionaire: How Legendary's Thomas Tull Used Comics, China and a Secret Formula to Remake Hollywood', *Forbes*, 29 February. Accessed 4 February 2021. https://www.forbes.com/sites/natalierobehmed/2016/02/10/the-global-mogul/?linkId=21151285.

Robinson, Michael (2005), 'Contemporary Cultural Production in South Korea: Vanishing Meta-Narratives of Nation', in *New Korean Cinema*, eds Chi-Yun Shin and Julian Stringer, 15–31. Edinburgh: Edinburgh University Press.

Roebuck, Andrew (2020), 'The Weird World of Kongsploitation: From 1933 to 2020: Exploring the Wild World of Tokusatsu', Scriptphobic, 11 February. Accessed 20 September 2021. https://scriptophobic.ca/2020/02/11/the-weird-world-of-kongsploitation-from-1933-to-2020/.

Roedder, Alexandra (2014), 'The Localization of *Kiki's Delivery Service*', *Mechademia* 9: 254–67.

Rosen, David N. (1975), '*King Kong*: Race, Sex, and Rebellion', *Jump Cut: A Review of Contemporary Media* (6): 7–10. Accessed 10 August 2020. http://www.ejumpcut.org/archive/onlinessays/JC06folder/KingKong.html.

Ruh, Brian (2010), 'Transforming U.S. Anime in the 1980s: Localization and Longevity', *Mechademia* 5: 31–49.

Russo, Tom (2013), '"Pacific Rim" Is the Heartfelt Project from del Toro', *Boston Globe*, 6 July. Accessed 26 September 2021. https://www.bostonglobe.com/arts/movies/2013/07/06/pacific-rim-latest-heartfelt-project-from-guillermo-del-toro/aTU5X0wLpNaUe1GpbHqDUO/story.html.

Ryfle, Steve (1998), *Japan's Favorite Mon-Star: The Unauthorized Biography of 'The Big G'*. Toronto: ECW Press.

Ryfle, Steve (2005), 'Godzilla's Footprint', *The Virginia Quarterly Review* 81 (1): 44–63.

Ryfle, Steve (2014), 'Whitewashing Godzilla', *In These Times*, 14 May. Accessed 30 September 2021. https://inthesetimes.com/article/whitewashing-godzilla.

Ryfle, Steve, and Ed Godziszewski (2017), *Ishiro Honda: A Life in Film, from Godzilla to Kurosawa*. Middletown: Wesleyan University Press.

Ryfle, Steve, and Song-ho Kim (2016), *Yongary: Monster from the Deep* Audio Commentary. Kino Lorber.

Sakamoto, Azumi (2020), 'Frankenstein; or the Postwar *Kaijū*: Contrasting Interpretations of *Frankenstein Conquers the World*', in *Japan beyond Its Borders: Transnational Approaches to Film and Media*, eds Marcos P. Centeno-Martín and Norimasa Morita, 225–42. Tokyo: Seibunsha.

Santos, Simon (2008), 'Pinoy Sci-Fi #4: Three "Atomic Monster" Movies in the Fifties', Video48, 24 May. Accessed 17 August 2021. http://video48.blogspot.com/2008/05/pinoy-sci-fi-4-three-atomic-monster.html.

Sargent, J. F. (2013), 'How "Pacific Rim" Got Kaiju Wrong', *Film School Rejects*, 1 August. Accessed 27 September 2021. https://filmschoolrejects.com/how-pacific-rim-got-kaiju-wrong-c154c1499531/.

Schaefer, Eric (1999), *'Bold! Daring! Shocking! True!' A History of Exploitation Film, 1919–1959*. Durham, NC and London: Duke University Press.

Schilling, Mark (2007), *No Borders, No Limits: Nikkatsu Action Cinema*. Godalming: FAB.

Sconce, Jeffrey (1995), '"Trashing" the Academy: Taste, Excess, and an Emerging Politics of Cinematic Style', *Screen* 36 (4): 371–93.

Sconce, Jeffrey (2002), 'Irony, Nihilism and the New American "Smart" Film', *Screen* 43 (4): 349–69.

Sconce, Jeffrey (2007), 'Introduction', in *Sleaze Artists: Cinema at the Margins of Taste, Style, and Politics*, ed. Jeffrey Sconce, 1–17. Durham, NC and London: Duke University Press.

Scott, Suzanne (2017), 'Modeling the Marvel Everyfan: Agent Coulson and/as Transmedia Fan Culture', *Palabra Clave* 20 (4): 1042–72.

Sedgwick, Eve Kosofsky (1993), *Tendencies*. Durham, NC: Duke University Press.

Sexton, Jamie (2016), 'The Allure of Otherness: Transnational Cult Film Fandom and the Exoticist Assumption', *Transnational Cinemas* 8 (1): 5–19.
Shaw, Deborah (2013a), *The Three Amigos: The Transnational Filmmaking of Guillermo del Toro, Alejandro González Iñárritu and Alfonso Cuarón*. Manchester: Manchester University Press.
Shaw, Deborah (2013b), 'Deconstructing and Reconstructing "Transnational Cinema"', in *Contemporary Hispanic Cinema: Interrogating Transnationalism in Spanish and Latin American film*, ed. Stephanie Dennison, 47–66. Woodbridge: Tamesis.
Shaw, Deborah, and Armida De La Garza (2010), 'Introducing Transnational Cinemas', *Transnational Cinemas* 1 (1): 3–6. doi:10.1386/trac 1.1.3/2.
Shin, Chi-Yun (2008), 'Art of Branding: Tartan "Asia Extreme" Films', *Jump Cut: A Review of Contemporary Media* 50. Accessed 19 February 2016. http://www.ejumpcut.org/currentissue/.
Shin, Chi-Yun (2012), '"Excessive" Remake: From *The Quiet Family* to *The Happiness of the Katakuris*', *Transnational Cinemas* 3 (1): 67–79.
Shohat, Ella, and Robert Stam (1994), *Unthinking Eurocentrism: Multiculturalism and the Media*. London and New York: Routledge.
Siegemund-Broka, Austin (2015), 'Anne Hathaway Lizard Film Under "Godzilla" Attack in New Lawsuit', *The Hollywood Reporter*, 19 May. Accessed 15 December 2021. https://www.hollywoodreporter.com/business/business-news/anne-hathaway-lizard-film-under-796883.
Smith, Andrew, and William Hughes, eds (2013), *EcoGothic*. Manchester: Manchester University Press.
Smith, Iain Robert (2013), '"You're Really a Miniature Bond": Weng Weng and the Transnational Dimension of Cult Film Stardom', in *Cult Film Stardom: Offbeat Attractions and Processes of Cultification*, eds Kate Egan and Sarah Thomas, 226–39. London: Palgrave Macmillan.
Smith, Iain Robert (2014), 'Bollywood B-Movies: Cult Cosmopolitanism and the Reception of Indian Genre Cinema in the West', *Frames Cinema Journal* 7. Accessed 27 September 2021. http://framescinemajournal.com/article/bollywood-b-movies-cult-cosmopolitanism-and-the-reception-of-indian-genre-cinema-in-the-west.
Smith, Iain Robert (2016), 'Transnational Holmes: Theorizing the Global–Local Nexus through the Japanese Anime *Sherlock Hound* (1984–)', in *Media Across Borders: Localising TV, Film and Video Games*, eds Andrea Esser, Miguel Á. Bernal-Merino and Iain Robert Smith, 36–52. New York: Routledge.
Smith, Iain Robert (2017), *The Hollywood Meme: Transnational Adaptations in World Cinema*. Edinburgh: Edinburgh University Press.
Smith, Iain Robert (2019), 'So "Foreign" it's Good: The Cultural Politics of Accented Cult Cinema', *Journal of Media & Cultural Studies* 33: 705–16.
Smith, Iain Robert, and Constantine Verevis (2017), 'Introduction: Transnational Film Remakes', in *Transnational Film Remakes*, eds Iain Robert Smith and Constantine Verevis, 1–18. Edinburgh: Edinburgh University Press.

Sobchack, Vivian (2001), *Screening Space: The American Science Fiction Film.* 2nd edn. New Brunswick, NJ and London: Rutgers University Press.

Sobchack, Vivian (2004), *Carnal Thoughts: Embodiment and Moving Image Culture.* Berkeley: University of California Press.

Solomon, Brian (2017), *Godzilla FAQ: All That's Left to Know about the King of the Monsters.* Lanham: Applause.

Sontag, Susan (2009), 'The Imagination of Disaster', in *Against Interpretation and Other Essays* by Susan Sontag, 209–25. London: Penguin.

Stam, Robert, and João Luiz Vieira (1990), 'Parody and Marginality: The Case of Brazilian Cinema', in *The Media Reader*, eds Manuel Alvarado and John O. Thompson, 82–104. London: British Film Institute.

Standish, Isolde (2005), *A New History of Japanese Cinema: A Century of Narrative Film.* London and New York: Continuum.

Steinberg, Marc (2012), *Anime's Media Mix: Franchising Toys and Characters in Japan.* Minneapolis and London: University of Minnesota Press.

Stephens, David (2018), 'Toho Planning Godzilla Cinematic Universe, Shin Godzilla 2 Canceled', *Screen Rant*, 19 May. Accessed 17 October 2021. https://screenrant.com/toho-godzilla-cinematic-universe-shin-godzilla-2-canceled/.

Sugimoto, Yoshio (1999), 'Making Sense of Nihonjinron', *Thesis Eleven* 57 (1): 81–96. Accessed 6 May 2021. doi:https://doi.org/10.1177/0725513699057000007.

Sullivan, Kevin P. (2016), '*10 Cloverfield Lane* and the 6 Steps to Making a Secret Movie', *Entertainment Weekly*, 25 February. Accessed 9 September 2021. https://ew.com/article/2016/02/25/jj-abrams-10-cloverfield-lane-secrets/.

Sullivan, Mac (2017), '*The Great Wall*: Matt Damon, Zhang Yimou, Edward Zwick, and . . . Dragons?', *Film Criticism* 41 (3). Accessed 11 February 2021. doi:10.3998/fc.13761232.0041.309.

Suzuki, Eishirō (1908), 'Mysterious World: A Strange Story (Kai Sekai: Chindan Kiwa)', National Diet Digital Library. Accessed 10 June 2020. doi:10.11501/885790.

Tanikawa, Takeshi (2020), 'Kaiju Films as Exportable Content: Reassessing the Function of the Japanese Film Export Promotion Association', in *Routledge Handbook of Japanese Cinema*, eds Joanne Bernardi and Shota T. Ogawa, 113–27. London: Routledge.

Tatsumi, Takayuki (2014), 'On the Monstrous Planet, or How Godzilla Took a Roman Holiday', translated by Seth Jacobwitz ,in *The Liverpool Companion to World Science Fiction Film*, ed. Sonja Fritzsche, 69–85. Liverpool: Liverpool University Press.

Thornton, Niamh (2014), '*Pacific Rim*: Reception, Readings, and Authority', in *The Transnational Fantasies of Guillermo del Toro*, eds Ann Davies, Deborah Shaw and Dolores Tierney, 121–39. New York: Palgrave Macmillan.

Tilly, Chris (2018), 'Why Ultraman Isn't in "Ready Player One"', Fandom.com, 28 March. Accessed 26 September 2021. https://www.fandom.com/articles/why-ultraman-isnt-in-ready-player-one.

Toho Kingdom (2014), *VHS Box Art,* 5 October. Accessed 1 August 2016. http://www.tohokingdom.com/articles/art_boxart.htm.

Travers, Peter (2019), '*Godzilla: King of the Monsters* Review: Destroy All Mediocre Franchise Cash-Ins', *Rolling Stone,* 29 May. Accessed 30 September 2021. https://www.rollingstone.com/movies/movie-reviews/godzilla-king-of-the-monsters-movie-review-840895/.

Tryon, Chuck (2009), *Reinventing Cinema: Movies in the Age of Media Convergence.* New Brunswick, NJ: Rutgers University Press.

Tsutsui, William (2004), *Godzilla on My Mind: Fifty Years of the King of Monsters.* New York: Palgrave Macmillan.

Tsutsui, William (2010), 'Oh No, There Goes Tokyo: Recreational Apocalypse and the City in Postwar Japanese Popular Culture', in *Noir Urbanisms: Dystopic Images of the Modern City,* ed. Gyan Prakash, 104–26. Princeton and Oxford: Princeton University Press.

Tsutsui, William (2014), 'For Godzilla and Country', *Foreign Affairs,* 28 March. Accessed 4 December 2015. http://www.foreignaffairs.com/articles/141472/william-m-tsutsui/for-godzilla-and-country.

Tudor, Andrew (1989), *Monsters and Mad Scientists: A Cultural History of the Horror Movie.* Oxford: Blackwell.

TV Tropes (n.d.), 'The Mockbuster', *TV Tropes.* Accessed 16 September 2021. https://tvtropes.org/pmwiki/pmwiki.php/Main/TheMockbuster.

Uchiyama, Takashi (2020), 'Film and Other Video Contents (TV Program and Internet Video)', in *Perspectives on the Japanese Media and Content Policies,* ed. Minoru Sugaya, 115–44. Singapore: Springer.

UNESCO (2021), 'Lists of Intangible Cultural Heritage and the Register of Good Safeguarding Practices', *UNESCO,* 26 August. Accessed 26 August 2021. https://ich.unesco.org/en/lists.

Variety Staff (1995), 'Romanian Counts Prod'n Bounty', *Variety,* 14 August. Accessed 4 August 2021. https://variety.com/1995/scene/markets-festivals/romanian-counts-prod-n-bounty-99129646/.

Verevis, Constantine (2006), *Film Remakes.* Edinburgh: Edinburgh University Press.

Wada-Marciano, Mitsuyo (2009), 'J-Horror: New Media's Impact on Contemporary Japanese Horror Cinema', in *Horror to the Extreme: Chainging Boundaries in Asian Cinema,* eds Jinhee Choi and Mitsuyo Wada-Marciano, 15–37. Aberdeen: Hong Kong University Press.

Warren, Bill (2017), *Keep Watching the Skies! American Science Fiction Movies of the Fifties: The 21st Century Edition.* Jefferson: McFarland.

Weaver Hwang Hae-Rym, Teri (2005), 'Morgue Official in Korea Convicted of Dumping Chemicals Avoids Jail', *Stars and Stripes,* 20 January. Accessed 6 August 2021. https://www.stripes.com/news/morgue-official-in-korea-convicted-of-dumping-chemicals-avoids-jail-1.28241.

Webber, Roy P. (2004), *The Dinosaur Films of Ray Harryhausen: Features, Early 16mm Experiments and Unrealized Projects.* Jefferson and London: McFarland.

Wee, Valerie (2010), 'Visual Aesthetics and Ways of Seeing: Comparing Video Images from *Ringu* and *The Ring*', *Cinema Journal* 50 (2): 41–60.

Wee, Valerie (2011), 'Patriarchy and the Horror of the Monstrous Feminine: A Comparative Study of *Ringu* and *The Ring*', *Feminist Media Studies* 11 (2): 151–65.

Week in China (2018), 'Primed for the Pacific', *Week in China,* 6 April. Accessed 11 February 2021. https://www.weekinchina.com/2018/04/primed-for-the-pacific/.

Weintraub, Steve (2013), 'Guillermo del Toro Talks Getting Back in the Director's Chair, the Evolution of the Script, Creating the World on a Giant Scale, and More on the Set of PACIFIC RIM', *Collider*, 19 June. Accessed 26 September 2021. https://collider.com/guillermo-del-toro-pacific-rim-interview/.

Wessels, Emanuelle (2011), '"Where Were You When the Monster Hit?" Media Convergence, Branded Security Citizenship, and the Trans-Media Phenomenon of *Cloverfield*', *Convergence* 17 (1): 69–83.

Wikizilla (2021), 'Five Versions of the First Godzilla Movie | MONSTER PLANET', YouTube, 5 March. Accessed 17 August 2021. https://www.youtube.com/watch?v=J1yE5hlu2Dc.

Wikizilla (n.d.), 'Kraken', Wikizilla. Accessed 3 September 2021. https://wikizilla.org/wiki/Kraken.

Willemen, Paul (2006), 'The National Revisited', in *Theorising National Cinema*, eds Valentina Vitali and Paul Willemen, 29–43. London: British Film Institute.

Woerner, Meredith (2013), 'How Frank Darabont Will Return Godzilla to his Rightful Place as a Terrifying Force of Nature', *Gizmodo,* 11 November. Accessed 30 September 2021. https://gizmodo.com/how-frank-darabont-will-return-godzilla-to-his-rightful-5977982.

Wong, Julia Carrie (2016), 'Asian Americans Decry "Whitewashed" Great Wall Film Starring Matt Damon', *The Guardian*, 30 July. Accessed 11 February 2021. https://www.theguardian.com/film/2016/jul/29/the-great-wall-china-film-matt-damon-whitewashed.

Wood, Robin (1985), 'An Introduction to the American Horror Film', in *Movies and Methods*, Vol. 2, ed. Bill Nichols, 195–220. Berkeley: University of California Press.

World Nuclear Association (2021), 'Fukushima Daiichi Accident', April. Accessed 30 September 2021. https://world-nuclear.org/information-library/safety-and-security/safety-of-plants/fukushima-daiichi-accident.aspx.

Xi, Jinping (2014), 'Xi Jinping: Build a Socialist Cultural Power and Focus on Improving the Country's Cultural Soft Power', *People's Daily Online*, 1 January. Accessed 11 February 2021. http://politics.people.com.cn/n/2014/0101/c1001–23994334.html.

Xu, Gary G. (2007), *Sinascape: Contemporary Chinese Cinema*. Lanham and Plymouth: Rowman & Littlefield.

Yam, Kimmy (2020), '"Godzilla" Was a Metaphor for Hiroshima, and Hollywood Whitewashed it', *NBC News*, 7 August. Accessed 10 August 2021. https://www.nbcnews.com/news/asian-america/godzilla-was-metaphor-hiroshima-hollywood-whitewashed-it-n1236165.

Yang, Jing, Min Jiao and Jin Zhang (2020), 'An Alternative Discourse of Modernity in a Chinese Monster Film: *The Great Wall*', *Cultural Studies* 34 (4): 656–74. Accessed 11 February 2021. doi:10.1080/09502386.2019.1694050.

Yomota, Inuhiko (2007), 'The Menace from the South Seas: Honda Ishirō's *Godzilla* (1954)', in *Japanese Cinema: Texts and Contexts*, eds Alastair Phillips and Julian Stringer, 102–11. London and New York: Routledge.

Yomota, Inuhiko (2019), *What Is Japanese Cinema? A History.* Translated by Philip Kaffen. New York: Columbia University Press.

Yoshida, Emily (2018), '*Pacific Rim Uprising* Might Be the Most China-Bait Studio Release Yet', *Vulture*, 21 March. Accessed 11 February 2021. https://www.vulture.com/2018/03/pacific-rim-uprising-review.html.

Yoshimoto, Mitsuhiro (2019), 'Nuclear Disasters and Invisible Spectacles', *Asian Cinema* 30 (2): 169–85.

Young, James O., and Conrad G. Brunk (2009), 'Introduction', in *The Ethics of Cultural Appropriation,* eds James O. Young and Conrad G. Brunk, 1–10. Chichester: Wiley-Blackwell.

Zhang, Rui (2020), 'Disney's "Mulan" to hit Chinese Theaters on Sept. 11', *China.org.cn*, 3 September. Accessed 9 February 2021. http://www.china.org.cn/arts/2020-09/03/content_76666159.htm.

Ziff, Bruce, and Pratima V. Rao (1997), 'Introduction to Cultural Appropriation: A Framework for Analysis', in *Borrowed Power: Essays on Cultural Appropriation,* eds Bruce Ziff and Pratima V. Rao, 1–27. New Brunswick, NJ: Rutgers University Press.

# Index

*10 Cloverfield Lane*, 175
1964 Tokyo Olympics, 49, 59
1988 Seoul Olympics, 102
2004 Indian Ocean Tsunami, 222
2020 Tokyo Olympics, 21
*2-Headed Shark*, 187
*3 Ninja Kids*, 100
*300*, 198
38th parallel, 88
*42*, 198, 229n
*6 Ultra Brothers vs. the Monster Army, The*, 79
9/11, 10, 172–6, 222

*A\*P\*E*, 34, 78, 190–3
*A.I. Artificial Intelligence*, 206
*Aadi Yug*, 79
ABC, 56
Able, Whitney, 177
AB-PT, 55–6
Abrams, J. J., 172
ABRY, 198
accented cinema, 205, 207
Adams, Nick, 17, 58, 61, 228
adaptation, 19, 43, 80–2, 85, 91, 94, 120–3, 154, 171, 177–8, 182, 187, 192–4
Agent Orange, 111
AGI Direct, 198
Aiken, Keith, 70, 165–7, 218
Ainu, 49, 152
Akatsuka Fujio, 90
*Akira*, 31
*Alien*, 109
*Aliens*, 169
*All Monsters Attack*, 124, 132
Altman, Rick, 7, 52, 78, 175
AMC cinemas, 200
American Film Market, 107, 187
American International Pictures (AIP), 62, 64, 114, 116, 121, 138, 140, 161–2, 163, 189, 240, 241
American International Television, 240
*American Warships*, 184
Americanisation, 46, 81–2, 122, 139, 150, 167, 169, 171, 188–9, 216–17
Anderson, Joseph L., 50–1
Anderson, Wes, 151–2
Andrew, Dudley, 15
Anglo-Amalgamated, 189
Anno Hideaki, 47n, 235
*Apocalypse Now*, 178
Appadurai, Arjun, 18, 91, 99, 103
appropriation, 14, 17, 22, 33, 43, 48, 83, 85, 90, 112, 115–16, 146, 150–5, 164, 167, 169, 171, 182, 184, 192–4, 194n, 207–11
Argento, Dario, 131
Arirang, 89–90, 107
Arkoff, Samuel, 162
Armstrong, Robert, 34
Arrow Films, 77n, 118, 138
Asylum, The, 107, 150, 184, 186–7
Atkins, E. Taylor, 89–90
*Atlantic Rim*, 150, 184
*Atlantic Rim: Resurrection*, 184
Atlas Entertainment, 210
*Atragon*, 9, 55
*Attack of the Mushroom People*, 241
*Avengers Assemble*, 224
*Avengers: Age of Ultron*, 224
*Avengers: Infinity War*, 214

*Babel*, 177
Bae Doona, 110
Baker, Andrew, 226
Bakhtin, Mikhail, 80, 191
Ballesteros, Isolina, 177–8
*Bambi Meets Godzilla*, 146
Bandai, 69
Bang & Olufsen, 161
Bang, Poul, 1, 161
*Bangla King Kong*, 192–3
Bank of America Capital Investors, 198

## INDEX

Banno Yoshimitsu, 92, 218
*Barefoot Gen*, 31
Barr, Jason, 6, 7, 9–10, 35, 69, 78–9, 98, 155, 156, 163
Barthes, Roland, 152–3
*Batman Begins*, 198
*Battle in Outer Space*, 32
*Battle of the Planets*, 120–1
*Battleship*, 184
Bazin, André, 83
*Beast from 20,000 Fathoms, The*, 16, 17, 37, 38–47, 50, 58, 64–5, 133, 136, 156, 160, 162, 169, 195n
Beatles, The, 146
Beck, John, 60
*Behemoth the Sea Monster*, 156–61
Behr, Jason, 107
Behrens, Marla, 162, 195n
Bengtsson, Stefan, 218–19
Bergfelder, Tim, 11
Berghahn, Daniela, 16
Bernardin, Marc, 151–2
Berry, Chris, 103, 104, 107
Bhabha, Homi K., 80
Bikini Atoll, 24–5, 208, 216, 221
Binoche, Juliette, 220
Biollante, 42, 156
Biondi, Robert, 137
*Bionic Woman, The*, 123
Bixio, Franco, 133
Black Lives Matter, 115
*Black Panther*, 214
*Black Rain*, 31
*Blackhat*, 198
*Blair Witch Project, The*, 172
Blitz, the, 158–9
*Blob, The*, 10
Bong Joon-ho, 103, 108–10, 113n
Booker, M. Keith, 183
Bordwell, David, 194n
Borenstein, Greg, 216
Borenstein, Max, 216
Boss, Joyce E., 164
Botting, Fred, 4–5
Boyega, John, 212
Bradbury, Ray, 38–9, 46
*Brewster's Millions*, 214
British Board of Film Classification, 160
British Film Institute, 14, 21
Broderick, Mick, 23, 31
Brooks, Max, 210
Brothers, Peter H., 45–6
Brown, Millie Bobby, 202

Brucesploitation, 79, 92, 187
Bunraku, 8
*Burakumin*, 54
Burr, Raymond, 125–6, 128, 130, 140, 143, 152
*Bye Bye Monkey*, 190

Cabot, Bruce, 34
*Calamari Wrestler, The*, 240
Cannes Film Festival, 104, 190
Caplan, Lizzy, 173
Carradine, John, 54, 136–7
*Casablanca*, 12
Castle Bravo, 25, 168, 223
Castle, William, 135
centre–margins models, 18, 83–4
*Chaebol*, 102–4
*Chambara*, 3, 20n, 67, 69, 77n
Champion Festival, 62
Chan, Jackie, 230n
Chen Zitong, 213
Cheung, Hye Seung, 105, 108, 111
*Children of Hiroshima*, 31
China Film Group, 199, 209–10
Choi Eun-hee, 94–5
Choo, Kukhee, 93
Chow, Rey, 210
Chow, Stephen, 199
Christian, Paul, 40
Chûjô Shinji, 66
Chun Doo-hwan, 102
Chung, Hye Jean, 105–6, 108
Chung, Steven, 94–5, 98
Church, David, 241
Cinema Shares, 123
CJ Entertainment, 103, 107
Clark, Roger, 205
*Clash of the Titans* (1981), 165, 195n
*Clash of the Titans* (2010), 165, 198
*Classic of Mountains and Seas, The* (*Shan Hai Jing*), 7, 211
Clements, Jonathan, 77n
Clifford the Big Red Dog, 218
cli-fi, 222
climate change, 20, 113n, 218, 223, 227
Cline, Ernest, 206
Clouzot, Henri-Georges, 137
Clover, 10, 42
Clover, Carol, 155
*Cloverfield*, 10, 42, 175–7, 184, 217–18
*Cloverfield Paradox, The*, 176
*Cloverfield/KISHINI*, 176
*Codfish*, 80–1

Cohen, Jeffrey Jerome, 5
Cold War, 13, 24–5, 99, 139, 144–5, 156, 169
*Collider*, 203
colonial mimicry, 40, 80–1, 83, 107, 188–9, 192
colonialism, 22, 40, 59, 80, 86, 89–90, 94, 107, 112, 115, 151, 154–5, 181–2, 191, 232–4
*Colossal*, 182–3
Columbia, 162, 165, 170, 240
Combe, Kirk, 178, 180
Comicon, 207
Conan Doyle, Arthur, 37, 42, 122
*Conan the Barbarian*, 131
Conrad, Joseph, 178
Conrich, Ian, 157–8
Constantin Film, 85
contact zones, 59, 61, 138, 151, 201
Cooper, Merian C., 33, 38
co-production, 61, 64, 71, 83–4, 86–7, 102, 112, 116, 124, 138, 161–3, 190, 196, 199, 202–3, 210, 214, 228
Corman, Roger, 140
cosmopolitanism, 122, 153–4, 207–8
Cospa, 70
*Costinha e o King Mong*, 80, 190, 192
Covid-19, 109, 229
Cozzi, Luigi, 131–5
*Cozzilla*, 131–6, 146n
Crandol, Michael, 3–4, 46
Crane, Kenneth G., 137
Cranston, Brian, 220
Creature Double Features, 144
Criterion Collection, 14, 118, 138
Crofts, Stephen, 117
*Crouching Tiger, Hidden Dragon*, 197, 210, 213
Crown International Pictures, 57
Cthulhu, 178
cult film, 11–14, 114, 118–19, 122, 141, 186, 193, 208, 241–2
cultural exchange, 17–18, 32, 43, 45, 59, 62, 82, 87, 117, 129, 151, 154, 158, 168, 170–1, 176, 193, 202, 208, 229
cultural flow, 11, 18–19, 78–9, 83–4, 91–2, 94, 99, 116, 150, 154, 157, 162, 167–8, 202, 207, 217, 229
*Curse of Frankenstein, The*, 3

Daewoo, 103
Dafoe, Willem, 209
Daiei, 51, 62–70, 73, 77n, 121, 242

*Daigo Fukuryū Maru* ('Lucky Dragon No. 5'), 25, 27, 30, 158
*Daigoro vs. Goliath*, 102
*Daikaijū Mono*, 240
*Daimajin*, 50, 63, 67–70, 75, 98, 241
*Daimajin Kanon*, 69
*Daimajin Strikes Again*, 69
Dalian Wanda, 153, 196, 199–203, 209, 212, 214, 215
Damon, Matt, 209
Dance, Charles, 227
Daneen, Mike, 71
Darabont, Frank, 218
*Dark Crystal, The*, 226
*Dark Knight Rises, The*, 198
*Dark Knight, The*, 197, 198
*Dating Game, The*, 121
Davis, Darrell William, 103, 210
Davison, Doug, 218
Dawkins, Richard, 80
*Day the Earth Caught Fire, The*, 133
*Day the Earth Stood Still, The*, 51
Day, Charlie, 212
DC Comics, 124, 198, 215
de Bont, Jan, 165, 169
de Certeau, Michel, 153
De Laurentiis, Dino, 131, 190, 195n
Deadpool, 149
Debus, Allen A., 163–4
*Def-Con 4*, 145
DeKnight, Steven S., 212
Del Mar, Eddie, 129
del Toro, Guillermo, 152–3, 205–6, 212
Deleyto, Celestino, 178–80
DeMille, Cecil B., 160
Denison, Rayna, 76, 120, 206
Depardieu, Gerard, 190
*Departed, The*, 217
Derendorf, Kevin, 21, 83, 91
Dern, Laura, 163
Desilu, 57
*Destroy all Monsters*, 124, 138
*Detective Chinatown 2*, 214
Devlin, Dean, 166–7
Diffrient, David Scott, 105, 108, 111
dino-anthropomorphism, 163–4
Disney, 2, 100, 200
Distribution, 16–17, 74, 100, 104, 108, 116–21, 133, 157, 161–2, 170, 186–7, 189, 198, 202, 232, 235–7, 240–1
Distributors Corporation of America, 137–8, 160

*District 9*, 177
Ditko, Steve, 189
*Dogora*, 55
Donlevy, Brian, 156
*Dōsojin*, 69
Dougherty, Michael, 17, 228
*Dr Cyclops*, 189
Dr Pepper, 144–5, 165
*Dracula* (1897), 103, 164
*Dracula* (1931), 161
*Dracula (*1958), 12
*Dragon Tuka*, 103
*Dragon Wars*, 107–8
drillable texts, 225, 229
dubbing, 5, 14, 52, 74, 114, 119–21, 126, 128, 132, 138, 143–6, 161, 187, 241
*Dying to Survive*, 214

*Earthquake*, 134
*Ebirah, Horror of the Deep*, 124, 195n, 242
Eco, Umberto, 12–13
Edwards, Gareth, 17, 25, 176–7, 218–27, 234–5
Elba, Idris, 205–6
Eleftheriotis, Dimitris, 85
Elliott, Ted, 165
Embassy Pictures, 116, 125, 129, 130
Emmerich, Roland, 14, 165–8, 170
*Emperor and the Assassin, The*, 210
Empire State Building, 36–8
*Enola Gay*, 133
*Enola Holmes*, 202
Erb, Cynthia, 22, 33, 35, 37–8, 81, 191–3
Eros Films, 123, 159–61, 195n
Esser, Andrea, 122, 135
*Executive Koala*, 240
exploitation cinema, 11, 13, 20, 34, 43, 51, 55–7, 61, 70, 74–5, 82, 84, 114–25, 128–9, 130–35, 137, 140, 150, 154–6, 160–3, 165, 183–4, 186–8, 192–3, 229, 240–2

*Fairy and the Devil, The*, 113n
*Fangoria*, 135
Ferrigno, Lou, 131
Field, Robert Scott, 186
*Fiend without a Face*, 159
Film School Rejects, 207
Filmlab Palestine, 201
*Fireman*, 93
Fischer, Paul, 94–5, 98
Fisher, Austin, 83

*Five Days, The*, 131
Floyd, George, 115
Fog Horn, The, 38–9, 46
forensic fandom, 224–5, 227–8
Forster, Robert, 107
Foster, Michael Dylan, 8–9
*Founding of Ming Dynasty, The*, 79, 93
*Four Flies on Grey Velvet*, 131
Frank, Sandy, 121, 138, 242
*Frankenstein 1970*, 140
*Frankenstein Conquers the World*, 55, 58–62, 65, 79, 124, 138
*Frankenstein vs. Godzilla*, 61
Frayling, Christopher, 83
*Friday the 13th*, 140
Frizzi, Fabio, 133–4
Frontier Enterprises, 138
Fujiki, Hideaki, 21
Fukasaku Kinji, 75
Fukushima Nuclear Plant meltdown, 31, 71, 220, 222, 234–6
Fulci, Lucio, 134
Full Moon Entertainment, 184–5
Funakoshi Eiji, 64
Futursound, 134

*gaiju*, 21–2, 83
Galbraith, Stuart, 52, 57
*Galgameth*, 100–2, 107
Gallagher Jr, John, 175
Gamera, 7, 8, 9, 10, 42, 62–7, 70, 76, 77n, 87, 90, 92, 102, 121, 138, 140, 239, 242
*Gamera the Brave*, 67
*Gamera vs. Barugon*, 64, 241
*Gamera vs. Guiron*, 205
*Gamera vs. Viras*, 71
*Gamera vs. Zigra*, 92
*Gamera: Guardian of the Universe*, 239
*Gamera: Super Monster*, 47n, 67
*Gamera: The Giant Monster*, 3, 50, 63–7
Gamergate, 183
*Gammera the Invincible*, 63, 138
Gappa, 10, 169
*Gappa, The Triphibian Monster*, 50, 72, 73–5, 157, 164
*Garuda*, 78–9
*Genocide*, 70, 72
Gerow, Aaron, 48
*G-Fan*, 9, 137
G-FEST, 236, 237
*Ghidorah, the Three-Headed Monster*, 71
*Ghost Story of Yotsuya, The*, 3

*Ghostbusters*, 9
*Giallo*, 132
*Gigantis, The Fire Monster*, 56, 137, 160
Gilroy, Tony, 210
GINO, 14, 167–8, 233–4
Girara, 10, 71
Glaser, Ed, 133
globalisation, 1, 14, 16–18, 33, 46, 49, 52, 64, 81–2, 93, 107–8, 112, 120, 129, 139–40, 150, 162, 171, 179, 187–8, 215, 232, 242
glocalisation, 214
Go Ah-sung, 110
Goblin, 133
*Godzilla* (1998), 14, 20n, 42, 104–5, 123, 165–75, 185–6, 189, 211, 221, 234
*Godzilla* (2014), 20n, 25, 196, 204, 215–24, 235
Godzilla, 1, 2, 4–7, 9–10, 12–14, 21, 33, 37–8, 41, 50, 62–3, 71, 75, 78, 84–5, 89, 90, 92, 95, 99, 102, 106, 109, 112, 118, 120, 123, 148, 152, 172, 182, 200, 204, 225, 230n, 233, 236
*Godzilla 1985*, 116, 139–46, 221, 240
*Godzilla 2000*, 146
Godzilla Junior, 169
*Godzilla Monster Apocalypse*, 76n
*Godzilla Raids Again*, 52–3, 56, 133
*Godzilla Singular Point*, 238–9
*Godzilla vs. Biollante*, 42, 163
Godzilla vs. Charles Barkley, 165
*Godzilla vs. Destroyah*, 95, 195n
*Godzilla vs. Hedorah*, 92, 114, 218
*Godzilla vs. King Ghidorah*, 7, 8, 186, 227
*Godzilla vs. Kong*, 34, 184, 196, 228–9, 231n
*Godzilla vs. MechaGodzilla*, 123
*Godzilla vs. MechaGodzilla 2* (1993), 166, 195n, 227, 239
*Godzilla vs. Megalon*, 123, 241
*Godzilla vs. SpaceGodzilla*, 76n
*Godzilla vs. the Thing*, 241
*Godzilla, King of the Monsters!*, 26, 30, 115–16, 121, 125–9, 132, 135–6, 143, 150, 151–2, 154, 156, 160, 168, 221
*Godzilla: Awakening*, 216
*Godzilla: City on the Edge of Battle*, 238
*Godzilla: Final Wars*, 167, 233–4
*Godzilla: King of the Monsters*, 17, 184, 195n, 196, 197, 225–8, 231n
*Godzilla: King of the Monsters in 3D*, 140

*Godzilla: Planet of the Monsters*, 76n, 238
*Godzilla: The Planet Eater*, 238
Godziszewski, Ed, 28–9, 32, 54, 56–7, 61, 218
Godzooky, 149
*Gogola*, 16, 79
*Gojira* (1954), 6–7, 13–16, 18–19, 20n, 23–34, 37–9, 41–7, 48, 50–3, 55, 57–8, 61–3, 76n, 78, 81, 83–4, 86, 89, 115, 117, 126–7, 129–30, 132–3, 135, 137, 144, 155, 156, 158, 167, 169, 171, 175, 183, 187, 189, 208, 219, 221, 229, 232–3, 237
Gojiro, 149
Goldman, Edmund, 125
Goodman, John, 175, 223
*Gorath*, 55
*Gorgo*, 73, 74, 124, 131–2, 146n, 156–7, 159, 160–1, 164, 169
Gorman, Burn, 205
Gothic, 4–6, 11, 32, 35, 174, 181, 183, 218
Gough, Michael, 189
Great Kanto Earthquake, 31, 51
*Great Wall, The*, 196–7, 201, 208, 209–12, 214, 215, 228
*Great Yōkai War, The*, 77n
*Green Slime, The*, 75
Greene, Lorne, 140
gross national cool, 84
*Grudge, The*, 217
*Gundam*, 206

Halberstam, Jack, 5
*Half Human*, 53–4, 57, 62, 136–7, 160, 189
Hall, Stuart, 22
*Hallyu*, 103
Hamamura Jun, 31
Hammer Studios, 3, 11–12, 131, 156, 163
han, 86, 89, 93
*Hangover, The*, 197–8
Hanna-Barbera, 149
Hansen, Miriam, 81
Hantke, Steffen, 172
*Hanzo the Razor*, 77n
Hara Kazuo, 238
Harada Itoko, 71
Harris Associates, 64, 138
Harryhausen, Ray, 41–2, 163, 165, 195n
*Harvey*, 60
Hashimoto Kōji, 139

Hasselhoff, David, 131
Hathaway, Anne, 182
Hawkins, Sally, 219
*Heart of Darkness*, 178
Heffernan, Kevin, 55–7, 159–60, 189, 240–1
*Hello Mr. Billionaire*, 214
*Henshin*, 69, 75, 76n, 79, 91, 120
Herbert, Daniel, 43, 217
*Hercules* (1983), 131
Herman, Pee-Wee, 103
*Hero*, 210
Heumann, Joseph, 222–3
*hibakusha* cinema, 30, 45, 58–60, 149, 167
Hiddleston, Tom, 225
Higson, Andrew, 15, 30, 116–17, 120
Higuchi Shinji, 47n, 236
Hirata Akihiko, 44, 76n
Hiroshima bombing, 18, 23–4, 27, 31, 53, 58–61,115, 133, 159, 188, 216, 234
*Hiroshima mon Amour*, 77n
Hitchcock, Alfred, 126
Hjort, Mette, 197, 200–3, 211, 215
Hokkaido, 53
*Hollywood Reporter, The*, 151, 236
Honda Ishirō, 17, 19, 28–9, 32, 53–4, 56, 61, 136, 139, 151, 156
Honda Kimi, 29
Horiaki Yoshii, 60
Horror, 3–6, 20n, 21, 25, 31, 33, 35–6, 42, 44, 70, 72, 74, 86, 103, 114, 126, 157, 159–60, 164, 172, 174–5, 200, 216–18, 241
*Host, The*, 108–12, 113n, 236
*House of Dracula*, 160
*House of Flying Daggers*, 210
*Houseguest and My Mother, The*, 94
Huang Kaijie, 213
Huayi Brothers, 198–9
Hughes, William, 218
*Human Vapor, The*, 61
Hunman, Charlie, 205
Hunter, I. Q., 74, 123, 154–5, 187, 188, 190, 192
Hurricane Katrina, 222
Hutcheon, Linda, 141
Hutchings, Peter, 156
Hyams, Phil, 159
Hyams, Sid, 159
hybridity, 3, 12–14, 17, 21–2, 33–4, 40, 48–50, 55, 60, 64, 74, 83, 85–7, 91, 112, 116, 129, 151, 154–5, 164, 171, 175, 207–8, 210, 214, 217
hyperobjects, 219
Hyundai, 104

Ichikawa Kon, 66
IDW, 149
Ifukube Akira, 23, 27, 56, 69, 139, 226
Igarashi Yoshikuni, 30, 48–50, 126, 236
Im Kwon-Taek, 105
*In This World*, 177
Inagaki Hiroshi, 48, 76n
*Inception*, 197–8
Incredible Hulk, The, 131
*Independence Day*, 14, 166, 169
*Indiewire*, 109
*Infernal Affairs*, 209
*Ingagi*, 37–8
Internet Movie Database, 100, 242
*Invasion of Astro-Monster*, 71, 90
*Invisible Avenger, The*, 53
Iordanova, Dina, 83, 201
*Isle of Dogs*, 151–2
*It Happened One Night*, 179
*It! The Terror from Beyond Space*, 71
Iwabuchi, Koichi, 22, 49, 112, 217
Iwanaga, Frank, 127–8, 130

Jackson, Peter, 37, 192–3
Jameson, Fredric, 141, 223
Japan Film Export Promotion Association (Nihon Eiga Yushutsu Shinkō Kyōkai, FEPA), 70, 72–3, 77n
Japan Self-Defense Forces (JSDF), 44, 51, 57, 59, 66, 73, 93, 158
*Jaws*, 80, 108–9, 154–5, 187, 193
Jawsploitation, 154, 187, 190
JD.com, 213
Jefferson Airplane, 223
Jenkins, Henry, 153–5, 207, 242–3
Jet Jaguar, 124, 238
Ji Li, 213
*Jiangshi*, 103
Jiao, Min, 209, 211–12
*Jidaigeki*, 20n, 48, 52, 67 69, 75, 188
Jing Tian, 209, 212, 213, 228, 230n
Johnson, Derek, 215
Johnson, Dwayne, 214
*Joint Security Area*, 103
Jones, Doug, 101
*Jurassic Park*, 42, 108, 163, 165, 169, 177, 230n

*Jurassic World*, 9, 200
*Jurassic World: Fallen Kingdom*, 214

Kabuki, 8, 152
Kadokawa, 63, 69, 176
Kadokawa Daiei Studios, 69
*Kagemusha*, 32
Kaiju Transmissions, 188
*Kaijumax*, 149
*kaiki eiga*, 3–4, 42, 46, 67, 75
Kalat, David, 33, 45, 138, 139, 145, 146
*kame*, 63
*Kamen Rider*, 75
*kami*, 8, 46, 69, 77n, 98
*kappa*, 8, 73
Karloff, Boris, 60
Katô, Masaya, 171
Katsu Shintaro, 63
Kawakami Keiji, 72, 77n
Kawasaki Minoru, 240
Kay, Richard, 125
Kayama Shigeru, 16, 46, 54
Keitel, Harvey, 104
Kellaway, Cecil, 40
Kemmerling, Warren J., 143
Kerner Production, 218
Kerner, Aaron, 167
Kikuchi, Rinko, 205, 206, 228, 230n
Kim Jeong-yong, 92
Kim Jong-Il, 94–5, 99
Kim Kidŏk, 86
Kim, Chung-kang, 86
*Kinema Junpō*, 3–4, 188
King Brothers, 160–1
*King Dong*, 192
King Ghidorah, 7, 9, 42, 63, 71, 90, 225, 227
*King Kong* (1933), 16, 17, 23, 33–9, 41–2, 44–5, 46, 53–5, 73, 74, 78, 81, 84–5, 125, 131, 137, 150, 155, 157, 161, 162, 163, 183, 187–93, 232
*King Kong* (1976), 34, 78, 80, 131, 162, 190, 195n
*King Kong* (2005), 34, 37, 184, 192–3
King Kong, 9, 22, 42, 44, 61, 172
*King Kong Escapes*, 34, 124, 146n, 195n, 196
*King Kong Show, The*, 124, 195n
*King Kong That Appeared in Edo, The*, 188
*King Kong vs. Frankenstein*, 60
*King Kong vs. Godzilla*, 34, 54, 57, 61, 137, 196

*King Kong vs. Prometheus*, 61
*King of the Lost World*, 184
*Kinky Kong*, 192
Kino, Lloyd, 171–2
Kinoshita Keisuke, 70
Kiritachi Harumi, 64
Kiryu, 42, 240
Klattenhoff, Diego, 205
Klein, Christina, 197, 199
Kobayashi Masaki, 70
Kōchi Momoko, 44
Kokas, Aynne, 210–11
*Kong: Skull Island*, 25, 34, 196, 209, 212, 216, 223–5, 227, 228
*Konga*, 34, 156, 189
Kongsploitation, 34, 78, 155–6, 187–93
Korean Film Archive, 84–5
Korean War, 88
Kore-eda Hirokazu, 21
Koven, Mikel, 131–2
*Kraa! The Sea Monster*, 185–6
*Kung Fu Hustle*, 199, 210
Kurihara Yasushide, 28
Kurosawa Akira, 30, 31, 32, 44, 48, 52, 63, 70, 76n, 194n
Kusatsu, Clyde, 171
*kyodai hīro*, 75

*Lake House, The*, 217
Lan Yingying, 213
*Land that Time Forgot, The* (1974), 163
Larson, Brie, 225
*Last Broadcast, The*, 172
*Last Godfather, The*, 104
*Last Horror Movie, The*, 172
*Last Year at Marienbad*, 114
Lau, Andy, 209
Laugesen, Martin Hauberg-Lund, 218–19
Le Vision, 210
Le, Bruce, 79
Lee Kwang-ho, 87
Lee, Bruce, 187, 230n
Lee, Danny, 79
Lee, Nikki, 108–9
Lee, Roy, 217
Lee, Sangjoon, 11–12
Lee, Vivian P. Y., 83
Lees, J. D., 9–11
*Legend of the Seven Golden Vampires, The*, 12
Legendary East, 197–9
Legendary Entertainment, 9, 20, 25, 34, 52, 149, 195n, 196–231, 236–8

LeMay, John, 11, 13, 55–7, 188
Leong, Al, 171
Levine, Joseph E., 125, 135
Lewis, Jerry, 103
Lim, Bliss Cua, 30, 117
Lin, Dan, 218
Lobato, Ramon, 74, 100, 119, 184, 186–7, 237
localisation, 20, 49, 83, 99, 108, 116, 120–2, 125, 129–30, 132–3, 135, 136–41, 144–5, 151, 154, 187, 2174, 239, 242
*Lone Wolf and Cub*, 77n
*Lost Horizon*, 114
*Lost World, The* (1925), 37–9, 41–2, 73, 155, 164, 189, 232
*Lost World, The* (1960), 163
*Lost World: Jurassic Park, The*, 47, 164
Lourié, Eugene, 16, 37, 73, 131, 156–7, 160–1, 169, 194n, 195n
*Love & Peace*, 240
*Love and Monsters*, 196
Lovecraft, H. P., 149, 218–19
*Lovetide*, 53
Lucas, Jessica, 173–4
Lucas, Jon, 198
Lucasfilm, 200
Luckhurst, Roger, 5, 178, 181
Luu brothers, 205
Lysgaard, Jonas Andreasen, 218–19

MacArthur, Douglas, 216, 223
McCorkle, Brooke, 8, 25, 30, 33, 45, 51–2, 58, 63, 65, 92, 219
McCreary, Bear, 226
McDonald, Keith, 205
McFarland, Albert, 110–11
McGray, Douglas, 84
McKevitt, Andrew C., 139
McNairy, Scoot, 177
McNamara, Sean, 100
McRobert, Neil, 174
McRoy, Jay, 3
*Magic Serpent, The*, 75
Magnetic System, 133
Magnolia Pictures, 109
*Man of Steel*, 198
Manchukuo, 28
Manda, 9, 107, 238
Manifest Destiny, 11
Mann, Michael, 198
Marcos, Ferdinand, 129
marked/unmarked transnationalism, 201–3

Maron, Mel, 123
Maroon 5, 210
Martin, Daniel, 85–6, 89, 108
Martini, Max, 205
Martin-Jones, David, 83, 118, 201
Marvel, 148–9, 196, 200, 215–16, 224
Maser Patrol, 21, 83, 91–2, 151
Mastroianni, Marcelo, 190
Mathijs, Ernest, 13, 118
*Matrix, The*, 154–5
Matsui Hideki, 239–40
Mazdon, Lucy, 171, 217
MechaGodzilla, 42, 206, 227
Media Blasters, 138
media mix (*media mikkusu*), 76, 233, 238
Medved, Harry, 114, 116, 141, 146n
Medved, Michael, 114, 116, 141, 146n
*Meg, The*, 184, 214
*Mega Shark versus Mecha Shark*, 150
*Megalodon*, 184
Meikle, Denis, 12
Melchior, Ib, 162
memes, 20, 33, 43, 80–2, 90, 108–9, 149, 162, 182–3, 186, 190–3, 232–3
*Memories of Murder*, 112
*Men in Black*, 166
Mewes, Jason, 104
MGM, 75, 123
*Mighty Gorga, The*, 190
*Mighty Joe Young* (1949), 189
*Mighty Joe Young* (1998), 189
*Mighty Morphin Power Rangers*, 75, 185, 204
*Mighty Peking Man, The*, 34, 78, 190–1
Miike Takashi, 77n
Miller, Bodil, 162, 195n
Miller, T. J., 173
Miner, Steve, 140
Miniya, 6, 169
Misumi Kenji, 63, 69, 77n
Mittel, Jason, 224–5, 228
*Miyamoto Musashi*, 48
Miyazaki Hayao, 21
Mizuno Kimi, 58
Mockbusters, 20, 107, 150, 183–7, 192
Monarch, 25, 216, 223–5, 228
*Monkey* (TV series), 79
*Monster* (2008), 184
*Monster from Green Hell, The*, 137, 195n
*Monster Hunt*, 79
*Monster Hunter*, 196
*Monster Island*, 2, 150, 184, 186, 207
*Monster Seafood Wars*, 240

*Monster X Strikes Back: Attack the G8 Summit*, 240
*Monsters* (2010), 5, 176–81, 222, 223
*Monsters Unleashed*, 149
*Monsters: Dark Continent*, 181–2
MonsterVerse, 9, 25, 34, 196, 207, 212, 215–31, 235
*Monstress*, 149, 153
Moore, Scott, 198
Morse, Terry O., 26, 125, 135, 136
*Mothra*, 17, 54, 55, 66, 74, 76n, 228
Mothra, 7, 9, 63, 76, 140, 156, 163, 225–6, 228, 239
*Mothra vs. Godzilla*, 58
Motion Picture Producers Association of Japan, 164
*mukokuseki*, 22, 43, 94
*Mulan* (2020), 215, 230n
multilanguage versions, 161–2
Munro, Caroline, 131
Murase Keizō, 87
*Murders in the Rue Morgue*, 38
Murray, Robin, 222–3
MUTOs, 219, 221–2
*Mysterians, The*, 32, 50, 51, 76n
*Mystery Science Theater 3000*, 1, 121, 240

Naficy, Hamid, 193
Nagasaki bombing, 18, 23–4, 27, 234
Nagata Masaichi, 63
Nakagawa Nobuo, 3
Nakajima Haruo, 76n, 95, 226–7
Nakano Teruyoshi, 95, 139
Nakazawa Kenji, 31
Nam Jeong-im, 88
*Name that Tune*, 121
Napier, Susan, 31, 175, 236
Naruse Mikio, 70
NASA, 177, 180
national cinema, 2, 4, 11, 14–16, 19, 21–4, 26, 29–33, 37, 60, 64, 74, 78–9, 85, 115–18, 164, 170, 193, 199, 210, 233, 235, 238–9
National Diet building, 27, 38, 44, 89, 130, 135
national trauma, 18, 24–7, 32, 43, 45–6, 48, 51, 58, 83, 89, 105, 109, 115, 118, 126–7, 143, 154, 167, 169, 181–2, 191–2, 208, 219, 227, 232, 236
Natsuki Yosuke, 141
Neal, Peggy, 71, 77n

Neill, Sam, 163
*Neon Genesis Evangelion*, 194n, 206
Netflix, 176, 238, 240
network narratives, 155, 196, 216, 224
New World Pictures, 116, 123, 140, 142, 145–6, 240
*New York Times, The*, 200
Nielsen, Leslie, 140
*Nights of Lucrecia Borgia, The*, 160
*Nihonjinron*, 49, 54
Nihonmatsu Kazui, 50, 70
Nike, 165
Nikkatsu, 50–1, 70–5
Nō, 8
Nolan, Christopher, 198
Noriega, Chon, 25, 151, 168
Nornes, Abé Mark, 120, 161
nostalgia, 14, 104, 139, 141, 144, 146, 172, 238, 240–3
*Notzilla*, 196
NTT DoCoMo, 70
nuclear testing, 25, 39, 40, 43–5, 88, 168, 170

O'Brien, Willis, 38, 41–2, 60, 163
O'Regan, Tom, 43
Oda Motoyoshi, 53
*Oen-san*, 53
Ogata Akira, 238
Oh Young-il, 88
Okada Eiji, 71, 77n
Okinawa, 49, 53, 152
*Oldboy*, 217
Oliete-Aldea, Elena, 17, 18, 52, 78, 82
*One Million Years* B.C. (1966), 163
Ong, Aihwa, 232
*Operation Red Sea*, 214
Orange Sky Golden Harvest, 198, 230n
Oria, Beatriz, 17, 18, 52, 78, 82
Orientalism, 30, 116, 222
Orion, 140
*orochi*, 9
Osaka, 53, 59
*Osomatsu-kun*, 90
Otherness, 5–6, 13, 18, 25–6, 31, 35, 61, 89, 118, 120, 154–6, 168, 180–1, 208
Oxygen Destroyer, 44–5, 126, 226
Ozu Yasujirō, 21, 30, 70

*Pacific Rim*, 2, 152, 182, 184, 200, 203–8, 209, 212, 215
*Pacific Rim: The Black*, 230n
*Pacific Rim: Uprising*, 209, 212–14, 228

paracinema, 13–14, 118, 120, 139, 140, 146
Paramount, 56, 200
*Paranormal Activity*, 172
*Parasite*, 103
Park Chung-Hee, 86, 89, 102
Park Hae-il, 110
Park Jungman, 96, 98–9
Pascal, Pedro, 209
Passer, Dirch, 162
Peirse, Alison, 85
Peña, Elizabeth, 107
Perkins, Claire, 177
Perlman, Ron, 205–6
Perren, Alisa, 230n
Pestar, 93
Phillips, Alastair, 21
Pile, Steven, 172, 174–5
Pink, Sidney W., 161–2
*Pirates of the Caribbean*, 165
Pitillo, Maria, 171
*Plan 9 from Outer Space*, 137
*Planet of the Apes*, 190
Plummer, Christopher, 131
Poe, Edgar Allan, 38
*Pokémon*, 76, 167
*Pokémon Detective Pikachu*, 197, 229, 231n
Polito, Jon, 104
Polygon Pictures, 230n, 238
post-credits sequences, 148, 216, 224–5, 227–8, 231n
Pratt, Mary Louise, 59–61, 151
*Princess Mononoke*, 164, 167
Production Committees, 76, 145
*Project-G*, 46
*Pulgasari*, 78, 84, 94–9, 100–2, 112
*Puppet Master*, 184

Qingdao studios, 200–1, 213
*Quatermass 2*, 155–6, 158
*Quatermass Xperiment, The*, 155, 158
*Queen Kong*, 190
Quintana, Tessie, 129

Ragone, August, 61
*Rampage*, 34, 194, 214
Rankin-Bass, 64, 124, 138, 140, 146n
Rao, Pratima V., 152–3
Raphael, Raphael, 150, 191–3
*Rashomon*, 63
Raymond, Paula, 40
*Ready Player One*, 206

*Rear Window*, 126
Reeves, Steve, 131
Reno, Jean, 170–1
*Reptilicus*, 1, 161–2, 195n
Resnais, Alain, 77n, 114
*Return of Daimajin, The*, 69
*Return of Godzilla, The* (*Gojira*, 1984), 20n, 95, 99, 139–41, 144, 236, 238
*Rhapsody in August*, 31
Rhedosaurus, 39–42, 58, 169
Rhoads, Sean, 8, 25, 30, 33, 45, 51–2, 58, 63, 65, 92, 219
Rhythm & Hues, 230n
Richie, Donald, 50–1, 127
*Rick and Morty*, 148, 194n
Rikidōzan, 48–9
*Ring*, 43, 217
*Ring, The*, 217
RKO, 37, 42, 60, 162, 195n
Roberto, John, 137
Roberts, Eric, 186
*Robin Hood: Prince of Thieves*, 100–2
Robinson, Craig, 107
Robinson, Jackie, 198
Robinson, Michael, 86
*Robotech*, 206
Rodan, 148, 225–6, 238
*Rodan*, 32, 55, 138, 160
*Rolling Stone*, 227
*Romance Papa*, 94
Rosen, David N., 35–6
Ross, Harold, 125
Rossio, Terry, 165
Ruh, Brian, 120–1
Ryan, Mark, 74, 119, 237
Ryfle, Steve, 13–14, 16, 23, 28–9, 32, 38, 40, 45–6, 48, 51, 53, 54, 56–7, 60–1, 86–7, 124, 125, 128, 137, 140, 146, 165, 221–2, 226
*ryū*, 9

S.H.I.E.L.D., 149, 224
Saban, 75
*Saga*, 161
Saito Torajiro, 188
Sakamoto Minoru, 136
Sakamoto, Azumi, 59–60
Samsung, 103
Santiago, Cirio H., 129
Santos, Teodorico C., 129
Saperstein, Henry G., 61, 140, 165
SARS, 109
Sato Ichiro, 46

Satsuma Kenpachiro, 95
Sawaguchi Yasuko, 141
*Sayonara Jupiter*, 139
Schaefer, Eric, 123, 125, 131, 137
Schoedsack, Ernest B., 15, 33, 189
Schwarzenegger, Arnold, 131
*Science Ninja Team Gatchaman*, 120–1
science-fiction, 3–6, 31–3, 35, 39, 46, 50, 53, 69, 86, 127, 133, 139, 145, 164, 172, 175–6, 178, 186, 214, 241
Sconce, Jeffrey, 13, 118, 177
Scott, Suzanne, 224, 228
Scottsboro Boys, 35
Screen Gems, 240
*Sea God and Ghosts*, 113n
Second World War, 18, 21, 24, 59, 130, 158–9
Sedgwick, Eve Kosofsky, 5
Segura, Santiago, 205
Sekizawa Shinichi, 57
*Seven Samurai*, 48, 194n
*Seventh Son*, 198–9, 230n
Sexton, Jamie, 13, 118, 208
*Shaka*, 63, 77n
*Sharknado*, 150, 187
Shaw Brothers, 11–12, 79
Shaw, Deborah, 1, 16–17, 169–70, 204, 233, 235, 239
*Shē*, 90
Shearer, Harry, 171
Sheen, Simon, 100
Shelley, Mary, 60, 163
Sherlock Holmes, 122, 202
*Sherlock Hound*, 122
*Shikari*, 189
Shim Hyung-Rae, 103–9, 112, 113n
Shimura Takashi, 44, 53, 58, 66, 76n
*Shin Gojira*, 47n, 144, 220, 234–8
Shin Sang-ok, 17, 78, 94–5, 98, 100–2
*shinpa* melodrama, 70
Shinto, 8, 46, 69
Shipton, Eric, 53
*Shiri*, 103
Shiu, Kelvin Wu King, 198
*Shobijin*, 66, 76n, 228
Shōchiku, 50, 70–2, 77n, 188
Shohat, Ella, 117
*Shout, The*, 190
*Shrek*, 165
*Shutter*, 217
*Simpsons, The*, 2, 148
*Sin Nombre*, 177
*Skyscraper*, 214, 228

Smith, Andrew, 218
Smith, Iain Robert, 14, 33, 43, 79, 80–2, 91, 93, 117, 118, 121–2, 129–30, 141, 167, 193, 208, 217
*Snow Creature, The*, 53–4
Sobchack, Vivian, 6–7, 227
soft power, 20, 64, 84, 103, 197, 200–1, 210, 214, 215, 229, 233
Solomon, Brian, 233
*Son of Godzilla*, 6, 124, 131
*Son of Kong*, 189
*Son of the Dragon King*, 113n
Song Kang-ho, 110
*Songdomalnyeoneui Boolgasari*, 84
Sontag, Susan, 7, 31–3, 175, 218
Sony, 104, 123, 146, 167, 170, 172, 217, 234, 236
*Space Monster Wangmagwi*, 84–5, 91
spaghetti Western, 11, 20n, 114
*Speed*, 165
Spider-Man, 189
Spielberg, Steven, 47n, 80, 163, 169, 206, 230n
SRS Cinema, 93, 113n
Stahl-David, Michael, 173
Stam, Robert, 80–1, 117, 192–3
*Star Trek*, 91, 93, 113n
*Star Wars*, 120–1, 131, 149, 152, 200
*Star Wars: The Clone Wars*, 148
*Starcrash*, 131
Sternberg, Claudia, 16
Stewart, James, 60
Stoker, Bram, 164
straight-to-video (STV) movies, 100, 102, 150, 184, 186–7
Strathairn, David, 222
Sudeikis, Jason, 182–3
Suez crisis, 158
Sugimoto, Yoshio, 49
Suitmation, 8, 69, 76n, 99, 101, 104, 161, 167, 226, 233
*Super Giant*, 124
*Super Inframan, The*, 79, 124
*Super Sentai*, 75
Superman, 124, 198, 200
*Superman Returns*, 198
Suzuki Akira, 87
Swords, Travis, 143

*taiyozoku* (sun tribe) films, 51, 73, 77n
Takahashi Nisan, 63
Takano Koichi, 79
Takarada Akira, 24, 44

Takuma Shin, 141
Tamblyn, Russ, 17, 61, 228
Tan Weiwei, 210
Tanaka Ken, 141
Tanaka Shigeo, 64
Tanaka Tomoyuki, 24–5, 39, 46, 63, 136, 139–40
Tanikawa, Takeshi, 71, 77n
Tao Tie, 209, 211
Tarancón, Juan, 17, 18, 52, 78, 82
Tatsumi, Takayuki, 46, 47n
Taylor-Johnson, Aaron, 220
*Teenage Mutant Ninja Turtles*, 100, 102
Tempera, Vince, 133
Tencent, 213
*Terror of MechaGodzilla*, 55
Teshigahara Hiroshi, 77n
*Them!*, 10, 137
*Thing from Another World, The*, 39–40
Thornton, Niamh, 205–8
*Three Kings*, 182
Three Mile Island, 220
Timbaland, 210
*Time*, 105, 222
Titan Productions, 138
*Titanic*, 103, 164, 167
Titans, 195n, 218, 221, 227
Toda, Toshi, 186
Toei, 70, 75–6, 87, 124
Tōhō, 12, 14, 16, 19–20, 23–5, 27, 34, 39, 42, 44–6, 47n, 48, 50–64, 70–1, 75, 77n, 95, 107, 113n, 114, 116, 123–5, 127, 133, 135, 137, 138–40, 145–6, 149–50, 165, 167, 169–70, 172, 182–3, 208, 217–18, 221, 226, 229, 230n, 231n, 234–8, 241
Tōhoku Earthquake, 31, 220, 234
TohoScope, 56
Tokuma Shoten Publishing, 63
*tokusatsu*, 51, 70, 72, 75, 76n, 79, 91, 93, 95, 136, 205, 225, 240
*Tokyo 1960*, 129–30
*Touch of Satan, The*, 241
*Train, The*, 133
*Trancers*, 184
Trans World Releasing, 125, 129–30
*Transformers*, 230n
transgression, 4, 6, 13–14, 38, 80, 178, 232
transmedia, 103, 172, 176, 196, 207, 215–16, 224–5, 228–9
Travers, Peter, 227
*Tremors: Shrieker Island*, 196

Tristar Pictures, 100
*Trollenberg Terror, The*, 159
Trump, Donald, 180–1, 213
Tryon, Chuck, 155
Tsuburaya Eiji, 23, 38, 41, 53–4, 58, 61, 64, 77n, 79, 93, 136
Tsuburaya Productions, 58, 72, 75, 93, 149
Tsukamoto Shinya, 238
Tsutsui, William, 5, 7, 16, 18, 25, 28, 51, 113n, 124, 127, 221–2
Tudor, Andrew, 31
Tull, Thomas, 198–9, 215
*Turist Omer Uzay Yolunda*, 91, 93
TV Tokyo, 69
*Twilight Zone, The*, 75

UAV, 123
*Ultra Q*, 58, 75
*Ultraman*, 58, 75–6, 79, 84, 93, 149, 230n
*Ultraman: The Adventure Begins*, 75
United Productions of America (UPA), 61, 64, 123, 138, 140, 165, 240
Universal, 134, 153, 160, 162, 195n, 196–7, 200, 212
*Unknown Island*, 189

*Valley of Gwangi, The*, 42, 163
van Cleef, Lee, 41
*Varan the Unbelievable*, 55–8, 138
*Variety*, 100, 198, 204
Verevis, Constantin, 167, 217
vernacular cinema, 132–3, 135
Verokron, 93
Vertigo Entertainment, 217
Vertigo Films, 176
VHS, 57, 123, 130–1, 137–8, 146, 240–1
Vidal, Belén, 201
Vieira, João Luiz, 80–1, 192–3
Vietnam War, 86, 88, 111, 223
Vigalondo, Nacho, 182–3
*Voltron*, 206

*Wages of Fear, The*, 137
Wall Street crash, 35
Wang Jianglin, 200
Wang Leehom, 210
Wang Zhongjun, 199
Wanstead, Mary Elizabeth, 175
*War God*, 79
*War of the Gargantuas, The*, 62
*War of the God Monsters*, 92–3, 95, 107, 112, 113n

Warner Bros., 40, 137, 162, 163, 196–8, 200, 212, 229n, 230n
*Warning from Space*, 50–1
Warren, Bill, 160–2
*Wasei Kingu Kongu*, 188
Watanabe, Ken, 216, 224, 228
*Watchmen*, 198
Wazaki Toshiya, 71
Wessels, Emanuelle, 174, 176
Westerns, 11, 20n, 42, 83, 114
Whale, James, 60
whitewashing, 115–16, 126, 130, 150, 151, 168, 209, 221
Wikipedia, 100
Wikizilla, 37, 129, 195n
Willeman, Paul, 116
*Winter's Bone*, 182
wonhon, 86, 103
Wood, Robin, 25, 126
*World of Warcraft*, 199
World Trade Center, 190
*Wrath of the Titans*, 198
Wray, Fay, 34
Writers Guild of America, 198
Wu, Constance, 209
*wuxia pian*, 197, 209–10, 212

*X from Outer Space, The*, 50, 70–2
*X: The Unknown*, 10, 156
Xi Jinping, 200, 213
Xiaomi, 213
Xu, Gary, 216–17

Yagi Masao, 87
Yam, Kimmy, 115
Yamashita Junichiro, 64
Yanagisawa Shinichi, 71
Yang, Jing, 209, 211–12
Yasuda Kimiyoshi, 67
*Yeti: Giant of the 20th Century*, 34, 190
yōkai, 8, 9, 69, 73–4, 79
*Yōkai Monsters: 100 Monsters*, 77n
*Yōkai Monsters: Along with Ghosts*, 77n
*Yōkai Monsters: Spook Warfare*, 77n
Yomota Inuhiko, 26, 30, 63, 151
*Yongary: Monster from the Deep*, 78, 84–90, 91, 93, 95, 99, 109, 112, 113n, 241
*Yonggary*, 104–8, 112
*Young-gu and Daengchili*, 103
*Young-gu and the Dinosaur ZuZu*, 104
*Your Name*, 235
YouTube, 13, 16, 85, 117, 122
Yu Xiaowei, 213
Yuasa Noriaki, 3, 63–4, 66, 67, 69, 71, 92
Yueh-yu Yeh, Emilie, 103, 210
Yustman, Odette, 173

*Zarkorr! The Invader*, 185
*Zatōichi*, 63, 67, 76n
Zensho Cinema, 188
Zhang Jin, 213
Zhang Ziyi, 17, 228
Zhang, Jane, 210
Zhang, Jin, 209, 211–12
Ziff, Bruce, 152–3
Zilla, 14, 167, 233–4
*Zombi 2*, 134
*Zone Fighter*, 75
Zshornack, Zaldy, 129
Zwick, Edward, 210

EU representative:
Easy Access System Europe
Mustamäe tee 50, 10621 Tallinn, Estonia
Gpsr.requests@easproject.com

www.ingramcontent.com/pod-product-compliance
Lightning Source LLC
Chambersburg PA
CBHW051112230426
43667CB00014B/2541